Tex McCrary

Wars · Women · Politics
An Adventurous Life across the American Century

Charles J. Kelly

Hamilton Books
A member of
The Rowman & Littlefield Publishing Group
Lanham • Boulder • New York • Toronto • Plymouth, UK

⊗™ The paper used in this publication meets the minimum
requirements of American National Standard for Information
Sciences—Permanence of Paper for Printed Library Materials,
ANSI Z39.48—1992

For Tex . . .

Contents

Author's Note

It began with a phone call.

This is Tex McCrary. Do you know who I am?

The call came right after Joe Klein's cover story, "Will Powell Run?" in the October 10, 1994 issue of *Newsweek,* which mentioned that I had founded "Citizens for Colin Powell," a presidential draft. Tex reminded me of his close involvement with "Citizens for Eisenhower," said he felt Powell was the right person for President, and that he wanted to get on board.

We met the next day at the Hay Adams Hotel. Tex insisted on walking into Lafayette Park and sitting on the bench where Bernard Baruch had conducted his conversations in Washington. We talked about the roles of John Hay and John Adams—the hotel is located on the site of their adjacent houses—and their roles in American history, and how sad it was that our nation's choices for the only nationally elected office were so limited, primarily because of an Electoral College system, established in 1789 and unchanged for over three hundred years. It was clear that we thought alike.

Many conversations followed—at our home in Georgetown and the Yale Club in New York—over many a convivial glass. Each story reminded him of another, a fascinating high life of adventure, particularly in matters political. Eventually I said, "Tex, you should write a book. You've had a remarkable life. You are the last man standing who has lived through, and participated in, most of the formative events of The American Century."

Sighing, he said that others had suggested this, but that he still had future ideas and plans, and he didn't want to stop to look at his life in the rearview mirror. Then he added, "But by now you know it all. If you feel it's important, you do it."

This book is the result.

Chapter One

Texas, Exeter . . . and Yale:
The Education of a Future "Insider"

Tex McCrary was born October 13, 1910, on his family's ranch, "Wildcat Farm," in the "cotton country" northwest of Austin, Texas. His given name was John Reagan McCrary, and his long life was to span the American Century—from the time of the Presidencies of the two Roosevelts to the two Bushes—active in national affairs, politics and wars, in the company of many of the most influential men—and the most beautiful women—of the time.

National affairs seemed very remote during his early years. Other than the country school, his only exposures to life outside the ranch were the regular visits from New York of his uncle, Tom Taylor, and his aunt, whom he always called "Tante." As Taylor and his wife were childless, their nephew was soon to become an important part of their lives.

The American Century arose out of the rapid industrial expansion of the late 1890s. The driving force of the time was Mark Hanna of Cleveland, who convinced the owners of new industrial companies that they should enhance their power by combining their individual companies into "Trusts" with interlocking directors. Hanna's increasing influence enabled him to bring about the election of his protégé, William McKinley, as President of the United States in 1896. In 1900, McKinley chose the national hero of the Spanish-American War, Teddy Roosevelt, as his Vice President. Six months after McKinley took office, he was assassinated—and Teddy Roosevelt became President, bringing a new vitality and new approach to the office. He attacked the monopolistic power of the industrial "Trusts," causing the arch-conservative Mark Hanna to declare, "Now see what you've done. That damn cowboy is in the White House!" Hanna was right. Roosevelt's Presidency marked a major shift of political power—and other major changes were at work as well.

On January 10, 1901, near Beaumont, Texas, an oil well named "Spindletop"—in oil talk—"Blew in a Gusher," shooting a solid stream of hot oil more than one hundred and fifty feet in the air. Startled drillers ran for their lives. It took more than nine days to get the oil flow under control. Virtually overnight, Spindletop became a "Boom Town," with production of 100.000 barrels of oil a day. Spindletop was the beginning of the modern oil industry—and all that flowed from it. Speculators and investors raced to the site, among them a tiny startup, a small but experienced drilling team advised by a prominent Texas lawyer, Tom Taylor. He had developed a successful legal career representing banks and railroads, and through those connections had come to the attention of various Eastern companies, including Rockefeller's Standard Oil, the Mellon's Gulf Oil, and the Pew family's Sun Oil, all interested in promising oil properties in Texas. Taylor was a close friend of Robert S. Lovett—universally known as "Judge" Lovett—who had grown up in Texas, had become general counsel and director of the Union Pacific Railroad, and had moved to New York to become advisor to the prominent financier and railroad investor, E. H. Harriman. Following the dramatic success of "Spindletop"—and with Lovett's advice—Taylor had put together a drilling team of "good ol' boys" who had worked their way up in the Texas oil fields, as "The Texas Company" and was eventually able to convince them that the company should move its headquarters to New York, changing its name to "Texaco," in the process.

On December 17, 1903, two bicycle mechanics from Dayton, Ohio, Wilber and Orville Wright, invented the airplane, fulfilling man's ancient dreams of flight on a cold and windy beach at Kitty Hawk, North Carolina. Orville made the first flight, only one hundred and twenty feet. A man could throw as far. A boy could run as fast. A horse could carry more. But the Wright Brothers had opened a new dimension to human possibilities, and the world would never be the same again.

After having served as President for the remaining three and a half years of McKinley's term, Roosevelt was elected President in his own right in 1904. He rapidly extended American influence, began construction of the Panama Canal, made major increases in the American Navy and sent "The Great White Fleet," around the world—visibly establishing America's place as a world power. An American fleet under Admiral Dewey in Japan on a goodwill "Show the Flag" mission, sailed to the Philippines and destroyed an antiquated Spanish Fleet in Manila Bay. Spain, which had controlled much of the Western world since the Fifteenth Century, had lost its Empire. Freed from Spanish control, Cuba, the Philippines, Puerto Rico and Guam became American dependencies. Thus, virtually without planning, without prior public discussion or approval, almost by accident, America had become a world power.

In 1908, although eligible to serve another full term as President, Roosevelt chose not to run, in effect giving the office to his Vice President, William Howard Taft. Nevertheless, Roosevelt remained by any measure the most popular, most respected national leader and, by 1912, he had come to regard Taft as a passive figure, a failure—and Roosevelt again sought the Republican Presidential nomination for himself. When the Republican Convention nominated Taft, by a rigged vote, Roosevelt bolted the Republican Party to organize the "Progressive Party," popularly known as the "Bull Moose" party when Roosevelt replied to a question on his health, saying, "I'm as healthy as a Bull Moose." Taft and Roosevelt split the Republican vote, and as a result, the Democrat, Woodrow Wilson, formerly President of Princeton University, was elected President of the United States—but with a minority of the votes cast.

The First World War began in Europe in 1914. In 1916, President Wilson, campaigning as the man who "kept us out of war," won reelection and, immediately after his Inauguration for his second term in the spring of 1917, took America into the war, effectively saving France and England from the brink of a humiliating defeat by Germany. Fresh American troops turned the tide of the war and an Armistice ended the war on November 11, 1918. President Wilson went to Paris for the Peace talks, where he fell ill. He was attended by his personal doctor and his wife, who issued all communications, and the exact nature of his illness was not disclosed. Essentially, America was without an acting President for the following two years, until Wilson's Presidency ended in 1920.

But business was booming in America. Good times were at hand. The country didn't seem to need a President and elected Harding, a nonentity Republican who had not advanced beyond high school. Harding lasted one term and was followed in 1924 by Calvin Coolidge—with the slogan, "Keep Cool With Coolidge"—who seemed to spend much of his time secluded at his home in New England. Americans didn't seem to care. They wanted fun, and uninhibited "flappers" danced the "Charleston." It was the "Jazz Age." Finally, a competent man, Herbert Hoover, was elected President in 1928. However, by then it was too late. The post-war Depression, which had started in Europe, came to America with the Wall Street financial "Crash" in October 1929.

Tom Taylor regarded New York as the vital center of the country. Through his friendship with Judge Lovett, he had been impressed by Lovett's son, Bob—who had gone to Yale and had become a naval aviator and "ace" in world war one—and Taylor was convinced that his nephew would benefit from an education beyond the farm country of Texas. He argued that, while Texas was certainly growing, it was growing in a relatively isolated context, tied to the state economy, primarily agriculture, oil, and small service businesses—and Texans, like most of the country, were isolationist in their thinking. While oil production in Texas was growing fast, it was driven by corporate and financial decisions made in New York, by men who had to think, not only nationally, but increasingly with an international point of view. An education at a quality eastern prep school, then at great national university—Yale, for example—could not help but broaden the scope and range of a young man's thinking.

Taylor's advice was met with strong opposition from the boy's father, who had been the quarterback on the Baylor University football team, and who's vision was the vision of Texas, where "cotton was king" (he was later to become the head of the politically powerful Cotton Growers Association). Apart from the philosophical aspects of Taylor's argument, as a practical matter the McCrary family's cotton operations were experiencing difficult times, so much so that the cost of an expensive Eastern education might create serious family stress. At that point, Tante stepped in, saying that, as she and her husband had no children, Reagan would be their natural heir—and she believed that the greatest inheritance she could provide would be to make available the cost of the best education possible for her sister's son. Reagan's mother agreed with her sister—and the decision was made that he should go to Exeter, in New Hampshire. But his mother reserved the college decision for herself.

The young man was excited at the prospect of Exeter—but also a little frightened as he boarded the train alone in Austin, en route to New York. His uncle met him, and his waiting car took them downtown, past the great office towers, to his uncle's large office in the Whitehall Building. The flags of all the countries where Texaco did business were arrayed around the office walls. Large windows opened to the full expanse of New York harbor, glistening in the sunlight. The young man stood transfixed. There were two giant brass telescopes mounted on pedestals and focused by large sighting wheels. The harbor was filled with ships of all kinds, many under sail. Through the telescope Reagan could even read their names and home ports, exotic names from all over the world. He had no idea how long he stood there that day, or the many other days he visited in his uncle's office, absorbed in the sight—and marveling at the magnetic power of the city to draw the whole world to it.

Tom Taylor and Tante lived in a large, handsome apartment at Broadway and 68th Street, with a ready staff available for the frequent entertaining required by his position in Texaco. During his visit, his uncle showed him the sights of the city. When it came time to leave for Exeter, his uncle decided to come along. His chauffeur, "Donovan," in his crisp uniform and cap, was seated in the "chauffeur's box" of the Pierce-Arrow town car. The drive to Exeter was another revelation: the green country, forests, mountains, and rivers, all so totally different from the dry, open spaces of Texas. As they drove, his uncle said he felt sure that Reagan would fit in at Exeter, that he should be open to new ideas and experiences, become involved in many activities, get to know as many people as possible, learn how they think, and begin to understand what was happening in the country and in the world. He said that the country would need more people who could make others see things they had not seen before, who could affect the perceptions and understandings of others. He urged Reagan to look for those opportunities wherever, and whenever, he could. But, above all, he hoped that he would learn how to learn.

Although secluded in hills of New Hampshire just above the Massachusetts border and a few miles inland from the Atlantic, Exeter conveyed a national, and even an international, perspective. Fortunately, the new student was gifted with a natural, open, friendly manner. He fit in at once, and immediately acquired a new name—"Tex"— which followed him for the rest of his life. Because of his slim build, he did not make the varsity football squad, but he played quarterback on the junior varsity, and in the winter took up boxing. The boxing coach had remarkable insight. He sparred with Tex, then said: "You think fast; you're quick; look for opportunities—and react." That advice influenced Tex's life. He took advantage of all that the school offered, responding immediately to the academic challenge, and soon began to reach out into new areas of interest. Boston and New York newspapers provided his first introduction to national affairs and Presidential politics, and he began to write for the *Exonian*, the school paper.

Tex enjoyed his Exeter years; however, there were two experiences, one personal, one national, which left lasting impressions. The first event occurred in Calvert in his last year at Exeter. He was with old Calvert friends when they saw a well-muscled black boy diving off a bridge over the Brazos River. He was pretty good, and a small crowd of blacks and whites had started to watch him. Some local white boys whom Tex knew took offense. They sent the black boy a letter signed with a girl's name, asking to meet at night in a local empty barn. When the black boy showed up, the white boys beat him to death.

The second insight arose in connection with his newspaper reading. At the National Society of Newspaper Editors, President Calvin Coolidge had famously declared, "The Business of America Is Business." Soon thereafter the country was rocked by the

"Tea Pot Dome" scandal, the transfer of major national Naval Petroleum Reserves—at Tea Pot Dome in Wyoming and Elk Hills in California—to oil tycoons, Harry Sinclair and Edward Doheny. The transfer had been arranged by Coolidge's predecessor, President Harding's Secretary of the Interior, Albert Fall. Later, after Fall's death, it was discovered that Fall had received a bribe of $400,000 dollars. A major national scandal ensued. Tex was puzzled, and then angry, when Sinclair and Doheny managed to escape conviction. He discussed it with his uncle, who said, "Oil is energy. It is essential to all industrial development. Control of oil represents wealth and power. As such, it is a constant temptation for corruption. Sadly, scandal is a symptom of our times." Tea Pot Dome—and its implications of manipulation of the national government for private interests—was to linger in Tex's mind thereafter.

Through his Exeter years Tex had spent increasing amounts of time in New York with his uncle and aunt, who were becoming, in effect, his surrogate parents, and they opened other dimensions to his education. His uncle kept reminding Tex that when he himself was young, most of the country was predominately agricultural. Apart from the seaport cities, it was mostly a land of small towns and family farms, following traditional farming practices. The prevailing concerns were local, communication was limited, and the economic attitude was "laissez-faire" self-sufficiency. He had seen the railroads, the telegraph and the telephone connect the country. Distances, continents, oceans had been conquered, and Lindbergh had electrified the world by flying alone across the Atlantic in 1927 while Tex was at Exeter.

His uncle said that the world was changing very fast, that few people understood how fast, or what the changes would bring. America's entry into World War I had introduced a new role on the country—but the majority of Americans did not think about what that meant, or what the demands would be—and when confronted by them, they would resist. The crucial fact was that an accelerating curve of advances in science and technology was driving, and would continue to drive, the growth of industry. American industrial growth would surpass all other nations. And all industry depended on oil to provide the essential energy. He hoped that Tex would think about the accelerating rate of change, the importance of oil and its implications for America's future—and for Tex's future.

College was the next step. Yale had not been his mother's first choice. She was an admirer of Woodrow Wilson and she wanted Tex to go to Princeton where Wilson had been President of the university before being elected President of the United States. She was delighted with the beautifully landscaped campus and she picked out what she considered an appropriate student and asked where they might find the house where Woodrow Wilson had lived. It became embarrassingly apparent that the student not only did not know where the house was but also seemed to have no idea who Woodrow Wilson was. His mother turned and said, "They don't seem to teach the boys anything here." They left for Harvard where many of his Exeter friends were headed, but it didn't seem to fit what he had anticipated, and his mother was put off by what she considered sloppy dress and poor manners. Yale appealed to Tex at once. It looked and felt exactly like he what he expected of a great university.

Tex entered Yale in the fall of 1928, at the peak of the "Roaring 20s," a glittering, glamorous time of high living. Yale was, in some ways, a kind of continuation of Exeter, although on a much larger scale, offering a wider range of activities, all highly competitive and pursued very seriously, with an implicit sense that Yale was a preparation for positions of responsibility in national and international affairs—and that achievements at Yale would carry over into the wider world beyond.

He tried out for the for the Yale varsity football team but, as at Exeter, he was cut, as too light. However he became the quarterback on the 150-pound team and, in the winter, he made the boxing team, coached by the famous Yale coach "Mosey" King.

Having ridden horses all his life, Tex was delighted to discover that Yale had well equipped stables and a skilled polo team. Although an experienced rider, he was not trained for polo. However, he practiced with the team and got to know several men from Long Island who became close friends, Jimmy Mills, Mike Phipps, Pete Bostwick, and Stewart Iglehart, who introduced him to a glamorous life of polo, parties and pretty girls in the Old Westbury—Locust Valley area of Long Island—and all of his polo friends went on to achieve stardom on U.S. and international polo teams.

Yale was famous for its student publications, foremost of which was *The Yale Daily News,* followed by *The Yale Record*, a journal of commentary and humor, the *"Lit,"* a monthly magazine of literary commentary, along with a variety of other publications. *The Yale Daily News* had acquired a special gloss because of the successful 1923 launch of the weekly news magazine, *Time*, by Henry Luce and Briton Hadden, the two top officers of the *"News"* in the Class of 1920. Hadden and Luce were the talk of the campus, and each issue of *Time* was read, discussed and debated, favorably and unfavorably. The fact that two recent Yale graduates could not only achieve such quick success "on their own," and also become major national opinion-makers, was a source of great interest to Tex—especially when the prevailing Yale careers of the time involved a slow process of moving one's way up in big financial, corporate or family institutions.

Tex had hoped to continue his *Exonian* writing at Yale; however, the *Yale Daily News* had a forbiddingly long line of experienced school editors. The *Yale Record* had more openings, and covered broader topics. He signed up. The apprentice system at Yale is known as "heeling"—and, after successfully surviving the process, Tex was elected chairman of the *Record* in his junior year. The experience at the *Record* introduced Tex to the possibilities of journalism as a career, and its effect was compounded by reading Walter Lippmann's *Public Opinion,* which left the strongest impression of all the books he read at Yale. It posed a direct challenge to a fundamental concept of democracy in America, the necessary linkage of a "free press," to a voter informed by "objective" journalism—a principle deemed so crucial as to justify protection by the First Amendment of the U.S. Constitution: "Congress shall make no law abridging freedom of speech or of the press."

However, Lippmann's first chapter, titled "Pictures in Their Heads," attacked the idea of what constituted an "informed" voter, asserting that the "news," as reported in the press, was, in reality, distorted by "the hopes of men who composed the news organization." Thus the very basis of a democracy—"public opinion"—supposedly resting upon the judgment of an "informed" voter—was called into question. Tex was hooked! Lippmann went on to argue that "while men are willing to admit that there are two sides to a question, they do not believe that there are two sides to what is presented by the press as a "fact". Moreover, in modern circumstances, an "informed" voter in a democracy would require an "omni-competent" citizen, one who had personal exposure to the circumstances and conditions upon which the citizen was to vote. While this might well have applied to the six thousand citizens of Athens who, in the dawn of democracy, had formed the voting quorum in that city-state, it surely did not apply, more than two thousand years later, to the millions of American voters making judgments on complex national and international affairs far beyond their scope of knowledge.

In the Yale of those days, election by a "secret society" was regarded as a mark of high distinction. There were seven secret societies, each "tapping" fifteen men on "Tap Day," in May of the junior year. "Skull & Bones" was generally regarded as the most selective, followed by "Scroll & Keys." Tex was tapped for "Skull & Bones," a connection that was to open an extraordinary range of associations world-wide. Prior graduates such as Robert Lovett and Henry Stimson often attended "Bones" events and Stimson, the distinguished public servant and both Secretary of State and Secretary of War, said that in all his life and travels, he had always slept in the home of a "Bones" man. The traditional Yale song, "Bright College Years," speaks of the "friendships formed at Yale." That was certainly true for Tex, as those friendships were to continue to affect his life in many ways.

Meanwhile, talks with his uncle continued, who asked him what he was thinking, what were his plans for the future. Tex said that he enjoyed meeting people, that he wanted to know "what was going on," and the idea of reporting the "news" was very appealing. His uncle said he understood Tex's interest—but where would it lead? The "news" was focused on the immediate present. The attention span of the public was both shallow and short. Most people would cling to the familiar. Surely it was important to know "what's going on," but being involved in addressing the critical needs of the future was far more important.

As graduation neared, his uncle urged Tex to think hard about the implications of the accelerating rate of change taking place in America. This would, in turn, lead to concentrations of power in ever-larger corporations, accumulating massive capital. It would inevitably force changes in people's habits. The result was visible all around them—the automobile, highway construction, the population shift from country farms to big cities—and all of these things would require ever larger amounts of energy—energy from oil. While there were, at that time, considerable quantities of oil in America, far greater amounts would be required in the future, which would eventually force America to access oil reserves located overseas in remote areas, especially in the Middle East. His uncle said that Americans like to think of their future in isolationist terms—but they would not have that privilege in the future. The rapid growth of international markets, the corresponding need for more energy, for ever more oil, would necessitate international involvement by America. Texaco, and the other major oil companies, would become the leading companies in the world because the economies of all countries, whatever their state of development, would come to depend upon energy from oil. Despite the Depression, the demand for oil would continue to grow. The great oil companies would need the most talented people. Tex had already demonstrated that he had natural leadership qualities. He could look forward to a great future in Texaco—and his uncle, although always delicate in expressing his hopes, nevertheless had made it clear that he had his heart set on having Tex join his company.

Many of their conversations took place over lunch at his uncle's club, where they were often joined by "Cap" Rieber, a singularly engaging man, a native of Germany who had risen from tanker captain through Texaco's worldwide fleet operations, and was soon to become president of Texaco. Together, they gave Tex a troubling international *"Tour d'Horizon."* The murder of the Russian czar in 1917, the subsequent communist take-over of Russia under Stalin, the spread of socialist/communist activism had combined to destabilize politics all across Europe. Revolutions were inevitable— and were likely to result either in socialist/communist governments of the Left, or anti-communist dictatorships of the Right. England had sacrificed a generation of her best young men in the first World War as fatuous, benighted generals ordered infantry charges into German machine gun fire. As a result, England could barely afford to keep her Empire. Germany, although impoverished by the Versailles Treaty, was potentially the most productive country in Europe, but with an authoritarian culture and history that indicated a dictatorship was the most likely political result. (Hitler was to rise to power in 1933). France was hopeless, largely immobilized by fragmented and extreme political parties of both the Left and the Right. Mussolini had become the "Il Duce " of Italy, a dictator promising to save Catholic Italy from a "godless" communist take-over. Spain, also an intensely Catholic country, would likely accept a similar right-wing dictatorship under Franco.

The probable future consequences were ominous. Whether a dictatorship of the Right or a Communist dictatorship of the Left, none of the European leaders could address the fundamental economic problems—massive unemployment and the necessity for rapid industrialization—which would require ever-increasing supplies of oil, And, apart from the United States, none of the major industrializing countries had oil. Specifically, they pointed out that in 1912, a young Winston Churchill, then the newly appointed First Lord of the Admiralty—knowing that England's Empire rested on control of the seas—to increase the speed of Naval vessels, had converted the Royal Navy from coal (of which England had plenty) to oil (of which England had none). By that act, England's future became dependent on the oil of the Middle East. While America had oil of its own, neither Germany, France, nor Italy had oil, so they, too, had to look elsewhere: Germany to the Ploesti oil fields in Romania, and ultimately to the Russian Caucasus and the Middle East; France, to Algeria and Morocco; Italy, to Libya. While in the Far East, a newly expansionist Japan, also without oil, was dependent on the oil of the Dutch East Indies—and on oil from America.

Tex's uncle and "Cap" Rieber said that the growth of American industry would surpass that of all other nations—and no business in America had greater opportunities. Texaco's domestic oil reserves were a major advantage, compared to developed European nations, which would have to look for their oil requirements to areas of untapped reserves, primarily in what they called "the Petroleum Crescent" around the Persian Gulf, ruled by backward Islamic sheikdoms, now known as Saudi Arabia, Kuwait, Iraq and Iran. Control of access to such dependable oil reserves would inevitably become necessary for the national survival of the major industrial nations. Hence, the dislocation of oil resources, and the inevitable competition for access, would make future wars inevitable. Tom Taylor concluded, "The great wars of the past were fought over religion—but the wars of the future will be fought over oil."

Tex had no basis to dispute that dark conclusion, yet he didn't want to accept it, or base his future on it. The fact was that, no matter the logic of their position, to borrow Walter Lippmann's phrase, "the picture in Tex's head" of Texaco was of endless office work, boring meetings, financial reports, nothing he wanted to do. The conversations only increased his interest in exposure to a rapidly changing world, and the idea of journalism appealed to him even more. It was connected to the news, to what was happening, and to the interesting people who made things happen. It might even help to make things happen.

Serendipity, as it was to occur so often in his life, seemed to offer him a way out. He said he wanted to see more of the world before he made any career decision. Ted Thackeray, a professor at Yale whose son had gone through Exeter with Tex, owned *The Shanghai Advertiser*, an English language newspaper in China, and had offered Tex a job there. His uncle knew Tex was just marking time. He said, "You must do what you think is right for you. I'm not concerned about your future. You are a man with many gifts, and with a remarkable capacity for friendships. They will expand and enrich your life. You have all the qualifications for leadership. I am sure you will find your place."

He had seen in Tex the qualities that were to become the hallmark of his long and adventurous life; his ever-widening circles of friends and acquaintances; his talent for identifying critical issues; and his ability to persuade the right people to focus attention on those issues. And, most important, his lifelong commitment to the search for national leadership in America. His uncle was the first to recognize that, down the road, Tex would become an "insider" himself.

Tex caught a ride to Hawaii on a Texaco tanker. But by the time he reached Hawaii, the Japanese had begun to take control of Shanghai and *The Shanghai Advertiser* job was withdrawn. Tex was disappointed and, at the time, he wondered if he would ever get to Shanghai. Hawaii was filled with Yale men, "Bones" men, sons of the founding missionary families, and assorted other friends. There were lots of lovely ladies, and the surf was up.

By Tex's return, his uncle's health had declined to the point where there was no opportunity for more serious conversations between them before his uncle's death. Through the rest of his life, Tex thought often of his "Uncle Tom,"—such a remarkable man—how fortunate he felt to have had his support and guidance. And how remarkable his prescient vision, his perception of the coming dominance of oil, of its international conflicts—and its implications for wars of the future—all of which were to unfold and involve Tex, in various ways, throughout his life.

Chapter Two

Franklin Roosevelt's "New Deal": The Depression and Isolationism

After his carefree days in the relatively insulated environment of Yale University, the harsh reality of the Depression in New York came as a shock to Tex. Income levels had fallen to one-half the 1929 rate, national unemployment was at 25% in 1932, and conditions seemed to grow worse every day. He wanted to be a reporter, but he had difficulty finding a job. *The New York Herald-Tribune*, owned by the Reid family, friends from Yale, was laying off experienced people, as was *The New York Times*. He had been at Exeter and Yale with Jack Howard, whose family were owners of the Scripps-Howard publishing company and, through that connection, he finally found a job at the *World-Telegram*.

His social life was active, and in the course of debutante parties, he met Sarah Brisbane, the daughter of Arthur Brisbane, the senior editor of the Hearst newspapers. She was very attractive, a graduate of Foxcroft, the fashionable girls school in the hunt country of Virginia, and they shared a common interest in horses. In due course, she invited him to spend a weekend at her father's country estate, *Allaire,* in New Jersey, where Tex had time to talk at length with her father. As the relationship with Sarah continued, a friendship developed between the two men and Arthur Brisbane became a powerful influence in Tex's life.

Brisbane was a courtly man with wide-ranging interests. His father had been a prominent American socialist in his early years, but he came to believe that socialism was not realistic in this country because the ownership of private property was so widespread. He had begun his career on Charles Dana's *New York Sun*. When his obsessive work endangered his health, his family took him to live and study in France and Germany, where he immersed himself in history, philosophy, languages and literature, especially Voltaire, his favorite author, whom he quoted often. He returned to the United States and joined Joseph Pulitzer at the *World* newspaper, then the largest newspaper in the United States, where he rose to an editorship. In 1895 he was approached by William Randolph Hearst to become Hearst's senior editor. When Tex met Brisbane, he was the most widely read columnist in the country, and a powerful presence in New York.

The romance with Sarah progressed into a formal engagement, followed by an elegant wedding. Brisbane offered his new son-in-law a job at the *New York Mirror*—which he eagerly accepted. He and Sarah were invited to move into a suite in the Brisbane apartment, which occupied the top three floors of 1215 Fifth Avenue. Brisbane spent weeknights in New York, while Mrs. Brisbane usually remained in New Jersey, coming in only for major events. Tex normally accompanied his father-in-law to his office, generally driven in Brisbane's car, and sometimes in Mayor LaGuardia's car, as the Mayor's office was near the *Mirror's* office in what was then known as "Newspaper Row" on Park Place in lower Manhattan. His higher education in journalism began with Brisbane's advice: "Learn to write for people who follow the words with their finger and move their lips as they read. If you can learn that, then you can reach all people, including presidents and kings."

While the economic problems of the Depression were worldwide, much of the origin in this country lay with the static complacency of Republican presidents, of big businesses, and the men who controlled them, men who had failed to recognize and respond to the economic, political and social changes that had occurred. Industrial unemployment was terrible enough, but the potentially irreversible, problem was cultural—the destruction of the family farm as a productive, independent, respected way of life. Banks were foreclosing loans on farms all over America, a profound threat, both psychological and sociological, to the structure of much of American society. Previously independent, self-reliant farming families, now deprived of their way of life, their income and their self-respect, were forced to move to towns—where businesses were also laying off workers. The result was a national panic, reaching far beyond the imagination or capacities of conventional politicians or government officials. Americans had lost trust in the political system, and especially in the people at the top.

Brisbane said that the Depression had exposed a problem of government beyond a simple failure of leadership. An underlying danger to the country lay in the structure of the national government itself, a structure set forth in the Constitution and the Electoral College in the later part of the Eighteenth Century—really as a kind of bribe to address the perceived issue of that time, the small states fears of dominance by the states with fast-growing commercial seaport cities—Boston, New York, Philadelphia, identified as "Federalist," favoring a national government—a position strongly opposed by the states primarily dependent upon agriculture, dedicated to "State's Rights"—really a racist position especially important to the slave-owning planters in the Southern states. There was no national government—and no political parties—when the Constitution and the Electoral College were drawn up. The American Revolution was fresh in the public mind, linked with memories of the abuses of power by the King of England. To address those fears, the drafters of the Constitution placed the principal powers of government—to make laws, to tax and to make war—in the Congress, and limited the President's powers to execute the acts of Congress.

Tex asked Brisbane about his Uncle Tom's assertion of the accelerating rate of change, and its effect on the country. He was surprised when Brisbane replied that it was the same question which troubled Jefferson about the Constitutional Convention in Philadelphia in 1787, that changes in the country would be so rapid that a new

Constitutional Convention should be convened every twenty years, just to make the necessary adjustments. By 1932, after more than one hundred and forty years had passed, the number of states had increased from thirteen to forty-eight, each new state small in relative population, but each with two Senators and at least one Congressman. The result was a huge legislative shift of power from states with large populations to the smaller ones, turning the politics of the country ever more inward, further reinforcing the perverse effects of the Electoral College on the Presidential election process.

Brisbane recommended a book, *The American Commonwealth,* written in 1888 by an English Lord, James Bryce, with a critical chapter, "Why Great Men Are Not Elected President," citing the effect of state political leaders promoting "dependable" men, i.e., people dependent on state parties and state interests, rather than the national interest. Brisbane believed that, after Washington, Adams and Jefferson, only Lincoln and Teddy Roosevelt, could meet the test of "Greatness." However, he had high hopes for Franklin Roosevelt.

After World War I, the power of "Big Business" had determined the election of Presidents "captive" to business,—Harding, Coolidge and Hoover. These men were Republicans, and they believed that Calvin Coolidge was right to declare that, "The business of America is business." Brisbane didn't doubt that these men were sincere in their beliefs—but the country had been devastated by the decisions they had made. After the Wall Street financial "Crash" in 1929 President Hoover and the national business leadership had remained frozen, seemingly incapable of leadership or action. Americans were faced with desperate economic conditions, and they wanted a President whom they trusted to put the national interest ahead of private interests.

By 1932, the economic problems had become so acute that action was required— action beyond the capacity of individual states or of Congress, action that only a President could take. To Brisbane, Franklin Roosevelt was the only person with the character, imagination and courage capable of offering a meaningful response to the fears that paralyzed the country. But to address the magnitude of the problems, Roosevelt would have to assume unprecedented Presidential powers. He believed that Americans were fortunate to have Franklin Roosevelt, a man to whom they could relate; one who had endured a profound test of character in overcoming the crippling pains of polio, while retaining his buoyant manner and self-confidence; one whom they thought they "knew" on a personal level; a man in whom the American public could place their trust; a man of courage, who exuded strength by example; who understood that fears are the seeds from which panics spring; one who understood the desperate anxiety of the individual, "What about me?"

Roosevelt's positive campaign song, "*Happy Days Are Here Again,*" quickly established a powerful connection with the anxious American public. Then, his inspirational Inaugural Address with its famous line, "*The only thing we have to fear is fear itself—nameless, unreasoning, unjustified fear.*" He followed by defining his Administration with a dynamic name—the "New Deal"—the prospect of a strong national government to counter the abuse of power and wealth by national corporations—and introduced a blizzard of new proposals, the famous "One Hundred Days" of new legislative initiatives—the Emergency Banking Act, Public Works Administration, Agricultural Adjustment Act, Rural Electrification Agency, Civilian Conservation Corps, Glass-Steagall Act to separate commercial banking from investment banking (an Act repealed in the mid-1990s, to be followed by major banking scandals.) Roosevelt reached out to the nation to support his initiatives with his introduction of radio "Fireside Chats," an inspired innovation and a new level of political communication, reaching Americans sitting in their homes all across the country, seeming to talk to them directly, personally—opening his remarks: "My friends . . ." No other President ever reached so many in such an intimate, reassuring way. The role of the President added another dimension. And the country—and the economy—began to respond.

Brisbane told Tex that he wanted him to learn how the world works, that there is an "inside" to everything. It means getting to know the "insiders" of influence. Brisbane seemed to know everybody in New York who was worth knowing—and they all seemed to want to come to his office to talk with him. He introduced Tex to his visitors and generally had him sit in on most meetings, providing him with a wide exposure and a remarkable perspective on the nature of political power at that time in America, including personal connection with the two men, other than Roosevelt himself, most responsible for Roosevelt's election: William Randolph Hearst, who delivered the Democratic Convention delegate votes necessary for Roosevelt's nomination, and Joe Kennedy, Roosevelt's behind the scenes deal-maker and fund-raiser. Brisbane described Hearst as a reserved man, that it would take time to gain his confidence; whereas Kennedy's personality was far more open, someone who enjoyed talking to an interested listener, especially one whom he thought might be of use some day.

Tex looked forward to his first meeting with Hearst, but he was not what he had expected. Hearst was a large, bulky man, expensively but awkwardly dressed, with a retiring manner, not at all what he had imagined as the most powerful, willful and capricious publisher in America, owner of newspapers in most major cities, several national magazines, and a weekly newsreel, a man who lived in various palatial residences, with fabulous art collections and other displays of apparently unlimited wealth. Hearst obviously had great respect for Brisbane. Prior to their marriages, Hearst had asked Brisbane to live with him in his mansion on Lexington Avenue, and Brisbane had worked with Hearst for nearly forty years as his closest advisor. In view of their long association, it was surprising to learn of their different views of the world. Hearst, despite his regular summers in Europe and his collections of quantities of European art and antiques, remained an undeviating isolationist, whereas Brisbane, by education, and by conviction, was internationalist in outlook. They had resolved their differences by separating areas of responsibility, each being careful not to step in the other's field. Hearst exercised absolute authority over all matters of national politics and international relations, while Brisbane served as general editor and as the principal columnist.

Tex was fascinated to learn the role that Hearst had played in the Democratic Convention in 1932, particularly the "inside" aspects of an otherwise presumably party Presidential selection process. Although Roosevelt had established an early lead, he had been unable to increase it through three ballots. Former New York Governor Al Smith was close behind Roosevelt, and Smith's vote was solid, whereas Roosevelt's showed signs of weakness. The fourth ballot was crucial. If Roosevelt could not win the necessary majority, enough of his support would go to Smith to give him the nomination, it being assumed that the Depression conditions were so overwhelming that Smith—despite the reservations over his Catholic religion that had cost him the 1928 election—could easily defeat Herbert Hoover.

The stalemate meant that control of a block of key delegations could dictate the nomination. Hearst had anticipated the possibility, and was well prepared. Early in his career, he had seriously entertained a political career for himself, naturally looking to the Presidency. To that end, Hearst managed to get himself elected to Congress, but his ambition did not survive subsequent electoral losses, first for the Senate, then for Governor of New York. However, Hearst realized that his "insider" position gave him the opportunity to influence the Presidential election. While he was in Congress, Hearst had befriended a fellow Congressman, John Nance Garner of Texas. Hearst had maintained this friendship and, by 1932, Garner had become a respected U. S. Senator. Dissatisfied with the prospective Democratic Presidential candidates, Hearst, recognizing the potential value of control of the Texas delegation, along with the California delegation which Hearst already effectively controlled through his newspapers, declared his support for Garner for President—and he threw the powers of all the Hearst papers behind him. Garner, as a "favorite son," won the support of the Texas delegation and, with the support of Hearst's minions, captured the California delegation as well. With the Convention deadlocked—and with both Texas and California delegations, although formally pledged to Garner, effectively controlled by Hearst, Roosevelt's nomination then effectively lay in Hearst's hands.

With Kennedy acting as intermediary, Hearst bargained hard. He came from San Francisco and he distrusted Roosevelt, believing that his New York origin, his Anglophilic education at Groton and Harvard, made him an "internationalist." Accordingly, Hearst demanded commitments that Roosevelt would maintain an isolationist position and keep the United States out of the League of Nations and the World Court. Kennedy obtained the assurances demanded by Hearst, whereupon Hearst delivered the winning votes to Roosevelt—and obtained the Vice Presidential nomination for Garner. Brisbane was delighted at Roosevelt's 1932 victory, but he was troubled that Hearst and Kennedy were able to have such control over the nomination process.

Joe Kennedy visited Brisbane frequently, and Brisbane was intrigued, often amused, at the audacity and shamelessness of Kennedy's operations—and his personal life. Kennedy's habit was to drop in unannounced and, if Brisbane was out of the office, he would talk with Tex who, from these conversations was able to piece together a remarkable story of how "insider" power was achieved. Kennedy had grown up in the underside of Boston politics, had married the daughter of a prominent Irish "pol," John "Honey Fitz" Fitzgerald, and had handled the seamy side and quiet payoffs underlying Fitzgerald's rise in Boston politics and his eventual election to Congress—from which Fitzgerald was subsequently forced to resign for "election irregularities." With the coming of World War I, Kennedy got a job in the offices of the Bethlehem Steel Boat Division in Boston—which kept him out of the military draft—and exposed him to a rapid education in executive management, the realities of dock gang payoffs and union racketeering, as well as hard bargaining over large dollar amounts on ship contracts with Franklin Roosevelt, then Assistant Secretary of the Navy. After the war, Kennedy became a stockbroker, where his business experiences had provided inside information, and substantial rewards. When Prohibition outlawed the importation of liquor into the United States, Kennedy used his dock-gang acquaintances to become a "bootlegger," arranging to off-load liquor from cargo ships lying off the beaches of Cape Cod, and later off Long Island. Kennedy's "bootlegging" operations expanded in New York and Chicago, where he developed close connections with the "underworld" leaders in both cities. At a Harvard reunion, he earned the admiration of his classmates by providing generous supplies of "bootleg" liquor, and the chairman offered a grateful toast: "To Joe Kennedy, whose liquor tonight came ashore, like the Pilgrims, in small boats."

Despite his financial successes, Kennedy was frustrated by the anti-Catholic prejudices of the Puritan aristocracy of Boston—"where the Lowells spoke only to Cabots, and the Cabots spoke only to God"—and he moved his family to New York, where he quickly became a prominent Wall Street "pool" operator, manipulating the prices of stocks, a line of work which rewarded brains over pedigrees. While Kennedy was always financially ambitious, he also saw wealth as an instrument for the acquisition of political power—and he had Presidential ambitions for himself. He closed his investment activities in New York before the 1929 "Crash," and moved to Hollywood to enter the movie business which he saw, not only having major profit potential by transforming otherwise limited "talent" into glamorous national celebrity, but also the potential of "movies" to become a powerful influence on American attitudes, fashions—and politics. When Wall Streeters questioned him about the seemingly lower class aspect of the movie business, Kennedy replied that any business which can survive being run by a bunch of bankrupt furriers has to be a great opportunity. He gained control of RKO, thereby adding another dimension to his rapidly growing fortune—as well as learning the skills of Hollywood promotion and publicity. He also acquired, among his seemingly endless stable of girlfriends, Gloria Swanson, then the leading lady of Hollywood, as his long-time mistress, and thus attained a highly visible rank in the annals of Hollywood skirt chasing.

Among Roosevelt's reforms after his election, he had established the Securities & Exchange Commission to regulate the financial markets and correct the abuses (from which Kennedy and other "pool" operators had so benefited and which were perceived to be a significant factor underlying the "Crash" on Wall Street) and, to universal surprise, appointed Kennedy as Chairman. In view of Kennedy's own questionable Wall Street history, Roosevelt was asked the reason for his choice. He replied, "You know the old saying: Set a thief to catch a thief." Roosevelt's "New Deal" was the "Big Story" of the time. The country had responded to Roosevelt's "One Hundred Days" of reform legislation and conditions had improved markedly. Roosevelt gave one of his most memorable "Fireside Chats," asking Americans to ask themselves, "Are you better off now?" (Years later Tex was amazed when Ronald Reagan asked the same decisive question in his first presidential debate with Jimmy Carter). The answer to Roosevelt's question clearly was "yes."

However, Roosevelt then began to shift his focus. He became identified openly with industrial labor unions, many with socialist or communist connections, in what came to be called the Second New Deal. Labor leaders became regular visitors to the White

House, particularly David Dubinsky, head of the United Ladies Garment Workers union, and Sidney Hillman, of the Amalgamated Clothing Workers, whose influence in the White House came to be so strong that "Clear it with Sidney" was reputed to be a requirement for any new policy statement. Roosevelt's language also turned hard-edged, describing Republicans as "malefactors of great wealth" and speaking of "driving the money-changers from the temple." This drew outraged reaction from Republicans, already angered at Roosevelt's sharp income tax increases to pay for the new social programs, taxes which were immediately harshly attacked as a "soak-the-rich" policy.

Tex was impressed as Roosevelt skillfully disarmed the harsh Republican attacks. In a "Fireside Chat" he reminded the country of the story of a rich old New York gentleman who fell into the East River. A passerby dived in and saved his life, but the old gentleman's silk hat floated away—and the old gentleman spent the rest of his life complaining about the loss of his hat. Roosevelt's light touch delighted Brisbane. He said that Roosevelt personified the difference between good leaders and bad leaders: good leaders were innately optimistic, whereas bad leaders exploited fears.

In spite of Roosevelt's national popularity, new opposition arose from both the far Left and the far Right. The argument from the Left was largely economic. Senator Huey Long of Louisiana, a singularly corrupt man from a state of notoriously corrupt politics, advocated radical transfers of wealth from the rich to the poor in a program, "Every Man A King." From California came the "Townsend Plan," a demand for a national pension. From the right, a reactionary Catholic priest from Detroit, Father Coughlin, started a radio program which was to exceed, in percentage of audience, the market share of any of the virulent "Religious Right" behavior today. In the mid-1930s, these fringe, but primitive and intense movements, if combined, seemed to have the potential to constitute a third force which, together with the Republican anti-Roosevelt vote, might have denied Roosevelt the 1936 Presidential election. Brisbane hated the idea of religion-based politics. He thought that religious wars were a continuing curse on civilization. Despite the bitter opposition, Roosevelt easily won a "landslide" reelection in 1936 but, for Tex, the "Father Coughlin's" religious agitation in the mid-1930s was an eerie antecedent to the "Religious Right" now dominating the Republican Party of President George W. Bush.

For some time Brisbane's health had slowly deteriorated, and his pace slowed. But conversations continued. Brisbane stressed that communication and politics were inextricably related, and that advances in communication would drive politics, as Roosevelt's powerfully effective radio "Fireside Chats" had so clearly demonstrated. He urged Tex to push the limits of communication as far and as fast as possible, in new markets as well as in new techniques, always trying to work to a public purpose or benefit. Brisbane had seen photographs displace print in newspapers. Then, as advertisers grew in power, newspaper owners acquired radio licenses from the government, and he knew they would inevitably do the same when television became available, further eroding the objectivity of newspapers even more. Brisbane urged Tex always to remember Roosevelt's distinction between the public interest and the corporate interest. Brisbane feared—as Tex's uncle had predicted—an inevitable increase in corporate growth, consolidation, and power. At Madison Square Garden, just before the

1936 election, Roosevelt delivered a bold, vivid attack upon "business and financial monopoly, speculation, risk, reckless banking, class antagonism, sectionalism, and war profiteering," ending with a defining declaration, "I should like to have it said of my first administration that the forces of selfishness and lust for power have met their match. I should like to have it said of my second administration that in it those forces have met their master."

The force of Roosevelt's assertion pleased Brisbane, but by then he was a very sick man. In their last real conversation before his death, he returned to his basic conviction that the greatness of America lies in the ideals of its founders, the dedication to opportunity for a better life for all Americans. He was fond of quoting favorite language, particularly the pregnant language in Roosevelt's 1936 Nomination acceptance speech: "Governments can err, Presidents do make mistakes, but the immortal Dante tells us that divine justice weighs the sins of the cold-blooded and the sins of the warm-hearted in different scales. Better the occasional faults of a government that lives in a spirit of charity than the consistent omissions of a government frozen in the ice of its own indifference. There is a mysterious cycle in human events. To some generations much is given; of other generations much is expected. This generation of Americans has a rendezvous with destiny."

Brisbane's condition deteriorated steadily, and Tex sat by his bed all Christmas Day of 1936. Talking tired him, and he was silent for a long time, scarcely breathing, then he whispered his favorite phrase from Voltaire, "This is the best of all possible worlds." He did not speak again. After some time, a doctor came in, took his pulse, and said that his heart had stopped. After the family had left, Tex remained seated at Brisbane's bedside. Sometime in the early pre-dawn hours, he heard the door open. He knew someone had entered. He did not look around, but after some time, he felt a hand rest on his shoulder, followed by Hearst's voice, obviously deeply moved by Brisbane's death, saying "There will be times when you will not be able to print what you want to print—because it is my paper. But I promise you that you will never have to print something that you do not want to print." After a moment, Hearst left, silently closing the door behind him.

Chapter Three

Bernard Baruch and the "Gathering Storm" in Europe

Bernard Baruch was the ultimate "insider" of his time, a fascinating figure, a renowned investor who had left Wall Street in 1916, at the peak of his financial successes, to become personal advisor to President Wilson and head of Wilson's "War Cabinet" in World War I. At the end of the war, Wilson took him to Paris for the Versailles Peace conference, where Baruch became friends with Franklin Roosevelt, then serving as Assistant Secretary of the Navy, a relationship which continued during Roosevelt's time as Governor of New York and then on into the Roosevelt Presidency, where Baruch was a regular visitor for private meetings in the Oval Office. At Versailles, Baruch had also begun a friendship with Winston Churchill, and thereafter they made extended visits in each other's homes during the summers. When they first met, Tex told him that he had found the Luce and Hadden papers in the "Bones" archives, including a "dummy" proposed first issue of *Time* magazine with Baruch on the cover, describing him as "the most respected and influential figure in the country." It was the beginning of a long and rewarding friendship, one which was to open many new doors.

Baruch personified the image of a great public figure, tall, over six feet four inches, erect, formally and elegantly dressed, with a great head of carefully coifed white hair and pince-nez glasses clipped to his nose. His manner was reserved, marked with old-school Southern courtesy, and he was immensely attractive, both to men and to women. For all of his many other achievements, Baruch was surprisingly proud of his career as a varsity boxer at City College, and Tex's boxing experience at Exeter and Yale established a common bond. They often attended the then popular Friday night fights at Madison Square Garden. For a man with Baruch's impeccable dress and manner, Tex was surprised to see a large framed picture of Baruch from his days as a college boxer—stripped to the waist, muscular arms crossed—displayed in the elegant living room of his apartment.

Early in the relationship, they talked mostly of contemporary issues, the depression, the economy, politics. Baruch said that everything he had done had begun at City College, particularly because of a course called Political Economy—which integrated, not only economics and politics, but also history, geography sociology, and psychology, as well. He believed that this approach provided a much better "real world" perspective than the prevailing practice of universities today to separate the subjects, an approach which he regarded as impeding students in their ability to understand how the world really works. Baruch's experience as a stock trader and speculator had also been a great education, forcing him to have to see both sides of an investment—something that he also valued in his public service role—in relating economic factors to the public interest. He had based decisions on his own extensive independent field research, and reviewed each decision in the context of his Political Economy training. He was regularly asked how he made investments, and he enjoyed replying, "I just do what people want me to do. If everyone wants to sell, then I have to buy." However, he would never talk about "short-selling"—selling stock he didn't own in anticipation of falling prices—for which Baruch was even more well known.

In addition to boxing, Baruch was attracted to beautiful women. As their friendship developed, he and Tex would meet for dinner, where Baruch would escort a beautiful, and always talented, lady. At that time, Clare Booth Brokaw was Baruch's mistress. She was a fascinating woman, exceptionally bright, beautiful, witty, talented, charming—and ambitious. Baruch obviously was very taken by her, and it was apparent that she would have liked to marry him—but Baruch, despite the fact that he lived apart from his wife and that his liaisons were not hidden, was not going to marry her. Among other things, he was more than twice her age. When Baruch was at his home in South Carolina, Clare, who liked to be seen with men about town, would ask Tex to take her to dinner.

When Baruch introduced Tex to a new mistress, he knew their affair had ended. Shortly thereafter Clare called him, and their relationship took on a more intimate character. They also had common literary interests. Her play, *Abide With Me*, was going through pre-opening problems, and she was working on a new play, *The Women*. They talked about writing problems, how to make people "see" through the use of words, of the relationship between pictures and words, how one could evoke the other, and what kinds of words were the most useful—they called them "picture-words." They also talked about the seemingly strange attraction of intellectuals to communism. They concluded that, at least to a degree, it must arise out of need for the simplistic, total all-inclusiveness, of communist doctrine. Her anti-communism later became almost obsessive.

For all her talent, beauty, and ambition, Clare had deep inner insecurities which led her to seek romantic reassurance. She was great company—and Tex was far from her only admirer. Her goal was marriage to a rich, powerful man, one who could provide the security and access to power that she so deeply craved. Tex was not surprised when she married Henry Luce, despite his driven personality. Luce represented her ideal of the perfect marriage partner for her, but it seemed odd that she kept the marriage secret for months. Baruch simply smiled and said, "Women are to be admired, not understood."

Beneath the surface, there were many dimensions to Baruch. He had been born in South Carolina shortly after the end of the Civil War, the son of a prominent local doctor who had served as a Confederate medical officer. Both of his parents were Jews, his mother's family having come to America in the early 1700s—his great-grandmother had danced with General Lafayette during the American Revolution. He told Tex that until he was eleven years old and his father moved to New York, he did not realize that he was Jewish—because it did not matter in South Carolina where his family was regarded as an integral part of the community. However, in New York, a city of many immigrants, it did matter. Although his father's medical practice progressed slowly, it eventually came to include figures from the financial world.

Baruch became fascinated with finance and, after graduation from City College, went to Wall Street. His abilities were apparent—but his Jewish name foreclosed admission to the leading firms, so he went out on his own in 1887. He soon recognized that, although securities trading was very active on the New York Stock Exchange, and despite the large amounts of money involved, most of the trading was done on rumors or "tips," with very little accurate information. Baruch wanted "inside" knowledge. He was especially attracted by important natural resources, many of which were located outside the United States, copper, tin, rubber and oil, and he set out to learn for himself, first-hand. He visited the sites, befriended or retained the leading independent mining engineers, and learned the actual cost basis of each resource—which gave him a great advantage in judging prices of such commodities on Wall Street. He operated on his own—always keeping his information private—while acquiring the title, "The Lone Wolf of Wall Street. His "inside" knowledge enabled him to make his fortune, often in investments associated with the great names of the "Gilded Age" of finance, Morgan, Harriman, Hill and Guggenheim.

With his wealth secure beyond all personal requirements, Baruch was taunted by his father's challenge: "Now that you have more money than you can spend, what are you going to do to make your life count for something worthwhile?" As a dedicated doctor, Baruch's father regarded service to the public as the highest calling. Baruch had established himself as a national leader in the financial world. But, while the financial world was about money, the political world was about power. And, at that time, the path to national political leadership, like financial leadership, was not open to Jews. Nevertheless, Baruch recognized that there was an underlying, general similarity between political decisions and those in the financial world, in that each turned on a choice between two positions: in politics, Republican or Democrat; in financial markets, Buy or Sell. And, in both cases, the decision was usually made with limited information.

While Baruch never mentioned the subject, it became apparent that he came to see a potential opportunity to achieve a national leadership role for himself as a private, "inside" personal counselor to the most influential figures in this country and abroad. To emphasize that he was beyond personal or financial ambitions, Baruch closed his office on Wall Street and intentionally maintained a highly visible social life style, cultivating a public identity as a person of the South. He maintained a fabulous plantation, *Hobcaw*, in South Carolina, where his wife lived, and where he entertained with gracious hospitality, providing luxurious hunting and fishing opportunities. By establishing this South Carolinian identity, Baruch was accepted as a sympathetic figure by the powerful block of southern senators, as well as other prominent figures. He offered friendship, advice, favors, gifts, and money—never asking for anything in return.

As a practical matter, he spent divided his time between national decision-makers in New York, or in Washington, where senators and congressmen were usually local in origin, background and education, and lacked the scope of knowledge or reliable information necessary for decisions on major matters, particularly in the international area. As in Wall Street, Baruch found that decisions in Congress were also made upon tips, gossip, and rumors, often accompanied by discreet transfers of large sums of money. Against this limited base of information, Baruch's real experience became all the more valuable, while providing him with inside information on the direction of policy in Congress. He held person-to-person meetings with important figures on his favorite park benches, in Lafayette Square across from the White House in Washington, or in Central Park in New York, where his benches are commemorated with brass plaques. His advice came to be so highly regarded that President Wilson asked him to become Secretary of the Treasury, an offer he turned down on the ground that his investment background would inevitably be a source of criticism. Wilson later asked him to be chairman of the Democratic Party, which Baruch said he rejected without regret.

Baruch expressed his growing concerns over the increasing concentrations of power in business and in government, reinforcing his conviction of the necessity of maintaining the crucial separation between the public interest and the private interest. He said that the lines had become increasingly blurred. National wealth had come to be calculated in terms of corporate wealth. In the corporate world, management is highly competitive, more so in this country than anywhere else in the world. Growth is the goal. Profit is the measure. Time horizons are short. Personal rewards are high. Temptation abounds. It was evident that corporate "investment" in "government relations" offered high rates of return, as many businesses demonstrated. As unions had grown in power, they had begun to play the power game, sometimes with open socialist or communist leadership or affiliations. And senators and congressmen, particularly congressional committee chairmen, openly used the positions for personal benefit. Baruch concluded that it was not a pretty picture, and it was getting worse.

By 1936 Hearst, who had effectively delivered the Presidency to Roosevelt in 1932, turned all the editorial resources of his papers against him. Hearst's isolationist attitude had steadily intensified, and he thought he perceived in Roosevelt's decisions the influence of young "Jewish" advisors, with "internationalist" (meaning socialist and/or Communist) inclinations, anti-business attitudes and "soak-the-rich" tax policies. Although far more vehement, Hearst was not alone in thoughts in this direction. Even Harry Hopkins, as close as he was to Roosevelt, grew so concerned over the anti-business attitude of other New Deal advisors, that it was said that Hopkins had commented that the younger fellows around the President don't want to see a business recovery, they want the government to run the country.

Tex was increasingly involved in his work in New York and, after the birth of their son, Michael (named for his friend Mike Phipps) Brisbane McCrary, Sarah had begun living at the Brisbane home in New Jersey, where Michael was well cared for and Sarah could pursue her long-standing commitment to serious equestrian competition. As time passed, they both came to realize that they had married too young, and that

Bernard M. Baruch on his familiar bench in Lafayette Square, Washington

their interests were very different. Their lives drifted apart and, as a practical matter, their marriage had effectively ended.

Apart from the demands of his column in the *Mirror,* Tex maintained an active social life. He continued to see his Yale friends, Phipps, Iglehart, Mills and Bostwick, who were rising rapidly in the championship polo ranks. Polo championships were great social events—and horse racing, "the sport of kings," was not far behind. To minimize the weight factor, horse racing had acquired a preponderance of hired jockeys, but a few "gentlemen" jockeys remained, Pete Bostwick among them. Social distinctions were retained, as demonstrated by the shout of a jockey riding up to pass a tightly packed field near the finish of the race, "Out of the way, you sons of bitches— and you, too, Mr. Bostwick!"

In the company of his polo and horse-racing friends, Tex had met Jock Whitney, an "insider" by birth. Their similar, easy, open personalities meshed immediately, and Jock was to become Tex's closest friend for many years. Jock was the embodiment of the gentleman sportsman. His picture was on the cover of *Time* magazine, the only polo player ever so recognized. Jock was handsome, charming, and Jock could do— and did—almost anything he wanted, always with grace, courtesy, and the absence of pretense. He seemed to be the same to everyone—and everyone loved him. Tex described him, in Kipling's words, "he could talk with kings, nor lose the common touch." He had been heavy-weight boxing champion at Groton and they shared interests in what was going on, news, ideas, the theater, sports, And, of course, both were especially interested in beautiful women and having good times. Seeing who could have the most fun became a kind of competitive game between them.

There were pictures in Jock's home of the marriage of his father, Payne Whitney, to Helen Hay, the daughter of John Hay, then Secretary of State, friend and biographer of President Teddy Roosevelt. By inheritance, Jock had become the richest man in America. His sister, Joan, became the richest young woman—until that title was accorded to Doris Duke, the only child of "Buck" Duke, founder of American Tobacco, another "close friend" of Tex. Jock Whitney's *Greentree* team won the National Polo Championship in 1935, followed by Phipps and Iglehart's National wins in 1937 and 1938, riding with Jock's cousin, Cornelius Vanderbilt ("Sonny") Whitney's *Old Westbury* team. Through Jock, Tex came to know Tommy Hitchcock, the top scorer on Jock's team, recognized as America's greatest polo player. Before our entry into World War I, Hitchcock had left St. Paul's School to enlist in the French Lafayette Esquadrille as a fighter pilot, shot down several German planes, was himself shot down, imprisoned, and subsequently escaped.

Within this group were two others, Bob Lovett and Averill Harriman, both "Bones" men, both prominent "insiders" who also were to continue to play a part in Tex's life. In 1917 Lovett and a few had left Yale before his senior year, trained as a pilot in the Yale Unit and went into action in France, flying a British Sopwith "Camel" airplane from a field near Dieppe, where he had been initiated into "Bones" on the beach, after returning from a mission. He shot down several German planes, and returned an acclaimed "ace." He married the daughter of the Brown family, of Brown Brothers, and joined the firm, where he became a strong Republican influence in a firm with Democratic leanings from its origin in Baltimore. Dignified and reserved in manner,

Lovett was greatly respected. He later assisted Tex in his articles on the inadequacies of U.S. military aviation before World War II, served as Under Secretary of War for Air in World War II, then after the war, was Under Secretary of State, one of "The Wise Men" who, under General Marshall, reestablished the European economy, ending his most impressive public career as Secretary of Defense.

Averill Harriman was older, a taciturn man with none of the personal grace or charm of Tex's other friends. But, reticent as he was, he was respected for his tireless effort and dedication, first demonstrated at Yale. After a Harvard crew had defeated Harriman's freshman crew, he had applied for two months leave-of-absence from Yale and went to Oxford to study their techniques. His recommendations were adopted (amazing in itself) and he was named Yale varsity coach while still an undergraduate, even though he had never rowed in a varsity race. He was tapped for "Bones," joined the Brown Brothers firm—which in fairly short order became Brown Brothers Harriman—and became an important financial investor in Europe and Russia and, later, a policy advisor and international political emissary for President Roosevelt.

Jock Whitney was, naturally, the centerpiece of the social crowd, always with a beautiful girl on his arm, nearly always distinguished in some way, Tallulah Bankhead and Paulette Goddard, prominent among them. Someone remarked of Jock, "For a guy with only one yacht, Jock sure has a lot of girls, in a lot of ports." He took an interest in the movie business, financing projects with David Selznick. When Margaret Mitchell's book, *Gone With the Wind,* was published, he recommended it to Selznick, who turned it down. Jock then bought the movie rights for himself for $50,000. Selznick told him he was crazy to pay so much, and asked what made him do it? Jock said, "I read it." As the book's popularity grew, Selznick changed his mind, and wanted it for their partnership. Typically generous, Jock contributed it at his cost.

Meanwhile, Tex continued to talk with Baruch, who spoke of his summer visits with Winston Churchill, and of Churchill's escalating anxiety of war, as a "Gathering Storm," across Europe (a descriptive phrase which was to become the title of the first volume of Churchill's postwar history of World War II), of the British and French "appeasement" in the face of Hitler's military development and aggressiveness, culminating in Britain's Prime Minister Chamberlain's "surrender" of Czechoslovakia to Hitler at Munich in 1938. Baruch said that the most important aspect of the event was Czechoslovakia's strategic value to Hitler. Germany's greatest weakness was that it had no oil to operate its industrial and military machine—and control of Czechoslovakia placed Hitler next to Romania and its Ploesti oil fields, the only source of oil in Europe.

The innate isolationist strain steadily gained strength in America, inflamed by Senator Gerald Nye of Iowa who initiated a Senatorial investigation of the U. S. munitions industry, accusing the companies of having instigated America's entry into World War I to generate profits for themselves—at the cost of the lives of American boys. This incendiary accusation resulted in the Neutrality Acts to prohibit sales of U. S. arms abroad, thwarting Roosevelt's desires to aid nations threatened by Hitler's rising aggressiveness.

The developing national and international events absorbed Tex, both from what he had learned from Baruch and from what he saw and heard in New York, and he became increasingly frustrated at not being able to write about what he was learning in his column—which was strictly limited to people and events around New York City. He was particularly concerned about Baruch's implication of the likelihood of America being drawn into a European war, and it turned his thoughts to what he had learned of American aviation developments—that American military aviation was woefully neglected—just as it had been before America's entry into World War 1. He wanted to write about the issue, and he thought that, given Hearst's antagonism to Roosevelt, he might be able to get away with some critical coverage of the lack of American aviation preparedness.

Every Yale man of that time knew about the famous First Yale Unit of Naval Aviation, organized by a group of Yale undergraduates, funded by their fathers before America's entry into World War I, and before the Navy had a pilot training program. Trained in aircraft on Long Island Sound in the summer and at Palm Beach in the winter, the Yale Unit was led by Trubee Davison, Bob Lovett, Dave Ingalls, and other assorted old Yale names. [Author's Footnote: Tex was curious for more information about the Yale Unit and I was pleased to be able to add a few Yale Unit stories, as my uncle by marriage, Liv Ireland, was a member of the group.] The Yale Unit benefited from the support of Trubee Davison's father, the senior partner at the Morgan Bank which had been retained by the British government to arrange and finance British purchases in the United States. In this capacity Mr. Davison and his son, Trubee, had spent the summer of 1916 in England and France and had seen the growing importance of aviation in the war in Europe—and the virtual lack of development in the U. S. Based upon what he had seen, Mr. Davison had tried to persuade President Wilson of the need for greater aviation preparedness. However, in 1916, Wilson would not increase U.S. military spending, apparently to preserve his presidential campaign theme, "He kept us out of war." Then, after taking office for a second term in the spring of 1917, Wilson took the country into the war.

With their fathers' financial support, the Yale undergraduate volunteers had bought planes, hired instructors, put the Unit together—and were eventually able to receive formal recognition as the First Naval Aviation Reserve Unit. The American people acclaimed the heroics of Bob Lovett and Dave Ingalls, who became Naval aces in combat, flying English "Camels" and French "Spads." Twenty years later, with Europe again on the brink of another major war looming again in Europe, the American Congress and public did not seem to grasp the significance of the American backwardness in the development of military aircraft, particularly as compared to the major efforts which had been undertaken in Germany—and visibly displayed in the Spanish Civil War in 1936.

As Tex looked into the situation, he found conditions that shocked him. At the end of World War I, Germany had rejected the entrenched attitudes and prejudices of the old order of military leaders, and Hitler had been able to build an integrated modern military machine. This was not the case in France, England and the United States, where the military leadership remained stuck in their old ways—the cavalry continuing to be the socially preferred arm. However, Britain and France had, at least, established independent Air Forces, while the United States—where the Wright brothers had invented the airplane—had not been able to design and produce a military airplane capable of fighting in World War I—and thereafter had blindly permitted Army generals to retain an Army Air Corps, subordinated to the Army, and equipped with a small number of antiquated airplanes virtually until the Japanese attack on Pearl Harbor on December 7th, 1941.

A major part of the problem was structural. Congress, dominated by isolationists, of both parties, was addicted to "pork-barrel" appropriations for their own interests —behavior memorialized by Mark Twain's famous comment, " The only natural criminal class in America is Congress." The combination of "Battleship Admirals" and "Horse Cavalry" Army generals, indoctrinated by antiquated thinking at their respective military academies, Annapolis and West Point—where promotions were by influenced by seniority and tainted by favoritism from "old boy" secret societies—maintained strong hostility to aviation as a potentially competitive branch of the military.

For his articles, Tex interviewed a lot of people, Bob Lovett, Tommy Hitchcock and Jimmy Doolittle, among them. The articles described the extent of the problems, the lack of readiness of our Army Air Corps as a subordinated stepchild of the Army, all in all, a badly neglected military aviation situation. Tex was disgusted by what he had learned of Congressional behavior, and he concluded with a recommendation for an independent Air Force—with status equivalent to that of the air forces of the other major nations—as a separate Cabinet Department. The articles made the front pages of the *Mirror*, and the other Hearst papers—his first major articles on a national subject—and they drew a fair amount of public attention and comment.

Tex considered these aviation articles the most rewarding journalistic work he had done. Bob Lovett became so troubled by the information in the articles that he undertook a personal survey of the aviation industry across the country and filed a private report to the War Department. When Roosevelt appointed Henry Stimson as Secretary of War, Stimson named Lovett Under Secretary of War for Air, a post which had remained vacant since 1931, when General MacArthur had instigated the firing of Trubee Davison, the last holder of that position.

In August 1939, the "gathering storm," in Europe, which Churchill had predicted, broke with dramatic impact. Baruch said that the "appeasement" hopes of England and France had rested on the belief/hope that Hitler's natural enemy was Stalin and Russian Communism. But on August 23rd, 1939, Hitler and Stalin stunned the world (and especially Communist parties and their sympathizers in unions and academic circles who took their orders from Moscow, both in the United States and elsewhere) by announcing a German-Soviet Non-Aggression Pact. Overnight, Hitler, the former archenemy, was suddenly Communism's newest best friend. A week later, on September 1, 1939, Hitler invaded Poland, demonstrating the awesome power of his co-ordinated Air and Army "Blitzkreig." Poland was helpless.

Only twenty-one years after the end of World War I—"The War To End All Wars"—the world was on the brink of another catastrophic World War.

Chapter Four

"We Want Willkie!" "No Third Term!" . . . Roosevelt: "Your Sons Will Not Be Sent to Fight in Foreign Wars"

The 1940 Presidential election was a landmark event in America politics, a confrontation between the implied warning of the venerated George Washington that no President should serve more than two terms, in conflict with the towering presence of Franklin Roosevelt—by far the most dominant national leader since Teddy Roosevelt—who was seeking a third term. The national debate was played out in the context of the deep-seated public isolationist instinct, faced with the imminence of another world war, as Hitler's menace in Europe loomed ever larger, and Japanese militancy increased in the Pacific.

Tex had put a lot of work into the preparation of his aviation articles which had given him substantial "insider" information and it seemed incredible to him that, with the world on the threshold of another world war, the leadership of the Republican Party was so blindly and inwardly focused as to offer up as candidates for President two men so obviously lacking in experience and international exposure: Tom Dewey, the thirty-eight year old Governor of New York—credited with breaking the "rackets," an alliance of the Mafia, corrupt unions and judges in New York—but otherwise ignorant of the world; and Bob Taft, son of former President William H. Taft of Ohio, elected to the Senate only two years before, and whose only exposure outside the United States was a Yale College trip to Bermuda. Taft was an open isolationist, as was Dewey, although in a somewhat lower key. However, Dewey was handicapped by his appearance, small in stature, prissy in dress and manner, with a clipped little mustache. Alice Longworth, the daughter of Teddy Roosevelt, said Dewey "looked like the candy groom on a wedding cake." Despite his unleader-like appearance and manner, Dewey was the favorite of Republican party leaders in the East, while Taft led in the West.

Baruch wondered how, at such a crucial period, with Europe at war, and America on the edge of war, the Republican Party leaders in the Congress and in the states could believe that the country should be in the hands of either of these two men, so lacking in international interest and experience. Baruch said that the weakness of the candidates simply reflected the fact that the dictates of the Electoral College give all the Electoral College votes of a state to the winner of the most votes in that state, effectively focusing American politics on internal state issues. Moreover, state party bosses want a candidate dependent upon them, thus depriving the country of a true national leader with some understanding of the world. Baruch continued, "But that's all irrelevant for this election. Regardless of their lack of Presidential qualifications, neither Dewey nor Taft has any chance to beat Roosevelt. So, it all comes down to this: Does Roosevelt want us in this war? And, if so, how soon? Or, to put it another way—can we, should we—stay out?"

As America awaited Hitler's next move, Tex began an effort to recruit American volunteers as fighter pilots for the "*Eagle Squadron,*" of the Royal Air Force in England—an activity which he had to keep quiet around the office. Then he got a call from Baruch who said that Churchill's first act on becoming Prime Minister was to appoint Baruch's old friend, Lord Beaverbrook, as Minister of Aircraft Production, who was coming to America to buy U.S. warplanes for England. Baruch was giving a dinner for him and, because of Tex's pre-war articles on American aircraft Baruch wanted Tex to meet Beaverbrook.

In 1940, America was still strongly isolationist, but there were some signs that the isolationist press was weakening. Henry Luce, always committed to passionate support of China, had put Chiang Kai-shek and his wife on the cover of *Time* in 1938 and other journalists around the country were becoming more internationalist in their thinking. However, the isolationist Congress continued strict enforcement of the Neutrality Acts of the mid-1930s which embargoed American sales of arms to belligerent nations, and public opinion polls supported the isolationist position in Congress by well over 70%, while only 12% indicated acceptance of even limited arms sales. Nevertheless, Roosevelt was widely suspected of secret understandings with Churchill. Baruch said that Roosevelt's frustration was evident in private conversations, in which he said that it was hard to try to lead the country, and look over your shoulder, to find no one following you.

Such was the situation, when Wendell Willkie burst on the scene, an entirely new kind of Republican, big, bluff, open, a dynamic personality, a very attractive man, a fine speaker, a far more vital and appealing figure than Dewey or Taft, and with significantly more impressive credentials. He came from Indiana, had risen to be a prominent Wall Street lawyer, then was selected to head the largest U.S. electric utility corporation, Citizen & Southern, a proven executive, with extensive international interest and exposure. And, despite the powerful isolationist element in America, Willkie believed that America had an important role in the world.

The lift-off of the Willkie campaign had been carefully prepared by Henry Luce, who had made appropriate calls and visits to key people across the country and had assigned his top man, Russell Davenport, to organize a national Willkie campaign. Luce put Willkie on the cover of *Fortune* magazine, accompanied by a flattering article describing Willkie's forceful, experienced leadership. Well-organized "Willkie Clubs" suddenly sprang up in major cities. Drawn by the energy of the Willkie campaign, young people pitched in, Tex along with them, his first active step in what was to become a life-long "insider" search for national leadership for our country.

When Tex told Baruch of his commitment to the Willkie campaign, he was prepared for Baruch to show disappointment. But, to his surprise, Baruch said that was exactly what he would do—then, after a hesitation, apparently remembering his public posture as a key advisor to Roosevelt, he added, "If I were you." Baruch followed up with a piece of advice. He said that Tex should always remember that the two political parties, although "national" in name, are not really interested in good national government. They are dependent on the state parties—and they are based on the past. Baruch, who had grown up in the south, had regularly heard the phrase, "Vote the way your pappy shot." Some of that Civil War attitude lingered on today, in both parties. But it's bad for the country. The country needs national leaders who understand what's going on in the world, who are open to new ideas and are focused on the future. International trade and commerce are historically the primary source of new ideas—and they tend to appear first in the cities with international trade. Congress is driven by a seniority system which places power in the hands of committee chairman, typically from the agricultural midwest and south—not the first places to look for world awareness, or new ideas.

Although Baruch had steadfastly maintained his public role as a dedicated Democrat and advisor to Roosevelt (when Roosevelt had asked him whom he thought should be President, Baruch had replied, "Are you kidding me, Mr. President, or are you kidding yourself?"). However, Tex had detected a lessening of Baruch's enthusiasm for Roosevelt's policies on several levels. Baruch had supported federal government spending for public works, such as railroads, highways and similar activities, so long as the financing was self-liquidating from revenues of the projects. However, Baruch was visibly uncomfortable with Roosevelt's general welfare projects; he was opposed to federally funded old-age insurance, however carefully camouflaged by the name "Social Security;" and he was particularly concerned over Roosevelt's support from militant labor unions, which required "open voting," with "strong arm" voting enforcement.

Meanwhile, Henry Luce's campaign for Willkie was unrelenting. He pushed Willkie with two *Time* magazine cover stories, along with positive pieces in *Life*. He received, strong support from the Cowles brothers' papers in Minneapolis and Des Moines—as well as the Reid's *Herald-Tribune* in New York City. These early entrants were soon followed by many other papers and, as the campaign progressed, a majority of U.S. newspapers endorsed Willkie.

While Tex was committed to the Willkie campaign, the war in Europe remained his primary interest. As Willkie was entering the Presidential arena in the spring of 1940, Hitler's storm troopers occupied Denmark overnight and swiftly conquered Norway. In England, Chamberlain's government could not survive, and England turned to Winston Churchill as Prime Minister. In May, German "Panzer" tanks pushed through Holland and Belgium, completing an end-run around the undefended Belgian border of the French *Maginot Line*. France was helpless. A British Expeditionary Army, trapped by the German "Blitzkrieg" tactics of coordinated air and armor, left their weapons on the beach at Dunkirk—and three hundred thousand soldiers were rescued in an heroic exercise by a fleet of small British vessels, many of them private yachts handled by their owners, while RAF fighters provided air cover. Tex knew that the *Eagle Squadron* was committed and he wondered how many of the men he had recruited had been lost in that bloody engagement.

Joe Kennedy, then the U.S. Ambassador in London, declared, "England is finished." Roosevelt immediately replaced him. France collapsed and Hitler's tanks raced through the Balkans to Greece, seizing control of the Ploesti oil fields in Romania on the way, and by the late summer of 1940 Hitler had a base on the Mediterranean, a threat to Britain's "Lifeline of Empire" for oil from the Middle East and Asia. Tex thought of his uncle's prediction that the wars of the future would be fought over oil.

After his nomination, Willkie seemed to be off to a great start. Henry Luce turned his magazines, *Time, Life* and *Fortune,* into virtual campaign publications for Willkie, which, not surprisingly, reflected Luce's own strong personal convictions on the repudiation of isolationism in the United States and increased international involvement, not only in Europe but, importantly for Luce, in favor of China and Chiang Kai-shek. Luce reinforced his public positions with a stream of policy memos to Willkie—and it was evident that Luce saw himself as Secretary of State in a Willkie Presidency.

Tex wanted to see if the Democrats' convention was chaotic as the Republicans'. The Democrat convention began on July 15th in Chicago, a one-party Democratic city, and the wards and city government jobs were patronage positions of Democratic bosses, many with long-standing ties to the underworld. As a "cover" to make it appear that Roosevelt was not seeking a third term, Jim Farley, Roosevelt's Postmaster General, had quietly arranged a "draft" for Roosevelt. Joe Kennedy played a central role in all the preparations, as he had many "contacts" in Chicago from his 1920 "bootlegging" days. The carefully orchestrated Roosevelt "draft" began with a constantly booming shout, "We Want Roosevelt," which seemed to come from all sides— actually generated by amplifiers under the hall, and thereafter known as "the voice from the sewers," a reference to the political power of Chicago public worker unions. A massive "spontaneous" demonstration ensued. Roosevelt was nominated by acclamation, as Roosevelt wanted it, with no formal voting of any kind.

Roosevelt's planning and execution of his national campaign was impressive. Ever the master at framing issues, he established his campaign domestically in "New Deal" terms, as "us," the people, against "them," big business, and internationally as "democracy versus dictatorships." He devised an enhanced "Lend Lease" program of military aide for Britain, as a means of bypassing the Neutrality Acts prohibition of "sales" of military equipment.

After the fall of France in June 1940, Hitler had marshaled his full strength on the English Channel, and began preparations for an invasion of England. Churchill rallied the British nation with his famous "blood and tears, toil and sweat" speech. Through August and September, the "Battle of Britain," a bitter air war was fought. The Royal Air Force squadrons, joined by the *Eagle Squadron* pilots, flying the dependable *Hurricane* and the magnificent *Spitfire,* eliminated Hitler's hopes to achieve air superiority, and thus ended the threat of a feared German invasion.

Through the early fall of 1940 Tex divided his time between the newspaper and his work on the Willkie campaign, but his mind was on the war. Roosevelt sent fifty old World War I U.S. destroyers to England to counter the German submarine campaign in the Atlantic, in exchange for leases of British bases in Bermuda and the Caribbean. He followed with a proposed U. S. military draft, and opposition from isolationist Republicans in Congress became passionate. Montana Senator Wheeler declared that Roosevelt would involve America in the war and would "plow under every fourth American boy." Nevertheless, the Selective Service Act, the U.S. military draft, passed Congress in September. The only woman in Congress, Janet Rankin of Montana, then voted against the draft, as she had in 1917 prior to the U.S. entry into WW I, and for the same reason—that, as a woman, she would not be called to fight, so she felt that she could not vote to send men into battle. She had been voted out of office in 1918, was reelected in 1938, cast the same vote again, for the same reason, in 1940 and was thrown out of office again.

Tex mentioned Janet Rankin's vote to Baruch, who said, "That's the problem we have here. There's no respect for principle in Congress any more." He reminded Tex about Edmund Burke's *Reply to the Electors of Bristol*—in 1774 Burke wrote that once a representative is elected to Parliament, he is no longer "the member from Bristol," he is a member of Parliament. And, while he owes his district his judgment, for which they elected him, he would betray his judgment if he sacrifices it to conform to his constituent's opinions. Burke was right, of course, but his district promptly voted him out at the next election. And we have the same problem in Congress. It is run by committees; power lies in the chairman; the chairman is determined by seniority. In the One-Party South, once elected, seniority is virtually assured. While there is more change in the North, the agricultural states between the coasts, typically follow local interests, and tend to vote with the Democrats. As a nation we are not only isolationist internationally, we are isolationist internally.

The Willkie vote was steadily increasing through the fall, and a week before the 1940 election, it was so threatening that Roosevelt felt it necessary to declare in Boston (always with a heavily anti-British Irish vote), "I have said it again, and again, and again. Your boys will not be sent to fight in a foreign war." Willkie—recalling President Wilson's similar 1916 campaign slogan, "He kept us out of war," only to enter the war a few months later—said, "That son of a bitch! He's going to win." Willkie was right. Roosevelt's Boston reassurance to the American isolationist yearnings—while Roosevelt secretly had the U.S. Navy escorting cargo ships to England and attacking German submarines, facts not revealed until much later—had determined the election. Henry Luce extended the national policy memos he had sent to Willkie—originally intended as support for Luce's desire to be Willkie's Secretary of State—into a entire issue of *Life* magazine, proclaiming on the cover, *"The American Century,"* the first identification of a phrase which was to take permanent root in American thought and politics.

Hearst was outraged by Roosevelt's election. He printed a front-page sketch of the Statue of Liberty with a knife labeled FDR stuck in her back. For the first time since his promise at Brisbane's deathbed four years before, Hearst ordered Tex, by then editor of the Editorial Page, to print a bitter anti-FDR editorial. Tex resigned. He had no pressing family obligations to consider. He and Sarah had long been separated and their divorce had been final for some time. She was independently wealthy following her father's death and, like many of her contemporaries, seemed content with her life of school friends, country houses, and horses, and their son, Michael, was well cared for.

Tex talked with Baruch about the next step in his life. Baruch said—with heavy drama—"The fate of great nations hangs in the balance." In their conversations in the summers Churchill had laid out the strategic picture, as he saw it. Hitler has his dream of Germans as the "Master Race," destined to pre-eminence in the world—and he has his people believing it. His speeches were carried on the radio—but radio did not carry the impact of being there in person and hearing the pulsating repetitions of the massed audiences, "Ein Volk, Ein Reich, Ein Fuerher." Baruch said that behind its well-trained and disciplined military, Germany had an impressive science and industrial base—but all that industry required oil, which Germany didn't have. As Hitler saw it, only England and America stood in his way—and they had access to oil. To strengthen his position, Hitler had pulled Japan, and Italy, the other major totalitarian nations without oil for their industries, into the *Tripartite Agreement,* binding all to respond if one is at war.

At that time, Hitler's "Blitzkreig" seemed invincible. His armies were on the shore on the Mediterranean, England's lifeline to her Empire, and an imminent threat to England's access to the oil of the "Petroleum Crescent,"—the Persian Gulf—ringed by the Arab countries of Saudi Arabia, Kuwait, Iraq and Iran. Baruch said that oil is the key to the war. People think of oil as fuel, but they don't understand. Among industrial nations, oil is power. The great prize is the immense reservoir of oil in the Middle East. If Hitler gets control of that oil, England is finished. England has to maintain access to it. That means oil tankers—which are vulnerable to Hitler's U-Boats. It's a very dangerous time.

Tex said he wanted to get involved, to get over to England. Baruch thought it was a good idea, and in England he would need appropriate introductions. He said that Beaverbrook had been impressed by Tex's comments on U.S. military aviation when they had talked at Baruch's dinner for Beaverbrook in New York earlier in the year—and he would call Beaverbrook and tell him of Tex's interest. In short order, arrangements were made for him to go to Canada, hook up with the Royal Canadian Air Force for a flight to England. And Beaverbrook would take it from there.

Beaverbrook's immediate response caused Tex to realize, for the first time, that he had become an "insider" himself. He had a farewell dinner with Baruch, who wished him well, hesitated, then added, "You'll enjoy England. And, remember, just because we speak the same language, it doesn't always mean we think the same way. Pay attention over there. You'll learn a few things—and the trip will do you good."

By arrangement, Tex flew to Montreal, dealt with some paperwork, and then took off for London in a U.S. PBY, a Navy patrol bomber, one of the first U.S. aircraft released to England after Roosevelt's "Arsenal of Democracy" speech in early December. The Brits, perhaps with their literary heritage, preferred names for their aircraft and called the PBY, the *"Catalina"* a long-range flying boat with a high wing containing two radial engines perched on a pedestal above the hull, a noisy, slow, awkward-looking aircraft, but very useful to the Brits for long-range reconnaissance in their battle against the seriously threatening German U-boat campaign in the North Atlantic. The pilot was Homer Barry, a Texan who had joined the Royal Canadian Air Force and trained with the *Eagle Squadron* recruits in Texas.

The flight in the winter weather was from Montreal, via Bermuda, the Azores, to Prestwick, Scotland. The last leg inbound from the Azores was a night flight, to avoid interception by patrolling German aircraft. McCrary sat alone in a side "blister" gun turret, looking at moonlight on the ocean, wondering what the future would hold.

By dawn they were flying over a cloud layer. Dead-reckoning navigation indicated that they should be near Prestwick—and they started to let down through the clouds.

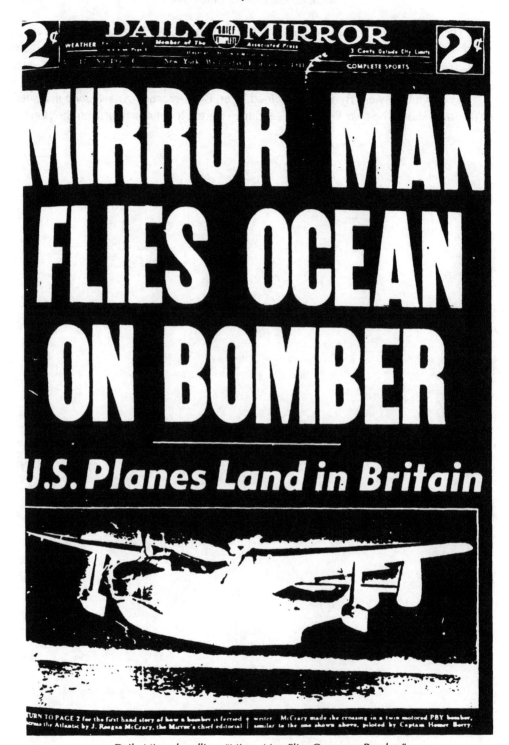

Daily Mirror headline: "Mirror Man Flies Ocean on Bomber"

Chapter Five

The RAF "Eagle Squadron"
and Lord Beaverbrook

Explosions of anti-aircraft fire shattered Tex's approach to the coast of England. The PBY was badly hit, one engine shot out, but Homer Barry managed a crash-landing in the harbor of Pembroke Dock near the western tip of Wales. They were picked up by a Royal Navy launch; the sailors apologized for bad communications ("the buggers at Signals didn't tell us you were coming") gave them a shot of whisky, and put them on a train.

Tex arrived in London, to the sound of Air Raid sirens signaling the beginning of the nightly German blitz. Jock Whitney had told him to go directly to the bar of the Dorchester Hotel, where his favorite cousin, Whitney Straight, an RAF fighter pilot, would likely be attending a nightly squadron party. The party was in full swing when he arrived. Straight greeted him warmly, introduced him around—and the party lasted into the early morning.

Straight's squadron, No. 601 "City of London," was part of the Royal Air Force Auxiliary Air Force. In their relaxed and quirky way, the RAF, in addition to its regular units, had separate categories of reserves, which, like The Auxiliary Air Force Squadrons, were recruited from, and named for, a particular area. Recruitment was carefully screened for social acceptability, and all pilots were commissioned officers, while Volunteer Reserve squadron's pilots were generally non-commissioned sergeants. It was commonly said, "Auxiliaries are gentlemen, trying to be officers; Regulars are officers, trying to be gentlemen; and Volunteers are neither, trying to be both."

"City of London" was also known informally as "the Millionaires Squadron." In addition to Whitney Straight, Lord Beaverbrook's son, known as "Little Max," was a member, as well as several others of aristocratic background—and the pilots' behavior reflected the circumstances of their life. One was assigned to the task of avoiding the tight restrictions of gas rationing for private automobiles, which were inhibiting the pilots' social lives. This officer, thinking to simplify his task, simply bought a gas station, later discovering to his dismay that its reservoir tanks were nearly empty. Fortunately, another squadron officer was a director of the Shell Oil company, and could arrange deliveries.

The social aspect of the RAF intrigued Tex. Proper tailoring was an important attribute of class distinction. RAF fighter pilots who had fought in the Battle of Britain identified themselves by leaving the top button of their tunic unbuttoned. In addition, elegant squadron pilots had their tunics lined with scarlet silk, perhaps having something to do with the scarlet tunics of the Household Cavalry regiments. A further embellishment was the delicate insertion of one's handkerchief up the left sleeve cuff. This casual attitude and assumption of privilege naturally drew criticism. As the war progressed, many pilots from other squadrons became high-scoring "aces." Tex later came to know one of the most outstanding pilots, Johnny Johnson, who was convinced that he had been denied admission to an Auxiliary Air Force squadron because the interviewing officer had discovered, during an obligatory glass of sherry, that he was "not a fox hunting man."

601 Squadron had distinguished itself in the *Battle of Britain* during the summer of 1940. Naturally the squadron was justly proud of, and recognized for, its record. Churchill had memorialized the achievement of the RAF fighter pilots in his famous speech:

> "Never in the field of human conflict
> has so much been owed by so many to so few."

Beaverbrook's *Evening Express* carried a banner headline written by Beaverbrook himself:

> "Not Duke, nor Earl, nor Baron, nor even Prince,
> but Pilot, that is England's new Nobility."

Tex was impressed by the apparent welcome shown him by 601 squadron members, which he at first attributed to Whitney Straight's introduction; however, he came to see they were fond of Americans for another reason, their deep respect and affection for Billy Fiske and his wife, Lady Rose, the Countess of Warwick. Billy Fiske was an American, born in Chicago, educated at Cambridge, and a close friend of many of the pilots in a dashing playboy kind of prewar life, skiing, driving race cars, flying planes. He had married Rose in 1937 and was an international banker living in New York when the war broke out. He called his friends in 601 and said, "I'm coming over to join you." The RAF, well accustomed to accommodating special situations, put Billy through tactical training and posted him to 601 at Tangmere, a RAF fighter base on the Channel coast. He and Rose lived in a little cottage near the field. During the "Battle of Britain," Rose would watch the *Hurricanes* and *Spitfires* take off, see their contrails curving high overhead, hear their machine guns fire. Then the pilots would land, and walk over for cocktails in the garden in the long warm summer evenings of 1940. Billy was a natural pilot, became one of the highest-scoring pilots, in fact, shot down a Heinkel bomber virtually over the field. One day, in a dogfight over the Channel, he was hit, his engine on fire. He made it back to the field, his *Spitfire* a mass of flames. A rescue team pulled him out of the cockpit—but too late to save his life. He was the first American fighter pilot killed in the Royal Air Force.

Fiske's fellow pilots loved Rose, tried to take care of her, adopted her, invited her to their parties. She obviously appreciated their attentions and, because he was an American, she seemed pleased to talk with Tex. He was immediately attracted to her, tall, lean, erect, her dark hair streaked with silver. She liked to talk about Billy and their life. One afternoon in London they went to Westminster Abbey where she showed him Billy's name in the Roll of Honor listing the three hundred seventy-five airmen killed in the Battle of Britain. Then she took him to St. Paul's Cathedral where there was a tablet commemorating him as the first American pilot to die in defense of England.

PILOT OFFICER WILLIAM MEADE LINDSEY FISKE, RAF
AN AMERICAN CITIZEN WHO DIED THAT ENGLAND MIGHT LIVE

Beneath it in a glass case were his RAF wings which his friends had cut from his tunic. The Countess of Warwick made a deep impression, and they continued to see each other as often as they could.

Shortly after his arrival in London, Tex had written the story of the PBY flight, of the "friendly fire" shoot-down, and of the rescue by British sailors. A reporter from Hearst's *Harper's Bazaar* was in London looking for a story, and he gave it to her. The story was brought to Hearst's attention and he printed the story on the front page, under a picture of a patrol plane similar to the PBY in which Tex had flown to England. And, despite their past differences, Hearst cabled that he wanted Tex to be a war correspondent for his papers.

Beaverbrook was recognized as the "Press Lord" in England, because his papers had the widest circulation. He gave weekend house parties at his country house, *Cherkley Court*, including Americans whom he thought might be influential on Britain's behalf in America. As an American war correspondent for the Hearst papers, Tex was invited regularly. One of the features of a Beaverbrook house party was a game in which every guest was required to offer a written comment on British-American relations. Comments were read aloud and judged on an anonymous basis. Tex's offering was: "Americans look down on the British—with the greatest of envy." It took the prize for that weekend. Shortly thereafter, he was invited to dinner at Churchill's country house, *Chequers*, where Churchill spoke brilliantly—and almost exclusively—throughout the evening.

Like Brisbane and Baruch, Beaverbrook saw in Tex qualities worth developing, and he provided him with an extraordinary education and range of introductions, helping him understand differences in attitudes and politics between the countries. Previously, Tex had understood American isolationism as a long-standing attitude rooted in the security provided by the Atlantic and Pacific Oceans—but he had not understood that England had its own kind of internal economic, political and social isolationism. Beaverbrook pointed out that, while the disillusionment following World War I and the effects of the worldwide depression were troubling in the United States, America benefited from a far more flexible social, economic and political structure, which had enabled Roosevelt's "New Deal" leadership to restore hope and vitality in America. But such was not the case in England. The same men, with the same lack of leadership that had cost them so dearly in World War I, continued in power.

Beaverbrook was a member of the House of Lords, the repository of the ancestral wealth of England, which was, not surprisingly, controlled by the Conservative (Tory) Party. As the Depression had worsened, profits had declined, while taxes were rising, driven by the rising influence of the Labour Party in the House of Commons. Accordingly, the conservative Tories anxiously watched the spread of Bolshevik mass rioting and violence in Europe. They regarded Russia with horror, and feared the spread of radical influence in England, in unions and in the Labour Party (which was to remain socialist throughout the war, and come to power at its end). Moreover, socialist-communist philosophy was spreading in the heart and bastions of the "Old Boy" system, at Oxford and Cambridge. The Oxford Union had voted publicly "not to fight for King and Country," and there was a growing awareness, of communist influence, even active subversion, notably, the "Cambridge Spies," Philby, Burgess and Maclean (who not only betrayed England, but later penetrated the top levels of the CIA and our State Department).

Internationally, Hitler's aggressive rearmament was obviously a threat. But in the House of Lords at that time the greater threat had seemed Russian Communism—as Hitler had come to power by destroying Communist agitation and restoring stability in Germany, thus giving rise to the hope and belief among the upper classes in England that Communist Russia was Hitler's natural enemy. From this perspective, it seemed possible that Hitler's military threat could be turned eastward by letting him take Czechoslovakia, creating the prospect of confrontations at a common borders between Germany and Russia.

Although a long-time leader of the Conservative Party, Beaverbrook believed this approach was folly, and he was further riled that the House of Lords had overtly concealed certain embarrassing information and actions that the British public ought to know. Tex was amazed to hear from Beaverbrook that official documents had been destroyed, records restated, and diaries rewritten to conform to desired results of the "Old Boy" system. Duplicity reached the level of conspiracy, both as to the past and the present. Most significantly, current military status was deliberately overstated publicly, lest the costs of rearmament lead to higher tax rates. These facts were hidden under the cover of the Official Secrecy Act.

Winston Churchill was the strong voice of opposition in the House of Commons, then controlled by the Conservative Party. Beaverbrook thought Churchill deserved a wider audience and he provided a regular column for Churchill in his newspapers. Certain serving ministers and military officers, also concerned by the cover-ups of His Majesty's current Government, quietly provided information to Churchill, which permitted him to raise embarrassing questions in the House of Commons. Unlike the hereditary members of the House of Lords, Members of Commons had to face the voters—and the voters read Beaverbrook's papers and Churchill's columns. Churchill's questions became so embarrassing to the government that he was threatened with prosecution for treason under the Official Secrecy Acts (Tex noted the similarity to Nixon's attempts to prevent the *Washington Post* and *The New York Times* from printing the *Pentagon Papers* during the Vietnam period.)

With the collapse of France in May 1940, and facing the prospect of an invasion of England by Hitler, Prime Minister Chamberlain's Government could not continue. The King and the House of Lords sought to maintain continuity with a new Conservative Government to be formed by the fatuous Lord Halifax, but public disaffection was too strong—and demanded new leadership from the elected House of Commons. Winston Churchill was the only realistic choice. He immediately appointed Beaverbrook Minister of Aircraft Production.

It was essential for England to secure more aircraft wherever it could, in whatever way possible. England was effectively bankrupt, but Beaverbrook pressed on regardless, placing orders of unprecedented size for American planes and parts. His agents went to Henry Ford, seeking additional production of the British Rolls-Royce *Merlin* aircraft engine, but Ford refused, unwilling to produce a foreign product (General Motors continued to produce its own Allison engine which was not effective over fifteen thousand feet, but which, inexplicably, continued to be supported by the U.S. Army Air Force engineering department at Wright Field, the Army Air Force research and development headquarters in Ohio.) Beaverbrook's agents then went to Packard—and Packard was licensed to build the *Merlin* engines which powered the outstanding British aircraft, the immortal *Spitfire*, the *Lancaster* and *Mosquito* bombers—and, ultimately, the U.S. P-51 *Mustang,* a decisive factor in the victory in the air war.

Beaverbrook knew that England could not pay for the purchases and he talked about this openly, saying, "I'll get it on the 'cuff,'" tugging at his shirt cuff for emphasis. Beaverbrook and Churchill were well aware that President Roosevelt was sympathetic to England's plight, and knew that these purchases were providing increased employment in the United States, which would be put at risk by any restrictions. Beaverbrook operated with great subtlety and discretion—and on many levels. He seldom went to an office—but his power and influence were ever present. Churchill and Beaverbrook both understood the potential power of publicity to affect public opinion, not only in England, but importantly in the United States—and Beaverbrook's country weekends for selected American journalists were just one part of this effort.

On May 20,1941, Rudolph Hess, deputy leader of the Nazi Party, flew alone in a German Messerschmidt ME 110 to Scotland, repeatedly circled the ancestral estate of the Duke of Hamilton, presumably looking for a landing field, then jumped by parachute. Whomever he planned to meet did not appear. His plane crashed nearby and Hess was taken prisoner. He was held in total confinement through the war, was tried and convicted on lesser charges in Nurenburg at the end of the war, and remained in total confinement until his death, his message still kept secret. The Duke of Hamilton was a noted anti-Communist and a part of the British aristocracy known for partiality toward Hitler. The Hess case was locked in official secrecy—and remains so today— but it was assumed that Hess's mission was to try to arrange through the Duke of Hamilton for England to join with Hitler in a war with Russia. Thirty-two days after Hess's flight, on June 22, 1941, Hitler launched his Blitzkrieg into Russia. The Russian army fell back, with devastating losses. By November, Hitler's tanks were on the outskirts of Moscow.

Even though subdued by wartime restraints, the high end of social life in London was far different from the "café society" life which Tex had known in New York. For generations, British aristocracy had maintained extremely flexible marriage standards. Men were at liberty at all times, while women were free after they had produced an heir to the title. In the tight aristocratic circles of British politics, titled ladies were frequent participants in political, and associated bedroom intrigue. All of the uncertainties of wartime inevitably contributed to the social atmosphere and behavior. Beaverbrook understood this, as well as all other aspects of politics. And Pamela Digby Churchill was his eager associate.

Tex met Pam through Lady Jean Norton—a great beauty, Beaverbrook's mistress, and a close friend of Pam's mother, who filled him in on the background. The Digby family was both aristocratic and wealthy, but followed a quiet country life. After her debutante season in London, Pam was determined not to return to that country life, and permitted herself to be invited for weekends in Paris with older gentlemen of her social circle. At the beginning of the war, aged nineteen, she met Churchill's son, Randolph, who had drunk and slept his way through life and was then pursuing the wife of a mutual friend, Lady Mary Dunn, whose husband was on duty overseas. However, Lady Mary was temporarily involved with Bill Paley, and introduced Randolph to Pam. Facing imminent active duty overseas himself, Randolph was desperate to sire a son to provide continuity to the Churchill line. Recognizing the advantages of a proper marriage (and telling her friends that she couldn't think of anything else to do) Pamela married him. Shortly after their marriage, Randolph was ordered to the Middle East and Pam in due course performed her duty and bore a son. A modest complication arose in that the wife of Churchill's cousin, the Duke of Marlborough, had also recently borne a son whom they had named Winston Spencer Churchill. Prime Minister Churchill demanded that the name was his. After some huffing and puffing, the Duke ultimately relented. The Duke's son was renamed Charles, and Randolph and Pam's son became Winston Spencer Churchill. Meanwhile, Randolph's life of drink and gambling continued overseas, resulting in debts far beyond his means to repay. For Pam, the marriage was over, but to help Randolph she went to Beaverbrook and asked for help. Beaverbrook told her he would do nothing for Randolph, but would provide her "presents" to start a new life. Pam accepted eagerly, fascinated by continued exposure to the "great game" of English politics. Beaverbrook understood Pamela Churchill's interests, and he also understood that Winston doted on Pamela and openly discussed affairs of state in her presence. Beaverbrook had no discomfort at using her as he thought best. Edward R. Murrow's nightly news broadcast, "This, is London," was the most powerful voice of Britain's wartime condition into the United States. Tex watched with interest as Beaverbrook set Pamela up in an attractive apartment, provided for her expenses—and introduced her to an easily-smitten Murrow.

Roosevelt's election in November of 1940 had permitted him greater freedom for aid to Britain, a program openly referred to as the "Special Relationship." For this role, Roosevelt had chosen Averill Harriman as his representative, formally designating him as "Expeditor" of the "Special Relationship." Harriman was a Groton graduate, as was Roosevelt, and Roosevelt believed strongly in the character benefits derived from those who had experienced the influence of the famous Dr. Peabody at Groton, which was modeled on the great English boys schools, Eton, Harrow and Winchester. Presumably, Roosevelt's choice was made in the belief that the British leaders would deal more comfortably with a man they could consider to have a "gentleman's" education. Harriman, of course, felt right at home in London. At Harriman's briefing before his departure, Harry Hopkins advised him to get to know Pamela Churchill, saying, "she knows everything in London—and she is very good looking." Beaverbrook arranged a dinner at Lady Cunard's upon Harriman's arrival. Pamela was seated next to Harriman. Nature took its course.

Over dinner one night at Claridges Harriman told Tex that he was very anxious to have his daughter, Kathy, join him in London; however, U.S. government relations precluded travel by any family member of a U.S. officer serving in a war zone from accompanying him. That rule did not apply to individuals who had recognized assignments, such as newspaper associations. Tex had known Kathy in the United States, and he suggested to Harriman that he could arrange to bring her to London to work with him as a researcher for the *Mirror*. Harriman was delighted at this prospect. Kathy duly arrived, was introduced to Pam, who asked Kathy to share her house.

Tex continued to spend a fair amount of time with his friends from the 601 Squadron, where he learned more about the military aviation situation. Lend-Lease U.S. aircraft were beginning to arrive in England—and received serious criticisms of their inadequate performance, the same weaknesses Tex had described in his 1939 articles in the *Mirror*. 601 Squadron had been singled out to receive the American Bell P-39 fighter, with the Allison engine. 601 Squadron, as well as other similarly equipped RAF units, found the P-39's performance as a fighter totally unacceptable for air combat, and immediately shipped them all to Russia, where the Russians used them as an anti-tank aircraft. The American Curtiss P-40 (also with the Allison engine) followed, some improvement over the P-39, but it too was judged inadequate to engage German fighters. The RAF sent the P-40s to the African desert to replace the antiquated biplanes, Gloster *Gladiator* fighters, then engaging the Italians on that front. The early models of the pride of the U.S. Army Air Force, the B-17 *Flying Fortress* bombers, were also considered unacceptable for combat purposes—lacking self-sealing gas tanks, power-operated gun turrets, and tail gun protection—and were deemed suitable only for coastal reconnaissance duties, as were the first B-24 *Liberator* heavy bombers, which came a year later.

Tex was struck by the similarities between the embarrassment over the fact that no U. S. airplanes had been fit to fly in World War I, and the continued, and obvious inadequacies in the latest U. S. military planes in 1941. In his reports from London for the *Mirror,* Tex duly commented on the similarities to his 1939 articles. This attracted attention in the United States and the editor of the *Mirror,* Charlie McCabe, a close friend, asked him to come back for a visit in New York, where he had arranged for him to provide radio news commentary with the respected radio news commentator, H.V. Kaltenborn. After one of his reports Beaverbrook sent Tex a cable which delighted him.

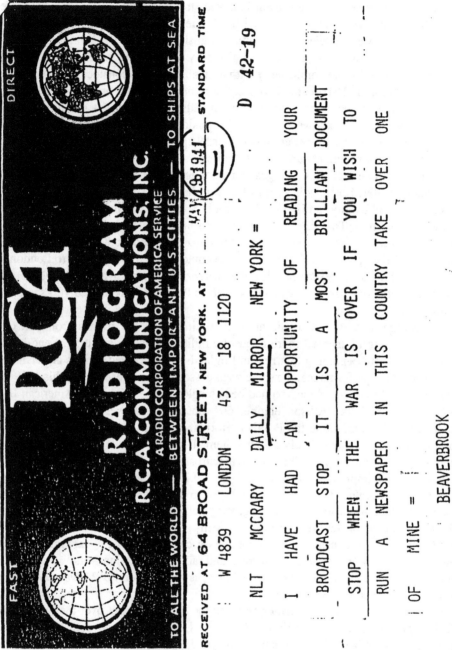

RCA Radiogram from Beaverbrook

While in New York, Tex was introduced to Jinx Falkenburg at the Schubert Theatre on the opening night of an Al Jolson comedy, *Hold On To Your Hats*, in which Jinx played a cowgirl—and stole the show. She was young, startlingly beautiful, vital, wholesome, athletic, with a fresh, open manner. She was a junior tennis champion in California, later runner-up to national ladies champion Pauline Betz. She had been on the cover of the *Saturday Evening Post* at sixteen. A whirlwind national modeling career had followed and she had been on more than a hundred magazine covers. He set up an interview. Jinx said that he was "professional" to the point of rudeness—but she knew then that he was the man for her.

When they met, Jinx was "Miss Rheingold." After a nation-wide beauty contest, the Rheingold company put her face on billboards all over the country, followed by a major, year—long, national promotion tour. Because of what he had seen and learned of problems with American aircraft in England, Tex wanted to follow up on recent developments in this country, which meant visiting Los Angeles, the largest aircraft design and manufacturing center in the country. He timed his quick visit with Jinx's schedule, met her family, and was further impressed. The Falkenburgs were the core of the younger social set at the West Side Tennis Club, the tennis citadel—and watering hole for the Hollywood crowd in that tennis-mad time in Los Angeles. Jinx's father was a mining engineer and the family had traveled with him through Europe (Jinx was born in Barcelona) and South America before moving to Los Angeles. Jinx's mother, Mickey, was a fine tennis player herself, and Jinx, and her brothers, Tom and Bob, all rose to national ranking (after the war, Bob Falkenburg won Wimbledon).

Tex returned briefly to England, coming back to New York in time for the Yale-Harvard football game at the end of November 1941. He talked with Baruch, who seemed very troubled. Baruch said that there were things going on in Washington that he feared would bring the country into the war—sooner, rather than later. Baruch had many people keeping him quietly informed on economic and strategic matters—and oil was at the top of the list. Baruch noted that Japan had no oil resources of its own, and imported its oil requirements, half from America and half from the Dutch East Indies. Apparently, no U. S. oil had been shipped to Japan since August of 1941. Oil shipments were administered by Harold Ickes, Secretary of the Interior, and Ickes wouldn't do anything unless Roosevelt wanted it done. Japan has no choice. It has to go to war to get oil. The Dutch East Indies is the primary source of oil in all of Southeast Asia. Without control of access to the Dutch oil, Japan cannot continue its industrial development. It would be basically helpless and would have to take over the Dutch East Indies. Since Teddy Roosevelt took responsibility for the Philippines, that's been America's forward base in Asia. The Japanese will fear a U.S. threat from the Philippines to their oil supply line from the Dutch East Indies. They will have to attack. America will have to respond. That means America will be at war with Japan. Under their obligations in the *Tripartite Agreement*, Germany and Italy will have to declare war on America. And America will have to declare war on Germany.

Tex was startled by the starkness of Baruch's statement, but the logic was compelling. Baruch asked if it made sense to Tex. He replied that when he was at Yale his uncle had told him that the wars of the future will be fought over oil. Baruch smiled, "Your uncle was a very wise man."

Chapter Six

Pearl Harbor, December 7, 1941:
"Flying Fortresses" over Germany

December 7, 1941: The Japanese delivered a devastating surprise bombing attack on Pearl Harbor in Hawaii. Roosevelt delivered his "Day that will live in Infamy" speech—and declared that "a state of war exists" with Japan. Two days later Hitler declared war on the United States. And two days after that, the United States declared war on Germany. Twenty-one years after the end of World War I, America was again at war.

A totally different mood infused the country in which the forces of isolationism had been so strong. Tex wanted to volunteer for pilot training, but he was just over the age limit (his younger brother was to became a decorated Navy pilot in the Pacific) and he was wondering what to do, when he got a call requesting that he come to Washington to meet with General "Hap" Arnold, Commanding General of the United States Army Air Force (he later learned that the suggestion for the meeting had come to Arnold from Bob Lovett, then Assistant Secretary of War for Air). Arnold said that Tex's 1939 articles in the *New York Mirror* had been helpful, especially in the argument for an independent U.S. Air Force. The war in Europe was daily demonstrating the importance of air power; however, Arnold said that the reports on the inadequacies of U.S. military planes as experienced by the British was not helpful to what was still known as the Army Air Corps. Tex said facts were facts. Arnold pointed to a chart with the projected performance figures for planned new aircraft, and said, "We can't talk about these yet, and we don't want you on the outside. We'd rather have you with us." Tex said, "Then sign me up." Arnold stood up, shook Tex's hand, commissioned him a Captain in the United States Army Air Corps, and said that orders would be sent immediately to report to Officer Training School in Miami Beach. "After graduation," Arnold told him, "You will be sent to England for public relations duty." The Army Air Corps, soon to be renamed as the Army Air Force, had taken over the Roney Plaza Hotel, an elegant resort hotel on Miami Beach. It was filled with newly-commissioned officers like Tex, including many old friends from Yale and New York. The training was intense—and with a visible connection to the war.

With their traditional supply of oil from the Dutch East Indies cut off, England depended on a steady stream of oil tankers from South America, which passed a few miles offshore from Miami Beach—where German submarines were waiting. American anti-submarine forces were committed to the North Atlantic to protect American troops and supplies en route to England. All of the Florida coast was under total blackout. When Jinx came through on her "Miss Rheingold" tour, after late dinners together, Tex would take her on to the roof of the hotel, where they could see the horizon lit by burning oil tankers, torpedoed by German submarines.

[Author's Footnote: My father was going through training there at the same time. Tex enjoyed the story that the Duke of Windsor (and former King), then officially Governor-General of the Bahamas, was also in residence in the Roney Plaza Hotel, as the Bahamas were essentially undefended and the Brits didn't want a King of England to be kidnapped. As Officer of the Day, my father had the delicate duty of dealing with the Duke of Windsor's repeated violations of the blackout requirements on his penthouse. He eventually had his sergeant remove all the light bulbs except one in an inside bathroom.]

After graduation, Tex passed through New York, en route to report to Major General Ira Eaker, commander of the Eighth Air Force in London—and he called Baruch to get his thoughts. Baruch was typically direct. He said that it would be a tough job. Political pressure would be intense. Roosevelt wants to prove our power quickly. Our bombers are the only available weapon of attack. Our top Army Air officers are dedicated to achieving an independent air force and have built their careers around an unproven concept of strategic daylight precision bombing, based on the B-17 *Flying Fortress*. We have damn few planes and even fewer trained crews. Expectations are artificially high, both here and in Britain. Neither the Germans nor the British have been able to mount a successful daylight bombing offensive in the face of enemy fighter opposition. So it all comes down to whether the crews of the *Fortresses* can sustain the heavy losses inevitable in the build-up of an effective daylight strategic bombing offensive, and, if so, can such a bombing force reduce German strength to the level necessary to permit us to invade successfully?

The last few days before Tex's departure were sad for both Tex and Jinx. She wanted to get married, but Tex knew that there were risks in store for him, and he didn't want to have Jinx become a war widow. He took her to a farewell party Jock gave for him at "21." Jock didn't help the situation with Jinx when, as he shook hands to say goodbye, he said, "God damn it, McCrary, you get to have all the fun—and I can't go with you, because Betsey Cushing is divorcing Jimmy Roosevelt to marry me."

In England, Tex reported to Major General Eaker at the Eighth Air Force Headquarters on Grosvenor Square in London. Eaker wasted no time, saying that General Arnold had written him saying that Tex would be helpful with public relations. Eaker told Tex to roam around and try to find out what's going on. Correspondents would be coming soon—that meant trouble and Tex would have to handle it. He gave him an order referencing Arnold's letter, which he said would get him anywhere in the Eighth Air Force. Eaker ended, "Now, I'm busy as hell. Get going. Try to learn something."

With Eaker's order in hand, and his own Jeep, he was free to move around pretty much on his own. He signed up for aerial gunnery school, visited air fields, talked with the pilots, checked in with the *Eagle Squadron*, with Beaverbrook, with Whitney

Straight and the 601 gang—and he called Lady Rose. She asked him to come for a drink that evening at her charming little house on Mount Street, a kind of elegant mews between Grosvenor and Berkeley Squares. Time had not reduced their mutual attraction—which soon ripened into a full-scale romance.

War has a demanding immediacy. It takes over people's lives, including Tex's. One tends to live in the present. In later years, when he talked of his experiences, what he had done, what he had learned—he said that while it was happening, things simply seemed to move too fast, there really wasn't time to think, or analyze. That only came later. Soon American war correspondents began to arrive, as predicted, all looking for a "hot" story—but there was no "hot" story. In the panicky environment after Pearl Harbor, and fears of Japanese attacks on the West Coast, the initial plans for the build-up of the Eighth Air Force had been curtailed. As a result, the Eighth Air Force, the designated instrument for the heralded U.S. air offensive against Hitler's Germany, was left with a single combat unit, the 97th Bomb Group, with twenty-four B-17 "Flying Fortress" bombers. The 97th flew their B-17s to England, arriving in late June 1942. Naturally every effort was made to fly the first combat bombing mission of the Eighth Air Force as soon as possible, although support and training took some time.

The first target was the railroad yards in Rouen, France, just across the English Channel. The 97th Group was commanded by Colonel Frank Armstrong. [Footnote: The acclaimed movie, *Twelve O' Clock High,* was loosely based on Armstrong, whose lead role was played by Gregory Peck. It was written after the war by Colonel Beirne Lay, a good Yale man who was, himself, later shot down while in command of the 487th Bomb Group, but escaped capture and was eventually able to return to England.] Tex told Armstrong that he wanted to go along. Armstrong led the mission, and another pilot that day was Paul Tibbitts, later to be the aircraft commander of the B-29 *Enola Gay,* the plane that dropped the atomic bomb on Hiroshima, whom Tex ran into in Japan three years later.

The first combat mission of the Eighth Air Force took off from Grafton Underwood, northwest of Cambridge, on the 17th of August 1942, a beautiful sun-lit summer day. It was Tex's first flight in a B-17. He sat behind Armstrong, watching as the mission formed up into two flights of six B-17s each—twelve B-17s, the total offensive capability that the Army Air Force could put in the air that day. The flight was relatively short and they saw few German fighters, probably because they had a fighter escort of four squadrons of *Spitfires.* The target was clear; they dropped their bombs, and returned in a buoyant mood. The first flight buzzed the field, while the second flight, with General Eaker on board, landed somewhat more decorously, to be greeted by thirty enthusiastic correspondents. The plane in which Eaker flew was named "*Yankee Doodle,*" a publicity opportunity seized upon by the correspondents. The crews were all in flight gear, but the General was prevailed upon by the correspondents to change from his flight suit into dress uniform and pose climbing out of the "*Yankee Doodle*" hatch. It was obvious that the raid was a symbolic operation—only twelve B-17s—and the Americans knew they had a lucky break going to Rouen, both with good weather and the lack of German fighter opposition. However, in Washington General Arnold had issued a pretentious statement: "The successful attack on Rouen verifies our policies of precision bombing of strategic objectives, rather than the mass bombing of large city-size areas." Although intended for American readership, Arnold's statement, implying a higher moral tone, was, understandably, seized upon in England as direct criticism of RAF bombing policy, and a gross insult to Britain. Suddenly, Tex had a serious public relations problem.

At that time, the RAF Bomber Command was the only offensive weapon available to the British against Germany. The Bomber Command was headed by Air Chief Marshall Harris, a most ambitious and aggressive man, publicly known as "Bomber" Harris. Anticipating the arrival of the first American B-17s, Harris had mounted a "one thousand plane" raid on Cologne, dramatically larger than any prior raid, which was naturally highly publicized in the British press—and compared to the Americans' first mission—twelve B-17s to Rouen—not to our advantage. [Footnote: Subsequent inquiry determined that, of the one thousand bombers cited by Harris, a substantial number were obsolete, twin-engine aircraft, *Wellington* bombers, and even some *Oxford* trainers; this is not to minimize the British effort, but merely to indicate the magnitude of the political pressures involved.] With Harris's support and open advocacy, a British press campaign began, calling for the Eighth Air Force bombers to be put under Harris's command to increase the aircraft available for the RAF night bombing offensive against German cities.

The RAF argument struck at the core convictions of the Army Air Force—the hope for an independent U. S. Air Force after the war—and the timing could not have been worse, for the RAF proposal had a superficial plausibility. Inevitably, the British press made the issue front page news, and the U. S. journalists in England naturally reported it back to America, not a helpful story. To address the problem, Tex recommended the formation of a Combat Photography Unit, which would let the American people see directly the roles that the men of the Eighth Air Force were performing. Good photographs could help to establish an emotional connection, and generate positive press to counter the negative, abstract "numbers" game. Eaker, who had come to appreciate Tex's ideas, liked the proposal: "Good idea, McCrary, you seem to know the right people, go get them, you're in charge." Tex did know the right people, and recruited top photographers from *Life* and other photo services, as well as movie people. The unit took shape quickly, produced positive results.

Meanwhile, Tex's romance with Lady Rose had progressed rapidly, and the announcement of a formal marriage engagement was carried in both the London and New York papers in the fall of 1942. Jinx read about it in a Hedda Hopper column in the *Los Angeles Times,* and sent Tex a sharp note, ending "I hope you enjoy your Thanksgiving turkey."

Tex's engagement to Lady Rose resulted in entry into another "insider" category—inclusion into elevated social circles, including formal dinners with English aristocrats, where many of the men, as well as some of the women, held high government positions and were exposed to secret military and strategic matters—matters which were restricted to senior officers in the American military—but which the Brits discussed openly at dinner parties. The conversations recalled visions of the Empire, of Suez, India, Singapore and Hong Kong—coupled with the threat to the essential oil supply from the Middle East and the continuing fears of German submarine sinkings of oil tankers en route to England. It seemed remarkable that, despite the explosions of German bombs, of flickering lights and ambulance sirens, there was little thought that England might be different after the war.

The American military preference was for a rapid buildup for an invasion of France, as soon as militarily feasible in 1943, seemingly the quickest and least costly way to defeat Hitler—and to assure Stalin's continuation in the war (it was believed that Harry Hopkins had earlier visited Moscow and had promised Stalin an invasion in Europe, possibly in 1942). However, Churchill had strongly opposed the cross-Channel invasion, saying that he dreaded the sight of the Channel red with British blood. He painted a dark picture of Hitler's armies, one already advancing deep into Russia and potentially moving southward to the vast oil fields of Baku on the Caspian Sea, while Rommel had taken his *Afrika Corps* nearly to Cairo. This raised a great panic of an imminent breakthrough by Rommel in Egypt, the loss of the Suez Canal, then moving unopposed, through Saudi Arabia to the Persian Gulf. The result would have been catastrophic, securing German control of the oil of Arabia, a strategic necessity for Germany, while simultaneously cutting England off entirely from the Empire, India, the Far East possessions, and Middle Eastern oil, the life blood of British military and industry. A further corollary was the possibility of a German linking with a Japanese westward offensive across Asia to India.

For Churchill, preservation of the Empire was always foremost and he argued forcefully for an immediate landing of an American army in North Africa at Rommel's rear, forcing Rommel's withdrawal from Egypt, and thus ending the imminent threat of German penetration into the Middle East and access to its precious reservoirs of oil. Churchill's position was strongly opposed by Roosevelt's military advisors who were convinced that Rommel's dramatic advance was overextended and would, in any case, be forced to withdraw for lack of fuel supplies (as was proven to be the case). Nevertheless, Roosevelt sided with Churchill, and agreed to postpone the planned cross-channel invasion from 1943 to 1944, and to divert U.S. air and ground forces to Churchill's preferred "Peripheral Strategy" in the Mediterranean, rather than the direct cross-Channel plan of the U.S. military advisors. Accordingly, U.S. forces, previously committed to Britain, were diverted to North Africa, to land at Rommel's rear, in Tunisia, in November of 1942.

For the Eighth Air Force, committed to the aerial offensive against German industry, the Roosevelt-Churchill meetings meant diversion of already seriously inadequate reinforcements at the worst possible moment—to a newly formed Twelfth Air Force to be based in North Africa under the command of Jimmy Doolittle. Additional Bomb Groups for the Eighth from the United States arrived slowly through the fall of 1942, in various levels of preparation. The inevitable effect was the further reduction of the Eighth Air Force operations, already impacted by approaching European winter weather with cloud cover obscuring targets.

With U.S. operations lagging, the British press continued to push for an RAF takeover of the Eighth Air Force bombers. Inevitably, this coverage began to spill over into the United States through the reports of U.S. correspondents—which put pressure on General Arnold who, in turn, began to make unrealistic demands upon an already overburdened Eaker. This continued to be a major public relations problem, even though the combat photos were helping a bit. It was essential to shift the argument, to refocus the U.S. correspondents away from the RAF " numbers game," how many planes, how many raids, etc. But, so long as that was all the information available to them, that's what the correspondents would write about—which of course simply fed the RAF position. Eaker felt, understandably, that he had to defend the Air Force position, that the daylight precision bombing strategy—with different aircraft capabilities, different equipment, higher altitude performance, could perform in important ways that the RAF could not. But, however much he felt it his duty, Eaker was the wrong man, in the wrong position, to make the best of that argument to the British. It was inevitable that the British press, no matter how much they respected Eaker personally, would come to cast him as just another general, jealously trying to hang on to his command. Tex didn't look forward to trying to deal with that argument with Eaker.

Then Tex learned that Jock Whitney had been commissioned as a captain, had gone through the Intelligence School at Harrisburg, and had orders to come over to be assigned to the Eighth Fighter Command. Many officers could handle that job but Tex knew that Jock might offer part of the solution to the larger political problem. Tex went to Eaker with the recommendation that the Eighth Air Force would benefit, particularly at this time, from a well-connected back-channel relationship into that critically influential, aristocratic inner circle of British leadership—and that Jock Whitney had ideal qualifications for that role. Tex outlined Jock's background, his post-graduate years at Oxford, the fact that he had spent several months of every year of his adult life in England in close association with the very top levels of British society—in the great blue-blooded sports, polo playing, horse racing, fox hunting, bird shooting, lady chasing and drinking. He was considered "one of them"—with an easy intimacy permitting him to do and say things they could not easily accept from another American.

At first, Eaker evidenced a certain skepticism. Tex pressed on, pointing out that there were certain bits of information potentially helpful to the current argument which neither Eaker, nor any present member of his staff, could touch. There were intimations of a sense of class concern about "Bomber" Harris, that perhaps he was rather coarse, particularly in his enthusiasm for stressing the multiples of thousands of German civilian deaths resulting from each of his "area" bombings of German cities. More to the point, there appeared to be reasons to question the accuracy of Harris's bombs. Reports of a survey (later confirmed by Churchill's science advisor, Lord Cherwell) indicated that only twenty-five percent of RAF bombs hit within five miles of their targets, and in the heavily defended industrial Ruhr Valley, the ratio dropped to only ten percent. Eaker knew he couldn't go near such sensitive subjects—but he could see that some of this, discreetly discussed, might be helpful in the context of the argument for daylight bombing. Eaker became more interested, "McCrary, does your friend Whitney play poker?" Tex assured him that he did, indeed, play poker—but unfortunately perhaps not too skillfully. Eaker looked up, "Very well, he can work with you. Have new orders cut for him—and set up a poker game as soon as he gets here."

All went well upon Jock's arrival. Eaker immediately recognized Jock's value in the ease with which the Brits responded to him. Jock was promoted rapidly to become liaison officer with the British (and he also arranged—very skillfully—to lose regularly at poker with Eaker and the other generals). Eaker's opposition to the RAF takeover proposal was reworked—from a narrow, defensive argument for the Eighth Air

Force's strategic bombing position—to a tight affirmative case for a militarily effective, mutually benefiting, coordinated strategy—combining U.S. daylight and RAF night attacks—giving the enemy no respite to fight fires, repair damage, recuperate, or restore morale.

The timing was fortunate. Churchill and Roosevelt had secretly scheduled a meeting in Casablanca in French Morocco in January of 1943. There was no advance notice of this meeting until General Eaker got a call from General Arnold to come to Casablanca at once. Eaker flew down, fearing that Churchill had been persuaded to accept the RAF proposal. Tex heard of the meeting later from Jake Smart, a young colonel, General Arnold's right hand man, and a member of the Air Advisory Council. The Joint Chiefs, General Marshall, General Arnold, and Admiral King, were led to believe that the conference was intended as a small gathering for Churchill and Roosevelt to discuss future policies, so Roosevelt was accompanied only by his Joint Chiefs and their personal aides. Instead, Smart said that the British showed up with staffs in full array, in the British phrase, "foot, horse and guns," and with future plans fully staffed-out in all details. Smart said it was a "set up" for an RAF take-over of the Eighth Air Force operations; hence the hurry-up call for Eaker. As Smart told the story, when it came time for Eaker to appear on the agenda, Churchill was in a grumpy mood, barely acknowledging Eaker's presence. Eaker handed Churchill a single sheet of paper. Churchill began to read, mumbling, half aloud, "Round the clock, round the clock, hit the devils round the clock." Then, after a pause, "You have not convinced me, but I will withdraw my objection to your proceeding—and I'll be watching." For the Eighth Air Force, a hastily drawn, and ineffectually broad order was issued, the *Combined Air Offensive*: U.S. bombing by day, British by night—striking German oil production, rubber, and machine tools. All lying beyond the range of available fighter protection.

Apart from the problems it created for the Eighth Air Force, the most critical national policy decision of the Casablanca Conference was the declaration of the Allied war aim declaration as the "Unconditional Surrender" of the Axis powers. It seemed that the declaration arose without advance preparation or consideration. Smart said that at a small lunch with Roosevelt, Churchill, and Marshall, after a pause in the general conversation, and with no apparent prior discussion, Roosevelt said, "I think our war aim should be unconditional surrender." And, after some pause, Churchill said, "I agree." Smart, and the military men, were stunned when they were told. They voiced private concerns to each other and feared that the starkness of the demand would eliminate the prospect of an early German surrender to avoid brutal Russian occupancy. As a result, the war would likely be far more difficult and costly, both in time and lives— even more so with respect to Japan, who might otherwise be more likely to make a demilitarized peace if they could keep their Emperor. Eaker's advocacy had won a reprieve for the Eighth Air Force—but it came at a heavy price. Now, the Eighth had to prove that it could strike the targets designated at the Casablanca Conference, all lying deep within Germany, without fighter protection.

The first deep penetration target was the railroad marshalling yards at Hamm, the funnel for distribution of the production of the Ruhr Valley, the industrial heart of Germany. It was heavily defended by German fighters. The mission took off on March 4,

1943, and Tex went along, flying with the 97th Bomb Group. [Footnote: Tex's description of the missions to Hamm and Huls are extracted, and slightly abridged, from *First of The Many* by John R. McCrary and David E Scherman, published in 1944 by Simon and Schuster, with an introduction by Lieutenant General Ira C. Eaker. Apart from Tex's vivid recollection of these two missions, the book is otherwise primarily a collection of assorted human interest pieces from early in the war.]

I needed good pictures of German fighters—and I didn't want to send photographers from my unit without going with them. There was a different feeling about this mission, the first deep penetration raid, on the strategic railroad center at Hamm, a palpably higher level of tension and a long flight—all without fighter cover. I rode in the radio compartment behind the cockpit, just below a gunner with a 50-caliber machine gun mounted above. The weather was clear and the German fighters hit us as we started our bomb run. Suddenly the gunner above me abruptly lurched against my back, knocking me into the passageway down on top of the curved top of the revolving belly ball turret. I saw blood washing down the rubber-matted floor. I had never seen so much blood before. It was strangely impersonal—just so much red paint. Then I looked behind me. The gunner was crumpled on the floor. Blood was burbling out of a wound in his back. The best we could do was two hypos to relieve his pain.

Now his gun was my responsibility. I wished I had paid more attention to lectures at gunnery school. I grabbed the handles of the 50-caliber and looked out at the rest of our flight. Impressions flitted by so fast. The B-17 flying next to us—a bomber looks funny with its bomb bay hanging open—like a little boy with his pants down. German fighters, Messerschmidts and Focke-Wulfs climbed up behind us, in our six o'clock position, out of range, crossed over on top, then rolled into a diving attack from the twelve o'clock high position on our nose, which was defended only with its single .30 caliber machine gun. I tried to remember the rules for deflection firing, the stuff about wing spans, and the number of sight rings to lead your target. But all I could think of was the instructor's advice, "Just keep pressing the triggers, and keep your lead in his eyes." By my count, I think perhaps a dozen German fighters came into my gun sights. Did I hit anything? I have no idea. I just tried "to keep my lead in their eyes." I also learned something else important. You can't help feeling better with a gun in your hands; it is far more comfortable to pull a trigger than to just sit there. Other German fighters, including twin-engine Ju-88s, were forming up behind us, waiting for a wounded Fortress to drop back out of formation, and then they would dive on the crippled plane like birds of prey. Our pilot called the tail gunner, asked how many B-17s were still behind us? The tail gunner's reply was chilling, "There aren't any." I looked back. All I could see were German fighters A JU-88 was flying just out of range. He began a slow turn in, and I swung my gun on him. Little hot balls of tracer danced out along the trajectory—but my tracers fell behind him as he passed underneath. Suddenly the German fighters were gone. Even with the roar of the motors, there seemed to be a huge silence. The wounded gunner was quiet, deeply sedated, and his pulse was very faint. The sight of the English Channel was very welcome on the way back. The pilot, Oscar O'Neill, eased our ship onto the runway. Ambulances pulled along side. Our gunner was stretchered out through the side entry, as gently as men who admire courage can lift a mortally wounded boy. He died in the ambulance.

Out of the group of twenty-four planes, five were lost over the target, five made emergency landings, only fourteen made it back to the base in flyable condition. The combat loss was over twenty percent—bad odds, not to mention another twenty percent unflyable. Losses were running well over the rate of replacements. The crews could figure it out for themselves. Headquarters established a regulation that bomber crews would be rotated out of combat after twenty-five missions.

It seemed to be a good idea for morale purposes to make a movie of the first bomber to make twenty-five missions, and Tex had some Hollywood volunteers in his Unit. Willie Wyler, who had just finished making *Mrs. Miniver*, that wonderful movie of England in wartime, was the ideal person to direct the bomber project. They didn't have a name because they wanted the movie to carry the name of the bomber that made the twenty-fifth mission. They also started a gunnery training film. Clark Gable came over as a Air Force captain to work on it. He went through gunnery school and flew five combat missions. Tex and Clark were friends from when Jock was involved with the *Gone With The Wind* movie and, when Jock came over, they all had good times together, joined sometimes by Jimmy Stewart, who led a B-24 Group.

Tex continued to fly missions for the 25-mission bomber film, flying with the old 97th Bomb Group. He liked the way O'Neill handled his crew and his plane, bringing *Invasion* back from the Hamm mission. It was too damaged to fly again and he soon had *Invasion II*. Tex flew several more missions with O'Neill. Sometimes he rode in the waist, where he could look out over the guns, but he also liked to ride up in the nose with that beautiful, clear bay window and a view of the whole majestic bomber stream soaring along in front. And then there was "*Our Gang.*" Tex went with them on June 22, 1943, to Huls, the largest German synthetic rubber facility, even deeper into the Ruhr Valley than Hamm—the deepest penetration raid yet. In an effort to mislead the Germans, the initial course was across the North Sea, making it look like an attack on sub pens at Kiel, then a sharp turn south for the long haul into the Ruhr valley, all at altitude, five hours on oxygen in the freezing cold. Tex's description:

> We climbed out slowly, gaining altitude over the North Sea, oxygen masks on. Then we saw the first enemy fighters, flying parallel, out of range, checking us out, trying to guess where we were going, probably under ground control. The German fighters had a different paint job, milk white all over, perhaps transfers from the Russian front. They seemed to be waiting for the bomb run, when the B-17s would have to fly straight and level. As we started the bomb run, the fighters came at us from twelve o'clock high. Our pilot, Smitty, started his "coach's drone" over the intercom: "Okay, okay, get set. They're lining up, here they come. Reach out for him, nose gun. Now hit him, top turret. Tap him goodbye, tail. Look out! Here's another on the nose." Suddenly, a Fort pealed out of the element ahead, straight up and then over, so close one could see into the cockpit, a furnace of orange flame. One parachute opened as a man bailed out of the waist. Another parachute fouled the tail, and the man was jerked right out of his harness. Another man bailed out of the nose hatch, on fire. His chute did not open. And then the whole Fort exploded. I braced against the padded walls of the radio compartment, camera cocked for a shot of the bomb fall from the flight above us. Suddenly—in combat everything seems sudden—there were white puffs along our left wing—20 mm. shell bursts—with a sharp crackling like gravel thrown against a tin roof. Smitty cut in: "Okay, top turret? Okay, waist guns? Okay, navigator and bombardier? Okay, tail?" And then, as an afterthought, "Okay, cameraman?" The Focke Wulfs piled in, their 20m/m hits ripping holes in the

wing outside my window against which I was holding my camera. Instantly, a sheet of orange flame blasted by the window. Amazingly, my first thought was, "God damn it, no color film!" Then came panic. The radio operator shouted, "FIRE, left wing!"—then, "Stand by to bail out." The crew tugged on parachute harnesses. My eyes were fixed on the fire on our wing. It would grow in length and fierceness, then shrink back inside the wing, then belch out again. I don't know how long it lasted; it seemed like forever. At the bombardier's shout, "Bombs away," Smitty peeled off into a dive. The other gunners and I were lifted off the floor by the "G" forces, our gear floating around in the air, and then, as he pulled out, we were all dumped into one corner in a heap, ammunition boxes, odd bits of radio equipment, cameras, thermos jugs, etc. Then we realized it was quiet. No fighters. After a bit, a gunner shouted, "The bastards are back. Twelve o'clock, high." I looked out, there they were, the black specks of fighters with their white vapor trails streaming behind them. Then another voice, "Don't shoot, they're Spitfires." An escort, flying out to the edge of their range to cover our return. The tension snapped, somebody started singing. It was the largest mission yet, one hundred eighty-six Forts made it to the target. But it was costly, the loss rate was about the same as the Hamm mission.

One morning Tex was sprawled out on the grass in the sun in his flying clothes beside a B-17, waiting to take off on another mission, when Colonel Ordway, the head of intelligence for the Command, came out in a jeep to order Tex yanked out of the bomber, telling him it was a direct order, that he had been flying too many missions. Tex began to raise hell, and the navigator said, "Listen, McCrary, you're a goddamn fool. What are you griping for? Why do you have to have somebody order you to get out of this thing? Don't you know people get killed up there?" Tex mumbled something, but he really couldn't answer that for himself.

The bomber movie was coming along well. They had great combat photographs and the competition was mounting to see which aircraft, and which Group, would get to make its twenty-fifth mission—and get to go home. The 97th Bomb Group had been there longest, and they had a substantial lead. Oscar O'Neill and his *Invasion II* were four missions ahead of *Our Gang* and *Memphis Belle*, also of the 97th. On the twenty-third mission, *Invasion II* didn't come back. Tex sat through intelligence debriefing. Everybody wanted to know who had seen *Invasion II*, had anyone had seen her go down, etc. Finally, a gunner of another ship spoke up, said he thought he had seen *Invasion II* dropping down, on fire. Everybody jumped in, "Any parachutes?" "Yeah, I think I saw some." "How many, how many?" "Maybe five, maybe six." The crew was ten. Families get a telegram, "We regret to inform you that your son has been reported missing in action."

After O'Neill's *Invasion II* went down, Smitty's *Our Gang* didn't come back from its twenty-third mission, so Bob Morgan's *Memphis Belle* became the first B-17 to complete the designated twenty-five combat mission tour. Morgan was ordered to fly the *Belle* back to the U.S. for a major publicity tour. The 97th Bomb Group had been the first and, in Tex's mind, the best. He had flown with them on their first mission, and on many others. The average mission life of a B-17 in the 97th Group was eleven missions, and only about ten percent of all the crews finished twenty-five missions. By the end of its first year, it was so shot up that its morale would go down again and again. The casualty rates were among the highest of any military units, anywhere.

For all that duty and courage could áccomplish, it was apparent that the German fighters were increasing in numbers. The commanders and the intelligence people didn't want to believe it because of the number of German fighters claimed as shot down by our Flying Fortress gunners. However, later records indicated total claims exceeded the total number of the entire number of German fighters deployed. This was not all the fault of the gunners over-claiming. It was simply very hard to tell in combat when several gunners on different planes were often firing at the same target, and each gunner saw pieces come off—or thought he saw pieces come off—justifying in his mind a legitimate hit. In the raids they were currently flying, there were over one thousand gunners. Everyone knew that the claims had to be exaggerated—but the size of the claims was justified as good for morale—and it enabled the Air Force generals clinging to the "Flying Fortress Invincible" theory to persist in their beliefs.

The *Combined Bombing Operation* order of the Casablanca Conference produced virtually impossible objectives. Nevertheless, an overly ambitious operation was planned for the summer of 1943, "Blitz Week," beginning with an attack on the massive oil facilities at Ploesti in Romania—then producing more than two-thirds of German oil supplies—and known to be the most heavily defended single site in all of Hitler's empire. Ploesti lay well beyond the effective range of B-17 *Flying Fortresses* flying from English bases; however, Ploesti was within the range of B-24 *Liberators* flying from North African bases.

The *Liberator* had been designed a few years later than the B-17—named to compete with the dramatic name identity established by the *Flying Fortress*—and it had some advantages. It was faster, could carry more fuel, a heavier bomb load, and had a longer range, which would enable B-24s based in North Africa to make the flight to Ploesti—but without escort fighter cover, the risks of the standard Eighth Air Force bombing practices were simply too high to contemplate.

A new plan was required. Abandoning all of the concepts of precision bombing from high altitude, the Ploesti mission was based upon a low-level attack, right on the ground, hopefully benefiting from surprise, Tex got pulled into the job by Colonel Jake Smart, now General Arnold's "Special Projects" man, who wanted to try an experiment, a precision-timed attack by B-17s flying from England and B-24s from bases in North Africa. The Ploesti mission would require the closest coordination in identical briefings at bases both in England and Africa.

The project was extremely hush-hush. The B-17 crews could be briefed in England, but for the B-24s crews coming from Africa, Colonel Smart wanted to have the Ploesti mission briefing put on a sound movie film. Tex set to work in a little soundproof studio, talking into a mike, and wondered how his words would sound to a bunch of kids down in the desert somewhere who knew nothing about a place named Ploesti. They would have to believe what they heard, fly their hearts out to take their Liberators into the target, and their lives would depend, in part, on what Tex told them.

He was assigned a remarkable British character, Wing Commander Lord Forbes, to work with him. Forbes used to write a page in the *Sunday Express* for Beaverbrook, flying all over, writing about the places and things that he saw. He had been in the Balkans when the war started, where he used to fly the diplomatic pouch between Belgrade, Warsaw and Bucharest—just for fun. With this background, he signed up with the RAF. The Brits knew they had an unusual talent in Forbes, and they moved him from Special Operations into Special Projects.

The Ploesti Mission Film was a mixture of technical navigation data, pictures for the bomb run on scale models of each target, some comedy tricks to emphasize the don'ts and dangers" of the job, and finally, some basic geography. When the film was finished, Tex asked Forbes if he was satisfied, but Forbes piped up, "You Americans have never learned to read a map, geography is a blind spot with you. All you Yanks know about the Danube is that Strauss wrote a waltz about it." Then he added, " I think we ought to take a look at the flight plan ourselves." Tex told him he was crazy, they couldn't take a B-24 in there without giving the mission away—not to mention perhaps getting themselves killed pointlessly. Forbes said, "Nonsense." He would ring up a chap he knew in a *Mosquito* recon unit. They would fly at altitude to Greece, then drop down on the deck to the turn at the critical Danube checkpoint, and pick up the Initial Point for the bomb run. Tex said, "That sounds just wonderful. And how do we get back?" Forbes had a ready answer: to obscure their flight plan from the Germans, they'd turn away and overfly another major target area, maybe Berlin, on the way back. He said not to worry, the Jerries are used to recon *Mosquitos* flying alone. They know they can't climb up and catch one, so they don't bother. And you know we'll both feel better if we've flown it first ourselves.

The *Mosquito* was built of plywood, and in its lightweight recon version, the *Mosquito's* twin Rolls Royce "Merlin " engines flew it as fast as a *Spitfire*. They flew to Bengasi in Africa, caught some sleep, then took off, and were over Romania at first light. They confirmed the route and the key Danube crossing, and were back in England before dinner. They were a little tired—but Forbes was right, they did feel better, having flown the mission route themselves.

The Ploesti mission took off from North Africa on Sunday, August 1st, 1943, the opening of "Blitz Week." Eighth Air Force B-17s, painted bottle-green, and Twelfth Air Force B-24s, painted in sand-pink desert camouflage, headed north across the Mediterranean, over Greece, and then down on the deck into Romania. As they approached the Ploesti oil fields, they were flying 250 miles an hour 50 feet over the ground. Then it happened. A leader made the wrong turn—and the defenses were even worse than had been feared. The losses were a shock. One hundred seventy-five B-24s took off on the mission. Only thirty-three were fit to fly the following day. Fortunately all were not shot down, as many were scattered in crash landings from the Middle East through the Balkans and across the African desert. Tex was anguished as he saw more troubles to come, more bombers, longer missions, and still no escort fighters to protect the bombers.

The culmination of "Blitz Week," was a coordinated attack, code named *Stiletto*, calling for simultaneous strikes to divide the German fighter defenses. The Eighth Air Force, in England, would hit crucial targets: the Messerschmidt fighter factory at Regensberg, and the key German machine tool and ball-bearing factory complex at Schweinfurt. The key to the mission was simultaneous attacks to force German fighters to defend two separate targets at the same time.

Then General Spaatz in North Africa, decided to get in the act with his Twelfth Air Force, flying from North Africa to England, to enlarge the attack into a three-pronged effort, by bombing the Focke-Wulf fighter factory at Weiner-Neustadt while the B-17s of the Eighth Air Force were to make simultaneous attacks on Regensburg and at Schweinfurt. Timing was crucial.

Both Spaatz and Eaker were under tremendous pressure from General Arnold, back in Washington, to step up the war. But the summers are not the same in Washington and London. Low clouds and heavy rain in England delayed the takeoff of the Eighth Air Force bombers, while in Africa, an impatient Spaatz decided not to wait, thereby sacrificing the intended benefit of the coordinated attack to divide the German fighter defense. Spaatz launched his bombers from Africa on August 13th, a 13-hour flight from Africa to England, with a bloody stopover at Weiner-Neustadt, another twenty-five percent combat loss.

Despite Spaatz's having ignored the potential benefits of splitting the German fighters by three simultaneous attacks, nevertheless, the Eighth Air Force might still gain some advantage from the two simultaneous attacks on Regensberg and Schweinfurt. Curt LeMay was leading the Regensburg mission and was scheduled to fly on to land in Africa. In England, the weather forecasts grew progressively worse, and the takeoff order was further delayed, and LeMay apparently feared that if he did not take off immediately, his aircraft would arrive in Africa after dark, when the landing would be too treacherous. LeMay had mechanics in Jeeps with flashlights leading B-17s through the fog to the active runways, Jeep crews aligned the pilots on the runways, and the pilots took off on instruments. Lemay led his mission alone to Regensberg. German fighters, alerted by their radar, were waiting. One hundred forty-six B-17s took off, nineteen aborted, one hundred twenty-six "effectives" reached the target, twenty-four were shot down in combat, one crashed in England, and fifty were unflyable without major repair.

The weather remained below minimums in England and the Schweinfurt mission did not take off for several more crucial hours. The German fighters had had time to land, refuel, rearm and meet the oncoming B-17s. The price was high. Two hundred thirty B-17s took off; forty-two aborted; thirty-six were shot down in combat; seventeen crashed in England; and one hundred twenty-one were unflyable.

The Eighth Air Force could not mount a major effort again until October 14th, 1943, "Black Thursday," another massive attack on Schweinfurt. Another catastrophic loss. Three hundred twenty bombers out, sixty-two aborts, two hundred fifty-two "effectives" over the target, sixty shot down in combat, seventeen crashes in England, one hundred twenty-one unflyable without major repair.

The numbers spoke for themselves. It was now inescapable that, without escort fighters to protect the bombers, the Eighth Air Force was unable to achieve the air superiority necessary to accomplish its strategic bombing mission over Germany. Eaker was told by his maintenance chief that, at the rate they were losing aircraft, before long they would have only one B-17 left to launch. Eaker said, "If that's the case, I'll be on it."

At that darkest hour for the Eighth Air Force, help was on the way—the P-51, the finest fighter since the *Spitfire,* an aircraft which could have been escorting our bombers long before—but a fighter which the Air Force had steadfastly refused to buy. After the war, Herman Goering, Marshall of the German Luftwaffe, was interrogated by Allied officers. He said that he knew Germany had lost the war when he saw P-51 fighters over Berlin.

Tex believed that those P-51s came to be there, at such a crucial time, because of Tommy Hitchcock, more than any other single person. Hitchcock knew that he would have trouble pursuing his plan to make the P-51 the essential escort fighter if he had to work under Air Force bureaucracy. He arranged with Bob Lovett, Assistant Secretary of War for Air, to have himself assigned as an attaché in the Embassy in London, outside of the Eighth Air Force command.

Hitchcock had an apartment in Grosvenor Square and when Jock Whitney arrived, he moved in with Tommy. They all were together having a drink after Tex had come back from the Huls mission. Hitchcock was an intense man — focused, quiet, reserved. He asked Tex to describe the mission. As Tex talked, Hitchcock became more agitated, finally almost shouting, "Insanity, madness." Despite a frightful record of losses, the Joint Chiefs issue directions, not for escort fighters, but instead to bomb German oil and military production facilities without fighter protection. The damn fools can't see that if they don't get escort fighters, they're going to lose the ability to attack anywhere. We have the best escort fighter in the world — the P-51 — but headquarters won't accept it!"

The outburst was totally unlike Tommy, and it caused Tex again to take a closer look at the fighter business. He didn't need much encouragement; he'd been on the missions and seen the loss of life personally. Naturally, there was a special place in his heart for the *Eagle Squadrons*, for which Tex had recruited pilots, which had expanded into three *Eagle* squadrons and, after America entered the war, all were incorporated into the United States Army Air Force as the Fourth Fighter Group. In their combat tour, both in the RAF and the USAAF, the *Eagles* amassed the highest-scoring record of any fighter unit — much to Tex's personal satisfaction. The Eagles flew *Spitfires* and, like all other pilots who ever sat in a *Spit* cockpit, they loved them. The *Spitfire* is, of course, a unique aircraft, graceful beyond description, and as responsive as a polo pony. All of the Eagles' *Spitfires* carried the RAF roundel insignia on their wings. With their transfer to the Eighth Air Force, the Eagles wanted the U.S. star on the wings — but nobody had a suitable description or model. A mechanic who was Jewish volunteered a Star of David, which was copied and painted on the wings on top of the RAF roundel.

Tex visited the *Eagles* whenever he could, and always tried to talk to Don Blakeslee. Blakeslee had had more than one hundred-twenty fighter missions with the RAF, with a number of victories to his credit, before coming over to the Fourth Fighter Group as a squadron commander, and later as the C.O. He was a great pilot, a great leader — and he loved the *Spitfire*. However, for all of its great qualities, the *Spitfire* had been designed as an interceptor, primarily for defensive purposes, and had limited range, a combat radius of no more than one hundred fifty miles. It was of no use for the longer strategic bombing missions. But with the neglected fighter aircraft development program in the pre-war years, the United States didn't have much on the drawing board. In an effort to gain a little more range, and not much at that, the *Spits* were taken away from the Eagles and replaced by the P-47, a fighter with more than twice the weight.

Don Blakeslee led the first mission in P-47s. He got on the tail of a *Messerschmidt,* followed it down and destroyed it. When he got back to base, he was congratulated, and the intelligence officer said, "Well, that fight certainly proves the P-47 can out-dive the *Messerschmidt.*" Blakeslee, in his laconic way, delivered a fighter pilot's judgment: it ought to be able to dive, because it sure can't climb. The P-47 was not the answer to the escort fighter problem, but headquarters in Washington wanted to put forward the best case possible for the plane, and it was given a fearsome name, *Thunderbolt.* The *Memphis Belle* film had generated a good public response, so Tex's unit was asked to make another, titled *Thunderbolt* [Author's Note: Both *Memphis Belle*, and *Thunderbolt* are still available in video]. The 56th Fighter Group, known as the *"Wolf Pack,"* also got the P-47. It was commanded by Colonel Hubert "Hub" Zemke, and it was chosen for the film. Zemke was a dedicated career officer, with all of the leadership qualities, but without the flamboyance of Blakeslee. When the film was finished, he was sent back to the United States for a tour with the *Thunderbolt* movie. When he returned to combat, leading his Group on an early mission, an inexperienced wingman flew into Zemke's plane. He was lucky to get out, landed by parachute, and was made a prisoner of war. In his prison camp, as a full Colonel, he was the ranking officer. One day the German commander of the prison camp came to him and said, "I want a roster of all of the prisoners who are Jews " Zemke replied, "We are all Jews."

How the P-51 finally came into being is a tangled tale, one of institutional obstinacy, powerful personalities, conflicting visions and ambitions, and above all, Congressional politics and pork. Tex had developed much of this background in his series in the *Mirror* before the war—and it was evident that a lot of bad thinking was involved. An Army Air Corps (before elevation to the higher status as the Army Air Force) engineering study had indicated that large aircraft could fly as fast as small aircraft; contributing to an assumption that fighters had no significant performance advantage over bombers—and thus were not needed for escort duty. As evidence of the state of confusion then extant in the War Department, General Arnold, chief of the Air Corps, stated in his postwar autobiography that he did not know of the speed and performance of German and British fighters until he was told by Charles Lindbergh in 1938, after Lindbergh had made inspection tours of German aviation arranged by the Army attaché at the Berlin Embassy. Apparently reports from Army attaches went to the Army General Staff at the War Department—and were not shared with the Air Corps. But it was hard to believe what seemed to be the case. Surely Arnold and senior officers went to movies and saw newsreels. England won the Schneider Cup race in 1929 in the beautiful Supermarine S.6, a forerunner of the *Spitfire*, which flew 400 miles per hour, despite the weight of pontoons, and with an early prototype of the Rolls-Royce *Merlin* engine!

Long before America's entry into the war, Air Corps leaders had a single goal—to win independent status for a U. S. Air Force. When war came, they were determined to win the war, and win it in a way which would achieve their goal. The senior top career officers like Arnold, Spaatz and Eaker believed that the full potential of air power could not be developed while being starved for funding by the Army and the Navy. There needed to be a showing of an independent, strategic mission for an Air Force.

The obvious answer was the capacity to deliver major destruction to the enemy, beyond the capability of the Army, limited by the frontline, or the Navy, limited by the shoreline. This was not a fighter function and, with that in mind, those early, dedicated planners concentrated on bomber development, hence the *"Flying Fortress"* which they felt could operate without fighter escort. Having fought for the strategic bombing concept so zealously for so many years, they could not believe—or admit—that it could fail.

In his 1939 articles on U.S. military aviation, Tex had written that six B-17 bombers, with then Lieutenant Curtis LeMay as navigator, had intercepted the Italian passenger ship *Rex* over six hundred miles off the East Coast, demonstrating the potential of the *Flying Fortress* as a weapon—and as a tremendous threat to the Navy's protected preserve. Orders were immediately that no Army aircraft could venture more than one hundred miles offshore. Requests for B-17s in 1938 and 1939 military procurement budgets were turned down on the grounds that military aircraft of the Army should be limited to ground-support activities. Thus, a decision that fighter engines need not operate above fifteen thousand feet.

Our country has produced many "unsung heroes," people with the wisdom and skill to get around closed minds and institutional bureaucracy, and Tommy Hitchcock was one. The British knew him well as a polo player, and they respected him, as he respected them. He recognized that aviation was a fast-moving field and he believed that Britain's experience in World War II, the *Battle of Britain* particularly, had taught them things that the U.S. had not yet had the opportunity to learn in the fighter business. Hitchcock wanted to learn, and he had the full support of our Ambassador, John Winant, former governor of New Hampshire, who had replaced Joe Kennedy in 1940. Winant had a son who was a B-17 pilot in the Eighth Air Force. He understood what Hitchcock was working on—and he knew what escort fighters would mean for his son (whose B-17, unescorted, was later shot down over Germany; fortunately, young Winant was captured and survived). Hitchcock went to Central Gunnery School for the top level of RAF fighter pilots. Then to the RAF Leadership School. Then engineering and technical studies.

Hitchcock told Tex that they had finally solved the fighter problem. With a little tinkering, the *Merlin* fit beautifully into the nose of the P-51, and it had performance like no other aircraft in its time. Above all, it could fly far beyond the range of any other fighter. This was the aircraft that could solve the problem of the catastrophic losses of the B-17s and B-24s. Hitchcock cabled Bob Lovett, who immediately came to England to see first hand. Lovett got the decision lifted out of the bureaucracy—and things started to move fast. The first P-51s began to arrive in England after the tragic second Schweinfurt mission, the darkest hour of the Eighth Air Force.

Don Blakeslee—leader of the *Eagle Squadron* and now commander of the Fourth Fighter Group—was picked to test fly the P-51. He landed and said, "This airplane can win the war. How many can I have and how soon can I have them?" The supply officer said, "Well, the Air Force regards this airplane as a tactical ground support airplane, and they will be assigned to the Ninth Air Force for that purpose." Blakeslee said, "Like hell," and he went to the top. They asked him how long he felt his pilots would need to transition into the new airplane. Blakeslee said, "Give them to me, and my boys will learn to fly them on the way to the target." That's when Goering saw them over Berlin.

Tommy Hitchcock had finally won his battle. He had one last request: he wanted command of a group of P-51s. Eaker knew how Tommy felt about his plane, and he told him that he could have his group. Tommy wasn't a man to wait inactively. To further increase the range of the P-51, an internal fuselage tank was installed behind the pilot. When full, the tank shifted the center of balance of the aircraft toward the tail. It could take off easily and had no problem in normal flight—but it created an unstable condition in acrobatics. Tommy continued to make regular test flights, always with careful preflight checks. When Tommy began high altitude acrobatics, the ship came apart in the air. Tommy managed to get out of the cockpit. His body was found with a half-opened parachute. The accident report pointed to a possible defective indicator on the auxiliary fuel tank which falsely indicated "empty." He was buried near a polo field in England, and in tribute to a great gentleman and sportsman, a memorial service for him was held in Saint Paul's Cathedral.

There are still some P-51s flying, in air shows and military displays—a few with the checker board nose paint scheme of the Fourth Fighter Group, the old *"Eagles"*— and whenever Tex heard that unmistakable sound of a *Merlin*, he always looked up and thought of Tommy Hitchcock.

Chapter Seven

War in the Mediterranean: England's "Lifeline of Empire"

After the losses of the October 1943 Schweinfurt raid, the Eighth Air Force operations were shut down. It was a solemn period for Tex, made more so by the cold, clammy London weather. He and Lady Rose were entertained at lunches and dinners but he was depressed by the thoughts of the empty places, the terrible loss of lives, the many friends gone. He wondered about his brother, flying off a carrier in the Pacific. Mail was slow.

The respite did, however, provide time to reflect on the course of the war in other theaters, and Tex was troubled by the consistent pattern of opposition between the British and the American formal strategic positions. By the spring of 1943, the Germans had been driven out of North Africa and Roosevelt and Churchill had met in Quebec to reach a final decision on the next phase of the war. Churchill had successfully pressed his "Peripheral Strategy," that the Allies should land in Italy, progress up the Adriatic coast, pass through the Alps, follow the "Ljubliana Gap" into the Danube plain to Vienna—and thence to Berlin. It was evident that Churchill's position was intended to recapture England's prewar influence in the Balkans, and secure the "Lifeline of Empire" to Arabian oil, to India, Singapore and Hong Kong. Moreover, Churchill surely also saw it as a way to reduce Stalin's prospective postwar Communist political power in Eastern Europe.

Roosevelt's military advisors persisted in their position that sound military strategy called for concentrating their forces in a single, major effort on the cross-channel invasion to destroy Hitler's army, that it was dangerous to divide their forces, particularly in an effort to advance British post-war political ambitions. Nevertheless, Roosevelt had again accepted Churchill's "Peripheral Strategy," calling for a series of Allied invasions, first North Africa, then Sicily as a stepping stone into Italy. American troops under General George Patton landed in southern Sicily, in parallel with a British army under General Montgomery. Patton, an aggressive cavalry officer, was determined to take the Sicilian capital, Palermo, before Montgomery, who was noted for his hesitant, delaying tactics. The result was a clear win for Patton, the surrender of Sicily, and the humiliation of Montgomery. But with serious personal cost to Patton. The hard-driving general, angered at what he took to be cowardice, had slapped an enlisted man, an act which, under any other circumstances, would have forced Patton's retirement. However, Eisenhower, already concerned over hesitant performances by other generals, formally reprimanded Patton, and kept him under wraps for future needs.

Faced with the loss of Sicily and an immanent Allied invasion, the Italian government had deposed Mussolini—who went into hiding—and surrendered Italy to the Allied Command. A relatively small number of German troops remained in Italy however, and the limited range of U.S. fighter air cover, based in Sicily, dictated a landing at the nearest access from Sicily, the Italian port of Salerno, south of Naples. The landing was planned for September 1943. Limited resistance was anticipated, with the expectation of a quick advance to Rome.

General Dwight D. Eisenhower was the overall Allied Commander, with British General Harold Alexander as field commander in Italy. The Allied force consisted of the American Fifth Army, under Lieutenant General Mark Clark, and the British Eighth Army under General Sir Bernard Montgomery, (knighted for his performance in Egypt) along with several divisions of French African troops. A giant American fleet assembled for several days in plain sight offshore, giving the quick responding German troops and artillery time to move into defense positions. Tex heard that the U. S. Navy commander asked General Clark when he wanted the big Navy guns to commence a massive barrage, standard procedure before troop landings, "to soften up the enemy defenses." He was astonished when told that Clark had replied that he did not want the naval fire support because he wanted the landing to be a "surprise." The landing met entrenched resistance, and took heavy casualties. Clark signaled a request to be taken off the beach, leaving his men under fire. Eisenhower denied Clark's request—but, to the consternation of all, did not remove Clark from command. [Footnote: Steve Ambrose's biography, *Eisenhower: Soldier, General, President-Elect* reports Eisenhower as saying that "Clark should fight with his men," and "I knew I should have given that command to Patton." Leading journalists had earlier asked Eisenhower about the Patton "slapping" incident in Sicily and Eisenhower had asked them to hold the story, saying that "Patton is indispensable to the war effort—one of the guarantors of our victory."]

Unfortunately, a few days after the Salerno landing, the muckraker journalist Drew Pearson published the Patton story—with the unfortunate result that Clark remained in command in Italy. The whole Italian operation seemed to Tex to be a wasted effort. The road to Rome was open, no German troops stood between. However, as at Salerno, Clark dug in on the beach and did not press an advance—a delay which gave the very able German General Kesselring time to establish initial defenses at Salerno, and to put in place a major defensive position across southern Italy, the *Gustav Line*, utilizing the treacherous Appenine Mountains to block the road to Rome. The highway, which had been considered an easy passage, cut through a narrow mountain pass dominated by Monte Cassino. After nearly two months of costly fighting, Naples finally fell in October, but what should have been a rapid movement on to Rome, dragged on, costly in lives and time, and holding up the U.S. advance well into the winter. Meanwhile, the British Eighth Army under General Montgomery had moved easily up the flat coastal plain on the east coast of Italy, and eventually captured the large airfield at Foggia.

When the British and American armies were finally joined, given the delays from Clark's bungled landing at Salerno, logic dictated that the situation should be re-evaluated. Italy had surrendered, the Italian troops had laid down their arms, and Mussolini had gone into hiding. The great harbor of Naples was a secure supply base and the Foggia air fields were easily capable of handling foreseeable requirements. German troops, while well dug in on the Gustav line, did not pose an offensive threat, and there was little, if anything, of military value short of the Alps. A thoughtful evaluation would have indicated that there was little further to be gained in Italy, and throwing Allied troops against the formidable Apennine mountains and the *Gustav Line* in winter seemed foolhardy.

Meanwhile, word had circulated around Headquarters in London that the overall strategic situation had begun to turn against Hitler. The Russians had won an immense tank and infantry battle at Kursk during July and August of 1943, the first major defeat for Hitler. Roosevelt and Churchill met in Cairo in November 1943 — joined briefly by Chiang Kai-shek, who obtained assurances for protection of his position in China — and then proceeded to meet with Stalin in Tehran on the Black Sea. As Tex heard the story, Stalin used his position, enhanced by his victory at Kursk, to opposed the thought of Allied troops in Eastern Europe, and instead had demanded an invasion on the French coast. If the Allies were unwilling to accede to his demands for an invasion by May of 1944, Stalin declared that he would have his army in Berlin by that time, and would negotiate a separate peace with the Germans. Churchill and Roosevelt protested that they had plans for a landing within that time frame. Stalin had immediately asked: who will command? As Churchill and Roosevelt hesitated, Stalin knew; no commander, no plan.

Thus confronted, Roosevelt and Churchill had been forced to a decision. It had been generally assumed that, since the Americans were providing the great preponderance of military strength, the overall commander should be an American. General Marshall was expected to be selected because of the universal respect accorded him; however, Roosevelt surprised everyone, reportedly saying he could not sleep nights if General Marshall were out of Washington. American troops would carry the heaviest burden, and, faced with the necessity for an immediate decision, Eisenhower was the obvious choice. [Footnote: as Steve Ambrose's biography sets out: "He had been battle-tested in North Africa, had demonstrated that he could get along with difficult Allies, understood the complex, delicate interrelationship of teamwork and unity of command." And, above all, "when asked the nature of Eisenhower's leadership, the universal response was, Trust. Everybody liked Ike, responded positively to his outgoing personality. His hearty laugh, infectious grin, relaxed manner and constant optimism were irresistible. He provided an overriding impression of vitality, of an immensely alive human being who enjoyed his job."]

Tex was delighted at the announcement of Eisenhower's appointment, but the Tehran talks also resulted in new strategic decisions and major changes in command. Jimmy Doolittle was picked to take over the Eighth Air Force. Eaker, of course, felt that the job should continue to be his as a result of his past work. However, as far as Arnold was concerned, the sands had run through the glass for Eaker. Arnold was known to have a problem with his own temper, and he could not overcome his frustration at the results of the Eighth under Eaker's command, whatever the obvious extenuating circumstances. The change of command took place at end of 1943. In a kind of consolation, Eaker was given command of the Mediterranean Allied Air Force that, on paper, was larger than the Eighth Air Force. But there was a catch. Eaker's command would be largely administrative and diplomatic. The big decisions of the Eighth would be made in London—and Doolittle would make them. Tex admired Eaker, ever the good soldier, who hid his enormous disappointment. He took command of the Mediterranean Allied Air Force—and took Tex and Jock Whitney with him.

Tex's orders were for an immediate departure, forcing an especially painful decision. He and Lady Rose had been formally engaged for some time, they had entertained, and been entertained, in the best circles, and she wanted to get married before he left. He had no idea what might happen to him, or where he would end up. He also knew he wasn't going to change what he was doing, and he knew there were serious risks ahead. Under the circumstances, he didn't think marriage was the right thing, for either of them. They were both miserable over the parting.

The situation in Italy was entirely different from London, different in location, in job, in closeness to the war, and in personal relationships. Eaker, and Jock, now serving as Political Officer, were deeply involved in diplomatic and administrative matters. Tex had his Combat Photo Unit staffed with good people, with clear assignments—along with an overview on correspondent's activities. But, as a practical matter, he was his own boss. He began to feel like a reporter again, more or less free to move around, see what he wanted, do what he wanted.

Now he had a chance to cover a war first-hand, at the front. Wars are ugly, brutal, ghastly things, but, in the midst of all the horror, some wonderful, fascinating people perform acts of incredible heroism and inspiration. While he was no longer directly involved in the combat missions of the Fifteenth Air Force operating out of Foggia, Tex did have ready access to B-25s—part of the Tactical Air Force operating from a local field, a rugged, twin-engine medium bomber, with great short-field capability that enabled it to get in almost anywhere—the plane Jimmy Doolittle had chosen to fly off a Navy carrier for his daring raid on Tokyo early in the war.

As for location, this part of the war was being fought in one of the most beautiful areas of the world. Allied headquarters was in a magnificent palace, built about a hundred years before by the kings of Italy as their summer residence in Caserta, a small mountainside town about thirty miles north of Naples, chosen because of the climate and the view of the Bay of Naples, the Sorrento Peninsula and the Isle of Capri just beyond. Tex was told that Eisenhower had picked Caserta, not for the view, but because he, better than any other Allied commander, understood the need for unity of command, cooperation and teamwork among the top Allied commanders. He wanted all the decision-makers of the Allied Mediterranean Force Headquarters located together, away from the fleshpots of Rome. (Later, he picked Versailles, instead of Paris, for the same reason). The story was told that, in the course of his inspection of the area, Eisenhower was taken by boat around the island of Capri and, noticing imposing villas, wondered to whom they belonged? An eager aide replied, "The largest is yours, General, and the others have been taken by General Spaatz and General Clark. Eisenhower ordered that no officers of his would have those villas. However, after the decision of the Tehran Conference to bring him to command in London, Eisenhower returned to Washington for briefings, which left Mark Clark (who Eisenhower notably did not take with him to England) in command of U.S. troops in Italy, while General Montgomery remained in command of the British troops.

Allied headquarters in Caserta, Italy

Tex recalled his time in Italy as a kind of kaleidoscope of events and experiences. By the time Tex and Jock arrived at the Allied headquarters in Caserta, a very active social life had already developed in that magnificent setting—and Jock and Tex did their duty as they saw it. British General "Jumbo" Wilson was the Allied commander in the Mediterranean and he was also billeted in the Kings Palace. The Brits gave delightful parties in their elegant, nonchalant style, bemedalled generals, Guards officers, members of the Royal Rifle Brigade, distinguished by their green uniforms with black buttons, with beautifully-tailored Indian or kilted Highland troopers serving drinks, with bagpipes playing in the background and the sight of the sunset across the bay. Jock arranged a comfortable insulated tent set-up in a mimosa grove beside the stream running down through the magnificent gardens to the Palace.

Attractive ladies seemed to be charmed by Tex, and he soon met General Wilson's personal secretary, Lady Hermione, Countess Ranfurly, an engaging, handsome woman with another remarkable English story. Her husband had been called up early in the war and had been posted to Cairo. She wanted to follow, but British regulations precluded a spouse's travel to war zones. So, taking her butler, Whitaker, with her, she booked passage from London to South Africa, where she hitchhiked by various ingenious stratagems, and through numerous hardships, to Cairo. Her titled presence was highly visible, and an obvious violation of official regulations. But this posed only a temporary problem for Hermione's ingenuity. She went to "Jumbo" Wilson and he, recognizing talent when he saw it, made her his secretary. As the British army advanced in the desert, her husband advanced with them—and was reported missing in action. Her butler had by then caught up with her in Cairo, and they moved with General Wilson when he took command in Caserta. After a long wait, she finally learned that her husband had been captured, badly wounded, and had be transferred to a hospital in Italy, where they were eventually re-united. [Footnote: Tex gave me her telephone number in England and asked that I call her. A charming conversation. Long widowed, she and Tex had remained friends, visited back and forth through the years. She talked warmly of wartime in Caserta, as if recalling a long house party, with "Jock" and "dear Tex." After the war she was prevailed upon to write her story. With typical wit, she titled the book, *To War, With Whitaker.*]

The war was nearby, active—and stalemated. Based upon what he saw, and came to learn, he believed that the failure to reconsider the military value of an Italian campaign was one of the most costly decisions of the war, both in terms of poor generalship and pointless American casualties. After four months of heavy losses, Clark had advanced only forty miles from Naples, giving the Germans time to establish an impasse at the foot of the dominating Monte Cassino, which towered over the narrow pass on the road to Rome. It was hard to believe that Clark had thrown the untested 36th Texas National Guard Division—in its first exposure to combat—as the point of the first assault. The two lead regiments were virtually destroyed as effective fighting units. Then, the supporting 45th Division, another National Guard unit, recruited from the Rocky Mountain states, was mauled nearly as badly.

The citadel of Monte Cassino was capped with the venerable Fifteenth Century Monastery of St. Benedict. Clark, frustrated by the failure of frontal assaults on the mountain, demanded that Air Force strategic bombers be committed to a massive air attack on the Monastery. Other field commanders maintained that there was no evidence of any German defense from the Monastery. Nevertheless, Clark continued to demand the raid—and one hundred thirty-five B-17s obliterated the Monastery. The German First Parachute Division, generally regarded as the best German division, was defending the area, and it was later learned that its commander, General Frido von Senger und Etterlin was, ironically, a lay member of the Order of St. Benedict—and had forbidden any military use of the Monastery buildings. However, once our bombing had destroyed the Monastery, he had his troops dig into the ruins, rendering the citadel even more defensible.

General Clark, having made little progress against the well-led and well-entrenched German defenses at Monte Cassino, determined upon a flanking maneuver, an amphibious landing at Anzio, behind the German defenses, A large force landed, unopposed, with a clear approach to Rome. But, as at Salerno, Clark did not advance and, once again, simply dug in on the beach. The Germans troops to the south at Monte Cassino were in imminent danger of being cut off and captured, responded quickly, established positions on high ground, and pinned down the Americans on the Anzio beach.

Tex was angry, and wanted to see the action for himself. Martha Gelhorn, an attractive correspondent, then married to Ernest Hemingway, wanted to come along. They had a rough ride on an LST and splashed onto the beach. They borrowed a Jeep, and thinking it might be good for the troops to see a pretty girl driving, Tex put Martha behind the wheel and she drove up and down the lines. The GIs loved it. Then a German machine gun opened fire, the bullets kicking up dirt around the Jeep. She spun the Jeep around and floored it. And she was cheered as she walked in the chow line for dinner in the Officer's mess. But they were depressed at what they had seen. Clark's pattern of landing unopposed and digging in on the beach, had given the high ground to the Germans and the whole Anzio exercise was another bloody failure on Clark's record. Worse, it reflected on the whole Army decision process that a general with Clark's record should be kept in command positions. It seemed beyond West Point favoritism, it smelled of powerful political protection.

Back at Caserta, the Monte Cassino battle was turned over to the British X Corps, commanded by General Richard McCreery, with whom Tex had become friends, partly because of the similarity of their names. Tex asked for a tour of the battlefield, a mountainous wasteland of rocks, winter mud and devastation. In the course of this visit He got to know John Huston, the great movie director, who, with total lack of concern for his own welfare, had filmed the bloodiest battle scenes Tex had ever seen on film. General Clark's censors, anxious over Clark's indefensible pattern of decisions, and the resultant heavy losses, were eager to protect Clark from the possible effect of this film. They seized what they thought was Huston's only copy; however, Huston had another copy. Tex sent it through to the United States with other film from his combat photography unit—and the film went into eventual movie distribution as the now-famous movie of war, *The Battle of San Pietra*. Monte Cassino held out until the middle of May 1944, continuing to resist massive attacks, first by the 4th Indian Division, then a New Zealand Division, until, finally, a Polish Division, eager for revenge against the Germans, carried the citadel and raised the Polish flag on the peak.

Meanwhile, Tex was flying back and forth to London, where the German V-1 pilotless flying bombs continued to strike. On one of his trips, he ran into Lord Forbes who said, with that wonderful casualness, that since they had had such a "splendid flight to Ploesti," Tex might like to fly with him again in a *Mosquito,* this time on a mission over the suspected German missile research center at Peenemunde, where the Brits believed that there was secret rocket work in progress—which was later to appear as the V-2 rocket bomb—but at that time the Brits had not been able to discern the level of traffic. The top RAF photo interpreter, Constance Babbington-Smith, went with them. They flew over Peenemunde as dawn was breaking. Babbbington-Smith's photos revealed heavy truck tracks in the dew on the grass, indicating high levels of traffic. A major RAF bombing raid followed, and so damaged the facility that the German V-2 rocket program was substantially affected.

The German missile development was intriguing to Tex, and he took Jim Rand, a friend from New York, an engineer by background, and part of the Rand family of the Remington Rand Corporation, in a Jeep to look at the U.S. supply operations in Salerno Harbor. The Germans were continuing to bomb the harbor and Rand pointed up and said, "That's something different." There seemed to be two German JU-88 bombers attached, one on top of the other, like "Siamese Twins." As they watched, the planes separated, one beginning lazy circles at altitude while the other headed down toward the cargo ships. As it neared one of the ships, the descending JU-88 began to make abrupt adjusting turns, and crashed into the water beside the ship. Rand said, "That's got to be a pilotless aircraft, radio-directed from the other plane." Tex thought about the continuing high level of losses of the Eighth Air Force crews and bombers, and he wondered what was happening in U. S. development of pilotless weapons. He asked around, but no one seemed to be thinking that way. [Footnote: Years after the war, when General Arnold published his autobiography, *Global Missions,* he revealed that Bill Knutson, head of General Motors, had proposed building a similar pilotless aircraft for the U.S. but Arnold had rejected the idea as too complicated. Tex wondered how many bomber crews might have been saved. Another aspect of the "fog of war."]

Early in the war, a few African-American soldiers were trained as pilots and were formed into an all-black unit, the 99th Pursuit Squadron, commanded by Colonel Benjamin O. Davis, then operating out of the air field complex at Foggia. Tex got a B-25 and went over for a visit. Davis's pilots were still flying the antiquated P-40s they had flown in ground support in North Africa. Two additional squadrons had been formed, were combined into the 332nd Fighter Group and assigned to the Fifteenth Air Force to fly bomber escort. Many soldiers and airmen came from the South where racial prejudice was widespread at that time. A story circulated that white officers, newly assigned to temporary duty under Colonel Davis, had said that they would refuse to salute a black man, regardless of his rank. Hearing this, Davis hung his uniform tunic, with his silver Colonel eagles on the shoulders, behind him. He told his adjutant to inform the white officers, who had been talking in the bar the night before, that they should report to Colonel Davis and, whatever their personal feelings, they would salute the uniform. Any act of insubordination would result in immediate disciplinary proceedings.

As he expected, Tex was impressed with Colonel Davis. They spent some time together, met some of his pilots. Davis told him that, despite many requests, they were the only bomber escort outfit operating without P-51s. Everything about Davis, and his unit, was impressive. Something was clearly wrong in the system. Toni Frizell, a famous fashion photographer from *Harper's Bazaar*, came through Caserta as a correspondent and asked Tex for some ideas for good pictures. He sent her over to see Davis and the 332nd. She brought back some extraordinary photographs, many noble, powerful, distinguished faces, set against the silhouettes of their fighters. Tex asked her to leave copies with him, as he knew that Eleanor Roosevelt and Harry Hopkins were coming through Caserta shortly thereafter. He told Mrs. Roosevelt the story of Davis and the 332nd. She asked if there was anything she could do to help. Tex told her that above all else, Davis wanted the new P-51s for his unit, so that his men could have first-line fighters to escort the bombers all the way to their targets in Germany. In remarkably short order, the long-desired P-51s arrived. Some bomber pilots, born in the South, had asked that their Groups not be escorted by the 332nd. Davis had his boys paint the tails of their planes red, and he had the word passed to the bomber pilots, "Look out of your cockpits. If you see a P-51 with a red tail, you can be sure no German fighter will get to your bomber." No bomber escorted by the 332nd was ever lost to enemy fighters. Davis ended a distinguished career as a Lieutenant General in the United States Air Force—and the Tuskegee Airmen hold a place of high honor in America. Tex remained friends with several of them until his death.

There were a few Free French units operating in the area and Tex heard that the famous French aviator-author Antoine de Saint-Exupery was flying with one of them. Today he is best remembered for his children's fantasy book, *The Little Prince*, but in the 1930s, St. Ex was the poet of aviation, and his pre-war *"Night Flight"* and *"Wind, Sand and Stars"* are timeless reading. Some of Tex's pilot friends had introduced him to St. Ex. in New York before the war. In 1940, he was a French reconnaissance pilot. When France collapsed, he escaped to North Africa, then to the United States, where he was lionized in literary circles. St. Ex. was almost obsessed by his concern over what he foresaw as a steady advance of totalitarian politics, afflicted with deep anxieties for the future of political and religious freedom, constantly saying, "What can man do? What must man do?"

With the prospect of the invasion and liberation of France, St. Ex pulled every one of his considerable strings of influence to get back into the air as a military pilot. His goal was to join his old French photo reconnaissance unit, Groupe 2/33, now flying P-38s under U.S. command. He got his wish, but, as an intellectual long known for his preoccupied absentmindedness, he had an unfortunate tendency to land his plane without lowering the landing gear. Eventually his commander grounded him. St. Ex was distraught, once again pulled out all the stops, begging to fly again for the invasion of France. The French Air Force Groupe 2/33 was based in Corsica, under the overall command of the Mediterranean Allied Air Force. Tex knew generally of St. Ex's situation, but it reached his desk through a call from a friend, John Phillips, of *Time* magazine, who asked for his help. Tex put a call in to St. Ex's commander, who began to recite the history of St. Ex's accidents. Tex asked, "Colonel, how many flyable P-38s do you have in your unit?" Answer: thirty-five. "How many pilots?" Answer: twenty-five. "It sounds to me that you can let St. Ex fly five more missions. We have plenty of P-38s available. Let us know if you need any more."

Corsica was an important staging area for *Operation Dragoon*, the code name for the invasion of the French Mediterranean coast. As invasion preparations accelerated, Tex was back and forth to Corsica, and took the opportunity to look up St. Ex. A remarkable man, they had long conversations, over several bottles of wine. St. Ex was tormented by the conflict between his idealized vision of France—and his hope for France's potential contribution to the destiny of Mankind—but he was also deeply pessimistic regarding the chaotic condition of French politics. Tex told him that he was regarded as one whose vision would be important to the future. St. Ex was silent for a time, and then just shook his head. Then Tex asked him the question that Tex couldn't answer when it was asked of him in England: "Why do you want to fly these dangerous missions?" Without pause, St. Ex said, "So I can sit in the presence of pilots—and be silent." St. Ex's P-38 disappeared on a photo reconnaissance mission over France. German records show no interceptions on the day in question. The cause of his disappearance remains a mystery. Tex believed that this was surely the symbolic departure that this poet of the air would have chosen.

After the long and bloody struggle at Anzio, the Army had finally broken out in the late spring of 1944. German General Kesselring declared Rome an "open city," and so no longer a military objective. Had General Mark Clark moved off the coast, as his orders directed, he could have cut off and captured the German forces at the *Gustav Line* farther south, effectively ending German military capabilities in Italy. Instead, Clark again delayed, marshaling his forces to lead a triumphal march into Rome, with Caesar-like embellishments. While Clark was preparing for his personal parade, the German troops in the south on the Gustav line escaped to take up new defenses farther north. Again, Tex couldn't understand why Clark was not removed from command.

Clark's delays had given the Germans time to regroup the forces and establish the *Arno Line,* running along the Arno River from Pisa through Florence to the east coast between Ancona and Rimini. The Air Force staff made every effort to avoid another Clark fiasco, and a plan was developed to cut off a German escape by bombing out all of the bridges across the Po River behind Florence. The plan was known as Operation Mallory Major—named for Bill Mallory, an Air Force intelligence officer a couple of years ahead of Tex at Yale, a famous football player from Memphis, known as "Memphis Bill", whom Tex had met in "Skull & Bones" Naturally, Mallory wanted to fly on the mission. His operation was a success—but his plane did not return. Another fine man lost.

Florence, like Rome, had been declared an "open city" by the Germans but it was a transportation center with substantial rail facilities nearby. It was important to take these facilities out of service, and not to damage the venerable structures of Florence itself. The painful memories of Monte Cassino lingered. Tex was assigned as part of a four-man team, including the bombardier who would lead the mission, to slip into Rome to the Vatican for an analysis of maps and advice from Church figures on the most important buildings that must be preserved in Florence. The mission waited for a clear day and the targets were hit without damage to the historic structures.

Jake Smart had been promised command of a bomb group, if he could ever get General Arnold to let him off his staff. Jake finally broke loose and got his group, the famous old 97th, now based at Foggia. Tex didn't know about it until he got a call from Jake. In less than three months, he had led his Group on twenty-nine missions. When

Eaker finally pulled him off operations and moved him up to the Wing headquarters, they finally had time together. Tex told him that he hoped somehow to get out to the Pacific where his brother, Douglas, was a Navy carrier pilot. Jake told him that there was something to think about. There was a new weapon that may end the war quicker than expected, and there would be a need for a group of top correspondents to cover the end of the war from the Air Force side. He said that Arnold liked Tex, and Smart thought that Tex could be in line to lead that unit, if he wanted. Tex told him to put his name in wherever way he thought best.

Meanwhile, the Air Force had faced a continuing problem trying to hit targets in East Germany at the very far edge of our bombers' range. An ideal solution would be shuttle raids, hitting the targets, then landing in Russia, refueling and rearming, and mounting another raid on the way back. Diplomatic efforts got nowhere with the Russians for more than a year, but something eventually was worked out. The raid was scheduled by the Fifteenth Air Force to take off from Foggia and land at Poltava in the Ukraine at the end of May 1944. Eaker wanted to lead this mission, his first since the first Eighth Air Force mission to Rouen, France, nearly two years before, and flying again with that old Group, the 97th. Eaker had his B-17 painted with the name *Yankee Doodle II* to commemorate that first mission. Naturally, Tex talked his way on to the mission. Just before they took off, Tex heard that Jake Smart had been lost in a raid on Weiner-Neustadt.

The Poltava mission included two other Groups, with a heavy escort of P-51 fighters. They bombed railroad yards at Debrecen in Hungary, and landed in Poltava on the first of June 1944, where they were met by Averill Harriman, our Ambassador to Russia, and his daughter Kathy, whom Tex had known in London. Pretty Russian girls greeted them with flowers, and Russian generals, loaded with medals from shoulder to belt, took them to dinner. They had been warned of the endless vodka toasts and the need to keep a clear head, if possible. For all the welcoming celebrations, there was a remarkable lack of preparation for the B-17s. Fuel was available only in fifty-gallon drums, which had to be siphoned by hand, causing innumerable delays. At twilight a single plane passed high overhead. It looked like a German ME-210. They wanted to send up some P-51s to knock it down, assuming it was a German reconnaissance plane, but the Russians said that no takeoffs could be permitted without prior approval from Moscow. They told the Russians to get it; they answered that all radio communication was out of order. In three hours, flares lit up the sky. The shiny new B-17s were easy targets. Two-thirds of their aircraft were destroyed on the ground, a clear set-up. But why? What game were the Russians playing?

Eaker was programmed to fly on to Moscow. Harriman acted as if Tex had done him a great favor in getting his daughter Kathy a job with the *New York Mirror* in London so she could stay with him in England during the war, and he asked Tex to come along and stay in the Embassy for a few days while Eaker was attending meetings. Kathy told Tex that she had grown closer to her father in Moscow than she had ever been before, but that he was bored and frustrated in the isolation of that post. She didn't trust the Russians. As Tex understood, she and her father had been taken to witness the disinterment of the bodies of thousands of German soldiers, who had been buried in the Katyn Forest, shot in the back of the head with their hands bound behind their backs.

The Russians wanted to convince the world that the Germans had been killed by the Polish underground in the previous summer. Averill had the Embassy issue a press release accepting the Russian position. Kathy wondered why the bodies were dressed in heavy winter uniforms. She felt her father was far too sympathetic and too trusting of the Russians. Tex said that Averill was probably acting under Roosevelt's instructions. Kathy replied, "That's even worse. It means our whole policy is wrong."

When Tex got back to Caserta, he ran into Bill Donovan, head of the OSS, which had a major headquarters in Caserta. It always amused Tex that the OSS station was code-named PALM BEACH (which was also its radio call-sign). Donovan passed through from time to time, staying at the elegant Harrison Williams villa on Capri. He told Tex that Serge Obolensky, whom Tex had known in New York, was running an OSS parachute school nearby, and the OSS would be glad to have him. That sounded interesting—so Tex looked him up. Serge was the same as ever, a dashing, gallant adventurer. He said that if Tex wanted to see a different kind of war, with some fascinating people, he should take his parachute course, and tag along on a few OSS jumps. He told Tex about Brigadier Fitzroy Maclean, the legendary British undercover operator, famous for his spectacular exploits in kidnapping Axis leaders in the Middle East and performing daring raids across the Sahara Desert to blow up *Afrika Corps* supplies. Among Maclean's many other attributes, he was known for a characteristic eccentricity in his choice of military dress, parachuting into hostile operations in his kilt with hand grenades in his "sporran" pouch.

The idea of the parachute program appealed to Tex, and he signed up for the six-jump qualification course. The initial jumps were at about five hundred feet, through a large door of a Douglas C-47, the military version of the DC-3, which the Brits called *"Dakota."* Tex said he had some qualms at first—but the thing to do is not to think, just do as you're told. He said it was kind of fun—afterward. Obolensky recommended that Tex make a jump with one of the OSS teams, called *Pathfinders*, which dropped behind German lines, said that he had an interesting operation in mind, and the OSS would brief him on the details.

Tex went back to Caserta, and waited for his *Pathfinder* mission. Whatever else they were doing, Tex and Jock managed to squire a number of ladies around during their time in Caserta. One day Tex got an OSS message—"Donovan to McCrary—Duke arriving tomorrow 1400 hours. Meet plane." Jock knew more Dukes than Tex did, but he had no better idea which Duke this was. It was raining torrents when it came time to meet the plane. Tex started for his Jeep, and Jock said, "For God's sake, Tex, you can't pick up a Duke in a Jeep in this rain. Take the ambulance outside." Good idea. As the B-25 landed, Tex pulled up beside it. One gets out of a B-25 by dropping out through the bomb bay. From the outside, the first thing one sees are legs. These legs were in officer's green trousers. The figure bent low under the bomb bay doors, dressed in trench coat and officer's cap, then stepped forward, and a woman's voice said, "Tex, darling, it's Doris Duke." They used to see quite a bit of each other in New York before the war. She always said that she wanted to get married, but that no American man knew how to be a husband to a truly rich woman—they simply didn't know how to act. Now she said she had finally met the right man, a British Colonel, who had just been ordered from Caserta to Sardinia. Tex made a call, found out the

Colonel's location, told her pilot to fly her to Sardinia. She gave Tex a big hug and kiss, and took off. A few days later she was back. Her Colonel had been killed just before she arrived. She was truly heart broken. Tex squired her around, found her a job heading up a rest camp. She outclassed everybody in her performance. She was so good that Tex got her credentials as a war correspondent.

Tex worked hard to get correspondents to see the war first-hand. He had an interesting inventory of aircraft available, B-25s and "droop snoop" P-38s with a clear plastic nose replacing the guns, and offering the best imaginable view. Some P-38s had been converted originally to permit a bombardier to lie in the nose and lead conventional P-38s on fighter-bomber flights—but the droop-snoops were spectacular planes for observation or photography. When Tex held correspondents' briefings, he always offered some "hairy" flight plans. He wanted them to see as much of the war as possible. Many correspondents preferred to go back to the local bar, but Doris was always the first to put up her hand for the "hairiest" flights, over the Brenner Pass being her favorite (the Germans still held everything in the north), and she shamed a lot of correspondents into taking flights they wouldn't have otherwise chosen for themselves.

Then the OSS got in touch and told Tex that he was scheduled to drop with a jump team on August 14, 1944, the night before the invasion of southern France, *Operation Dragoon* (Churchill insisted on the name, saying that he had been "dragooned" into approving it, as he had previously wanted to invade through the Balkans). When Jock learned that Tex was scheduled to go, he naturally wanted to go, too—but he wasn't jump-qualified. However, Jock was determined to get a combat mission during the war. He got hold of Bill Donovan and wrangled his way on to another mission, going in by fishing boat.

A few days before his jump was scheduled, Tex flew to Corsica and joined up for briefings with his OSS team. The OSS had rigged a small parachutist motorcycle to carry all of his photo gear. This equipment was rigged to break loose when his parachute snapped open, to hang down below him so that he could land relatively less encumbered. It didn't work out that way. Tex jumped at low altitude, at night on a static line, his chute opened immediately—and he was in the trees, big trees, his equipment package hung up on a higher branch, leaving him suspended upside down. He realized someone was shouting at him in German. Then Tex saw him, holding a rifle. Tex struggled out of the tree, still a little groggy. Dawn was breaking. Tex pointed to his equipment. The German nodded, gestured with his rifle for Tex to pick it up. An OSS "partner" had been assigned with Tex. He showed up behind the German soldier with his Tommy gun, and spoke quietly in German. The German guard dropped his rifle. None of them knew what to do. They went inside a nearby shed. They could tie the German up, but they didn't want to leave him and have him talk—and they didn't want to kill him. They tried to think of a plan. Suddenly two trucks pulled up in front, and German soldiers surrounded the shed, demanding their surrender. Prisoners again. But now the Germans didn't know what to do with them. They all stood around looking at each other. They could hear gunfire, planes and bombs coming steadily closer. The Germans talked on their radio, then got up and pulled out, leaving them alone. They looked around—nobody in sight, so they started to walk down a road, "to the sound of the guns" —but the gunfire didn't last long. Soon they saw a German convoy coming. They ducked into the bushes and the Germans passed without paying any attention. Then another came by the same way. Tex took some pictures. They realized that the Germans were withdrawing. After a while, a farm truck came by, picked them up and took them into Marseilles, now in Allied hands. Two days later Tex was back in Caserta.

Jock was not so lucky—he was reported missing in action. Then Tex received a penciled note—he never learned exactly how it reached him—addressed: Col. Tex McCrary, Hqs. Med.A.F, Caserta. "Tex, you son of a bitch. Now I'm having more fun than you are." Eventually Tex learned Jock had been a prisoner of war for several weeks, but Tex didn't get the full story until they got together in New York in June 1945, when he was, by then, on his way to the Pacific.

Jock's fishing boat had gotten him ashore safely as the Germans were withdrawing. However, Jock and his team were overrun by a German unit, were sighted, and took cover in a farmhouse. The Germans brought up a tank. Jock was the ranking officer— and he surrendered his group. The Germans held him in a farmhouse (where he left the note to Tex), then herded them into larger groups of prisoners, first in trucks, then into a POW camp, then into boxcars on a train which moved slowly and only at night to avoid Pete Quesada's P-47s that strafed everything that moved in daylight. In the middle of the night, while the train was moving, Jock and several others jimmied the lock, and jumped from the train. They split up and Jock eventually was picked up by the French underground and brought back to American troops.

When Tex returned to Caserta, after his brief period as a German prisoner himself, he ran into Bill O'Dwyer, then a brigadier general, later to be mayor of New York City, who was on his way back to New York. They talked about the war, which both then thought might be slowly drawing to a close. Tex had also been thinking about what life might be like for him after the war, and that led him to think about Jinx. He asked O'Dwyer to call Jinx for him. On his first day back in New York, O'Dwyer, by chance, ran into Jinx on the steps of the Astor Hotel and said "I've got a message for you from a guy in Italy, who has gone crazy, jumping out of airplanes behind enemy lines, all sorts of nutty things." Jinx was thrilled. She had read in a gossip column in the *Los Angeles Times* that Tex and Lady Rose had ended their engagement and she had been hoping to hear from him. She wrote him immediately. After exchanging messages of increasing warmth, telling of her life since they had parted, of acting in movies—the eventual total was twelve—and traveling on USO tours to entertain troops. Jinx wrote that she would be going on a USO tour to the China-Burma-India theater, with a stopover for a few days in Cairo in December 1944. Perhaps he could meet her there? He could. They had four happy days together—and the word "marriage" came up. Jinx left Cairo ecstatic, and Tex went back to the war.

By then, the main war theater was in northern Europe and Tex followed the news closely. After the D-Day landing in Normandy on June 6th, 1944, Eisenhower's advance had become bogged down in the farm hedgerows of Normandy. Eisenhower had to have an aggressive general to break out—and, of all his generals, George Patton was his choice. Patton, the old cavalry officer, scorned infantry tactics, moving slowly and covering the flanks. An old Army-Air Force controversy had fought over the close support of ground forces. Patton wanted to move fast, not be slowed down covering his flanks. He got together with General Pete Quesada, who committed to cover Patton's flanks from the air, with his P-47s, a "first" in military history. Each service, ever jealous of its prerogatives, used separate radios, creating constant communication problems. Quesada put Air Force radios in Patton's tanks so that tankers could call in direct air support from Quesada's fighters overhead—"take out that anti-tank gun behind the hedge row on the left side of the road"—a level of cooperation which became a major contributor to the successes of the American Army in Europe. Patton's tanks raced out of Normandy, with Quesada's P-47 fighter-bombers covering the flanks, and were able to encircle and destroy two German field armies trapped in the "Falaise Gap." With Quesada's air cover, Patton pressed on. Paris was liberated at the end of August 1944, and Patton wanted to go on to Berlin. It was thought that the war might be over before the end of 1944.

Tex had heard about Pete Quesada long before they finally met in England when Quesada came up to London with Jimmy Doolittle to take command of fighters in the Eighth Air Force, just before Tex went to Italy with General Eaker, and their paths crossed often thereafter. Quesada was the kind of man people talked about throughout the Air Force as a "comer." The story was that in the late 1920s, Millard Harmon, then an Air Corps Major and later a revered General, worked part-time as a referee in college football games—and saw Quesada quarterback an underdog University of Maryland football team to an upset victory over Penn State. Always on the look-out to recruit young pilots with leadership potential, Harmon finally found Quesada life-guarding at a public beach—and persuaded him to become an Army pilot.

Gifted with great intelligence and natural charm, Quesada excelled at everything, and in the early 1930s became the personal pilot for Trubee Davison, then the Assistant Secretary of War for Air, and founder of the Yale Unit of Naval Aviation in World War I. On weekends, Quesada flew Davison back and forth from Washington to Davison's home in Locust Valley on the North Shore of Long Island. He met all the top people—all of whom he impressed and who were ready to advance his career. Davison later had Quesada fly him around Africa on a National Geographic project. His career advanced rapidly as World War II approached, and Eisenhower took him as commander of the Ninth Air Force in North Africa. Quesada was viewed as a future head of the Air Force. However, toward the end of the war, and looking to an inevitable inter-service battle in Congress over an Independent Air Force, a political decision was made to favor Hoyt Vandenberg, the nephew of a powerful senator and with very limited combat command experience, over Quesada, putting his path to the top command in jeopardy.

By the winter of 1944, the Allied armies were divided into two lines of attack: a northern drive along the coast, under Montgomery, intended to take Antwerp and open the harbor to Allied supplies; and a southern drive, under Patton, which was advancing straight into Germany, with the prospect of taking Berlin and ending the war in 1944. Montgomery, always jealous, and wanting a part in the victory, claimed he needed the gas from Patton's tanks. Eisenhower, apparently believing part of his role was to maintain positive British participation, shut down Patton's advance to supply Montgomery—who characteristically stalled some more. Even British historians recognize Montgomery's hesitancy as a great military blunder, unnecessarily prolonging the war for many months—and leaving an opening for a surprise German attack on the American troops under Montgomery's command in the north.

The result was *The Battle of the Bulge*, the largest land battle by Allied forces. Patton, driving toward Berlin, shifted north to relieve the embattled Americans. The ensuing battle was fought under winter blizzard conditions through the end of 1944—a highlight being the relief of the trapped 101st Airborne Division, who called themselves the "bloody bastards of Bastogne." The battle was Germans against Americans, the single most costly battle of the war—seventy-five thousand American casualties, including nineteen thousand dead. British Field Marshall Montgomery sat out the battle, declining to provide support. There were only two hundred British killed in that action. Tex was furious. The price of political decisions.

As 1945 began, the major battle continued in Germany and the Italian front became a kind of sideshow, with the Army stalled in winter weather in the northern Italian mountains. Meanwhile the Russians were advancing in the Balkans, as Churchill had feared, with little German resistance. Tex wanted to see what was happening in an area that had so concerned Churchill, and he wanted some photos. He arranged to fly in the nose of a droop-snoop P-38 as part of a fighter mission to strafe a German troop train in Yugoslavia. The P-38s found the train, hit it hard, and banked away. Tex asked his pilot for one more low pass over the smoking wreck. As he was looking through his camera's viewfinder, he saw tracers flashing by. He looked up to see what, at first, looked like German Messerschmidts. Then he saw red stars on their wings—Russian fighters, YAK-9s. Tex's droop-snoop P-38 had its guns removed from the nose to make room for the passenger, so they had no choice but to drop the landing gear as a sign of surrender, and follow the Russian lead. They were led to a nearby field, forced to land, and briefly interrogated. They were told that the train they had thought was German was, in fact, a Russian troop train—and their strafing had killed a Russian general. This caused Tex considerable concern but, to his surprise, the Russians didn't seem to want to deal with American prisoners, and he and his pilot were handed over to Tito's partisans.

Tito's headquarters was in a Yugoslavian duke's palatial hunting lodge. They were loosely guarded, and Tex walked into an elegant reception hall with a marble floor of black and white squares. A large, heavy man in a disheveled British uniform was lying on the floor, mumbling, obviously drunk, moving brandy bottles on the squares. Tex took a second look. It was Randolph Churchill. He said he was playing chess, and wondered if Tex would play a game with him. While Tex contemplated the prospect, an educated British voice behind him said, "I'm Brigadier Maclean. Who are you?" Maclean was head of the British liaison mission to Tito.

The Maclean episode went on to become another of Tex's most unusual and innovative World War II experiences. At that point, Tex's status was somewhat uncertain, although the Russians were ostensibly allies, his plane had strafed a Russian train and apparently killed a Russian general. On the good side, however, Tex and his pilot were with the respected British liaison officer. It seemed that the Russians took losses in stride, and they paid little further attention. Maclean said Belgrade would fall shortly, and he needed to visit another part of his unit. It was rugged country, and he planned to parachute in. Tex asked to go along, told him that he had been jump-qualified by

Obolensky, and that he had jumped into France. Tex didn't mention how it had worked out. Maclean said, "Splendid. Come along." It was another low-altitude jump with a static line and Tex was on the ground moments after his chute opened. (And yes, Maclean did in fact jump in his kilts, with a grenade in his sporran!)

Tex enjoyed the chance to talk more with Maclean, and he was impressed at how well Maclean got along with Tito's dedicated communists. He asked Maclean about Randolph Churchill's role in his command and he said that Randolph had begged for a chance. He had recognized that he had made a mess of his life. It was not easy being Winston Churchill's son. True, he drank excessively, but never on duty, and he had proven himself dependable and fearless in action. Maclean thought Randolph should have a chance to vindicate himself, so he had kept him on.

Tex asked Maclean for his thoughts about the future. Maclean told him that he feared that as soon as the war came to a close, the socialist Labour party in England would bring Churchill down, with promises of major new social benefits. However, the Labour party leaders were old-line socialists, incompetent for the leadership required in the post-war period, and he feared the worst. As to Yugoslavia, Tito's communists were tough and dedicated Yugoslavs. But they did not want their country ruled by Russia. Maclean believed that there was an opportunity for a constructive relationship for economic development with Tito, but he feared that anti-communist political pressures in the United States and England would likely inhibit effective political engagement.

Belgrade fell shortly thereafter, and Tex went into the city with Maclean. Belgrade had aspects of a handsome old Central European city, but Russian troops had already stripped anything moveable. Russian officers were trying to put a better public face on the rapacious role of their troops, and they had brought in the *Bolshoi Ballet* to evidence the high level of Russian culture. Maclean asked him to think up something on our side. Tex suggested that he get hold of Thornton Wilder—a fine writer and dependable Yale man, the author of the play, *Our Town*—who was an Air Force major in Caserta, an intelligence officer with Mike Phipps. Maclean loved the idea and it was arranged for Wilder to be flown over to put on a Belgrade production of *Our Town*. Maclean thought it might be useful to ask Tito's mistress, a recognized Yugoslav actress, to play the leading female role. Encore after encore! Personalities always affect politics.

Tex caught a ride back to Caserta on a C-47 supply plane. He had maintained friendships and connections with the OSS and learned in April that Italian communist partisans had captured Mussolini in Milan. The front was in a fluid condition, and he was able to get through quickly. However, the anticipated opportunity for Mussolini to be handed over to Allen Dulles of the OSS was preempted by the partisans, who, to enhance their own position in postwar Italian politics, wished to have the privilege of executing him. He and his mistress were machine-gunned, and then strung up by their heels in the village square. Tex arrived shortly thereafter, and got some photographs by way of documentation. He was impressed by the human consideration of the obviously enraged partisans who had been disturbed at the thought of Carla Patacci's skirt hanging down. With a surprising sense of modesty and decorum, the partisans had tied her skirt to her knees, providing her at least that dignity in death.

For all practical purposes the war in the Mediterranean Theater was over. The Italians never seemed to have ever had their heart in the war, and Tex was troubled by the military decisions he had seen in the Italy. So many soldiers, so many civilians, had been killed to no purpose that he could see. Why hadn't Roosevelt stood up to Churchill and passed Italy by? Churchill was dreaming of a British Empire that time had left behind. And the whole bloody Monte Cassino and Anzio operations brought no benefits that he could see. He felt strongly that Mark Clark should have been relieved of command at Salerno and, for Monte Cassino, Anzio, and Rome he should have been retired from the service.

By the end of April 1945, the active war in Europe was effectively over, and Tex's role as leader of a team of correspondents to cover the war in the Pacific was working its way through Washington. He was eager to press this forward when he heard that General Patton was flying to Salzburg on a secret mission to rescue or ransom the famous Lipizzaner horses. This was too good a show to miss. Tex grabbed Doris Duke; they jumped into a B-25, and flew to Salzburg. They landed without incident, the B-25 the only evidence of a U.S. presence. Shortly thereafter a C-47 come in, followed by a C-46 with trucks and a jeep. Patton got out of the C-47, theatrically uniformed as always, riding breeches, cavalry boots glistening, pistols on either hip. Doris and Tex were standing nearby, in uniform, and Patton, seeing them, whom he took to be strangers, naturally assuming that news of his supposedly "secret" mission was no longer a secret. He strode toward them, obviously angered, slapping his boot with his riding crop. Tex had no idea what he was going to do when, just as he drew close, Doris Duke removed her cap and let her hair fall, saying, "Georgie, darling, it's Doris." Patton stopped momentarily, threw his arms out, grabbed Doris, lifted her in the air, twirled her about, put her in his Jeep and roared off. Patton's aides said he was having dinner with some Russian generals. Tex waited around Salzburg with Patton's guys. The next morning, Patton's Jeep returned. Doris stepped out, opened her trench coat, revealing her uniform covered from her shoulders to her waist with Russian medals.

When Doris and Tex got back to Italy, Clare Booth Luce appeared. Determined to have an established position of her own, along with that of wife to Henry Luce, Clare had gotten herself elected to Congress from her home district in Connecticut and was using her Congressional travel privileges to get around the world. Rome fascinated her (later, after her conversion to Catholicism, she got Eisenhower to appoint her Ambassador to the Vatican). Clare came to dinner at Doris Duke's apartment in Rome and, after dinner, Tex walked Clare to her car. Clare knew that Tex and Doris had been involved with each other, off and on, through the years, and Clare gave him some advice, " Just remember, Tex, the man who marries the Duke becomes the Duchess."

Then Tex got a message that General Eaker wanted to talk to him.

Chapter Eight

War in the Pacific: MacArthur and Hiroshima

"God damn it, McCrary, you're the luckiest bastard I know. Despite all your skylarking and general tom-catting around, General Arnold is going to let you pick your own play group to go on a vacation tour around the Pacific with a bunch of high-priced toys. I can't believe it."

General Eaker had been in meetings with Generals Arnold, Spaatz and Doolittle while Tex was in Salzburg. Eaker said he was going to tell Tex inside stuff, straight from the top, but it's stuff he had to know to do the job. The cover story was that he was just another Air Force officer in charge of a bunch of correspondents coming out to cover the end of the war in the Pacific. But his real job was to do whatever he could to make sure that the Air Force's role was seen by the American people as the strategic weapon in the defeat of the enemy—not only in this war, but in the future. That was essential to the achievement of an independent U.S. Air Force.

Eaker noted that Tex had flown the missions, seen the pictures, read the reports. He knew what the Air Force had done to Germany. Tex should take his correspondents over via Europe, and show them a couple of bombed German cities along the way. The B-29 is a lot more formidable strategic weapon than the old B-17s and B-24s. We can hit the Japs a lot harder and their cities are much more vulnerable. No modern society can endure the kind of destruction the Air Force can now inflict. That's why it's so important for our country that the Air Force's strategic capability be recognized.

Eaker said that Tex should expect trouble. The authority structure in the Pacific is a mess. Unlike what Eisenhower had as Supreme Commander in the European Theater, there is no unified command in the Pacific. The Navy thinks it owns the ocean. And it goes without saying that General MacArthur thinks he's God. Admiral Nimitz has promulgated an order prohibiting Air Force bombing of Japanese ships or carrying out any offensive operations more than ten miles off shore unless under Navy command. The better minds of the Navy understand that in the future they will have to go into the air and under the water—and they are hungry for big land-based aircraft like our B-29s. So that's the problem. The Army and the Navy both want our control of the air. MacArthur has already seduced a bunch of big name correspondents. And the Navy has had a steamroller public relations operations since John Paul Jones. Ships are photogenic as hell. So here's where you come in. Arnold wants the Air Force to have a group of correspondents, who haven't already been seduced, to be led by one of us. You get to pick them. God knows you're not much—but you're all we've got who seems to be any good at this kind of thing. You'll get a clean set of orders signed by Arnold and co-signed by Marshall—that should keep you out of MacArthur's jails. You will also have your own censor authority with new direct radio communication to Arnold so MacArthur's censors can't muzzle you. Pick your correspondents, equipment, aircraft and support. You'll get everything you ask for.

Tex thought he was through, but Eaker kept on. He said there was something else to think about. Roosevelt's death has created a lot of uncertainties. The British Labour Party, a bunch of socialists, is trying to overthrow Churchill. Stalin is taking control of Eastern Europe. As far as the Army Air Force is concerned, we've got a problem with this new President, Truman. General Arnold worked like a dog to wean Roosevelt away from his love of ships and his days as Assistant Secretary of the Navy, and now we have Truman as President, a man who never went beyond high school, who has no experience in foreign relations, no travel abroad other than being a short-term Missouri National Guard artillery officer from the last war. Roosevelt kept Truman completely in the dark about everything.

At the Air Force meeting in Cannes, Arnold got a very troubling letter by courier from Bob Lovett saying that the Air Force was not being represented in Truman's top meetings. Apparently, Truman's closest confidante is some Missouri lawyer he got commissioned as his Naval aide and is now his inside lawyer, a guy named Clark Clifford. Our take on him is that he is a snake in the grass, only out for himself. Truman's other cronies are also questionable. He spends his evenings on the Navy yacht, drinking and playing poker with lobbyists and old Senate pals, while Clifford gets their drinks and sings songs for them. Arnold thinks General Marshall can keep things steady for a while, but we've got to try to get an Air Force aide next to Truman, if we can. We talked it over in Cannes, and all agreed it should be Pete Quesada. Eisenhower and Bradley love him. He flew Ike in a P-51 over the beaches in Normandy, and Ike liked it so much he made Pete fly him half way to Paris before he'd go home. Quesada has the rank and the experience—and he is the most charming, socially adept guy we've got.

Eaker said that, down the road, Doolittle would be taking the Eighth Air Force to the Pacific, where he'll be parallel to LeMay's Twentieth Air Force in the Strategic Air Command. Obviously, both MacArthur and Nimitz want control of the B-29s, but Arnold has worked out a deal with Marshall to keep overall control of the Strategic Air Command in Arnold's hands in Washington, with Spaatz to have operational command of both LeMay's Twentieth and Doolittle's Eighth Air Force, when he gets there. What this means is that when we get our independent U. S. Air Force, Spaatz will get the top job, for old time's sake. For the future, our best bet for commander is Quesada—unless they have to take Vandenberg, as a bribe to his Senator uncle not to cut Air Force appropriations

Tex asked what Eaker was going to do. He said he was going to be stuck in Washington at headquarters with the title of Deputy Commander of the United States Army Air Force—but what he was really going to be doing was to watch the contractors build the goddamn Pentagon. He said, "When I heard what Arnold was going to let you do, I even asked him to let me trade places with you—but Arnold said I had too much rank." Rumors were flying everywhere. The invasion of Okinawa was going badly, more slowly and with higher casualties, more than 30%. Everybody assumed that the planned invasion of Japan's home islands was going to be even more bloody. Tex was worried about his brother, flying in the Pacific. Air crews who had completed their combat tours over Europe, and had expected to go home, were now getting brief home leaves, with further orders to combat units in the Pacific. LeMay had already stepped up the B-29 offensive against Japan. All of the top commanders wanted new combat assignments to further their post-war careers. Tex understood what a bitter pill Eaker's new assignment was for him.

Tex's orders for his return to Washington required a stop in London. He cabled Beaverbrook, who asked him to dinner, saying that he wanted Tex's insider's impression of what he had seen in Italy. Tex told him of the confusions, the shifting of commands, the whole question of what we were doing in Italy to begin with. Why had Churchill pushed Roosevelt so hard, what was he trying to accomplish? Beaverbrook said that Churchill was a truly great man, dedicated to preserving England's historic role in Europe, the Balkans, the Mediterranean, and throughout the Empire. Whatever the questionable decisions, they were washed away by the victory. Beaverbrook believed that the defeat of Hitler had vindicated Churchill's leadership, and he was convinced the voters would reject the Labour Party in the forthcoming elections. Tex asked how Beaverbrook could be so sure, and Beaverbrook said "I'll bet you ten thousand dollars, ten to one." Tex said he didn't have one thousand dollars. Beaverbrook said that he was so confident he would make it easy for Tex. "I'll give you a ten to one against your one hundred dollars." Tex flew to Washington the next day, then soon left for the Pacific—and forgot about the bet. However, Tex was right. At the moment of final Victory—to which Churchill had carried them, virtually single-handed, the British people turned him out of office, to elect an incompetent Labour government. When Tex returned to New York from the Pacific, Beaverbrook's waiting check was a welcome surprise.

Tex's orders called for arrival in Washington the first week of June, 1945, for final briefings, and to pick up his unit and equipment for the Pacific. Take-off for his mission was June 11th. The informed Air Force view was that the invasion of Japan would take place later in the fall. In the midst of this, Tex got the great news that Jake Smart, who had been reported lost over Weiner-Neustadt, had survived as a prisoner. Smart had intimated that a new weapon might be available to accelerate the end of the war. It began to occur to Tex that the war might be over somewhat sooner.

When Tex was leaving Italy, he got a cable from Jinx in Los Angeles, saying that she would be in New York on June 10th, leaving on the 11th for another USO tour, and she hoped they could get together. Tex tried to reach her, but could not get through. Tex called Charlie McCabe, his editor at the *Mirror*, and asked him to find Jinx and tell her that Tex would meet her in New York on June 10th. And he added, "Tell her I'm ready to talk about marriage." Tex was certainly looking forward to seeing Jinx when his C-54 landed at Bolling Field for his briefings in Washington. The props had barely stopped turning when a grinning sergeant pushed a ramp up to the door and handed Tex a new copy of *Life* magazine, with two pages of their "Life Goes to a Party" feature, describing a big party given in Hollywood by Clark Gable and Paulette Goddard for Jinx Falkenburg, who was leaving for New York to marry Tex McCrary.

The fact that Jinx had announced their imminent marriage to the world without notice to Tex came as a bit of a shock. He had expected that the subject would come up, but not so soon, and certainly not spread all over *Life* magazine. His mind tended to wander during his briefings at Air Force headquarters. He raced through his duties in Washington, and flew to New York on the morning of June 10th, 1944. Charlie McCabe and Jinx had made all the plans. Charlie's limo took them to City Hall, where Judge Pecora was waiting to marry the happy couple. The clerk asked for Tex's Wasserman blood test (which required a ten-day waiting period). Tex didn't know what to say. Charlie McCabe simply handed over a slip of paper. The clerk nodded, said the Judge was waiting. The ceremony was brief. They got back into the waiting limo and Tex asked Charlie about "his" Wasserman. McCabe said he had gone to a doctor, given Tex's name and his blood. Tex asked what he would have done if his blood had come back positive? They had a celebratory dinner at "21" with Charlie McCabe and Joan Crawford, who was then living with him, and Jock and Betsey Whitney—after which Tex and Jinx went to the Whitney apartment for the night. They left the next morning, Jinx with her USO tour and Tex flew back to Washington to pick up his correspondent team.

The McCrary unit was assigned two B-17s, one configured with high-powered short-wave radio sets to permit direct communication to Headquarters in Washington, outside Navy or MacArthur censors. The other was a modified "Command" B-17 with the waist gunners' windows replaced with Plexiglas, the interior and bomb bay reconfigured with seats, with some effort at soundproofing and heating. Tex had the name *The Headliner* painted in large black letters on the nose.

There was considerable interest among top correspondents to join his unit, so Tex could take his pick. Clark Lee of the *International News Service* was an old China hand, had been all around Asia, spoke a bit of the languages; Bernie Hoffman, a top photographer from *Life* Magazine; Vern Haugland, the aviation editor of the *Associated Press* who had worked with Tex pre-war in recruitment for the *Eagle Squadron*; Bill Laurence of the *New York Times*; Homer Bigart of the *New York Herald Tribune*; Charles Murphy of *Fortune*; and George Silk, from *Life*, Frank Fulton of NBC; Bill Downs of CBS; Jim McGincky of *United Press*; who had been part of Tex's OSS team when they jumped into France, along with several others. The correspondents wore officer's uniforms with no insignia of rank. And all of them were eager to get to Paris, their first opportunity to visit that seductive city since the beginning of the war.

When they got to Paris, "liberation" celebrations were still in progress, and the reporters were eager to join in. There was some trouble getting them reassembled. They flew on to Hamburg, which had been almost totally destroyed by an RAF "firestorm" bombing attack. Tex had seen the strike photographs, but they could not convey the damage visible there on the ground, then on to Dresden, another horrendous effect of the firebombing of a beautiful city. These cities had been selected particularly to show the effects of firebombs—in anticipation of General LeMay's new policies for the B-29s of

Tex and his son, Michael in front of the "Headliner" just before takeoff.
(Note: Tex's British battle tunic, with Parachute "jump wings," left chest.)

the Twentieth Air Force. LeMay had determined to abandon the long-defended daylight bombing approach used in Europe, and had adopted city-wide night firebombing techniques in Japan. The B-29 had been designed as a high-altitude precision bomber (as a follow-on design from Boeing, manufacturer of the B-17), but the wooden construction of much of the Japanese cities suggested a different approach to LeMay. Japanese night fighters and anti-aircraft artillery were not radar-controlled, and LeMay determined to launch low-level incendiary night attacks. LeMay removed the turrets and guns from his B-29s so they could carry larger loads, fly at night, bomb from low altitude, with new, larger and more effective incendiary bombs. Initial attacks demonstrated the effect of this approach, and he had launched a massive attack on Tokyo on March 9th, 1945. The results exceeded anyone's expectations. A firestorm swept the city; eighty-four thousand Japanese were killed and an additional one hundred sixty thousand injured. Tex later heard that LeMay had advised Arnold that he believed Japan could be brought to surrender by bombing alone, without the necessity of an invasion.

From Germany, they flew on to Naples, a beautiful day, the Alps glorious through the clear nose of the B-17. Tex had had no time to tell Doris Duke before his sudden wedding to Jinx—but Doris had seen the news, and sent him a cable, "What about me?" Great lady and great sport that Doris was, she put a big party for Tex and his group. They flew to Cairo; then on to New Delhi. The reporters wanted to see more of the city, but Tex kept them on schedule.

Next, over "The Hump," that incredible stretch of towering, majestic, unforgiving mountains, range upon range, to Chungking. They looked around, talked to a few people, and had long conversations with the U.S. Ambassador, Patrick Hurley, Secretary of War in the Hoover Cabinet, a seasoned and respected figure in Washington, later to become a Senator from New Mexico. Hurley said that the Chiang problem was even worse than they knew, that Chiang was both crooked and weak, dominated by T.V. Soong, the venal head of Chiang's wife's family. Hurley said he had told Soong outright that the trouble with him and his whole gang was that all they thought about was money and themselves and they should wake up to their responsibilities to their country. Despite his warnings to Roosevelt about Chiang's weaknesses and corruption, Roosevelt had made it clear to Hurley that his duty, above all else, was to keep Chiang in the war against Japan, preferably in cooperation with the Yenan communists (as Mao's army was then known), rather than depleting resources in civil war against them, fully recognizing the possibility that Chiang was capable of making a private deal with the Japanese to keep him and his family in power.

Listening to Hurley, Tex thought of his talks with Kathy Harriman in Moscow about Averill's seemingly oblivious support of anything Stalin did, regardless of the intransigent lack of Russian cooperation. Kathy had maintained that Roosevelt's instructions to her father as Ambassador was to do everything possible to keep Russia from a separate peace with Germany—doubtless the same message Hurley had received regarding China. After Roosevelt's death, Truman fired Hurley. Tex later heard that James Byrnes, Truman's new Secretary of State, had convinced Truman that Hurley's efforts to get Chiang and Mao together (as Roosevelt had ordered him to do) indicated that Hurley was sympathetic to Communists. Another factor was that T.V. Soong and the China Lobby had become massive financial supporters of the Truman Administration and of influential Congressmen. The extent of the postwar power of the China Lobby reached everywhere.

Tex was later amused by an interesting personal sidelight. Roosevelt had sent Wendell Willkie, who had opposed Roosevelt in the 1940 election, on a goodwill tour around the world. Willkie was known to be—as it was called in those days—a "ladies man." During Willkie's visit in Chungking, Madame Chiang, apparently angry at Chiang's flagrant attention to his mistresses, took up a visible romantic relationship with Willkie.

Willkie had written *One World*, a best-selling book urging international cooperation, which was considered to be an early step toward the formation of the United Nations. Tex was puzzled that—despite the wide public acclaim over Willkie's book, with its strong advocacy of international cooperation and free trade—Republican isolationist policies in Congress did not diminish. Tex thought that Willkie's death from a heart attack in the fall of 1944 was a great loss for the country.

Tex left Chungking with mixed emotions. Despite the seemingly endless corruption of Chiang, his family and his government, he was impressed with what he saw of the Chinese people, dedicated and hardworking, under the most miserable conditions. And he could hardly imagine how much worse conditions must have been for Mao's forces fighting Chiang's army. Without the massive U.S. support, Chiang and his family could not have survived. Tex wondered what China's future would be.

On the flight to Manila, he had a long talk with Clark Lee, bright, tough, fearless, every bit the romantic image of a "foreign correspondent," known for his experience in the Far East. He had gone to the Pacific as a reporter for the Associated Press in 1936. He and his wife had lived in Tokyo, Hong Kong and Shanghai, a very attractive, popular couple—who knew everyone worth knowing. By the fall of 1941, all of the informed people in Shanghai knew war was coming very soon. When the Marines at the U.S. Consulate in Shanghai were pulled out in September 1941, Clark sent his wife and young daughters back to their home in Honolulu. One of Clark's contacts was a Japanese army sergeant, the son of a prominent Tokyo family who had been born and educated in Southern California. The sergeant gave Clark a discrete warning of "unpleasant" things soon to come, noting that a Dutch freighter was leaving for Manila the next day, and that further departures were "unlikely." Lee caught the boat, planning to go home to Honolulu, but when he reached Manila, the Associated Press ordered him to stay on. He moved into the Manila Hotel, where General Douglas MacArthur lived in a splendid penthouse.

Lee told Tex that by late 1941 alarming signals were already apparent in Manila. Most of the military and diplomatic families had gone home, and only essential personnel were left in place. A Japanese attack was anticipated—and everybody knew that the Japanese favored surprise attacks, particularly on Sundays. MacArthur's briefings dismissed concerns of imminent danger to Manila, stating that the Japanese intentions were toward Indo-China and the Dutch East Indies. MacArthur said that any risk to Manila would not occur until after January of 1942 at the earliest, and that the War Department in Washington had set the warning date for the late spring. MacArthur had the U.S. fighters and bombers lined up wing-to-wing in rows on Clark Field, and the Navy had their ships moored together in the harbor, to protect them from local sabotage, just like at Pearl Harbor.

Lee was awakened early on Sunday, December 8th (Manila time) 1941, with a call from the Associated Press office in Honolulu that Pearl Harbor was under Japanese aerial attack. He raced to MacArthur's headquarters but there was no sign of activity. The duty officer had no comment on Lee's report of an attack at Pearl Harbor. Lee told him to turn on his radio and wake MacArthur. But apparently MacArthur did nothing all through the day, no aerial patrols, no alert to the land forces or dispersal of aircraft or Naval vessels. Nine hours later Japanese bombers virtually wiped out most of the U.S. military airplanes—still lined up as easy targets on the runways—and sank or damaged most of the naval vessels in the Philippines. MacArthur's behavior has never been explained.

Tex was fascinated by Lee's account. Without aerial protection, the Navy soon pulled out their remaining ships, except for a couple of submarines and a few PT boats. Lee followed MacArthur's retreat from Manila to the Bataan Peninsula. MacArthur then retreated with his family to the Gibraltar-like island fortress of Corregidor, ordering most of his troops to hold out on Bataan, where survivors lived through the infamous "Bataan Death March." MacArthur, his wife, young son, and his public relations officers left on PT boats, to escape to Australia. Lee made his way on foot, down the Philippine island chain, eventually catching a rusted-out tramp steamer to Australia, where he reported for a time, and then hitchhiked a ride on a Navy patrol bomber to Honolulu for a visit with his family. Then he had joined up with the Navy, coming back on a aircraft carrier for the battle of Guadalcanal, flying on bombing missions during the battle. He had ended up with MacArthur again for the invasion of the Philippines.

Tex pressed him for his judgment of MacArthur. Lee started off by saying that he didn't know how anyone could really describe MacArthur adequately, a compelling personality, larger than life, a gifted actor, living out a self-idealized vision of himself as an historic military commander/statesman. MacArthur was a distant cousin of Franklin Roosevelt, whom he regarded as a lightweight politician, but one who was also a great actor, playing out his own role. MacArthur was absolutely fearless, when it was visible, consistently exposing himself unnecessarily to enemy fire, especially when troops or correspondents were witnesses, always behaving as if he felt himself protected by some kind of a special destiny.

The McCrary group landed in Manila, where the grandiosity of MacArthur and his worshipful staff reminded Tex of stories of Hearst at his castle in California, only on an even vaster scale. The correspondents were given extensive tours over a couple of days, including lengthy inspections of massive amounts of equipment and fleets of cargo ships preparing for the invasion of Japan, all leading up to a formal briefing by Major General Charles Willoughby, MacArthur's chief intelligence officer. Tex had been looking forward to seeing him. Willoughby had been born in Germany, entered the U.S. Army in World War I, claimed aristocratic heritage, and became aide to the then-Major Carl "Tooey" Spaatz, (also German-born) commander of the U. S. Army pilot training program at Issoudon in France, where Willoughby's petty and demanding disciplines, combined with his boot-licking behavior toward Spaatz, apparently did not leave him many friends. However, he had moved on to attach himself to MacArthur, where Willoughby's sycophantic approach found ready acceptance. MacArthur seemed attracted to his European background, his fluency in languages, and extreme right-wing philosophies. Clare Booth Luce had not made a secret of her affair with Willoughby before the war. Tex was aware of Henry Luce's sexual dysfunction, and was acquainted with the surprising range of Clare's sexual appetite, so he was curious to see what she had found so attractive in Willoughby. The World War I pilots in France were right. Willoughby was a self-important, sycophantic, overbearing phony—who could tell a good story.

Willoughby's briefing was lengthy, a presentation of MacArthur's unquestionably impressive career; a description of MacArthur's campaign from Australia to the Philippines—all as an unctuous introduction. The key point of Willoughby's briefing was to emphasize MacArthur's genius as a military commander by stressing the relatively small number of casualties incurred by MacArthur's campaign in the Pacific, as compared to the total U.S. casualties experienced in Europe (an implicit negative reference to Eisenhower)—but the comparison was built on obvious errors. It did not include the loss of MacArthur's entire army in the Philippines before he left his troops and escaped with his family to Australia. Moreover, it included in the European numbers the very high cost of the invasion of France and the ensuing battles in Germany—significantly incurred as a consequence of British Field Marshall Montgomery's diversions and delays—while not recognizing the anticipated costs of the invasion of Japan, which MacArthur himself had stated would likely cost over one million U.S. casualties. Tex had warned his group that they were not on friendly ground, and it would not be a good idea to question Willoughby too closely. They should learn what they could, but not make things unnecessarily difficult for themselves.

Tex had dinner with *Life*'s star team of Carl and Shelley Mydans, both caught up in the cult of MacArthur admirers. This was not entirely gullibility. In foreign theaters in wartime, correspondents are really almost totally dependent—for transportation, housing, food, and all outside communication—upon the relationship with the commanding general, which in MacArthur's case required a bended knee. The Mydans seemed to believe Willoughby's line, and repeated MacArthur's own comments from an interview MacArthur had given to the *New York Herald Tribune*, in which MacArthur said that Eisenhower and his generals had made "every mistake that supposedly intelligent men could make;" and that, "if MacArthur had been given just a portion of the forces sent to North Africa in 1942, he could have retaken the Philippines in three months." The Mydans' conversation continued along this line and, as the dinner and the drinks progressed, Tex's guys began to show increasing skepticism. He tried to get them out before too much damage was done, and he was worried that the word of the conversation would get back to MacArthur's ever-present security staff.

The extent of MacArthur's censorship and security apparatus amazed Tex. It had served to conceal repeated instances of his overt disobedience of orders which did not suit him from the Joint Chiefs, and it covered up his major blunders, Manila itself being a good example. First, his still inexplicable inaction for nine hours after learning of the Japanese attack on Pearl Harbor—nine hours during which the Navy had put ships safely at sea—a lapse of duty contributing to MacArthur's loss of most of the defense capabilities of the Philippines, not to mention the human cost.

Mac Arthur was shameless. After his return in 1944, he misinterpreted reports of Japanese troop movements within Manila as a withdrawal from the city, causing MacArthur to issue a statement that Manila had "fallen" to him, after which he failed to occupy the city, thereby permitting the Japanese "Rape of Manila"—the bloodiest Japanese atrocity of the war. MacArthur's security had been able to keep the episode largely unreported throughout the war, and generally ignored thereafter.

The climax of the MacArthur theatrics occurred in his presentation the next day. He had extraordinary stage presence, and was conducting a masterly recitation of great generals and great campaigns in history, with references and comparisons to the current situation. MacArthur was very good, obviously enjoying himself, and his face was flushed with enthusiasm. He was embarking on a description of Japanese culture and philosophy when his chief of staff, General Whitney, came up behind Tex, tapped him on the shoulder, and asked to see his orders. He handed them over. Whitney looked at them quickly, frowned, and withdrew to a corner to read them more closely. Whitney then walked up to MacArthur, in mid-sentence, and whispered to him. MacArthur's face blanched, he hesitated for a moment, took Tex's orders, glanced at them, and then stalked from the room, leaving his presentation unfinished.

Everyone stood up, in some uncertainty. Tex nodded to his men to leave quietly and get back to the hotel. As he followed them out, Whitney came back into the room, stopped him, and asked if he had any other copies of his orders. Tex had many copies, and he did not want to come under MacArthur's command, so he told him no. But being the kind of guy Whitney was, he probably couldn't be sure that there wasn't a copy, so he would likely hesitate before trying anything drastic, such as confining Tex and his group to quarters without communication. In any case, Tex didn't want to wait to find out. He caught up with his group, told them they were leaving Manila immediately for Guam. Tex never found out what caused MacArthur's reaction. He assumed MacArthur must have been angered, perhaps even felt threatened—if that's possible to imagine—that someone had come into his domain without being subject to his control. Fortunately, Tex's other copies of orders were in the B-17—and it was good to be in the air and out of MacArthur's reach.

At Guam, they picked up the rest the of the unit, Air Force support personnel, equipment, and aircraft, including C-46 transports and a P-51 Mustang fighter, which Tex had ordered specially modified into a two-seat "piggy-back" version, similar to the one in which Pete Quesada had flown Eisenhower over Normandy after D-Day. Jimmy Doolittle had recommended Captain Sandy Moats, a ranking ace from the Eighth Air Force, as pilot. Tex told him that he wanted to go in close, land on short strips, things like that. Could they do it? Sandy said, "No Guts, No Glory." Tex said, "That's it! Get that painted on the nose." It was the beginning of a wonderful relationship.

Jimmy Doolittle was putting his headquarters together at huge Kadena airfield on Okinawa, and Tex flew over to see him in the P-51. Doolittle said he expected to have his Eighth Air Force "mission-ready" soon. They both knew the war would be over before too long and their talk turned to talking about the future. Doolittle pointed at the B-29s landing outside his office, saying that those long-range airplanes would mean the end of America's isolationism. He said that one had already been forced down in Russia, and " those bastards will copy it. After the war things will have to change. America can't go on pretending that the rest of the world doesn't exist."

Tex later learned that, a few days before Hiroshima, General Spaatz called Doolittle and told him that the Atom bomb mission was going to take place and, likely, end the war, adding that Doolittle should fly a bombing mission before that date if he wanted to get combat credit for the Twentieth Air Force in the Pacific war. Doolittle thanked him for the courtesy, but said that he wouldn't risk a man for a meaningless mission credit. Spaatz told him that, after his record with the Eighth Air Force in Europe, getting the Twentieth into action against the Japanese would earn him his fourth general's star. Doolittle said he could not accept a fourth star before Ira Eaker. They both had to wait several years, but Tex was happy they both finally got what they richly deserved—but he always suspected that they wouldn't have had to wait until long after the war if they had been West Point graduates.

He then flew back to Tinian, to catch up with Bill Laurence, the highly respected science writer from *The New York Times,* assigned to his unit. Laurence had gone on ahead to Tinian and was involved with a secret project. Tex's security clearances gave him access, and after a few talks with Laurence, it was clear what was going on, the project that Jake Smart had earlier intimated to Tex was in the works. Laurence had been fully exposed and briefed on the A-Bomb project and was scheduled to fly the first mission.

The day before the take-off for Hiroshima, Laurence told Tex that General Groves, commander of the A-bomb project, had pulled him off the flight on the grounds that he might be shot down, tortured, and reveal A-bomb secrets to the Japs. Tex asked Groves if he could go—he pointed out that he knew no A-bomb secrets—but no dice. Paul Tibbetts, with whom Tex had flown the first Eighth Air Force mission from England in 1943 was the aircraft commander of the B-29 *Enola Gay,* but the pilot who actually flew the plane was Bob Lewis. Tex told Lewis that, since Laurence had been cleared for the mission, but had been grounded for other reasons, there should be some first-hand written record of the actual event. He gave Lewis a reporter's notebook and a kneepad to strap on his leg—and asked Lewis to keep notes throughout the flight. The date was August 6, 1945. The attack plan called for a sharp turn away from Hiroshima immediately after release of the bomb. Lewis did so but, after the flash, he looked back at the mushrooming cloud—and wrote on his kneepad, "My God, What have we done?"—words which lead every story of the A-bomb, even now, more than sixty years later.

When Lewis landed, he gave the note pad to Tex, who lent it to Bill Laurence who wrote the prize-winning *New York Times* article, using Lewis' notes and quotes. Henry Luce put the picture and Lewis' words on the cover of *Time.* Tex kept in touch after the war and, years later, when he learned Lewis was dying of cancer—and needed money badly—knowing that Malcolm Forbes was collecting materials on the war, called Forbes and told him the story of Bob Lewis and his notebook. Forbes said, "Bring me that notebook and I'll give you a check for $85,000 for Lewis—thanks for giving me the opportunity."

After the Atom bomb obliterated Hiroshima, attitudes begin to change, and Tex could see that the war would soon be coming to an end. The second Atom bomb was dropped on Nagasaki on August 9th. On August 12th, the Japanese Emperor, Hirohito, spoke directly to his subjects, the first time they had ever heard his voice, and declared "hostilities have ceased."

President Truman, with British approval, named MacArthur Supreme Commander on August 15th. MacArthur immediately issued orders that no Japanese surrenders should take place anywhere in Asia before the formal surrender to him on the battleship *Missouri* in Tokyo Bay on September 2nd.

A friend with Navy connections tipped Tex off that MacArthur was arranging the deck of the Missouri without Air Force representation. MacArthur needed the Navy— and the battleship *Missouri*—and the Navy was going to fill the sky over the ceremony with carrier-based planes. The Air Force was effectively being cut out of the picture entirely, ostensibly on the grounds that the Army Air Force was part of the Army, therefore adequately represented by MacArthur himself. Tex immediately called Barney Giles, the Deputy Commander of the 20th Air Force, telling Barney that General Arnold was concerned that his pilots were not flying, and were likely losing their navigational skills. Barney reacted, as Tex expected, "Goddamn it, McCrary, our boys can do anything, etc., etc." Tex said, "Well, Barney, MacArthur and the Navy are planning the surrender ceremony without any Air Force participation. Do you think you can arrange to fly five hundred B-29s over the *Missouri* at five hundred feet at 0900 on September 2?"

Tex sent an alert to General Arnold, recommending that Arnold send Doolittle, thinking that MacArthur couldn't keep out of the surrender ceremony the man who had led the first strike on Tokyo after Pearl Harbor, and he passed the word on to Doolittle. As it turned out, he was wrong. General Arnold sent Spaatz (the old West Point game). Doolittle came to Tokyo, but MacArthur kept him out of sight. Personally, Tex had hoped that the B-29s would be a surprise for MacArthur, perhaps even drown out part of his speech. But he also knew that news of the operation would leak—and that both MacArthur and the Navy would try to kill it. So he suggested that, if opposition surfaced, the Air Force should say that the B-29s were intended as an Air Force tribute to MacArthur and the Navy. The B-29 fly-over was in flights of three— low, loud, long, and most gratifyingly impressive.

Emperor Hirohito, god-like to the Japanese people, had broken his celestial silence to tell his nation that the war was over—but was it? The fanatic resistance of Japanese soldiers seemed to increase as U.S. forces moved ever closer to Japan. Kamikaze pilots had inflicted heavy casualties in the battle for Okinawa—and seven million Japanese soldiers waited in their homeland. Despite the Emperor's decree, a number of kamikazes had declared that, in becoming kamikazes they had already died to this life and were, therefore, no longer bound by the Emperor's decree. As such, they intended to perform their ritual of sacrifice for the honor of the Empire. No one really knew what to expect when the McCrary group landed in Japan.

Clark Lee, with his many years of experience in the Far East, had another perspective on the situation, and he clearly understood MacArthur better than any of the group. What they had seen was the negative, the sycophancy, the showmanship, the overstatements, the derogative comments on contemporaries, and the manipulations of MacArthur's censorship. But Lee pointed out that MacArthur's many years of experience in the Orient had given him a deeper understanding of Japanese culture, of their profound respect for authority, and, particularly the oriental concept of "face." MacArthur had forced the Japanese emissaries to come to him, at his headquarters in Manila—where he kept an Olympian distance, refused to see them in person, and required them to work out arrangements with his subordinates.

The first advance parties of the invasion force were to land at Atsugi air base on Tokyo Bay between Yokohama and Tokyo on August 26th, to be followed by MacArthur himself on August 28th, well before the arrival of any substantial United States military forces in Japan. This seemed to many to be a considerable risk, but MacArthur cavalierly shrugged it off, saying he understood the Japanese respect for authority better than his critics.

No U.S. aircraft were permitted to land in Japan before the occupation, but Tex laid on a flight for the correspondents over Hiroshima. He planned to take off later in his P-51 and catch up with them. While he had been engaged in the planning of the B-29 flight over the surrender ceremony, Clark Lee had seduced the others with tales of the mysteries and delights of Shanghai, of wine, women and song, and other possibilities. They told Mark Mangan, the B-17 pilot, that plans had changed, that they were to take a look at Shanghai instead of Hiroshima. They had taken off before Tex learned of the changed flight plan, but he knew he could catch them in the P-51.

It was a great flying day; Mount Fuji was in the clear with its sparkling white cap of snow. They flew across the South China Sea until they could see the yellow mud stain of the Yangtze River far out in the sea. Then they swung south along the Whang Poo river to Shanghai, where they saw the B-17 flying low above the Shanghai Bund, the elegant roadway and esplanade along the river, lined with the formerly elegant hotels and offices of prewar Shanghai. The boys on the B-17 were startled, and frightened, when somebody shouted, "Fighter at four o'clock!" Tex called them on the radio, told them that they couldn't get away from him so easily. Lee had the B-17 fly right down on the rooftop of the Metropole Hotel, where he had been friends with the Swiss manager before the war. Then Mangan changed the prop pitch, and the roar must have rattled windows all along the Bund. The street began to fill with people. Lee dropped a note to his hotel manager friend, something to this effect: Ed, I'm in the B-17 up here. I have some friends with me, and we want to stay at the hotel. Go up to the balcony of my old room and give us signals. If the Japs are shooting up the town or we can't get through, wave your hands crisscrossed over your head. Otherwise get some taxis to meet us.

While Lee was arranging his social schedule, Tex had been examining the area from the air. There were two Japanese military fields outside of the city, with Japanese fighters lined up on both sides of the runways—and there was no apparent activity. Tex radioed the B-17, telling them to "stop trying to knock the tops off those buildings and follow me. We've got a spot to land." There was a big racetrack on the south edge of the city with a long straight grass infield. Sandy Moats was sure he could get the P-51 in, and he thought there was enough room for the B-17. He dragged the P-51 in on the edge of the stall, and set it down in a swirl of dust, with plenty of room to spare. A crowd of Chinese ran out on the field. Sandy gunned the P-51 around and taxied right at them, to make room for the B-17, which landed behind him.

Before they could climb out, they were surrounded by Chinese, all smiling and clapping. After a few minutes, uniformed Japanese began to arrive in trucks. Lee went over to a car parked nearby and asked to be taken to town. In the back seat was a senior Japanese naval officer with a pidgin-speaking Chinese interpreter, who said, "This Japanese mastah, numba one Japanee Navy, wanchee surrender Japan soldier-man American." Lee pointed toward Tex. The Japanese officers came over and gestured toward the B-17. The B-17, *The Headliner*, had been left in Okinawa for minor repairs, and Tex had borrowed Jimmy Doolittle's B-17, which had three general's stars on the nose. Tex was in flying clothes and the Japanese assumed, reasonably enough, that the stars on the plane indicated Tex's rank. They pointed to the administration building where the Japanese commander bowed formally, and presented his sword to Tex, in surrender.

Tex didn't want to get in any more trouble with MacArthur over accepting the Japanese Commander's sword, so he explained to the Japanese commander that occupation troops would be coming in due course. Then there would be an official ceremony, and the Japanese commander should keep his sword for the formal ceremony. Meanwhile, he should, "carry on."

Tex caught up with his men at the Shanghai hotel, where a party was already in full cry. They wanted to know what had gone on, and he told them that the Japanese commander had surrendered Shanghai to him—but that they had all better keep it quiet. Before long, the word got out that Lee was in town, and an amazing number of friends—and lots of attractive ladies—began to show up, telling stories of the occupation, including tales of thriving businesses carried on across the Chinese and Japanese lines, dealing in American equipment and supplies which Chiang Kai-shek's people were openly selling.

When the time for take-off from Shanghai neared, there was some difficulty finding everybody and getting them on the B-17. They got back to Okinawa—most of the group fighting serious hangovers, before shaping-up to take off before the advance party for the occupation of Japan in the predawn of August 26th. General MacArthur would make his ceremonial grand arrival on August 28th, 1945.

Most of the advance party were coming up in transports, all intricately planned and scheduled. But Tex, as usual, was on his own—and his P-51 was the fastest of all. He and Sandy Moats took off from Okinawa early on a cloudless morning, climbed to 20,000 feet to conserve fuel, flew northwest for about two hours, then picked up the Japanese island of Kyushu. They dropped down and flew along the western coast of Kyushu for nearly an hour, then crossed the straits between Kyushu and the west end of Honshu, the major island of Japan. It gave Tex an eerie feeling to look down at such a beautiful island—and think that its people had been our deadly enemy for more than four years.

He and Moats were eager to try to be the first to see Hiroshima at low altitude. As they approached the west end of Honshu, the location of Hiroshima was clearly visible, facing south on a bay, with mountains rising behind. Moats looked over his shoulder at Tex questioningly, Tex nodded. Moats pulled back the power, lowered the flaps, tipped the P-51 on its wing, and they spiraled down. For a moment they couldn't fully grasp what they were seeing. The place that had been Hiroshima—previously a substantial Japanese city,

A senior Japanese officer surrendered to Tex

Tex sitting on his P-51

more than three hundred thousand inhabitants—now was obliterated, lifeless, marked by a few rough, grayish-white concrete ruins on the waterfront, with a wide area behind, cut by river channels, and marked by rectangular whitish streaks where streets had been. They leveled off, and began slow, wide circles, as slow and as low as they could fly without stirring up the ashes. They were mostly silent, awed by what they saw. Tex believed that, other than high-altitude photo reconnaissance flights, they were the first to fly at low level over the site of the world's first use of the Atom bomb.

Tex had seen major bombed-out cities before—he had been in the European Theatre since 1941, flown combat missions with the Eighth Air Force over Germany. Hamburg and Dresden were the worst—but they were recognizable as war scenes, with buildings burned-out, but still standing, and with people visible. But Hiroshima was altogether different. What had been an undamaged, fully functioning city had been flattened into lifeless gray gravel—akin to what he then imagined as the surface of the Moon.

They flew on to Atsugi, the huge Japanese military air base on Tokyo Bay between Yokohama and Tokyo, where they landed—and taxied by rows of Japanese fighters lined up beside the runways, painted in the Kamikaze colors of the Japanese suicide pilots, but with the propellers removed. *The Headliner* came in shortly behind them, and as Clark Lee got out, one of the Japanese officials present addressed him in pidgin by name. "Ree-san! Ree-san, Herro, herro. So grad you return Japan." He was a former waiter from the Grill Room of the *Imperial Hotel* in Tokyo where Lee had lived before the war. The group went on to Tokyo, to the *Imperial Hotel*, designed by Frank Lloyd Wright to withstand earthquakes, and still intact despite our bombings, which had heavily damaged the rest of the city. Several others of the team had stayed there before the war—and the same staff remembered them and gave them their old rooms. Everywhere they went the Japanese seemed eager to please, acting as if the war had not been deadly hostile and cruel, but rather some kind of a remote, impersonal act of nature. It gave Tex, and all of group, a strange, eerie feeling.

In Tokyo, Clark Lee was greeted by a Princeton graduate, Japan's interpreter at important world conferences since the early 1920s. Clark asked, "What's going to happen?" His Princeton friend said that he had gone to Manila with the Japanese negotiators, and they had asked MacArthur for a delay. MacArthur thought they were stalling—but they weren't. They were afraid they could not control their hotheads. He pointed to the rows of Japanese fighters lined up, and said that Atsugi was the home of three hundred kamikaze pilots, some of whom flew over Tokyo dropping leaflets saying they intended to fight on, regardless of the Emperor's surrender. A number of them had committed hari-kari by diving their fighters into Tokyo Bay, while other diehards attacked Radio Tokyo and tried to seize the station. But they had been gotten under control, and the guns and propellers had been removed from the fighters.

Tex walked around the street with several of his group. At first there was fear and caution on both sides. The Japanese people were badly in need of reassurance about contact with Americans, and the sight of strange uniforms and white skin gave them a shock. But after the first few hours, as the Japanese became more accustomed to seeing these Americans walking through the streets, they discovered that Americans did not intend to rape women or kill children, and the tension grew less. What developed was remarkable—not a single instance of sabotage, not a wire cut or a gas tank set afire, not a single shot fired.

The Japanese acted as if the war had been erased, as if it had never happened. They would stand in front of still-smoking, bombed-out buildings, laugh and smile, and say, "Oh, so sorry, city not beautiful. Had bad earthquake," or "Everything burn down." These cheerful, smiling people walking the streets had sons and brothers who had tortured or killed captured American pilots, who had staged the Bataan death march, who had starved thousands of Australian and Dutch prisoners, who had bayoneted little Filipino babies—and who had relatives who had died under our bombs! It was hard to reconcile.

To the GIs in the Pacific, Tokyo Rose's nightly radio broadcast had made her the best-known Japanese, perhaps next to Prime Minister Tojo. Lee found her through Japanese contacts before the American military had begun to investigate and he smuggled her into the *Imperial Hotel* with her husband, a Portuguese–Japanese named Philip d'Aquino. Her name was Iva Ikuko Toguri, Los Angeles-born, pleasant-appearing, with long braids, looking about twenty. Her pay as Tokyo Rose was about six dollars a month. She said she had liked life in the United States, and hated the restrictions of wartime Japan. But for her six dollars a month she wrote and broadcast every night a script designed to try to make American servicemen lose their will to go on fighting.

The Tokyo Rose interview was interesting, but it was also the beginning of trouble. MacAthur's Counter-Intelligence Corps had lost face when Tex's correspondents found her first and, after the story broke, the Army ordered Tokyo out-of-bounds to correspondents. Typically, the CIC decided that the way to execute this order was to put sentries on the bridges over the river between Yokohama and Tokyo. Apparently it didn't occur to them to think that the McCrary group was already in the city.

The next day, Lee made another strike. Through a Japanese reporter Lee had known prewar, aided by a carton of American cigarettes, he found out the location of Prime Minister Tojo's home, a modest house by American standards. He had a pleasant interview, and agreed to come back the next day. At the Army breakfast for correspondents, the briefing officer announced that Tojo was first on the list of war criminals and would be arrested by the Counter-Intelligence Corps that day. Lee raced back to the *Imperial*, grabbed George Burns, the photographer for *Yank* magazine, who was breakfasting on Spam, and yelled, "What do you want to do, Burns, sit there and eat Spam, or see Tojo kill himself?" Tex went with them. By the time they got to Tojo's house, the lane was beginning to be crowded. Tojo came out and said, "No pictures," and went back inside. They could smell incense. It took the Counter-Intelligence Corps three hours to find the place. When they arrived, the CIC people broke down the door—and the sound of a shot rang out. Tojo had shot himself sitting in his chair. He was lying on his back, breathing faintly, and began to speak slowly. He said that his was a just war, but his country's strength was exhausted. Americans had the right to take the person responsible for the war, but he did not wish to stand before a jury. He said he had tried to shoot himself in the heart, instead of the head, because he wanted the Japanese people to recognize that it was Tojo, and that the Americans had not substituted somebody else's body.

People kept pushing into the room, grabbing for souvenirs. Tojo lay on his back. Brundidge, a former police reporter for the *New York Daily News*, rolled Tojo over and said, "The bullet exits the back and makes a bigger hole, so there's more blood — you'll get a better picture." Burns, the photographer from *Yank* magazine, stepped in front of Tex to take the picture. He then went to the chair in which Tojo had shot himself, found Tojo's bullet in a pillow, and put it in his pocket. Then the Counter-Intelligence Corps finally got into the room. Two GIs grabbed Tojo's arms, and two others took his feet. As they picked him up, more blood flowed. Somebody said, "That'll finish the son-of-a-bitch!" By this time a doctor had arrived. He looked at Tojo briefly and said, "I noticed a lot of blood in there. It looks like somebody turned him over, and he had a hemorrhage. That was good judgment. If they hadn't given him an opportunity for the blood to drain, it would have gone to his lungs and drowned him. Best thing you could have done for him. That saved him for the hangman."

The Counter-Intelligence people weren't at all happy to find that Tex and his people had been there ahead of them, especially right after the Tokyo Rose episode. Tex thought it was time to get out of Tokyo for a while. He got the gang together and took the B-17 from Atsugi to let them have a look at Hiroshima. They flew through heavy storms, and landed on a fighter strip that they had located in the P-51 a few days before. A Japanese naval surgeon served as a guide, and he had arranged automobiles to drive them 28 miles to Hiroshima. He said, he was glad it was raining as it soaks up the radioactivity. Apparently they were the first Americans to reach Hiroshima, before the first scientific investigators arrived. As they drove into the city, they passed parts of buildings, still standing, but burnt-out, with roofs and walls gone. As they got closer, the effects of the bomb increased. Major damage began approximately four miles from the spot where the bomb exploded, at about fifteen hundred feet in the air. The level of destruction grew steadily, and they came into an area of complete devastation. The ground looked as if it had been gone over with a giant rake,

Tex's group returned to Kure, enplaned, and flew further south to Nagasaki. The city faced the South China Sea, just south of the great naval base at Sasebo (and about one hundred fifty miles below Korea — where Tex was to return five years later as a correspondent in another war). The weather at Nagasaki was rotten and they didn't try to find a field. But they did have a chance to circle and make some slow, low passes — again, the first Americans, so far as they knew, to have had a chance to see Nagasaki close-up from the air. A few days later, they were able to land and go into the city. Nagasaki's location was not level, and the effects of the blast were more uneven than in Hiroshima; however, in some ways the devastation was more awesome, because of the pockets of buildings, heavily damaged, but still standing, in the midst of surrounding destruction. Compounding the psychological impact of exposure to Hiroshima, Nagasaki left a kind of shock effect. Bernie Hoffman, a top *Life* magazine photographer, had wrapped his camera and film in lead foil to shield it from radiation. He took a few photographs as they walked through the city. But, as they were getting ready to leave, Tex saw him deliberately stripping film from his camera. Hoffman said, "There's nothing left here to shoot." He did save one shot. *Life* ran it on a full page, a marble head of Christ, split in half, the only identifiable object in that scene of devastation.

These war-hardened reporters were all deeply affected. What they had seen was literally overwhelming—its significance beyond their capacity to comprehend. The group was silent on the plane, all thinking the same thing, so Tex said, "I don't think we should write about what we've seen yet. I don't think they're ready for it back home. But, it's up to you. Remember, if one of you is going to, then you must tell me, because then we all have to." They honored his request. One of them, Fred Fulton, gave up journalism, became a Mormon missionary, and later returned to Japan.

After Tex and his group had left, John Hersey paid his visit. The result was his masterpiece, *Hiroshima,* which became a landmark in journalistic history when *The New Yorker* gave it an entire issue, without advertising.

MacArthur's decision to retain Hirohito as Emperor—and to exempt him from war crimes charges—shocked everyone. Clark Lee and others argued strongly that the Japanese wanton atrocities rivaled Germany's, and certainly it was impossible to imagine General Eisenhower absolving Hitler of war crimes and maintaining him as Chancellor of Germany. However, it became evident that MacArthur had his own vision for the future of Japan—under his direction—and to carry out his plan MacArthur knew it was essential to maintain the cohesion of the Japanese people and their extraordinarily disciplined loyalty to their Emperor.

Back in Tokyo, the group got word that MacArthur intended to have Tex court-martialed for taking his unit to Hiroshima without authorization (apparently he hadn't yet heard about Nagasaki), and the Counter-Intelligence Corps were beginning to harass Clark Lee and some of the other correspondents, threatening arrests. It was clear they were not going to be able to see or to learn much more in MacArthur's Japan.

Tex felt he had discharged his assignment to do all he could to make sure that the Air Force was adequately represented at the Japanese surrender. Now there was a once-in-a-lifetime opportunity—to be the first American reporters to visit the liberated capitals of Asia. Tex told his people to fan out around Tokyo, go to every PX, buy all the booze, candy, silk stockings, etc., they could find, and be ready for takeoff in the *"Headliner"* at four in the morning. Tex and Sandy Moats hated to say goodbye to their wonderful P-51, *"No Guts, No Glory,"* the first American plane into Shanghai, and the first to make low-level inspection passes over Hiroshima and Nagasaki.

As commander of his unit, Tex could write his own orders, if necessary. And the *Headliner* conveyed authority of its own. Aviation gas was available at every allied air base.

So they took off, curious about what they would find.

Chapter Nine

A "Victory" Tour through Asia: Intimations of Wars to Come

Tex began to come to grips with the fact that the war was finally over on the long flight to Hong Kong. America had won the war—but what did that mean? What was the war really about? What did peace mean? Tex was about to learn about Asia, about the war—and about the peace.

Chungking and Shanghai had been his first lessons. The Shanghai visit had been enlivened, of course, by the Japanese surrender to Tex—but it was important to him also as the place where he had intended to take his first job, as a reporter on *The Shanghai Advertiser,* when he graduated from Yale. Tex had often wondered, had that job developed, what Shanghai would have been like before the war. For Tex, the reality of what he had seen in Chungking and Shanghai was nothing like the romanticized Yale-in-China educational program, or Henry Luce's missionary and political fantasies.

However, the elegant style of pre-war Shanghai life was evident in the imposing classic European bank and hotel buildings along the Bund, the great avenue on the riverfront. But the Japanese occupation had been oppressive and brutal. To meet their raw materials shortages, they had stripped everything moveable, from the great bronze lions in front of the Hong Kong and Shanghai Bank, to the doorknobs and shower-heads in the hotels. Nevertheless, despite their brutality, and despite the loss of the war, the Japanese had brought lasting change through their message of the end of European domination: "Asia for the Asiatics." Shanghai, long the romantic international city, was rapidly becoming a Chinese city, but only "Chinese" in a cultural sense, not in the form of a responsiveness to a cohesive national government. The massive Black Market in U.S. goods supplied to Chiang's government, openly sold everywhere, evidenced the obvious corruption of Chiang Kai-shek, his family, and his leadership. What Tex had seen and heard in Chungking and Shanghai, though the visits were brief, had made it clear to him that continued European control over Asians was long past.

Hong Kong was the next stop. Tex said he never forgot his first impression: the magnificent sight of the inbound approach to the Hong Kong's airport; around the Peak of Hong Kong island, still predominantly green and undeveloped; the harbor, filled with sampans under sail and gray warships flying the Union Jack; then the final approach to the runway lying between the Kowloon mountains and the bay.

Whereas Shanghai was a Chinese city with a European flavor, Hong Kong was a kind of "little England" superimposed on top of a large Chinese base. When the old Brits said, "The sun never sets on the British Empire," they were thinking of Hong Kong. But Hong Kong, too, had been changed by the war. The "Taipans," the officials of the great British trading firms, Jardine Matheson, etc., who had been taken prisoner, had now resumed their old positions. Tex was entertained in grand style, but the Taipans had not recovered their prewar confidence and air of superiority. Chinese bankers and businessmen were cooperating with the English, but the new relationship, while not fully equal, was certainly not the toadying subordination that it had been. The buildings on Hong Kong island were still closed and sand-bagged, but that great Victorian edifice, the *Peninsula Hotel,* in Kowloon, was largely undamaged—and filled with Taipans. They had to know that their world had changed—but their attitude toward the Chinese remained pre-war: "Insolent beggars! We'll soon put them in their place."

Despite the patronizing attitude of the Taipans, Tex was fascinated by what he saw and learned of the potential of the Chinese, justly famous for their energy and business acumen. Hong Kong had become a great center of wealth creation, generally attributed to the skills of the Chinese, but also because those skills could function freely under the protection of English law and order, enforced by impassive Sikh police—and all tax-free. It is popular to attribute Hong Kong's success to its origins as a trading center—but the original base of its trading wealth was opium—opium financed, manufactured, transported and distributed by the British, the French and the Dutch throughout the European colonial empires in India, China, Indo-China and Java. Not only was opium immensely profitable in itself, it was also presumed to offer a tranquilizing relief to subjected peoples. Before the war the Japanese had undertaken the manufacture and export of opium, and they continued the practice in their occupied countries. Chiang Kai-shek understood the threat of opium, and had been making headway in curbing its use in China—while profiting from its distribution elsewhere in Asia.

The Taipans clung to their belief that Winston Churchill could make good on his statement that he "had not become Prime Minister to preside over the dissolution of the British Empire." But Hong Kong was exposed by geography and history. Tex was fascinated by the story. At the start of the Twentieth Century, the British, concerned over the expansion of Czarist Russia in Asia, had entered into a treaty with Japan—the first modern treaty between a Western and an Eastern nation. Japan then went to war against Russia, won a decisive victory, and acquired Korea and the Kwantung Peninsula. In World War I the Japanese joined the Allies and the Japanese Navy escorted Australian and New Zealand troops to Europe, gaining some Pacific island bases in return. By 1922, with the United States and Canada concerned over growing Japanese influence, the British did not renew the Japanese treaty. At the World Naval Conference in Washington the British agreed with the Japanese not to fortify Hong Kong, in return for the Japanese agreement not to fortify their Pacific islands. The

British promptly began to build their great naval base in Singapore, to which they moved much of their fleet from the Pacific, as the American fleet extended its influence towards the Philippines. As a result of the British move of its military and naval forces to Singapore, Hong Kong was not well defended in 1941 when the Japanese attacked.

As the Taipans regained control in 1945, they gradually reinstituted their prewar social policies. The Peak was the great physical and social symbol, while the city itself spread around the harbor. Wealthy Chinese could have homes halfway up the Peak, but the top was reserved for Taipans. After the war, this arrangement became complicated by the fact that the Japanese had erected a large concrete monument to their conquest on the highest point. Naturally the Taipans intended to tear it down until it was revealed that the Japanese—in furtherance of their political concept of "Asia for the Asians"—had mixed the bones of the dead British soldiers and sailors into the monument. But the British determination to demonstrate their authority was strong—and the monument eventually disappeared from Hong Kong. Kowloon, across the harbor, was functionally part of Hong Kong—but the land just beyond the border was controlled by Chinese Communists loyal to Mao—a dark shadow looming over Hong Kong's future.

Although the visit was brief, Tex was intrigued by Hong Kong. The vitality of the place was compelling. After the war he came back on visits, and bought a newspaper there for his son, Michael. And it was the success of Hong Kong's landfill real estate development that, years later, inspired Tex to promote the concept of Battery Park City in New York to David Rockefeller

Tex didn't know what to expect when he landed in Bangkok. Just before their arrival Thailand had been an enemy, an ally of the Japanese all through the war. Now they claimed they were on our side. English-speaking Thai Air Force officers, well mannered, squared away, met their plane, eager to welcome them and assist in every way possible. They said that the past was the result of a few "bad" politicians, but now the Americans were their friends.

It's easy to like the Thais. The country was the cleanest and the prettiest in Asia. The people were open and friendly, without the demeaning deference of peoples who had been subject to colonial rule. Prior to the war, Thailand had been the only independent country in Asia, thanks to a mutual agreement between the British and the French that both would benefit from a buffer state between the major British colonies—the Malay States, Burma and India—and the French in Indo-China.

Despite Thai independence, the British influence in Thailand had been strong—reflected charmingly in the movie, *Anna and the King of Siam*. But there were major differences between the British attitude and the American. The British now seemed to regard Thailand as an enemy. They insisted upon the destruction of a seven hundred mile railroad which the Japanese had built with Thai forced laborers and captured British soldiers—the brutal treatment commemorated in *The Bridge On The River Kwai*—across the isthmus of Thailand, which would shorten by nearly two thousand miles the trade route by sea from the Orient to Europe, previously controlled by the British.

From the point of view of world trade, it was obvious that the railroad, and a proposed ship canal paralleling the railroad, would have been a substantial aid to the development of Asia—but the British saw it as a threat to their monopoly of sea traffic on the round-about requirement of trade through the British port of Singapore, where all traffic became subject to the "Imperial Preference" that all traffic move on British transport at rates set by the Brits.

It began to dawn on Tex just what the British ideas of freedom and democracy for Asians were. Tex had always been strongly pro-British—but that was because he had seen the best of them, in their country, fighting for their own freedom. Now he was beginning to see something quite different, and not at all appealing.

The Chinese minority was another problem developing in Thailand. It was approximately 15%, and everywhere the Chinese went, their energy and enterprise made them far stronger economically than their numbers would indicate. Moreover, the Chinese sent their money back to China. The gentle, peace-loving Thais did not know what to do with their Chinese, especially with the spreading civil war in China and the prospect of a victory by Mao's communists.

A small OSS team had landed in Bangkok the day after Japan surrendered. Among them was an interesting OSS captain, Jim Thompson. He had been an architect in New York before the war, a sensitive man who had gone to St. Paul's and Princeton. He and Tex had friends in common—and they struck up a quick friendship. The OSS team was living in the old *Oriental* hotel, a sprawling former palace overlooking the river, which had once rivaled the *Peninsula* in Hong Kong and *Raffles* in Singapore. Even though sadly neglected, the hotel had great romantic charm, evoking visits of Noel Coward and Somerset Maugham. Thompson and Tex were fascinated by the place. They could see the inevitable postwar expansion in air travel and international trade— and the opportunity for international hotels. Much of the future business would be American. They were both drawn to the *Oriental* as an obvious opportunity—and Tex talked of coming back to make it happen. However, their lives, like so many wartime friendships, took different routes. Jim Thompson returned, directed the restoration of the *Oriental*, and created his world-famous artistic Thai silk industry. His disappearance many years later is still a mystery, and presumed to be an assassination related to his undercover work for the CIA.

While Thompson slept under torn mosquito nets in the then ramshackle *Oriental*, Tex's group stayed as guests in the King's palace during their visit, as a demonstration of national friendship. They were entertained lavishly, given sumptuous dinners attended to by lovely, graceful Thai girls. Thailand was very seductive.

From Bangkok they flew to Saigon in French Indo-China, looking forward to the storied pleasures of the "Paris of the Orient." They landed in a fierce rainstorm on a short, rain-slick runway. The B-17 had to brake hard—and blew a tire. They were met by an RAF officer, who told them, "Don't you know you've dropped into the middle of a war? The natives are rebelling. I'll get some Gurkha soldiers to escort you into town." After a long wait in the rain, they were taken in trucks into a dark city. The best hotel was full of cowering French. They had done nothing during the war, and were frightened at what was happening around them—so the British had moved in, "to maintain order." Tex and his group were put up at the *Majestic Hotel*, which had been the Japanese headquarters until a few days before—still without heat, with flickering lights, thoroughly unpleasant.

The next morning, the Frenchmen in fresh tropical whites began their daily parade with their ladies on the *Rue Catinet* from the Saigon Cathedral to the Mekong River. Tex was met by Lt. Colonel A. Peter Dewey, the head of a small OSS group. Dewey had parachuted into Saigon on VJ Day, had obtained the release of one hundred thirty-six interned Americans, and had gotten them started back to America. Now Dewey said he was "looking after U.S. interests," by which he meant Standard Oil, Texaco, etc.—which the British didn't like—and they especially didn't like an eight-man U.S Air Transport Command unit setting up an aviation radio facility at the Saigon Airport. That seemed natural enough to Tex—but it infuriated the British, who saw it as part of a plot to extend U.S. airlines through "their" part of the world. They were very concerned about their economic future. Britannia had ruled the waves since Trafalgar, but now they recognized how important airlines were going to be in the new postwar world trade. Secure in their maritime trade traditions, the British had lagged behind in development of long-range commercial aircraft before the war and, in their desperate early days of the war, had sacrificed the development of transport planes to produce fighters and bombers. The U.S. was way ahead, with big Douglas, Lockheed, and Boeing airliners.

Apart from the character and attitude of the French, the underlying problem of French control of Indo-China lay in its population base. Out of a total of twenty-eight million, twenty-three million were Annamite people, who were determined to end the hated French domination—and had sided with the Japanese for that purpose. In March of 1945, and anticipating their own defeat, the Japanese commander, pursuant to the Japanese message of "Asia for the Asiatics," had set up an Annamite government, the Vietnam Republic, which was supported by Chinese based in Hanoi, and loosely associated with the Yenan Communists of Mao. At the end of the war, the French had asserted their claim to control, with a thin layer of squabbling Vichyites and Gaullists, a mixed bag of third-rate people. And the Annamite Vietnam Republic began armed rebellion.

While the French cowered in Saigon, the British moved in and General Gracey took charge in characteristic British colonial style. Gracey was a old Tory, a mindless "Colonel Blimp." He saw the Annamite rebellion as another "native" disturbance to good order, discipline and authority—not to mention British Colonial influence. He told the Annamites that he intended to disarm the Japs, then he double-crossed them, and instead used Japanese troops to attack the Annamites (an approach also used by the Dutch in the East Indies to fight the rebellious Javanese).

To the colonial "Colonel Blimp" mind, the OSS was an element of American elite intellectuals with leftist democratic ideas, bent on subverting proper British control of the natives. This attitude of the British—and General Gracey's stupidity—cost Colonel Dewey his life.

The local people hated the French, didn't like the British—and looked to the Americans as their liberators. They responded eagerly at the sight of American uniforms—and were disappointed to learn that Tex's group was only a journalist unit, transients, like the handful of Air Transport Command radio station people and Colonel Dewey's half dozen OSS men—none representing the U.S. occupation troops they had hoped for. But to the mind of British General Gracey, all Americans represented a potential disturbance, and Dewey and the OSS seemed a real threat. Gracey had set up "security" perimeters patrolled by Gurkha soldiers, beyond which he warned it would be "dangerous" to go. This was silly on its face. There was no danger; the locals welcomed Americans. Gracey's "security" perimeter was solely intended to maintain his control—and to give the French a place to hide. The only risk was not being identified as Americans.

The correspondents' obvious and increasingly unmilitary behavior, coupled with their preference to remain in hotel bars, or lower dives, provided a considerable level of self-protection. Not so, Colonel Dewey. He carried himself with military dignity and acted upon the assumption that America's presence should not be controlled by, or confused with, arrogant British autocracy. Tex liked Dewey. He lived outside Gracey's "security" perimeter, and went where he chose in a Jeep, flying the American flag. Gracey couldn't stand it—and he finally hit upon the ultimate "Colonel Blimp" solution. He called Dewey in and told him that he must not fly the American flag on his Jeep. Dewey naturally protested on national sovereignty principles. Gracey rested his case on a higher level, declaring that only Generals were permitted to fly flags; further, Gracey would have Dewey arrested and imprisoned for any disobedience of this order. Then Dewey's second-in-command, Captain Joe Coolidge, of the presidential family line, while trying to rescue some French nuns and school children, was shot in an Annamite ambush, unrecognized in his Jeep without the American flag. In the ensuing American protest, Gracey was dismissive, saying that proper orders must be obeyed.

The following day, Colonel Dewey asked two of Tex's group, Bill Downs and Jim McGlincy, to meet him for lunch at the OSS house, outside the "security" perimeter. While they were waiting for Dewey to arrive, heavy shooting broke out nearby. They were given carbines and told to defend themselves, if necessary. A wounded and bloody OSS officer staggered in with the news that Colonel Dewey had been shot and killed driving toward a Annamite roadblock, unrecognized by new troops without his customary American flag. After a fire fight around the house, the Annamites drew back. Downs and McGlincy escaped, pretending they were drunks, singing American songs, staggering down the road, waving whisky bottles.

Tex's correspondents put the news of Dewey's death—and General Gracey's role—out on the news wires. The news reached Lord Louis Mountbatten, the British Supreme Commander in Singapore, and Mountbatten ordered General Gracey to report to him immediately. Tex had known Mountbatten from dinners with Lord Beaverbrook in London in 1941, and he and Lady Rose had seen him socially thereafter. Tex remembered him very favorably, one night especially. When Eisenhower came to London, he was a chain smoker—four packs a day. He sat through his first speech-filled official dinner as Supreme Commander as long as he could, finally lighting up just before the toast to the King. Sacrilege! The newspapers were filled with comments of the uncouth American general who presumed to smoke before the toast. Another dinner followed shortly. Ike dreaded the ordeal. But, as soon as the guests were seated,

Mountbatten stood, raised his glass, "Gentlemen, the King." With the toast behind him, Ike smoked contentedly through the dinner.

Tex's B-17 was the only plane available to make the flight to Singapore. They were ready to go, and he agreed to take Gracey with them. He wanted to see how Mountbatten, whom he then thought was the best of the "Royals," would handle a jackass like Gracey. The correspondents didn't like the idea of having to ride with Gracey in the plane. None of them would speak to him, and he sat silent and alone throughout the flight.

Singapore, even more than Hong Kong, was the imperial citadel of the British East Asia empire. The massive Singapore naval base had been built, partly by trade profits resulting from the eighty thousand ships that put into Singapore annually, and partly from the competitive advantage of "Imperial Preference," which granted control of the export of the raw material resources of the region, rubber, tin and, importantly, opium, exclusively to British cartels.

When they landed in Singapore, Tex experienced the attitudes of a British colonial Supreme Command Headquarters. A supercilious young RAF officer pulled his Jeep up to the B-17, and asked for the commander. Tex identified himself as Colonel McCrary. The officer said, "Let me see your papers, old boy." Tex couldn't let that young sprig get away with that. He said, "The Supreme Commander asked me to drop in— and, by the way, you can let him know that I've had to give his commander in Indo-China a ride down in my plane."

They were taken to the famous *Raffles Hotel*, a monument of the Empire, named after Sir Stafford Raffles who had planted the Union Jack and built British power throughout the area. *Raffles* is featured in all the romantic stories of the Orient, a long, rambling building, its porches once filled with rubber planters, opium and tea merchants in white suits drinking gin. When Tex got there, it was filled with British businessmen and planters recently freed from Japanese prison camps. Having just seen the rebellion in Indo-China, Tex asked whether troubles were brewing in Malaya. The planters said there would be no trouble, that they knew how to handle the colored people here—the French and the Americans don't. The French are too weak, the Americans are too soft. You try to treat natives as equals. "Just can't do that, old boy."

Tex and his group were invited to meet with Mountbatten at Government House, who played his role with his natural aplomb, bounding upstairs in his tropical whites, shorts and knee socks, every bit the picture of a proper British officer. As Supreme Commander of the Southeast Asia Command, his unspoken mission was the reestablishment of the colonial empires—for England, naturally, India, Burma, Malaya, Singapore, and Hong Kong—but also for French Indo-China, and the Dutch East Indies.

After Mountbatten's graceful introductory courtesies, the correspondents asked for his comments on the investigation of General Gracey's conduct in connection with the death of Colonel Dewey. Mountbatten calmly said that Colonel Dewey's death was entirely the fault of Colonel Dewey; he had refused General Gracey's offer of an escort of Gurkhas to protect him and he had chosen to live and travel outside of General Gracey's designated security areas. Furthermore, Colonel Dewey was not part of

Mountbatten's command—he belonged to General Donovan. In saying that, Mountbatten stylishly threw his arm across his chest to cover his lower face, signifying the mysterious cloak-and-dagger image of the OSS. To him that seemed to explain it all—not his responsibility. Actions of British colonial officers were not subject to question. Mountbatten excused himself to change for dinner, returning in an immaculate green dress uniform with four rows of decorations, attended by Lady Mountbatten, equally elegant.

Tex couldn't believe this was the same man he had known in London, when he had thought he was the best of the "royals." Mountbatten's attitude in that imperial setting was perfectly representative of British authority and power in the Orient—but the sun was setting on the Empire. After the war Mountbatten became Viceroy of India—and Lady Mountbatten became the mistress of Prime Minister Nehru.

Kipling's poetry had been a strong influence on Tex in his Exeter days and his exposure to the remnants of the British Colonial Empire reminded him of the words of Kipling's *Recessional:*

> Far called our navies melt away;
> On dune and headland sink the fires;
> Lo, all our pomp of yester years;
> Is one with Nineveh and Tyre.

Tex knew that he and his group would continue to be unpopular in Singapore, so they took off for Batavia, on the island of Java, the capital of what had been the Dutch East Indies. The history of the area fascinated him. Since early in the sixteen hundreds, the Dutch had controlled a vast island empire, stretching from Sumatra on the East, through Java, Borneo, the Sunda Islands, to New Guinea on the West, a seemingly endless source of wealth, first, from the spice trade with Europe, and then, in the Twentieth Century, from great reservoirs of oil. Tex recalled that Baruch had told him before the war that the Dutch East Indies were the crucial source of oil for all of Southeast Asia and, importantly, for Japan. When President Roosevelt cut off Japanese oil imports—half of Japan's requirements—from the United States in the summer of 1941, the Japanese knew that they could not survive in the industrial age without control of the oil of the Dutch East Indies. The Japanese had removed a British threat by the capture of Singapore and the sinking of the British fleet. America represented the only remaining threat to the Japanese—and after Pearl Harbor, they proceeded to invade and occupy the Philippines to deny the U.S. a forward base from which to cut off the crucial supply of oil from the Dutch East Indies. However, by the later stages of the war, U.S. submarines and bombers had reduced oil shipments to Japan from the Dutch East Indies to a virtual trickle.

Tex had only a sketchy knowledge of the history, but he knew that the relationship between the Javanese and their Dutch colonial masters had been bad. The leading prewar native leader was Dr. Sukarno, who had long and actively tried to get rid of the brutal Dutch overlords. When the Japanese easily overwhelmed the Dutch resistance and took control of the islands in 1941, as they had elsewhere, the Japanese maintained a native government, the Indonesian Republic, headed by Sukarno/ He worked with the Japanese and, in 1943, was appointed by the Japanese to head an independence committee for Java and Sumatra. Upon the collapse of Japanese occupation in 1945, Sukarno had proclaimed himself leader of an independent East Indies, and was determined to fight against any return to Dutch Colonial status.

Batavia was quiet on the first night after their arrival, except that Clark Lee got into a fight with a Nazi sailor from a German submarine which had been operating in those waters against U.S. shipping in cooperation with the Japanese. The next day the British landed, bringing with them the hated Dutch troops, equipped with U.S. Sherman tanks and P-47 fighters in Dutch markings. The Javanese had been expecting U.S. troops to be their liberators, and they were distinctly unhappy to see the hated Dutch. Sukarno had used his authority to impose a curfew to keep his people off the streets at night. All would have been well with any exercise of good judgment, but the Dutch wanted to show their power, so as long as they had the protection of British troops the Dutch arranged "incidents," which were used as excuses for repression—and a full-fledged revolution began. The British realized this was going nowhere, and withdrew.

Recognizing the universal native support for Sukarno, the Dutch were afraid to shoot him, so they had him confined to his home. Tex arranged a visit for his group. Dr. Sukarno had been schooled by the Dutch as an engineer, one of the very few to have received that benefit in a country where the Dutch had maintained the natives in the lowest literacy rate in the civilized world. Sukarno said that no agreement was possible with the Dutch because they had broken all promises and agreements made over the past two hundred years. The Japanese had given his people an opportunity for freedom—and they had taken it. He openly acknowledged his cooperation with the Japanese, and he also acknowledged his regret at some of the results. However, he pointed out that, after the British had withdrawn, the Dutch had used captured Japanese troops to fire on the Javanese, ample evidence of Dutch dishonor.

However, war has many paradoxes. As disliked as the Dutch were, the Javanese recalled that when the Japanese had conquered the Dutch East Indies, they had taken all of the Dutch and Anglos into prison camps—and separated the men and women. Tex and his group were present when the families were reunited. They had seen a lot of misery and death during the war—but they were not prepared for what they saw that day. Dutch husbands were waiting to be reunited with their wives after several years of separation. As their wives were led out, many of the Dutch wives carried Japanese babies in their arms.

After what they had seen, Tex and his group were ready to move on. But, given what he knew about the world demand for oil, Tex wondered about the future of the country. Having seen the arrogant attitude of the Dutch, and the reciprocal hatred by the Javanese, Tex didn't believe the Dutch could reestablish effective control. The oil of the Indies was a great prize, and many would fight for it.

All of this was very depressing. Tex's group was tired—and wanted to see something of the romantic image of the Indies. They flew on to Bali, which lived up to its billing. A spectacularly beautiful island. They were given a party, which lasted, by consensus count, for three days. When the last man was helped aboard the B-17, they took off for home. The hangovers lasted almost to Honolulu, where Clark Lee's charming wife had prepared an elegant luau.

It was wonderful to be back on American land. Despite the beauty of Hawaii, Tex was eager to come home, to see Jinx. He left the faithful old B-17, *The Headliner,* in Honolulu, and flew on to San Diego.

As Diamond Head slipped beneath the wing on his homeward flight, Tex thought about what he had seen and done. He and his team had started out from Japan—flushed with the victory over Japan—to learn more about the peoples and places they thought America had fought to liberate from the Japanese: Chungking, Shanghai, Hong Kong, Bangkok, Saigon, Singapore, and Batavia. Instead of people rejoicing in their freedom, they had found the Chinese engaged in a major civil war against the Chiang Kai-shek government that the U. S. was determined to support; French Indo-China in open revolt against the French; the Javanese hating the Dutch; British control in Hong Kong eroding; Malaya and Burma unstable, with rumblings of increasing unrest in India.

He had not really expected much of the French—he had seen something of their colonial behavior in Saigon—but they were even worse than he had expected. As far as he was concerned, the conduct of the Dutch was indefensible. And he had certainly expected better of the British.

All in all, the behavior of America's allies was very troubling. What he had seen was not what he had hoped to see, and not what Americans thought they had fought the war for. Instead, he had seen the reality of Colonialism. Outright oppression of great masses of non-white Asian peoples, for the benefit of white Europeans. True, the British had introduced a basic system of law and order in Hong Kong and Singapore, but that did not apply to the French and the Dutch colonies. It was hard to sort out the meaning of it all.

To most Americans, the war had been Roosevelt's war. His visions and his decisions had largely directed all actions, even after his death. And there were unresolved complexities about Roosevelt. There was the democratic, anti-colonial Roosevelt of the "Four Freedoms"—but who had acceded to the Churchill "who had not become Prime Minister to preside over the end of the British Empire." And there was the Roosevelt who had fought the dictatorships of Hitler and Mussolini—but had accommodated and supported the totalitarian dictatorships of Stalin and Chiang Kai-shek.

Except for a brief return visit from London before Pearl Harbor and his transit from Europe to the Pacific—when he had married Jinx—Tex had been out of the country for nearly five years. When he had left for London in 1940, Baruch had told him that he "would learn a lot." At that time, neither of them had any idea of what was to come—and he had certainly learned a lot in five years of war.

The war had changed everything. Roosevelt and Churchill, the great war leaders, were gone, Roosevelt had died in May 1945 and Churchill, who had won the war for England, was thrown out by the voters in the same month, to be replaced by an incompetent socialist Labour Government. In America, Truman became President, a man of whom the country knew little—and who, himself, knew little of the world.

En route to the Pacific in June of 1945, Tex had thought of the devastation he had seen in Europe, with half of Germany and all of Eastern Europe now under Stalin's boot. And what he had seen in Asia—Chiang Kai-shek's corrupt dictatorship in China, and the imperial attitudes of the Colonial governments of the English, French and Dutch—had convinced him that revolutions were inevitable all over Asia. What would they bring about?

And what about the Atom bomb? Clearly, it was something altogether different, a new kind of energy, entirely apart from what had been previously experienced. The Atom bomb had opened another dimension, awesome to contemplate, its power potentially unlimited. Tex tried to grasp its implications. What would it mean for the future of our country? What would it mean for the world? Was this a potential benefit, or was this a weapon threatening civilization as he had known it?

America's power was then supreme in the world. But Americans are not good at keeping secrets. Inevitably, bigger, more terrible, bombs would be built—by other nations. Images of Hiroshima and Nagasaki lingered in his mind.

Change was everywhere. But how much had America changed? Tex had learned from Roosevelt, and from the Willkie campaign in 1940, that America would respond to positive, vital leadership. But now Truman—picked for Vice President by a bunch of politicians in a hotel room in St. Louis—was President. He saw nothing in Truman's background to qualify him for the leadership of the country.

In the chaos and shambles of the post-war world, America would have to lead, and that would require a new kind of national leadership. The reality of a shrinking world would force Americans to choose as our President persons of international awareness and experience. Presidential power would inevitably continue to increase. But the process by which American Presidential candidates were nominated was fundamentally flawed.

Change was coming. He had seen more of the world than most and he wanted to be a part of that change. He wanted to do something, to get involved. But where? And how? He felt certain that he could go back to writing a newspaper column about goings-on in New York, but that had no appeal. He knew that what he had seen and done in the war had changed him—and he thought that it had likely changed the country as well. Symbolically, the intercontinental range of the B-29 had made the world a much smaller, closer place. Further scientific advances would inevitably accelerate the process. America might still be isolationist politically, but the men who had fought the war now knew that American leadership in the world was essential in ways it had never been before. Tex wanted to find a way to help others understand the leadership required in the post-war world. What could he do to help make that happen?

News radio had cut into the role of the print press to a significant degree. A number of great reporters, Ed Murrow foremost among them, had already established national reputations on radio. But the network chiefs allocated only fifteen minutes—after commercials, effectively only twelve minutes—to network news in the evening. A shocking indication of the low opinion of the interest and intelligence of the American public in the minds of the network owners. Tex knew it would be a struggle to try to break into that market.

Photography had always interested him and his command of the Air Force Combat Photo Unit had provided him with a certain reputation. Television, while not yet available, was on the horizon—and he was convinced that when it was introduced, it would become the dominant medium of communication. So that would be his goal. But how to start, how to get there?

And what about Jinx? Her personal grace and beauty provided instant recognition everywhere—and would make her a natural for television. But television was still in the future. It was worth thinking about. Jinx had been the top magazine "Cover Girl," traveled all around as "Miss Rheingold," made many movies, visited the war theaters on USO entertainment tours. Perhaps there might be a way they could work together?

When he landed in San Diego, Jinx was waiting.

Chapter Ten

Tex and Jinx: Pioneers in Television

New York in the fall of 1945 was not the same place that Tex had left five years before. And Tex was not the same man. The war had changed everything—the Depression mentality, the politics of fear and redistribution, the war itself. Now all were left behind. Franklin Roosevelt, the great leader who had dominated American politics, was gone, succeeded by his largely unknown Vice President, Harry Truman. Stalin, a brutal, aggressive dictator ruled Russia in the name of "Communism" and appeared intent on taking over Eastern Europe, devastated and impoverished by the war. In 1941 Henry Luce had proclaimed "the American Century"—devoting an issue of *Life* magazine to the subject. Now the idea was in the air everywhere. America was the leader of the free world, but what kind of leadership did America have?

Tex was married to the most beautiful girl in America, and naturally he wanted to introduce her to his friends. Jock Whitney welcomed them, put them up in his 10 Gracie Square apartment, and he and Betsey gave a couple of elegant parties for them. Tex hadn't seen Jock since they both headed into France with OSS teams on the day before the invasion of the southern French coast—Jock on a fishing boat and Tex by parachute—and both had been captured by the Germans. Tex had an easy escape, but Jock had a much harder time. They had a lot to talk about.

Tex and Jinx said they were looking for an apartment in the city. Jock nodded his head, of course, they would need an apartment, but they had to have a place in the country—and he had just the place in mind, the *Mousehole* on *Greentree,* his huge estate in Manhasset. Tex protested that he couldn't afford it, but Jock, being Jock, said, "Look, don't worry. You're my old friend. We lived together in the war, and I want you to live nearby." (Footnote: The *Mousehole* was an old farmhouse, beautifully restored, with a big kitchen, immense fireplace, opening into a large dining-living room. The house was later moved and reconstructed in a museum)

Tex took Jinx to see Baruch and, naturally, he was crazy about her, as Tex knew he would be. At their first, long dinner in Baruch's apartment in the Ritz Tower, Tex had hoped to get in a few words with him but Baruch talked to Jinx throughout, until he suddenly stood up and said, "I'm an old man, and must go to bed." He walked them to the door, shook Tex's hand, and said, "Tex, we have much to talk about. Call me." He then kissed Jinx's hand elegantly and said, "Oh, to be seventy again!"

111

For Tex the immediate problem was where to begin? His friends Brown and Ogden Reid, whose family owned *New York Herald Tribune,* offered Tex a column—interesting, but restrictive. Tex had seen too much, had had too much freedom for too long. He wanted to do his own thing. And there was Jinx to think about. She was at the peak of her career as a magazine "cover girl,"—but that's a brief career, at best, and controlled by other hands.

Tex kept thinking about radio, and television was even more intriguing. It seemed obvious to him that television would inevitably become the most powerful and effective means of public communication—and he wanted to be a part of it. But television was not yet on the market. However, radio had developed to the national network level (he liked to mention that the first national hook-up was for the Yale-Harvard football game in 1927) so radio seemed a reasonable place to start. Financial arrangements were different in those days. Corporate sponsors typically developed and produced the programs which were carried on the three networks. David Sarnoff's NBC was the largest, followed by Bill Paley's CBS, which had benefited from the wartime reporting of his star reporters Ed Murrow, Eric Sevareid and Walter Cronkite. The Mutual Network, which later became the base for ABC, was a distant third.

Tex's radio broadcasting before the war with H.V. Kaltenborn, although brief, had exposed him to most of the tricks of the trade. He was pretty well acquainted around New York, and he thought he and Jinx had a good start toward a saleable package for a program of their own. The prevailing judgment of the radio moguls in New York after the war was that the news was a serious matter, most interesting to men, and should therefore be presented in the evening when men would be at home. However, Tex couldn't believe that, despite the level of importance they seemed to attach to the evening news, the moguls only allocated fifteen minutes to it.

The daytime was mostly "light stuff" and "soap operas," devoted to women, with the youth programs, *Jack Armstrong, Captain Midnight* and *The Shadow* in the late afternoon. However, the mornings seemed to offer a window of opportunity. He and Jinx were convinced that the war had changed women's roles and attitudes, given them a greater interest and involvement in national and world affairs—far more than the radio moguls realized—and that there was an both an unfilled appetite, and an opening, for discussion of serious subjects in the morning hours.

While his ideas were taking form, Tex talked with Baruch. But before he could get to his future plans, Baruch wanted to talk about Tex's experiences and reflections on the war. Baruch seemed deeply troubled. He was disgusted that the British had ousted Churchill as Prime Minister and replaced him with Clement Attlee, whom Baruch considered intellectually limited, and politically locked in the British class warfare of the past. He was particularly curious about Tex's trip around Asia, his thoughts on Chiang Kai-shek and the civil war in China, the turmoil in the British, French and Dutch colonies—and especially, his opinion of MacArthur.

Baruch believed that the world was at a tipping point and America, as the strongest nation, inevitably must lead. He had a strong personal dislike for President Truman, whom he considered woefully inexperienced and inadequately prepared for the magnitude of problems facing America. Not only would America have to rebuild our allies in Europe, whose governments were weak and whose economies were in disarray, we would also have to deal with the difficulties of their colonial empires and we would have to help rebuild the economies of the defeated nations, Germany and Japan.

Moreover, Baruch was visibly distressed by Tex's description of MacArthur's imperial attitude and behavior in Japan. Baruch shook his head, saying that Truman simply wouldn't know how to handle him. Tex was surprised to see Baruch, usually so optimistic, now so troubled—and he said so. Baruch replied, "You're right. Let's stop talking about the world, and talk about you and Jinx."

Tex outlined his plan for a radio program as a steppingstone into television. Baruch warmed to the idea at once, saying that that's exactly what he should do. Introduce serious people and subjects; but keep a light touch. There was no competition. Tex and Jinx wouldn't have any trouble getting an audience. Through his exposures and experiences, Tex knew lots of people, and Baruch said he'd introduce him to anyone he didn't know. All of the major national and international figures called on Baruch. His support and frequent appearances on the show were to be very helpful.

Tex talked to a few people on technical and organizational matters, and then it was time to take the next step—to start at the top. Tex had known both David Sarnoff of NBC and Bill Paley of CBS in New York before the war, and had seen something more of them during the war when both had come to London to follow the interests of their companies. But they were very different men. Sarnoff had been born in Russia, immigrated as a boy into the United States, was a genuine pioneer in electronics, had created the Radio Corporation of America and had introduced the earliest national radio hookup. Paley was the son of a Philadelphia cigar manufacturer who had adroitly parlayed his inheritance into radio station ownership. During the war Sarnoff had put his substantial technical knowledge to work on military communication problems, while Paley seemed to be riding on the prestige of his lead reporter, Ed Murrow whose "This . . . is London" cue line was the most memorable radio voice of the war—and he seemed mainly interested in chasing girls, preferably with titles, Pam Churchill being one of his many conquests. For civilians in London, the strict rationing policies were inconvenient. The Army had recognized the potential help that Sarnoff and Paley could provide in public opinion, and therefore gave both of them the "assimilated" rank of colonel, which imposed no military duties, but did provide the considerable benefits of access to the Officers' Mess, PX privileges, and travel on military transport.

Tex had a lot more respect for Sarnoff than for Paley, so he took his plans to Sarnoff first. After exchanging a few war stories, Sarnoff listened to the plan, and said that he liked the way Tex thought. He agreed to put him on his New York radio station when the show was ready. Tex couldn't wait to tell Jinx. They didn't know what to call it. After a while Tex said, "I'll just open with 'Hi, Jinx'." So that became the title of their first show. Now they were on their way. Meanwhile Tex needed some income. He went back to Brown Reid and accepted his offer for a column in the *Herald Tribune* five days a week, which he called *"Close Up."*

Their first radio show aired on April 22nd, 1946—and they got excellent coverage, ranging from words like "sprightly" to "rather intense discussions of world affairs." Their favorite comment appeared in *Newsweek* cover story, "A soft-spoken, calculating Texan, Tex McCrary, inched up to a microphone and drawled, 'Hi, Jinx'. A voice with all the foamy substance of a bubble bath answered, 'Hello, Tex'." Naturally they favored celebrities, but unlike today's "celebs" most of whom are famous for being famous (for the infamous fifteen minutes), their guests were people of real achievement, ranging from political leaders, as well as Eleanor Roosevelt, Baruch and other prominent financial, literary and theatrical figures, to poets like Krishnan Menon.

Tex and Jinx were very happy living in the *Mousehole,* with Jock and Betsey Whitney only a short walk away across the beautifully landscaped *Greentree* property. The main Whitney house was beyond the enclosed tennis courts (both lawn and court tennis), the pool house and, of course, suitably away from the stables and the polo fields elsewhere on the property. There was another handsome home on the property, a classic white country wooden structure with green shutters, wide porches and gracious lawns, which Jock had rented to their Air Force friend, General Pete Quesada, and his wife Kate-Davis, the daughter of Joseph Pulitzer II, a war widow whom he had recently married. The scale, grace and dignity of that style of life is now lost forever, but it was wonderful to experience it at the time.

Meanwhile, Bill Paley's first wife, a cousin of Bill Hearst, fed up with Paley's relentless womanizing, had divorced him, and Paley intended to enhance his status with a marriage to Barbara Cushing Mortimer, recently divorced from the very social Stanley Mortimer, and a sister of Jock's wife, Betsey Cushing Roosevelt Whitney. When the old original Pulitzer estate, next to Jock's property, came on the market. Paley bought it immediately. Jock recognized that it would make Betsey happy to have her sister, Babe, living "next door" as it were. Everyone got along very well.

Some time later, Jock came to Tex and said that Pete Quesada had just told him that he had decided on a new opportunity in office real estate development in Washington and was going to have to move. While Jock was pleased to have Betsey's sister next to them, he feared that the famously domineering mother-in-law, "Gogs" Cushing, would want to move in if she learned that the Quesadas were leaving. To preempt that possibility, Jock wanted Tex and Jinx to move into the larger Quesada house immediately. Jinx had taken a couple of days off to have their first son, "Paddy," and they could use more room but Tex told Jock that he didn't know if he could afford it, given the need to finance their program. Ever generous, Jock insisted that, since Tex would be doing him a favor by keeping his mother-in-law off the property, he would only ask that Tex make the same minimal rental payment that he was already making for the *Mousehole.*

As their radio audience grew, they started a new radio show called "Tex and Jinx." Their shows began to be carried by other stations outside of New York, and all was progressing very satisfactorily. By mid-1947 they were well along to proving their case that their shows could attract a broad audience. They had an apartment at 10 East 63rd Street in Manhattan, which they also used as an office for Tex-Jinx Productions, Inc. It was decorated in modern Japanese style with shoji screens and prints from the Museum of Modern Art where Jock was a director. Finances were tight and they needed help badly. Every penny came out of their pockets, and they couldn't afford much. Len Safir, who was carrying the burden of the *Herald Tribune* column, brought his brother Bill from Syracuse University for a summer job. Bill was terrific, but he was soon drafted into the Army (where he changed the spelling of his last name because the sergeants had trouble pronouncing it). When Bill Safire was discharged, Tex

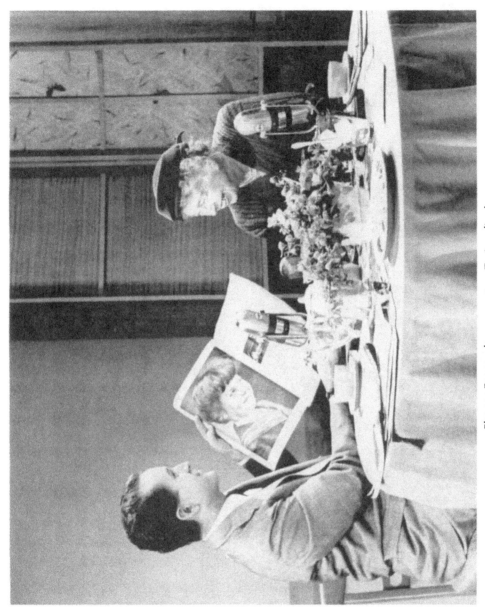

Eleanor Roosevelt as a guest on Tex's radio show

Bill Paley; Jinx; Mary Cushing Astor Fosburgh; John McClain;
Betsey Cushing Roosevelt Whitney; Jock, Babe Cushing Mortimer Paley; Tex

asked him to work full time and offered him $40 a week. Tex knew that he was good, and Bill liked the opportunity. He agreed to join up, but only if he could have a good secretary. There was a terrible scene when he found out that the secretary would be paid $60 a week.

For all the anticipation of the future of television, it was still a fragile activity—and a huge financial risk. In the oil industry, which Tex well knew from Texas, a "wild-catter" is a person who identifies, finances, and drills, his own well, independent of the giant oil companies. That's what Tex and Jinx were doing as pioneers in television. There were only a few thousand sets in America, expensive, tiny screens, poor definition, frequent breakdowns, many not even deemed worth repairing, considering the feeble programs available. There were only eleven television stations in the country, all local, with most programming local sports. Advertisers were reluctant pay for the tiny audience. Tex kept pointing out that the total TV audience just in the markets of those eleven existing stations totaled nearly thirty million people, about one-third of the then population of the United States. Brave talk, at the time.

The absence of major corporate sponsors made things difficult. There were very few trained people available and they had to do a great deal of the work themselves. Their first television show was at eight o'clock on a Sunday night in the summer of 1947. Bristol Myers was the "sponsor." They put up $200—which their two guests ate and drank away at a post-show dinner. It cost about $400 out-of-pocket for each weekly show—film, cameramen and film cutters. Swift & Co., the meat packers, came on board, at $300 per show—and they went on from there.

Newsweek put Tex and Jinx on the magazine cover on August 25, 1947, along with a positive story: "Television: The Wildcatting McCrarys."

They did everything they could think of to build audience and to emphasize the visual impact of the program. Tex adjusted his old newspaper formula, Headline—Picture—Caption—Quote, for television. Now Picture became the Headline, and he and Jinx were Caption and their guests became the Quote.

Igor Sikorsky helped serve as an early example of the kind of person they tried to interview. Sikorsky was one of the great original aviation pioneers, and the actual godfather of the helicopter. Tex had gotten to know him because Jock owned one of his S-38 amphibians, the same type of plane that Lindbergh had flown from Miami to Cuba to inaugurate Juan Trippe's Pan American international airline service. The S-38 was an ungainly-looking thing, but Jock, as one would expect, had Sikorsky fit it out luxuriously. It was slow, but it could land almost anywhere. Jock used to take off from one of his polo fields at *Greentree,* land on the East River for meetings or to pick up guests, then fly down to his Virginia horse country estate or to the South Carolina quail plantation and the McCrarys often came along. Sikorsky's helicopters had come of age in the military during the war, and were just on the verge of entering civil use. Tex called Sikorsky and asked him to pick them up in a helicopter at *Greentree,* fly them to Manhattan and land on the top of Radio City, where they produced their shows. Terrific television, dramatic setting, arresting action, Jinx stepping elegantly out of the helicopter. Perfect. It generated lots of follow-up coverage for the show, as well as for Sikorsky, who was delighted at the promotion of his product.

Tex and Jinx were rapidly becoming "the celebrity couple," "insiders" in the social world of New York, so Tex was not too surprised when Paley asked him to produce a television program for CBS. The market was improving all the time, and Paley's offer was too good to pass up, but with all the shows they were doing, it had to be something in their style, and not repetitious of their other programs. Tex hit upon the idea of presenting a weekly preview of coming events, Broadway openings, etc., most of which needed publicity and would be happy to contribute their services. CBS handled production costs and paid, for those days, a generous fee. They called the program "Preview." Paley gave them a prime-time spot at eight o'clock on Monday nights (when the Broadway theaters are "dark"). They were given top billing, and luck was running with them. Tex got his old friend Mary Martin to do the first show. She was opening with Ezio Pinza in "*South Pacific*," with Richard Rodgers' music and Oscar Hammerstein's lyrics, one of the greatest musicals of all time. What a kick-off!

With so much going on, so many programs and appearances, they needed more help. They started an apprentice program. Bill Safire had been the first of that remarkable bunch of eager, able, attractive young people. He became a close friend and went on to establish his impressive career as the highly respected columnist for *The New York Times* and the author of important books—one of which he sent Tex inscribed with what Tex considered the best compliment he ever received: "To Tex—who taught me all I know—but not all he knows!"

In addition to Bill Safire, there were other fine people—Schuyler Chapin, who flew C-46 transports over "The Hump" from India to China during the war, and who later became head of the New York Philharmonic; Hugh Downs; Gabe Pressman; Barry Farber; all of whom went on to have outstanding careers in television. Barbara Walters, fresh out of Sarah Lawrence, was the first of many talented women; her extraordinary television career speaks for itself. Another was Mary Olhberg, one of the very best. Mary married Ted Yates, who was so talented Tex couldn't afford to keep him. NBC made him a producer. He did great work, including winning the prestigious George Polk Award for Journalism for his reports from the war in the Dominican Republic. Tex gave a dinner for Ted with former Polk winners, in the course of which he asked, "Do you know who won the first award?" Nobody knew. Tex told them that it was Herbert Bayard Swope, for his coverage of the First World War—from the German side. The Arab-Israeli conflict was heating up into another war in 1956 and Tex asked whether any of the Polk winners would volunteer to cover that war from the Arab side. All said no—except for Yates, who went over immediately. When the shooting started, Ted, ever eager for the best photo, stepped in front of the lines. Israeli machine gun fire killed him. Mary was heartbroken. Bill Paley later made her a producer of *Face The Nation*, where she met and later married Mike Wallace. They remained close friends of Tex and Jinx.

Occasionally an attractive candidate didn't work out. Jackie Bouvier came down from Vassar after a "Prix de Paris" writing fellowship from *Vogue*. Jackie wanted to be a photographer. As a test, Tex gave her a Leica and told her to go around the city and shoot a roll of film of smiling faces. She came back the next day and told Tex, very sadly, that she couldn't find a single smiling face. There was a certain natural reticence in Jackie's manner; she was just too shy. She went on to Washington as a freelance photographer, and Charley Bartlett, respected Washington reporter and close friend of Jack Kennedy, introduced them, and was an usher in their wedding.

Tex tried to have a "public service" piece on his program whenever possible. He was overwhelmed with requests, and tried to give an interview to key public figures. It seemed that many of the more interesting things that happened in New York involved one or more of the Rockefeller brothers. Tex knew all of them. Each had evolved in his own niche. John was the eldest, a major philanthropist, and head of the family foundations, following on the works of his father, who had built the elegant Rockefeller Center; David was the banker, the power at the Chase Bank, and deeply involved in major real estate all over the world; Lawrence was a creative venture capitalist and, later, environmentalist; Nelson was the internationalist, and probably the most publicly visible: Winthrop was the playboy. He had courted Mary Martin and wanted to marry her, but the brothers didn't want a Rockefeller to marry an actress. Winthrop got even—he married "Bobo," a former Miss Lithuania.

Tex was particularly interested in what was happening in New York real estate. Bill Levitt was on the program a couple of times in connection with his "Levitt Town" housing projects for veterans. Then Bill Zeckendorf called with an idea for the depressed area of the former cattle slaughter yards on the East River from 49th Street to 42nd Street. Zeckendorf had taken an option on the stockyard property, and wanted to build a platform over the East River Drive to create an upscale office and apartment project, with lawns and terraces and a grand view of the East River. But Zeckendorf couldn't get financing from banks whose executives didn't see a market for people who would live "over the stockyards".

Zeckendorf's option on the land was nearly running out, and when Tex called again, he was worried at what he expected to hear. Instead Bill said, "Tex, I've got it. I woke up my wife and told her I'm going to put those bastards on the platform. She said, 'What bastards? What platform?' I told her the U.N., of course, on my platform." Tex called Nelson Rockefeller, told him to get together with Zeckendorf. As Tex knew he would, Nelson loved the idea. He got his brother, John, to buy the land and donate it to the U.N. It always made Tex happy whenever he drove by the handsome U.N building, which transformed the whole mid-town area.

After their second son, Kevin, was born, Jinx was back at work in a couple of days—with an idea. The GI Bill had made a major impact in America, giving GIs a college education and financing for their own homes. Jinx received a lot of mail, especially during her pregnancies, much of it from the wives of young GIs who couldn't afford to live in Manhattan, and were moving to Long Island—many to the nearby "Levitt Town"—and having babies. The rich families on Long Island had their babies in Manhattan, but it was clear that Long Island needed a hospital of its own. The population was expanding rapidly, but civic leadership hadn't kept pace for the kind of hospital which would be necessary. Some major civic stimulation was required. Jock's *Greentree* property was several hundred acres—and Jock's ownership also included a large parcel that was used by Jock for additional practice polo fields. Population pressure had made the land very valuable commercial property. It was ideal for a major hospital, but the commercial value was too great for the community to acquire. Jock had inherited the property from his father and, while he had no compunction about buying and selling land for investment and development, in Jock's mind inherited land was different, and he would never think of selling it simply for profit. Jock donated generously to the established Whitney charities, Payne Whitney Hospital, of which he was chairman, the Museum of Modern Art, the Payne Whitney Gymnasium and other buildings at Yale University, as well as many other benefactions. However, he was not drawn to initiate new projects which were not directly in his line of personal charitable interests. Jock would need some encouragement to make the idea his own.

Tex called Igor Sikorsky and asked for a helicopter to pick him up in front of his house on Christmas morning They hovered outside the windows of Jock's library, where Tex knew he and Betsey would be unwrapping presents, and then touched down on the lawn. Jock was delighted. Tex suggested they go for a ride. There were virtually no flight regulations for helicopters in those days and the weather was beautiful. They flew all around, hovered outside friends' windows and peeked inside. Jock loved it. Tex made sure that they covered all of the housing developments that were going up, as well as the slow, heavy traffic on the roads Tex asked Jock what would happen if he, or a friend, had a serious accident on one of his polo fields, a life-threatening accident which required immediate hospital attention. Manhattan might be too far. Long Island needed a hospital. They hovered a few feet over his Spinney Hill land, then landed in front of Jock's library and talked in front of the fire. Jock could see the possibilities.

The community would have to be energized to justify and support such a project. Tex suggested that it would help if the prominent families would take the lead in demonstrating support through major charity balls. Babe Paley got excited, and took a lead role. Babe did a great job, really put her heart into it. An organization was cobbled together, attracting the right mix of supporters, and for many years gave two annual events, an elegant *Winter Ball* in the handsomely decorated Coast Guard Academy gymnasium on the North Shore, and a big summer festival, called *Star Night*, with a slight "show biz" flavor at the Belmont Racetrack. Jeanne Vanderbilt chaired *Star Night*, and Mike Todd and Elizabeth Taylor arranged the theater. All of the top performers worked as volunteers. Lena Horne, one of the all-time great singers and a personal favorite of Tex's, was a regular for several years. Spinney Hill Road is now known as Community Drive—and Jock's polo fields became part of what is known as the North Shore–Long Island Jewish Hospital.

Tex seemed to know everybody—and although he had many good ideas of his own, was at his best putting the right combination of people together to bring an idea to fruition. Always forward thinking, Tex thought big, but recognized that the pieces of the puzzle had to be put together to complete the picture. Although he and Jinx were frantically busy, he was always willing to take on a new project—sometimes to the detriment of personal relationships, and almost always to his own finances—because deep within him he saw things that he felt "needed to be done" for the greater good of society, and, basically, he didn't like to say "no."

Chapter Eleven

Korea: The Forgotten War: MacArthur and Truman

The prevailing impression of Truman today seems to be that of a man of limited background and experience who, nevertheless, evolved into greatness as President. To Tex it seemed ironic, even perverse, that this elevation of esteem has come about as the result of a forced decision, made overnight, by President Truman in 1948—a decision which Truman did not want to make, one which ran contrary to his prior personal and political beliefs.

Tex had been in the war in Italy when Roosevelt died in April 1945 and Truman became President. His impression of Truman was derived almost entirely from Baruch, who described Truman as a kind of political "accident." He said that in 1944 Roosevelt was alert to the growing national concern over Communist influence, particularly in labor unions, whose voting support was critical for a Roosevelt reelection, but Roosevelt did not want to appear to be too dependant upon them. Therefore, it was important for Roosevelt to appear to move more toward the center. Roosevelt's sitting Vice-President, Henry Wallace, a brilliant scientist in agricultural genetics, but a man with left-wing associations, was more than Roosevelt wanted to carry into the election. So Roosevelt distanced himself publicly from the vice-presidential process, asserting that he would accept whatever choice the Party determined at the convention. Although Wallace led by a wide margin in the Vice-Presidential public polls, a bunch of competing state and local politicians in a backroom in Kansas City eventually compromised their differences by agreeing on Harry Truman.

Truman was then an obscure, second-tier Senator from Missouri, a hanger-on of the famously corrupt Pendergast political machine in Kansas City, a man who had not attended college, whom Roosevelt scarcely knew and who had no popular public support outside Missouri. Baruch told Tex that after the election, Roosevelt proceeded to ignore Truman, keeping him in his office in the Capitol, and seldom including him in White House meetings. When Roosevelt died in May of 1945, two months into his fourth term, Truman had apparently not been fully briefed on Roosevelt's February meeting with Stalin at Yalta, had only the most fleeting knowledge of a new military weapon, the Atom bomb, and was obviously ill-equipped to make informed decisions on the future role of the United States in Europe or Asia.

Baruch regarded Truman essentially as a man of conventional southern politics, narrow, clannish, suspicious, ignorant of large and complex national issues, far too hasty and impulsive in his decisions. He had surrounded himself with his old "cronies," a seedy bunch generally, particularly Harry Vaughan whom Truman had commissioned a brigadier general in the Army, and had made his personal aide—and who, along with other hangers-on, was soon involved in a variety of sordid "five-percent" kickback deals. Tex recalled that when General Eaker was briefing him for his mission to the Pacific, Eaker had mentioned Air Force concern that Truman had taken as his Naval aide an adroit, highly intelligent and ambitious young lawyer from Truman's home state, Clark Clifford, whom the Air Force regarded as a "snake in the grass" who would do anything to advance himself. Eaker's prediction proved accurate, as Clifford later rose to a position of great influence and political power in Washington for many years, until his later role in the Bank of Commerce and Credit bank scandal, his self-serving manipulation of Pamela Harriman's estate, and other unsavory matters, ultimately led to his disgrace.

However, in his role as Truman's chief political advisor, Clark Clifford was regarded as the architect of Truman's clever, come-from-behind 1948 Presidential campaign. Later, it came to light that Jim Rowe, an influential and highly respected White House lawyer for Roosevelt, had written and delivered to the White House a lengthy, detailed plan for Truman's election campaign, titled "The Election of 1948." In the memo, Rowe highlighted critical steps necessary to Truman's election: develop a strong stand against Russian aggression in Europe; satisfy the Jewish vote on the issue of Palestine; court the northern black vote, not only because it tended to vote as a block, but also because of its geographic concentration, it could affect the outcome in key states with large Electoral College votes, New York, Illinois, Pennsylvania, Ohio, and Michigan; purge himself of his tainted cronies; avoid all appearances as a "politician;" get out of Washington, travel around the country—and blame high prices and all consumer issues on the Republican-controlled Congress.

Truman adopted Rowe's recommendations—but Truman did not receive that memo from Rowe. Clifford read the President's mail before Truman, and apparently the contents of Rowe's memo were forwarded to Truman under Clifford's name. When the substitution was later discovered, Clifford justified it on the grounds that he knew that Truman had a grudge against Rowe's law partner, Tommy "the Cork" Corcoran and, because of his anger at Corcoran, Truman might not read the important document from Corcoran's partner.

In any case, the armed forces were integrated into a single Department of Defense in 1947 and Tex was pleased that the Air Force finally achieved its long-sought independence from subordination to the Army. Stuart Symington was named the as first Secretary of The Air Force, while James Forrestal, a naval aviator in World War I, was named as the first Secretary of Defense—however, he was soon incapacitated by a serious mental illness, which eventually led to his suicide, jumping from his Fitzsimons's hospital room. Truman then gave that critical position to Truman's chief political fundraiser, Louis Johnson, a man who seemed to have little other apparent qualification for the position. While the Department of Defense constituted a prospective organizational benefit, it did not improve the condition of the military. The defense budget, which had totaled $81 billion in 1945, had shrunk to $13 billion by 1947—and remained at this level through 1950.

Then, Truman's appointment of the revered General George Marshall as Secretary of State was to be the high mark of his Presidency. Marshall recruited an outstanding group of dedicated assistants, generally regarded as the most talented group of policy advisers ever assembled, who came to be known as the "Wise Men." Among them were Tex's friends, Bob Lovett and Averill Harriman, along with John McCloy, Charles Bohlen, George Kennan and Dean Acheson. Together, this group brought about a reversal of America's long-standing policy of isolation with new programs, the first of which was announced by Secretary of State Marshall in a graduation address at Harvard in June of 1947, the establishment of a massive economic aid program for Europe, which came to be known as *The Marshall Plan.* This was followed by *The Truman Doctrine,* a declaration of U. S. support for any nation threatened by Soviet expansion, a result of the Soviet takeovers of Czechoslovakia and the murder of Czech Prime Minister Ian Masaryk of Romania, the Soviet military invasion of Hungary, and pending threats to Greece and Turkey.

Then, on May 14, 1948, Truman made a most fateful decision. He recognized the existence of a new Jewish state in Israel. The announcement was made from the White House. Baruch told Tex that Truman's decision resulted from a contentious White House meeting where Secretary of State Marshall protested Clifford's presence, asserting that the meeting was solely a matter of foreign policy, not a matter of domestic politics and, therefore Clifford, the President's political campaign advisor, should not be present. Truman seemingly ignored Marshall's protest. Clifford took over the meeting and argued for the immediate, unilateral recognition of the Jewish state. Marshall responded that any such action was premature, that there was nothing to qualify for such action, no Jewish state existed, no government had been formed, no boundaries established. Further, any U.S. action should be taken in coordination with Great Britain, and other countries. He argued that the decision, if handled impetuously, and obviously for domestic political reasons in connection with the imminent 1948 election, would lead to lasting international difficulty. Truman, once again, ignored Marshall and followed Clifford. The result was a single sentence statement, corrected in long hand, issued from the White House, without contact with the State Department, Congress, or any other department of government.

In the summer of 1948 Truman effected the integration of black troops into the Army by an Executive Order of the President, rather than permitting the matter to go before Congress and face contentious delays. The practical effect was to begin the shift of the black vote from the Republican Party to the Democratic Party. Despite these significant steps, Truman had little public support before the 1948 election. His polls were in the thirty percent range, and falling. Accordingly, the Republican Party leaders thought anyone could beat him. They persisted in their habit of pushing a "dependable" candidate—one who could be counted on to do the Party's bidding—and they nominated the two-time loser, Tom Dewey, whom Tex and his friends had knocked out of the nomination with "We Want Willkie" at the 1940 Republican Convention in Philadelphia, and who had been smothered by Roosevelt in 1944. Nevertheless, even such a small-caliber candidate as Dewey was heavily favored, and appeared to have the election in hand.

Tex couldn't understand it, but Baruch told him it was important to recognize the existing political reality. At that time there were effectively four political parties in America: a moderate Democratic Party, liberal and international in outlook; and a narrowly conservative Southern Democratic Party, regional in outlook, and devoted to the racist traditions of the Confederacy, thinly disguised as "States' Rights." Republicans were similarly divided: a moderate Republican Party, national and international in outlook, based largely in the northeast and upper midwest; and a conservative Republican Party, in the Farm Belt and the west, with local concerns, small town businesses, and with a strong isolationist outlook. As a practical matter (and the result of the demographic distortions of the Electoral College) a functional coalition of conservative "states' rights" Southern Democrats and small-town conservative Republicans had controlled Congress for more than thirty years.

The Democratic National Committee tried desperately to keep the divided elements of the Democratic Party cobbled together, but the divisive elements were too strong. A far-left Democratic splinter group formed around Henry Wallace. Angry at Roosevelt's firing him from the Vice Presidency in 1944 in favor of Truman, Wallace had become a strong advocate of left-wing causes and started a new party, the "Progressive Citizens of America." Moderate Democrats rallied around Hubert Humphrey, the progressive young mayor of Minneapolis and staunch advocate of a strong human rights plank—which was bitterly opposed by the racist Southern Democrats. The Democratic National Committee, with strong Southern influence, made it clear to Humphrey that his future in the Democratic Party depended on his support for a weak, weasel-worded civil rights platform carried forward from the 1944 convention.

Humphrey regarded this as a "sell-out." After agonizing reappraisal, and long after midnight at the Philadelphia Convention, Humphrey rose to speak, the shortest speech of his long-winded life, eight minutes, rising to his passionate summation, "There are those who say that we are rushing civil rights; I say we are one hundred seventy-two years too late. The time has come for the Democratic Party to get out of the shadow of "States' Rights," and to walk forthrightly into the bright sunlight of "Civil Rights."

The Convention was swept up with enthusiasm, and endorsed a strong civil rights platform. Truman, in the White House, his traditional southern "States' Rights" convictions violated, allegedly called Humphrey a "crack-pot." But he slept on it—and recognized that Humphrey had opened the only possible path to his reelection. Truman came to Philadelphia and accepted the Humphrey platform. The conservative Southern Democrats bolted the party, formed a new "States' Rights" Party, called themselves "Dixiecrats," and nominated Senator Strom Thurmond of South Carolina for President.

Rather than fight the disparate wings of his party, Truman seized the opportunity to take the fight to the Republicans. He recalled the Republican-controlled Congress—otherwise planning to take the rest of the summer off for their own campaigns—back into session, and challenged them to address pending Democratic legislative proposals. He "barnstormed" around the country by train, speaking at every whistle stop. He ignored his Presidential opponent and lambasting Republicans, the famous "Give 'em hell, Harry" campaign—a relentless attack upon the "Do-Nothing Republican Congress."

The election was razor-close. The *Chicago Tribune* ran a famous banner headline, DEWEY DEFEATS TRUMAN, and other morning newspapers ran similar headlines. However, when the final votes were counted, Truman had won a narrow, but remarkable, come-from-behind victory over the complacent, over-confident Dewey. Initially, Tex was surprised at the outcome, but later came to understand, far more than he realized at the time, that Truman's change of political position was to shift the base of the Democratic party from racist repression to the party of civil rights. And this change was to determine much of the political future of the country. Following his election, Truman focused on meeting the continued Soviet advances in Europe. Thanks to the *"Marshall Plan"* and the work of the *"Wise Men,"* the North Atlantic Treaty Organization passed Congress with overwhelming bipartisan support. In 1949 Dean Acheson succeeded the retiring George Marshall as Secretary of State.

Meanwhile, there was concern over what was going on in Asia. The State Department—anticipating a takeover of China by Mao's Communist government—issued a White Paper on China, in effect placing the blame on the corruption of Chiang Kai-shek's Nationalist government. The response indicated the level of public confusion—as well as inconsistency. Polls showed that only twenty-six percent approved of Chiang as the leader of China; only twenty-three percent of Americans expected that China could escape the Communist takeover—and seventy percent believed that there was nothing that the U.S. could do about it But the American people, demonstrating inherent political perversity, simultaneously disapproved of the White Paper by fifty-three percent to twenty-three percent.

Chiang fled to Formosa with his relatives, the Soong family—taking with him the assets of the Bank of China and the art of the National Museum. Right wing Republicans and "Asia-Firsters" like Senator Bill Knowland, owner of the *Oakland Tribune*, took up the cry, "Who lost China?" It seemed obvious that Chiang had lost China—but reflecting a general sense that things in the Truman Administration were out of control, the "Who lost" charge caught public attention, was adopted by Republicans—and became all the more virulent when the Republican junior senator from Wisconsin, Joe McCarthy, waved a paper which he said contained the names of two hundred five State Department employees who were members of the Communist Party. Although McCarthy's charges were later to be totally discredited, the virus of "McCarthyism"—pandering to the most ignorant and prejudiced people—was to poison American politics for many years.

In January 1950, Secretary of State Acheson delivered a major speech at the National Press Club in Washington, declaring that the defense perimeter of the United States extended from the Aleutians to Japan to the Philippines, specifically excluding Korea and Formosa. The North Koreans took Acheson at his word, and invaded South Korea six months later, on June 25, 1950, another Sunday morning, just like Pearl Harbor. Both MacArthur, the theater Commander, and the Truman Administration, were taken totally by surprise—and both were totally unprepared.

Five years had passed since Tex had been exposed to MacArthur's imperial ambitions, and unpleasant memories came flooding back. Tex had watched with increasing concern and dismay as President Truman, Secretary of State Acheson, and the Joint Chiefs of Staff, had focused their attentions on Europe, while seemingly mesmerized by MacArthur, had permitted him virtual personal control over Japan and America's role in Asia. Less than a week before the North Korean invasion, MacArthur had confirmed to John Foster Dulles, then in Tokyo as an advisor in connection with the drafting of the final Japanese peace agreement, what he had repeatedly reported to the Truman Administration, that there were no military risks in the area, things were well in hand, there was nothing to be concerned about.

Upon receiving news of the North Korean invasion, Acheson phoned Truman, then at home in Missouri. An immediate response was required—and there were no plans. Although the Constitution places the power to make war in the Congress, that route risked long delays. Instead, Acheson recommended bypassing Congress and going immediately to the United Nations, then in session. Truman agreed and, while Truman was returning to Washington, Acheson was able to obtain a U. N. Resolution (the Russians were fortunately absent from the U. N. meeting) condemning the North Korean invasion and appointing General MacArthur as Commander of all U. N. forces. Acting in his new authority as U. N. commander, MacArthur immediately committed U.S. troops. Upon the North Korean invasion, the South Korean army had collapsed, and American troops in South Korea were driven to a tiny perimeter at the southern end of the Korean peninsula at Pusan. The situation was critical. An American Dunkirk—like humiliation loomed.

All of Tex's doubts from five years before, about MacArthur and his grandiosity returned. He wanted to get over there and see for himself what was going on. But first he wanted to talk to Baruch, who was just as upset as Tex. Baruch said they should meet with General Eisenhower, then President of Columbia University, and get his thoughts. They met with Eisenhower at the president's home at Columbia, and he, too, was deeply concerned about the situation. He knew all about MacArthur's arrogant behavior in the Pacific—he had endured several tough years as MacArthur's aide in the Philippines in the 1930s—and he had grave doubts about Truman's ability to control MacArthur. He said he thought it was a good idea for Tex to go over there, but Eisenhower cautioned, "This is a different kind of war; a limited war with no clear strategy or objective. It will be a lieutenant's war, not a general's war. Cover it at the platoon level, go out on patrols."

It would be pointless for Tex to apply for correspondent status with the Army. MacArthur had kept all his old sycophants, Generals Willoughby and Whitney, and they wouldn't have forgotten him. Instead, he called some friends and asked to be accredited with the Navy, so he could hook up with the Marines and go into Korea under Navy jurisdiction, outside MacArthur's direct authority. Meanwhile, Tex asked his television listeners for the names and military units of boys in Korea, and said he would try to look them up, get them on tape, then get the tapes back to Jinx for their program.

Before Tex arrived, MacArthur had pulled off a daring amphibious landing on September 15, 1950, at Inchon on the west coast of Korea. It was the kind of spectacular high risk/high reward maneuver MacArthur needed to overcome his failure to maintain proper surveillance before the North Korean invasion. The Joint Chiefs were unhappy at the risks of the Inchon landing—thirty-foot high tides, fast moving across nearly impassible wide mud flats—but MacArthur was provided with large forces, three hundred twenty ships, four aircraft carriers, and seventy thousand troops. In September the First Marine Division executed the difficult landing successfully. Seoul was quickly recaptured, the North Korean troops in the south were cut off, and the U. S. forces at Pusan were out of danger. MacArthur claimed personal credit for the victory. The United States public was thrilled at the apparent rapid turn of events from the seemingly desperate prospect at Pusan only three months before. But the old pattern of inconsistencies in MacArthur's decisions continued.

MacArthur's orders from Truman and the Joint Chiefs were to "restore the borders of South Korea." Once Army troops and equipment were ashore at Inchon, MacArthur ordered the Marines, who had carried out the assault landing, to board their ships, sail around the bottom of the Korean peninsula and stage a landing on the eastern shore of North Korea. In this, MacArthur had committed a classic military blunder. He had divided his forces, placing the Army on the west and the Marines on the east, separated by a major mountain range, virtually impassible in the approaching winter, and without effective coordination between them. The Army and the Marines each reported separately to MacArthur in Tokyo where MacArthur was out of touch with reality in Korea, and out of control from Washington. Regardless, MacArthur ordered the Marines to advance into North Korea. Northern Korea is mountainous, an area of precipitous peaks, a few primitive roads, with blizzards and ferociously cold winters. The Marines were still in their summer uniforms when they landed in early October—and they had just begun to move north by the time Tex caught up to them.

Meanwhile, concern grew over MacArthur's decisions and the divided U.S. forces. In Washington, President Truman, who had not been overseas, other than brief National Guard service in France in World War I, decided to fly to meet MacArthur on October 15th on Wake Island in the Pacific. Apparently, nothing was decided at the meeting. MacArthur was not restrained. Historians have no adequate explanations. Truman's approval ratings in the polls were below 30%, and falling, and Congressional elections in America were only three weeks away.

To cover his blatant disregard of orders from the Joint Chiefs to limit his activities to the South Korean border, after his return from Wake Island, MacArthur ordered the Marines to attack up to the Chinese border on the Yalu river, and declared, "I'll have the boys home by Thanksgiving." Apparently not wishing to disparage what appeared to be an imminent victory—the Joint Chiefs issued new, but ambiguous orders to MacArthur, authorizing him to "destroy the North Korean military forces," but an order carrying with it the requirement that all U.S. forces stop well short of the Chinese border, and to remain clear of any contact with the North Koreans. Only South Korean troops, or troops of other nations, were to approach the Chinese border.

When Tex arrived, he hooked up with the First Marine Division and, for all of his admiration for the Army troops he had known, the Marines were special. He talked his way into the good graces of the pilot of an old B-25 to give him an aerial view of the country and he crawled up into the plexiglas nose for the best view. The Northern part of Korea is a mass of high mountains, crisscrossing ranges, steep cliffs, virtually no roads, terrible weather conditions. It seemed inconceivable to him that a commander who had seen this terrain would have sent his men where MacArthur ordered the First Marine Division. But the Marines pressed on, in bloody battles, in frightful conditions, cold in their summer uniforms, virtually without transport, without close air cover, clawing their way across treacherous mountain ranges barely passable, especially in the rapidly deteriorating winter weather.

Tex interviewed individual marines on tape, took photographs, and sent them back to Jinx to put on the program, with the boy's parents, wife, or girlfriend present, if possible. And he followed Ike's advice, that "this was a lieutenant's war, go out on patrols." It was a new experience for him—frightening, and one which reinforced his admiration for the Marines. They patrolled at night, preferably without moonlight, not knowing if, when, or where they might be hit by the hidden enemy, where every sound triggered a flash of fear. He was fired on often, once highlighted by Chinese flares and pinned down under a mortar barrage. In a tank for the first time, Tex went out leading a patrol. Under fire, the tank took a direct hit. He was seated behind the driver and the turret gunner. Both were wounded, but Tex, lucky yet again, had just a few nicks, and some holes in his uniform. As he recalled them, those patrols seemed worse in many ways than his airplane combat missions in World War II. At least those missions were in daylight when everything seems easier if you can see. In addition, on missions in the air, the crew knew where they were, and when they were most likely to face combat. However bloody, it was fairly predictable, and relatively brief. On the line in Korea, it was dangerous everywhere, all the time.

The platoon leaders Tex was with were mostly just out of college, all volunteers, many from Yale, little prepared what they were getting into. The company commanders he met were mostly "retreads" from World War II, many recalled from families with children—they were there because they were Marines. He admired them all. As the Marines approached the Yalu River, the border of China, there were indications of increased Chinese military activity. The Indian government forwarded to Washington strong messages from China, warning that the Yalu was the border of their country, with important Chinese dams, electrical and manufacturing facilities on the river, which froze solidly in winter, permitting easy crossing of tanks and military equipment. China was unwilling to accept the presence of a potentially hostile foreign army on the opposite shore. Squadrons of Russian MIG fighters in Chinese markings arrived on the large military airfields across the river. Advance Marine patrols picked up prisoners speaking Chinese. All this was reported to MacArthur in Tokyo. Later, Tex learned that in spite of continued warnings from India, and other nations, advising Washington of the increasing Chinese anger, and the prospect of direct intervention, warnings passed on to MacArthur, he replied that he was fully informed, and confident that no threat existed from the Chinese.

Tex could still picture MacArthur, as he was in Manila in his Imperial Hotel Headquarters in 1945, surrounded by his lackeys, Whitney, his chief of staff, and Willoughby, in charge of intelligence, both telling him only what they knew he wanted to hear—making one of his dramatic briefings to correspondents, eager aides carefully unfurling large maps, MacArthur striding to the easel, saying, "I shall strike here," as he rapped his swagger stick on the map. All a fantasy, detached from reality. No one spoke the truth around MacArthur. In Tokyo, correspondents only learned what they were told—and, just as they had in the Pacific during World War II, MacArthur's censors controlled the release of information.

Advance units of Marines reached the Yalu River on Thanksgiving Day, 1950. A few days later, two hundred fifty thousand Chinese troops attacked the forward elements of Marines, whose equipment and support was strung out in a tiny trickle across treacherous mountains. On the west coast of Korea, the South Korean troops were panicked by the Chinese invasion and ran, followed by the U. S. Eighth Army. A sorry episode.

Tex could hardly describe the terrible conditions he saw facing the Marines. Some froze to death in their sleeping bags. Others, unable to get out of their sleeping bags in time, had been bayoneted by Chinese soldiers in sudden night attacks. Facing disaster, the First Marine Division began a remarkable military maneuver, its achievement not fully recognized because "retreat" is not an accepted word in the Marine vocabulary. In tightly disciplined fashion, the Marines fell back, one unit defending while a second withdrew through it, to take up a new defense position; then the first unit withdrew through the second to take up still another new line of defense. A difficult, brilliantly executed, courageous, disciplined achievement under appalling conditions. Facing fearful odds, the Marines marched out, carrying their dead, corpses frozen stiff, piled like cordwood. Tex saw only parts of this historic maneuver, but he shuddered whenever he thought about it.

Confronted with the magnitude of the disaster facing him, MacArthur responded by demanding more troops, four new divisions—the total U.S. strength at the time was ten divisions—and the U.S. had heavy commitments in Europe, where they were threatened by more than eighty Soviet divisions. Conditions in Korea were increasingly desperate. Tex saw a quagmire facing our forces—and had a total lack of confidence in MacArthur.

After the American retreat from the Yalu River at end of November 1950, the Korean war was stalemated. As a practical matter, MacArthur's leadership had failed, and it seemed inescapable that Truman should have removed him from command. But, ever grandiose, MacArthur spoke of invading China, using Chiang Kai-shek's Chinese troops from Formosa—and of using the Atom bomb When Truman was asked about MacArthur's threats to use the Atom bomb on China, he replied that as a theater commander MacArthur had the choice of weapons. How could Truman delegate such power to that megalomaniac! The Joint Chiefs, everybody in Washington knew what kind of a man MacArthur was, yet Truman and the Joint Chiefs left him in command for five more months of pointless bloodshed from December 1950 until April 1951. What were they afraid of? What could they all have been thinking? Finally, the military and political pressures became too much, MacArthur was relieved of his command and ordered home in April 1951. MacArthur wrote a letter to Congress declaring, "There is no substitute for victory"—and he instantly became the favored presidential candidate of the right wing of the Republican Party for 1952.

Truman ordered the war to stabilize at the 38th Parallel, and began efforts toward peace negotiations. Both sides were obstinate and the North Koreans would not agree to anything while Truman remained as President. As a result, the war dragged on for two more years, with casualties steadily mounting, ultimately nearly doubling the total casualties of the Korean War to fifty-eight thousand American dead.

Tex came back from Korea—outraged—and poured out his anger to Baruch—a furious castigation of MacArthur, of Truman, of the Joint Chiefs' timid, vacillating, hesitant treatment of MacArthur, his egregious, willful misjudgments, his folly in dividing his forces, his ignoring of intelligence and weather conditions, his outright insubordination of orders not to have U. S. forces approach the Yalu River—all of which had so blindly, senselessly, sacrificed so many gallant soldiers and Marines. Tex had seen enough bad decisions in World War II, but nothing seemed to him as bad as Truman leaving MacArthur and his sycophants in power.

Was anybody in charge? At the White House? At the Pentagon? And Congress! What were they thinking? Where was any leadership? All in all, a shameful lack of responsible government!

Chapter Twelve

"I Like Ike"

"It's time for you to talk to Ike, tell him what you've told me," Baruch concluded after Tex described what he had seen in Korea and his opinion of the Truman Administration's handling of the war. He said that Tex should meet him in Paris later in the spring and they would talk to Ike together. Baruch spent his summers in Europe and Eisenhower had returned to active duty as Commander of NATO after the outbreak of the Korean War.

Eisenhower and Baruch were old friends. In the late 1930s, Baruch had picked out Eisenhower as a promising young major, had befriended him, and they had stayed in touch over the years. Baruch said that Ike understood that there were many Americans who didn't much like what either Party had become—and they especially didn't like what they saw now at the top of either party, Truman, or Taft, whom the Republican state party bosses had picked up after backing three losing efforts with Dewey. The people in this country want a President they feel they know and trust, a true leader of the nation, not a figurehead of the special interests of either Party. There's a disconnect in the country between "Party People" and the rest of the country. That's true for both parties, but it's worse for the Republicans.

Baruch continued, saying that Ike had all these Republican Party people, kingmakers and hopefuls, the people who live off the party system, whispering in his ear. But that's not what he wants to hear. The Republican Party is too backward-looking for Ike. Taft and the Republican "Old Guard" have this crazy dream of repealing the New Deal. If Ike's going to be President, he wants the country behind him, the Real People. He doesn't want to seem to be in the pockets of the Party People. Remember, he is a military man, a strategic thinker. He said that Tex would have to show him a plan.

Tex knew what to do. A kickoff with a big rally in New York, well before the Republican Convention, independent of the Republican National Committee and the Party People, welcoming Independents and Democrats disillusioned by Truman's handling of MacArthur and the Korean war. He knew where to begin to look for independent support in the states. He and Jinx had met Eisenhower in Berlin in 1948 when they were part of a Bob Hope Christmas road show for the men who were keeping

Berlin alive with the Berlin Airlift. Eisenhower had come to the show and he had asked them to spend some time with him afterward.

Tex was then head of the Air Force Public Affairs Squadron—known as the "Iron Gate" Squadron because they met at the iron-gated restaurant, "21"—and he was asked to arrange and serve as master of ceremonies at a New York rally for the Air Force Association, a newly-formed national body of Air Force veterans and supporters, aircraft manufacturing corporations, etc. It was called the Air Force "Wing-Ding" and Tex asked General Eisenhower, recently named president of Columbia University, to be the honored guest. The Air Force rally filled Madison Square Garden, and Tex had taken the state chairmen back to "21" for a few drinks afterwards. All agreed that Truman was discredited by Korea, cronyism and corruption. The country needed a new leader—Ike. Later, the Navy asked Tex to give an event for the Navy League, an organization similar to the Air Force Association. Tex's brother, Douglas, a decorated Navy carrier pilot in the Pacific, was a leader of the organization, so Tex really couldn't say no. Another Madison Square Garden rally, then the chairmen back to "21", and the same unanimous support for Eisenhower for President—of either party! These men had put their lives at risk for their country, had seen more of the world, and knew that new leadership was required, and Tex knew where to call for commitments from all over the country.

He and Jinx met Baruch in Paris early in June 1951 and they visited Eisenhower in his apartment on the Champs-Élysées in the late afternoon. Perhaps suspecting their purpose, Eisenhower received them in a rather casual, off-hand manner, putting golf balls into a highball glass lying on the carpet. They exchanged pleasantries, while Eisenhower continued to stroke his putts. At a pause, Baruch came directly to the point, "Ike, at the Republican Convention next summer, you will be nominated for President—and you will win. Tex will explain."

Surprised by Baruch's sudden opening, Tex said, "It will begin in early 1952 with a well-publicized "Citizens for Eisenhower" rally which will fill Madison Square Garden. The theme will be, "I Like Ike." It will be even bigger than the Air Force "Wing-Ding" that Jinx and I put on in 1948 and that you attended. The American people are fed up with both political parties. They want a leader they feel they know and trust to end the war in Korea and deal with Russian threat of Communism in Europe. The rally will be keyed to the first Republican state primary, in New Hampshire, and while directed to the Republican Convention, it will be a "Citizens" campaign, independent of the Republican National Committee, and will reach out to include independents and disaffected Democrats, all voters disgusted with both parties."

While Tex was speaking, Eisenhower stopped his putting, sat down, laid his putter across his knees, and began to listen intently. Tex told him that he had gone to Texas, collected some Texas friends at the Shamrock Hotel and raised $200,000 dollars for expenses, then he persuaded other friends at Madison Square Garden to give him the Garden after the paying customers at a prize fight had left. Tex outlined the schedule of primaries, told him of the state support shown in his Air Force Association and Navy League rallies. He finished up with the associated "Citizens" plan leading up to the Republican Convention.

When he finished, Jinx asked one of what Tex called her "off-the-wall" questions—they always drove him crazy at their interruption—but she had the kind of intuition that made the "wrong" question be exactly the right question. Jinx said, "Why do you let them talk to you about politics like this? You've done so much for the country already." Tex wanted to wring her neck. But Eisenhower looked at her, rose slowly from his chair, walked to a table nearby, picked up a picture of his grandson and said, "For him."

Eisenhower then turned and said, "I'm going to get Mamie. Will you repeat what you told me? I want her to hear it." Mamie came in and sat quietly as Tex repeated his story. Eisenhower stood up and said, "That's very impressive. Thank you for coming." Baruch, Jinx and Tex said their goodbyes and went on to dinner. Baruch seemed very pleased. "That went very well. Now you've got your orders. You know what to do next."

When he returned to New York, Tex told Jock Whitney about Eisenhower's reaction to the meeting in Paris. Jock was delighted and set out to pass the word discreetly in suitable circles—while Tex alerted key people from the Air Force and Navy meetings at "21." Jock was a member of Augusta National, the famous Georgia golf club, home of the "Masters" Tournament, whose membership included perhaps the largest single collection of high-powered business leaders in America, dominated by the autocratic co-founder (with Bobby Jones) and powerful perennial chairman, Clifford Roberts, a New York investment manager. Part of Roberts' concept was to attract prominent national figures to membership—and he had begun to recruit Eisenhower right after the war, arranging a special guest membership for him, where Eisenhower became a very popular and regular visitor (the club later built "Mamie's Cottage" for him on the club grounds). Jock told Roberts, already an Eisenhower enthusiast, of Tex's meeting in Paris, and interest rapidly developed at Augusta.

[Author's Footnote: I worked in the Eisenhower Administration as a Special Assistant to the Secretary of Commerce, at the end of the Eisenhower Presidency, and with his introduction, I became Cliff Roberts' assistant in investment management in New York. Roberts told me that there were serious concerns arising from of the fact Truman had written Eisenhower, offering to step aside in 1948 if Eisenhower would run as a Democrat, and therefore many Republicans were concerned that Eisenhower was not a Republican. Roberts and Bill Robinson, President of the *New York Herald Tribune*, went to Paris to ask the question. Eisenhower replied that when General Marshall reached down through hundreds of senior officers to promote Eisenhower to senior commands before World War II, Marshall told him that the one thing which could destroy his military career would be any party affiliation or involvement in organized political activity—and, as a serving officer, Eisenhower continued to hold to that position. Seeing Robinson's face fall, Roberts quickly interjected, "Ike, let me ask you this. Do you think that, as a nation, we should try to grow the size of the economic pie, or fight over the size of the pieces?" Eisenhower answered, "That's easy. Growth is the only way to keep the American Dream alive for our growing population. You can't keep adding taxes endlessly without killing growth. You have to lead from the center."

Roberts turned to Robinson and said, "Well, Bill, that's good enough for me. He's clearly a Republican. Let's go." The Augusta group developed rapidly. Bill Robinson became the most visible figure, while Cliff Roberts operated more behind the scene. I asked Roberts how he had arranged the early Eisenhower financing, and he said that he had billed the Augusta members a "special assessment" on their club accounts. Roberts' word was law at Augusta.]

Leading Republican figures, seeing which way the Eisenhower wind was blowing, were eager to take positions for themselves, but Baruch, who had followed developments closely, warned Tex against the involvement of Republican political figures saying that they would all just jockey for position, elbow each other, make endless trouble. Baruch was right, as usual. Governor Dewey assertively pursued a role—but he had a mixed record with Eisenhower. Before he gave up on his ambitions for a possible third try for the Presidency, Dewey had tried, not too subtly, to influence Eisenhower away from thoughts of running. Later, he visited Eisenhower with suggestions that Eisenhower should run. Eisenhower was not impressed.

As word of the "Citizens" activities spread, Senator Henry Cabot Lodge of Massachusetts went to Paris in the fall of 1951 and told Eisenhower that it was time for professional Republican political party involvement in the "Citizens" effort. Eisenhower responded that as NATO commander he felt himself barred from any political connection. Thereafter, Lodge gathered a group of major corporate and financial figures in New York City, including Eisenhower's close friend, retired General Lucius Clay, then Chairman of the Continental Can Corporation; Governor Dewey and his lawyer, Herb Brownell; economist-banker Gabe Hauge; banker Winthrop Aldrich; fund-raiser Harold Talbott; Sig Larmon, head of the powerful advertising firm of Young & Rubicam, along with Jock Whitney, and several others. Lodge made the pitch that the "Citizens" effort needed a politically experienced leader, and he made it clear that he was available for the job.

Jock called with the news of the meeting, and said that, as Tex had feared, the group had agreed that Lodge could serve as chairman. Tex hated the idea of Lodge, a sitting Republican senator, and such a group of powerful New York corporate executives, financiers and even an advertising man, inserting themselves as representing the "Citizens" effort. Jock told Tex that, rather than have a divisive fight, the better course was to accept Lodge as, hopefully, the least doctrinaire of the Party People (and not apparently harboring secret presidential thoughts of his own, at least for that election) as co-chairman of the rally. Tex called Baruch, who predicted that things would not go smoothly. Before long, the political figures, Governors Dewey and Stassen, couldn't stand each other, and the fundraisers, eager for recognition, were intensely jealous, Talbott of Aldrich, Aldrich of Jock, etc., etc.

Tex had been working with Jackie Cochran as chair of the committee. She had an impressive record as a business person and Tex had met her years before when she was working for Bernie Gimbel's then wife, Sophie, as manager of Sophie's salon in Saks Fifth Avenue, where Jackie met Floyd Odlum, Wall Street financier, head of Atlas Corporation, with extensive aviation interests. While Odlum's wife was trying on dresses, Jackie told Odlum that she was working to save money to take flying lessons.

Odlum said he thought he could arrange it. In due course Odlum married Jackie. She became a famous aviatrix, won several national races, including setting a national speed record in an Air Corps P-35 fighter that Floyd had bought for her. She went on to organize and command the distinguished Woman's Air Service Pilot Corps ("WASPS") during World War II. They were prohibited from flying in combat, but they flew all the latest combat aircraft to advanced bases, flying at least as well, and frequently better than the male pilots. They were famous for faster trans-continental deliveries than the men, who seemed to like to spend more nights on the way. Jackie was a loyal trooper as well as a great executive, and she proved essential to the success of the "Citizens" effort.

The Eisenhower Madison Square Garden rally came off even better than Tex could have hoped. There were "I LIKE IKE" signs everywhere. After the audience at a prizefight had left, the Garden had filled, as he had promised Eisenhower, with eighteen thousand people inside, and many thousands standing outside on the street listening on loudspeakers. The event was covered on radio and television, with extensive national coverage as well. Orchestra leader Fred Waring led off with "The Battle Hymn of the Republic." Various celebrities followed, among them, Clark Gable (making his first appearance on TV), Humphrey Bogart, Lauren Bacall, Jinx (in tennis whites, hitting "I Like Ike" tennis balls into the crowd). Then a forklift placed a piano in the prize ring, and Richard Rodgers played while Mary Martin, on a telephone hook-up from London where she was doing *South Pacific,* sang "I'm in Love with a Wonderful Guy—Ike." Lodge delivered the keynote speech from the prize ring, and the rally ended with Irving Berlin leading the audience in singing his "God Bless America."

Tex had arranged for Spyros Skouras, head of Twentieth-Century-Fox, to film the rally and Jackie Cochran flew the film to Paris and showed it to Ike and Mamie. Jackie told Tex that they watched attentively, obviously deeply moved. At the film's end, Ike said, "Let's have a drink." Jackie stood, raised her glass and said, "To the President." Ike's eyes teared up, and he said, "Go back and tell them I'll do it."

Tex didn't know it at the time, but Jackie's delivery of the Madison Square Garden Rally tape to Eisenhower came at a most fortuitous moment. Just before her arrival, Senator Taft and former President Herbert Hoover, along with sixteen other "Old Guard" Republicans isolationists had released a letter demanding the recall of all United States troops from Europe—totally undercutting NATO, and all that to which Eisenhower was committed. Eisenhower had led an Allied army that had won the war against Hitler and he was dedicated to the idea that the United States should not abandon the opportunity of leadership for future peace. To Eisenhower, the Taft-Hoover letter was further evidence that he could not be comfortable with the country in the hands of the narrow, inward-oriented, turn-back-the-clock Taft Republicans.

In America, the President serves both as the head of state and as the chief of a political party. To the Party People, the latter role generally seems paramount. However, the President is, first and foremost, the leader of the nation. The American people are essentially positive by nature, and they are uncomfortable not liking their President. From his mentors, Brisbane and Baruch, as well as the best commanders

Jackie Cochran, Jinx, and Tex at Madison Square Garden

D D E

Supreme Headquarters
Allied Powers Europe
20 February 1952

PERSONAL

Dear Tex:

Spyros Skouras has just brought to me the special album you had
made up for my interest. I most sincerely thank you for your
thoughtful courtesy.

Just before lunch he produced a newsreel in which he had pic-
tured highlights of the Madison Square Garden rally. As you
know, Mrs. Odlum brought me a Kinescope of the same demonstration. From these pieces of evidence, as well as from
accounts of eye witnesses and participants, I have learned just
what an extraordinary thing you both did in producing such an
enormous rally under adverse conditions.

While, as you know, I firmly believe that American interests
demand that for the moment I remain outside the swirl of domestic political activity, it would be idle as well as false for me to
attempt to deny that I am deeply touched by the obvious energy
and conviction that you devoted to the Garden effort and by the
extraordinary enthusiasm shown by the great crowd of Americans
who gathered there. Even a clear personal knowledge of unwor-
thiness of such confidence cannot overreach the pride that I feel.

Won't you convey my warm greetings to Mrs. McCrary and, of
course, best wishes to yourself.

Sincerely,

Dwight D. Eisenhower

Mr. John R. McCrary
Co-Chairman
Eisenhower Bandwagon Committee
51 East 47th Street
New York, New York

Eisenhower's congratulatory letter to Tex from Paris

he had known during the war, Tex had learned how essential a positive attitude is to leadership, and he could never understand why the Republican Party seemed to remain through the years oblivious to this fundamental principle, and continued to convey negative attitudes, defined more by what they are against, rather than what they are for.

He believed that a major difficulty (in both Parties) was that so many people—their number ever-expanding with the exponential increases in political fundraising—lived off the system, with their prestige, income and power dependent on their Party position. He came to conclude that, to the Party People, defeat was preferable to the acceptance of an outsider who might threaten their position.

After the Madison Square Garden rally, Eisenhower agreed to have his name entered in Republican primaries, but declared that he would not campaign personally prior to the nomination. At the rally, Tex had featured New Hampshire Governor Sherman Adams and the importance of New Hampshire as the nation's first primary. Adams went to work, and Eisenhower won New Hampshire—with a twenty-five percent increase in voter turn-out—easily defeating Senator Taft, as well as the other candidates, Governors Warren of California, Dewey of New York, Stassen of Minnesota—and, much to Tex's pleasure, General MacArthur. The next primary was Minnesota. It was too late to get Eisenhower's name on the ballot, but his supporters began a write-in campaign, with Eisenhower finishing second, only a few thousand votes behind the very popular Minnesota Governor Stassen, who immediately pledged to deliver Minnesota's votes to Eisenhower at the Convention.

Meanwhile, Taft, in support of his campaign, had published a book on foreign policy, and had agreed to appear on an NBC television program called "Author Meets Critic." Tex arranged to be the critic. His first question was, "Senator Taft, how can you write a book on foreign policy when the only time you've been out of the country was on a vacation trip to Bermuda?" (Years later, Tex wondered why nobody asked George W. Bush a similar question.) Taft blustered, stormed out of the studio, and demanded that Sarnoff, chairman of RCA, the parent company of NBC, fire Tex. Sarnoff called him in. They both understood that NBC depended on Federal radio and television licenses, and Sarnoff could not afford to risk offending the leading Republican Senator, and potential President (Tex remembered Brisbane's warning that the immense profitability of national television licenses would eventually erode the independence of journalism). Sarnoff said that Tex could choose: resign or be fired. He resigned. Sarnoff said, "That's fine. And here's my personal check for the campaign."

The 1952 Republican Convention was a defining moment in American politics. Citizens for Eisenhower was the first effort to establish a truly "National" Republican Party, led by a nearly universally respected national figure. Also for the first time, a significant proportion of delegates were determined by state primaries in sixteen states—a process long envisioned as a democratic remedy for the prior disreputable delegate selection process by state party bosses. Eisenhower had gone on to win most of the Republican primaries by decisive margins that, together with national polling data, clearly evidenced a substantial public preference for Eisenhower over Taft. However, there were only sixteen primaries in 1952—and there were still opportunities for mischief by Party People furthering their own interests.

The Republican National Committee and local Party bosses—determined to preserve their power—were aligned behind Senator Taft, persistent in their belief, still asserted among many Republican "diehards" today, that if only a "true" Republican were nominated, there would be an outpouring of an otherwise invisible Republican "base." Regardless of all evidence to the contrary, they sought to maintain their power and control by any means available. Accordingly, they arranged hand-picked and controlled captive delegations from the "Solid South" Democratic states, where there were then no effective Republican parties, and the "delegates" so selected were political flotsam, mostly local hangers-on and patronage seekers. The Republican Party bosses made every possible effort to give the nomination to Taft. They further rigged the convention by their choice of speakers, selecting General MacArthur, now a jealous critic of Eisenhower ("he was a good clerk for me") as the keynote speaker, to be followed by the major address of each day from ardent Taft supporters, first, Herbert Hoover and then the infamous Senator Joe McCarthy.

Much to his credit, Cabot Lodge's had organized rival state Republican conventions in the southern states, open to the public, which elected delegate slates pledged to Eisenhower. The Republican National Committee asserted that their rules gave them the right to decide between rival delegations. Lodge then filed a "Fair Play" amendment to the Committee rules, the amendment to be voted upon by the majority of the delegates in the convention, with the challenged delegations not permitted to vote on their own admission. Tex noted the historic irony in Lodge's position. In 1912 Cabot Lodge's father, Henry Cabot Lodge, Sr., using tactics similar to those of the Republican National Committee in 1952, was able to deny the Republican nomination to the overwhelmingly popular Republican Teddy Roosevelt, giving the nomination to Senator Robert Taft's father, William Howard Taft. Whereupon Roosevelt had stormed out of the convention, founded the *Bull Moose* Party, split the Republican vote, thus permitting the Democrat Woodrow Wilson to win the Presidency in a three-way race.

Because of the manipulations and maneuvers of Party loyalists, the outcome hung in the balance. Anticipating possible problems, Tex had learned that the 82nd and 101st Airborne Divisions, which had jumped into Normandy on D-Day, were planning a memorial reunion. He persuaded representatives to come to Chicago, where the Republican Convention was being held. He arranged an invitation to their reunion for Eisenhower, who accepted—but said that, pursuant to his original declaration not to campaign before the convention, he would arrive at the paratroopers reunion, and leave immediately after the ceremony. Tex set up a presentation for Eisenhower by a Medal of Honor paratrooper, Sergeant Funk—who, at the critical moment in the presentation, forgot his lines. By custom, the Medal of Honor recipient is entitled to the first salute, regardless of rank. The Medal is worn around the neck on formal occasions and Eisenhower, seeing the Medal, saluted the flustered Sergeant, who returned the salute and stammered out, "You came to see us the night before we jumped. We'll never forget you." Eisenhower embraced him, turned to

Tex and said, "I'm staying. I'm going into that convention and shake the hand of every delegate."

Everyone, both inside the convention and the millions more watching across the country on television, understood that the ultimate decision would come down to the roll call vote on the "Fair Play" amendment. The initial count indicated that the large California delegation would provide the swing vote. Presidential hopeful Earl Warren was Governor of California, and the California delegation was pledged to vote for him as a "favorite son" on the first ballot. If the "Fair Play" amendment won, there was a chance that neither Eisenhower nor Taft would win the majority necessary for the nomination, in which case Warren hoped that he might become the nominee as a compromise candidate. Accordingly, the California delegation voted for the "Fair Play" amendment. Leadership within the delegation was split between the dedicated Taft advocate, Senator Bill Knowland, and Senator Richard Nixon. Lodge talked to Nixon and whispered the magic word "Vice President." Nixon called a caucus of the California delegation and, in a bitter struggle, won the support of the delegation. Tex often wondered what promises were made.

The Presidential roll call included two "favorite sons," California Governor Warren and Minnesota Governor Stassen. As the first roll call drew to its close, it was evident that Eisenhower, although leading by a substantial margin, would fall nine votes short of the nomination. Lodge was counting on the California delegation to be recognized first; however, the standard-bearer of the Minnesota delegation was a tall man, Newt Weed, who waved his standard so early and so vigorously that he was recognized first—and Minnesota switched its votes to Eisenhower, putting him over the top. In the celebration that followed the Minnesota switch—and little noticed except by Lodge—there was no need for a formal vote by the California delegation, thus Nixon was able to preserve his favorable relationship with the far right wing of the California Republican Party—a situation with ominous implications for the future.

The Eisenhower nomination was a gratifying moment for Tex. A "Citizens" movement had won the nomination from an entrenched, inward-focused, self-serving party structure that had previously been able to achieve its own ends by making its own rules. But, in this moment of victory, the loose structure of the "Citizens" movement revealed its weakness. It had been so focused on achieving Eisenhower's nomination—and it had all come together so quickly—that little attention had been paid to other crucial leadership positions, especially the Vice President.

Powerful corporate leaders like George Humphrey, who had previously supported Taft throughout the nomination, now asserted themselves. Cabot Lodge, looking to the importance of such people in fund-raising, gathered together a group, much as he had nine months before, including Party figures, Governors Dewey, Stassen and Warren, as well as corporate leaders, and argued that it was essential for the Republican Party to have a strong anti-Communist as Vice President, one who could bring the power of the California right wing, which favored the nomination of Richard Nixon, in the interest of "Party unity." The Party People, naturally, concurred—Nixon was a dependable Party captive—and the politically unsophisticated corporate figures did not fully anticipate the future problems from the passionate opposition of the isolationist Taft "Old Guard."

Tex was angry that all the work of the "Citizens" efforts could be so compromised. The Nixon recommendation was taken to Eisenhower, who was concerned with the leadership and direction of the country, and had little interest—and doubtless had given less thought—to Party reform or Party building. He respected the personal achievement of these powerful, successful businessmen who had supported him—and he was willing to accept their recommendation. His first act after the nomination was to walk across the street (a gesture well covered on television) to shake Taft's hand—and he came away believing that they could work together in the interests of the country.

Eisenhower had only been introduced to Nixon, did not know him at all, but did not object to the recommendation. However, his initial tolerance of the Nixon selection was to change very soon, with the revelation of a Nixon's "slush fund"—a paltry amount by the standards in today's politics, but the details of which further revealed Nixon's unappetizing "Red baiting" background and right-wing associations with Senator Bill Knowland, owner of the *Oakland Tribune,* and Harry Chandler, owner of the *Los Angeles Times.* Eisenhower wanted to drop Nixon immediately, but Dewey, showing his true colors, acted behind Eisenhower's back, advised Nixon to go on national television, give a exculpatory explanation for the "slush fund," and ask viewers to telegraph their approval—not to Eisenhower, but to the Republican National Committee. Nixon, without informing Eisenhower, gave the notoriously maudlin "Checkers" speech, defending his "slush fund" by implying that his "slush fund"—like his dog—was a gift from friends, and he wouldn't give up his dog, either. Tex thought that it was a sad reflection on the lack of American public political sophistication, that thousands of Americans, their sympathies touched by Nixon's dog story, telegraphed support.

And there was a further complication, toward the end of his speech, Nixon, claiming his own financial purity, stated that he was making public his tax returns—with the challenge that all candidates should do so. Nixon's alleged target was the Democratic Presidential candidate, Adlai Stevenson, but the shot struck Eisenhower, who had received a private Treasury Department capital gains tax ruling for his book *"Crusade in Europe,"* rather than the then confiscatory income tax rate over ninety percent. There was nothing Eisenhower could do—but he didn't forget.

The outcome of the election was never really in doubt, and it became inevitable when Eisenhower announced, "If elected, I shall go to Korea," thereby signaling the end of the hated, stalemated war. On election night, Tex and Jinx went with Jock and Betsey Whitney to Eisenhower's suite in the Commodore Hotel to watch the returns with Ike and Mamie. The Citizen's for Eisenhower campaign had overcome the narrow isolationist Republican forces to provide new positive leadership for our country, and hope for a world devastated by war. The country had responded to select a true national leader. It seemed the fulfillment of a great and rewarding effort.

Chapter Thirteen

"He Kept the Peace"

Dwight Eisenhower's election as President of the United States in 1952 was a remarkable personal triumph, recognition of the trust accorded him by the American public. Voter turnout increased by twenty-five percent, from 49 million votes for Truman in 1948 to 61.5 million for Eisenhower in 1952. Eisenhower's popularity at the top of the ticket carried Republicans to control of both houses of Congress for the first time in the twenty years since Roosevelt's first term election in 1932. The size of the Eisenhower vote nevertheless carried future problems, as Robert Taft, the conservative son of former President William Howard Taft, became the majority leader of the Senate, and the most powerful man in Congress.

The press covered the Eisenhower election as a victory for the Republican Party. But, while Tex was delighted, he saw it differently. To him the most important fact was the "split-ticket," the gap between the votes for Eisenhower and the far smaller vote for the Republican Congress. Few people seemed to notice that Eisenhower had been nominated over the strong opposition of Republican party regulars—and had been elected by a public which was dubious about the Republican Party—all of which carried implications of things to come.

After the election, the first order of business was the selection of the Cabinet. Eisenhower had said often that he was determined to restore order and dignity to the national government, which he felt had been tainted by the cronyism of the Truman Administration. Eisenhower would need a strong, politically astute Cabinet and Tex was disappointed that Eisenhower's first appointment was John Foster Dulles as Secretary of State. Eisenhower was certainly aware of Dulles' arrogant manner and narrow Presbyterian dogmatism, but he told friends at Augusta that he had picked Dulles because "he knows more international leaders than anyone except me." Eisenhower then turned over the Cabinet selection process to General Lucius Clay and Herbert Brownell, Governor Dewey's lawyer and close associate, while Eisenhower flew secretly to Korea for a first-hand examination before announcing his decision to end the war.

Tex didn't like what he saw coming. He understood that Eisenhower trusted Clay, but he also knew that Dewey's hand behind the scene meant trouble. While he was in

Korea, Eisenhower approved each recommendation of the Clay-Brownell committee, and individual announcements were made as if he were present in this country. Tex was particularly troubled at the lack of "Citizen's input. While Eisenhower had said he wished his Cabinet to serve as a policy team, instead the selection process produced a Cabinet of individuals with whom Eisenhower had little or no personal relationship.

The very forceful George Humphrey, head of the important Cleveland company, M. A. Hanna, a Taft man through the Republican Convention, became Secretary of the Treasury. Despite his rigid conservative views, expressed most vividly in his repeated demands for budget cutting to avoid a "recession which will curl your hair," he was to become the strong man in the Cabinet, and, as an Augusta member and frequent golfing and hunting partner, the closest to Eisenhower.

Charles Wilson, chairman of General Motors, became Secretary of Defense, apparently because as head of the largest company in America, it was hoped that he could establish some management control over the Pentagon. But, having seen the inept way that the auto manufacturers handled their union relationships, Tex felt certain that Wilson's obliviousness would be a problem. Almost immediately, Wilson refused the requirement to sell his large block of General Motors stock, an obvious conflict of interest in view of General Motors' large business relationships with the Federal government. When asked to justify his refusal, Wilson blithely replied that he saw no conflict because, "what's good for General Motors is good for the country."

Dewey's man, Brownell, then became Attorney General, a position which Eisenhower had also considered for Governor Earl Warren. When Eisenhower returned from Korea, he told Warren that he would get the first open seat on the Supreme Court. Shortly thereafter, the death of Chief Justice Fred Vinson opened a far more influential seat for Warren than Eisenhower originally had in mind. Nevertheless, Eisenhower kept his promise—which resulted in Warren's later emergence as one of the most important figures in the history of American jurisprudence by his achievement of a unanimous landmark Supreme Court decision on Civil Rights in 1954, *Brown v. Board of Education*, which required the admission of black children to previously segregated schools.

Tex was furious when he learned that his nominee, Jimmy Doolittle, clearly the best choice for Secretary of the Air Force, was rejected in favor of Harold Talbott in a deal rigged with Dewey to reward a major campaign fund-raiser. Much to Tex's satisfaction, Talbott was later forced to resign for soliciting business from Air Force contractors for a consulting company in which Talbott had an undisclosed personal ownership. Oveta Culp Hobby, whom Tex had recruited to become head of Democrats for Eisenhower, became the only woman in the Cabinet when she was selected as Secretary of Health, Education and Welfare.

Tex was disappointed by the absence of "Citizens" in the key Cabinet policy positions. He was convinced that this was more of Dewey's work—favoring "dependable" Party people—and that it would prove to be a serious weakness. Henry Cabot Lodge, the man who had slipped Nixon on to the ticket in the Chicago Convention, had lost his Massachusetts Senate seat—as he had always said he would, "whenever the Democrats find an Irishman in Boston with a clean record." And John Kennedy had proved Lodge's prediction. Lodge was offered the choice of White House Chief of Staff or

Ambassador to the United Nations, and he took the U.N. Governor Stassen chose the Mutual Security Agency, in charge of the Foreign Aid programs. The decisions of Lodge and Stassen reflected the emphasis that Eisenhower and the "Citizens" group placed upon international affairs, as opposed to the traditional Republican isolationist tendencies; however, it also had the effect of removing from a voice in the Cabinet, and from close counsel to Eisenhower, the most politically experienced representatives of the "Citizens" group.

When Eisenhower arrived in Korea, the U.S. commander was General Mark Clark whose continuation in positions of high responsibility, despite his performance in Italy during World War II, Tex regarded as another triumph of the "West Point Protection Society." Typically, Clark had arranged formal presentations and briefing, but Eisenhower had bypassed Clark, had gone to the front, interviewed soldiers, eaten from mess kits and quickly concluded that there was no justifiable purpose to Clark's strategy of fighting limited battles, hill by hill, with continuing casualties.

Eisenhower returned from Korea and announced that he would end the hated war. Tex was astonished that this most important event for the country, the stopping of the steady, pointless bloodshed, as well as the fulfillment of his campaign promise, was met with surly response from the newly Republican-controlled Congress. Eisenhower had pinned high hopes on Senator Taft's assurance of cooperation when he and Taft had shaken hands after Eisenhower's nomination. However, Eisenhower's interest was in governing, and neither he, nor any of the "Citizens," had given thought or attention to preparing a plan for establishing relationships with Congress.

The Congressional seniority system placed powerful committee chairmanships in the hands of the "Old Guard" people from the "safest" districts, principally from the Midwest and West, and typically from districts outside metropolitan areas, virtually all affected by the long-standing Republican tradition of American isolationism, and who traditionally operated in loose alliance with reactionary southern Democrats. Instead of using the Eisenhower victory to build the Party, the Republican Congressional committee chairmen, intoxicated by their newfound majority power—due entirely to Eisenhower's place at "the top of the ticket"—unburdened their pent-up frustration and anger from being out of power for twenty years into what could be described as a "witches' brew" of confused, vengeful, self-contradictory, and self-destructive proposals.

The Republican Congressional leadership seemed obsessed by the fear of "Communism," both as to subversion in the United States and to Russian expansion abroad. From what Tex had seen of the inefficiency and raw brutality of Russian military operations—reinforced by Kathy Harriman's comments of what she had seen and learned from her time in her father's Embassy in Moscow—Russia did not seem a realistic threat to America. And he had seen for himself that the "Communist" parties in the Balkans, in China, in French Indo-China, and Indonesia—although supplied in varying degrees with Russian arms—were principally "National" movements, aided and armed—but not controlled by Russia.

Then Senator Joe McCarthy of Wisconsin, a drunken, brutish thug, whose chief counsel was Bobby Kennedy, whipped fears of "Communism" into a flame by asserting that an extensive network of Communist spies existed in the United States government. Despite the fact that McCarthy was known in Congress to be an irresponsible alcoholic, and offered no support for his claims, nevertheless Republican leaders supported him—not necessarily because anyone believed him, but because most of McCarthy's attacks were upon Democrats. The Communist scare was heightened as the news leaked out that Stalin had died in early March of 1953 under mysterious circumstances and the question of his successor remained unknown, provoking uneasy speculation.

Apart from the riding the "Red Scare" scenario, the Republican Congressional leaders were dedicated to the traditional Republican "cut budget/cut taxes" mantra, perversely slashing the budget for NATO and Foreign Aid, both obviously important to counter Soviet expansion abroad. Eisenhower's commitment to free trade was the target of further Republican Congressional attack. The chairman of the powerful House Ways and Means Committee promoted a return to heavy tariffs on imported goods, reminiscent of the Republican Smoot-Hawley tariffs in 1930, generally considered a cause of the Depression. (Tex was surprised and disappointed to see, fifty years later, the current Republican President, George W. Bush, establish a thirty percent tariff on imported steel.)

Congress also proposed sharp reductions in the military, justified on the grounds that the United States should rely more upon the Atom bomb for its military requirements—this despite the fact that the United States had lost its Atomic monopoly, and the Soviets possessed Atom bombs of their own. It became more and more evident, not only how narrow and partisan, but also how intellectually isolated, how little exposed to the world, most Congressmen were.

Eisenhower was visibly disappointed at the behavior of Congress, particularly since he had counted on support from Taft who, as Senate Majority Leader, was associated with these perverse proposals. However, Taft was soon diagnosed with terminal cancer and resigned in the spring of 1953. The equally far right-wing Senator William Knowland of California was elected by Republican Senators to take Taft's place as Majority Leader.

The White House staff was unprepared for this multi-faceted obstructionism from Congress, and the most politically experienced men, Lodge and Stassen, were committed in other assignments. Eisenhower needed to counter, at least to some degree, the obstructiveness coming from Congress. Tex was asked to direct a weekly television program called "The President's Week," broadcast on Sunday mornings to "break print," i.e., to capture the headlines in the Monday morning papers and, hopefully, influence the public, and thus Congressional, attitudes for the week ahead. Eisenhower assigned his Press Secretary, Jim Hagerty, to work with Tex, who had his most talented men, Bill Safire as chief reporter, and Ted Yates in charge of production.

The assignment was to dramatize the President's side of issues and to focus on the importance of the President. The first program addressed the U.S.-Soviet confrontation, to emphasize the need for NATO and appropriate military capability and to counter the isolationist opposition of the "Old Guard." Tex had the camera open in ECU, extreme close-up, on his hands, each with a tweezer holding a live scorpion. He dropped the scorpions into a brandy glass, which was "miked" to pick up the sounds of their stingers, as the camera, again in ECU, full screen, watched them sting each other to death. As they writhed and stiffened, Tex's voice-over began, "As Robert Oppenheimer, father of the Atom bomb, has said, the world today is like two scorpions in a brandy glass . . . the USA and the USSR . . . a Balance of Terror."

On another program, Tex picked up the story which he had heard on election night when U.E. Baughman, Chief of the U.S. Secret Service, had briefed Eisenhower on security matters. He began the program, "In such a world as we face today, our guest has a very special mission. He is U.E. Baughman, Chief of the Secret Service. Chief, could you explain just what your job is? In the beginning the Secret Service was formed to catch counterfeiters. What's your job now?" The Chief took out of his pocket a little cloth, opened it on the table, and removed something that looked like a wad of chewing gum. He poked it with a red pen. Tex asked, "What's that thing?" He said, "That is to remind us of what our job is. This is the bullet that killed President Lincoln." Years later, when Tex thought about Kennedy's assassination and Reagan being shot, he remembered Baughman's statement.

While Tex had seen the vast corruption of Chiang's government in Chungking and Shanghai in 1945, he was startled at the magnitude of the overt, outright corruption by the China Lobby in Washington, a multi-million dollar operation organized to bribe influential U.S. Congressman to support Chang Kai-shek's government-in-exile in Formosa with steadily increasing billions of U.S. financial and military aid. Much of this U.S. "aid" money was then recycled by Chiang's agents back to Congressmen, particularly the top Republican Senators in power, Knowland, Bricker, Dirksen, Bridges, and others throughout the system, who also pressed for General MacArthur and his repeated requests to "unleash" Chiang's troops on the mainland of China. This pandering and plundering by Congressmen was reinforced by the endless favorable publicity of Henry Luce's magazines, which linked the China issue with the overall obsession with "Communism"

All this reactionary agitation was reinforced by Senator Joe McCarthy's irresponsible "Red Scare" spy charges, most unfortunately coupled with Eisenhower's puzzling reluctance to challenge McCarthy directly, which had become an open sore in the Administration and in the country. This eventually came to a head in the Army-McCarthy hearings, televised nationally, in which the long and disgraceful support of Joe McCarthy by right wing Republican Senators was finally brought to a close by a Senate vote to censure McCarthy. All Democrat senators voted for censure, except Jack Kennedy, who was recorded as "absent." The Irish vote is big in Boston. Republican senators split twenty-two to twenty-two, with most of the senior Republican senators voting for McCarthy's acquittal. Tex regarded this as further damning evidence of the continuing character problem of the Republican Congressional leadership. Fortunately for the country, McCarthy rapidly faded to an alcoholic death.

Tex continued to attend meetings with Eisenhower, mostly related to the upcoming 1954 mid-term election, and he was invited to a White House dinner.

Jock Whitney was also a guest at the White House dinner, as were Hagerty and Brownell, along with some corporate chiefs and fund-raisers. The conversation among the guests mainly dealt with the forthcoming 1954 election, and the risk of losing the Republican control of Congress. (Privately, Tex thought that from the way the Republican Congressmen were acting, a change might not be such a bad thing).

D D E

THE WHITE HOUSE

Augusta, Georgia
April 19, 1954

Dear Tex:

I wonder if it would be convenient for you to come to
an informal stag dinner on the evening of Monday,
May tenth. I hope to gather together a small group,
and I should like very much for you to attend if it
is possible for you to do so.

Because of the informality of the occasion, I suggest
that we meet at the White House about half past seven,
have a reasonably early dinner, and devote the evening
to a general chat. While I am hopeful that you can
attend, I realize that you already may have engagements
which would interfere. If so, I assure you of my complete understanding.

I shall probably wear a black or white dinner coat, but
business suit will be entirely appropriate.

With warm personal regard,

Sincerely,

Mr. John R. McCrary, Jr.
The Dorset
30 W. 54th Street
New York, N.Y.

Tex's invitation to a White House dinner

After dessert had been served, Eisenhower began to speak. He said that while domestic politics were important, his primary concern was how to keep the peace. He asked the group to think about the global picture. The world was divided between a democratic, industrialized West—the U.S. and northern Europe—confronted by the East, controlled by Stalin, a ruthless dictator with a powerful military, armed with Atom bombs, developing long-range missiles, and spreading Communist political ideology throughout Eastern Europe, Asia and the Far East. Then there was a "Third World," harboring powerful resentments from the oppressions of Western "Colonialism," as well as resentments of darker-skinned peoples against dominance by whites. All this was combined with deep religious hostility in the Islamic East against a Christian West, further inflamed by U.S. support of Israel, which people of the East regard as a "Second Crusade," an invasion of lands holy to Muslims by "infidels."

Eisenhower said that when he was a cadet at West Point a wise instructor had said that the most critical military decision was to distinguish between a war of necessity and war of choice. History revealed far more wars of choice, generally arising out of royal jealousies, religious politics or personal passions, and most often destructive to all sides of the conflict. Now science has developed vastly more devastating weapons, atom bombs and missiles. Future wars would leave survivors, but no lasting winners. America must beware of wars of choice. After Eisenhower finished speaking the room was silent. Conversation resumed slowly, with subdued talk, plans for golf games, a few jokes, and the evening ended quietly.

In addition to the problems in Europe, which naturally attracted more national attention, Tex followed events in the Far East. His 1945 Air Force tour through Asia, coupled with his experience in the Korean War, had left a lasting impression. He and Jinx had begun to talk about taking a trip around the Orient. In addition to Hong Kong, he wanted her to see Bangkok, with the restored *Imperial Hotel*, and where his wartime friend Jim Thompson's elegant *Thai Silk* business was attracting world attention. And Tex wanted Jinx to visit Saigon, to see what the French colonials were really like. However, these thoughts were soon overtaken by world events.

By 1953 the French were struggling to cling to their French Indo-China colonial empire. The Japanese had occupied the country in 1941 and then it had been administered by Vichy French officials under Japanese command through the war. Tex had been disgusted by the visible corruption of the weak and venal French officials he met in 1945 and, because of the corruption he had seen, he had not been surprised when a guerrilla war began under the leadership of Paris-educated Ho Chi Minh, supported by Chinese encouragement and supplies, much of it carried over a guerilla supply route from Hanoi in the north through Cambodia to the Saigon area in the south, known as the Ho Chi Minh Trail. In an effort to interrupt this supply route, the French sought to establish a military stronghold in North Vietnam. Thirteen thousand French Foreign Legionnaires were parachuted into a remote, isolated spot, Dien Bien Phu, a seemingly inaccessible valley surrounded by mountains. Their officers were confident that the Vietminh guerrilla forces could not bring heavy artillery up the mountains. They protected their exposed position in the valley by "fire bases" on several surrounding promontories (Tex was amused to learn that French soldiers had named each promontory for one of the mistresses of the French commander, General Christian de Castries). But the French had underestimated the resolve of the men they were fighting. Ho Chi Minh's soldiers manhandled heavy artillery up to the overlooking mountain tops, concealing the guns in caves and tunnels to protect them from attack by French aircraft, and began constant artillery fire on the French troops in the valley. The French were helpless, and pleaded for U.S. military help.

Admiral Radford, Chairman of the Joint Chiefs, with the support of the other Joint Chiefs, Senate Majority Leader Knowland and other leading Republican Senators, recommended U.S. intervention, including the use of Atom bombs. Based on his determination not to engage in wars of choice, Eisenhower refused, saying that he would not send American boys to fight in a war between Asian people on their land for the benefit of European powers. He did, however, provide the French with B-26 bombers and other military equipment. But the French position was hopeless and final French surrender took place in May 1954.

A Geneva Conference on Vietnam was convened in July 1954, as an effort to restore peace in the area. It produced a political decision, resulting in an arbitrary division of Vietnam into two states: South Vietnam, a Buddhist country, under a French-trained Catholic President, Ngo Dinh Diem, who ruled with his aggressive wife and brother, with support from the United States (read CIA); and North Vietnam, under Ho Chi Minh. The Republican Congressional policy was that Vietnam represented an Asian version of the Cold War "Domino Theory," calling for strong opposition to any Communist expansion anywhere. Tex thought this required a considerable stretch: first, that Ho was controlled, as opposed to aided, by China; secondly, that China was controlled by Russia, the old Korean War mistake. Blind to reality, and ignorant of all but internal U.S. political advantage, right wing Republican Congressmen adapted their old mindless attack on Democrats from, "Who lost China?" to "Who lost Vietnam?"

Then, Chiang Kai-shek reappeared in the picture in August 1954, rattling his sword about a "re-conquest" of China, and fortifying the tiny islands of Quemoy and Matsu, only eight miles off the coast of China. In response to Chiang's aggressive belligerence, the Chinese commenced artillery fire on Chiang's fortifications, and Chiang immediately sought U.S. support. The right-wing Republicans in Congress took up the cry, "Unleash Chiang"—more evidence of the financial "take" in Congress from the China Lobby. Admiral Radford and the Joint Chiefs again recommended that the U.S. intervene with Atom bombs to defend Quemoy and Matsu. Eisenhower once again refused and the crisis eventually calmed down.

Events then took a turn which really angered Tex. Eisenhower's principal international commitment was NATO, the North Atlantic Treaty Organization, in which France was not only a participant, but was the prime beneficiary as well—and the French took adroit advantage of their position. They, threatened to withdraw French troops from NATO unless the U.S. immediately committed U. S. troops and substantial military support to Vietnam. Tex was outraged at the presumption that, after America had sent its soldiers to save France from German conquest and occupation in two World Wars, at the cost a hundred thousand American lives, and was now protecting France with American troops in NATO, France should now try to blackmail America into their colonial war

The French blackmail demand for American troops in Vietnam, however outrageous, placed Eisenhower in a difficult and dangerous position. NATO was the centerpiece of Eisenhower's policy in Europe. The French situation in Vietnam was hopeless, and Eisenhower was determined to avoid having America drawn into a Vietnam war of choice. Eisenhower's response to the French was arrived at with great reluctance, he increased military supplies and equipment to the French, but he responded to De Gaulle's demand for troops only in the form of a limited number of military "advisors," all volunteers, mostly CIA, who were instructed never to wear U.S. military uniforms, nor to operate in American units. Instead, they were to dress informally, to wear "Hawaiian shirts," because Eisenhower knew that any "blood on the uniform" risked drawing America into war.

At the same time, things weren't going well on the domestic front. The sad reality was that money, in increasingly massive amounts, was calling the shots in Congress. The oil lobby was pushing a bill through Congress to deregulate natural gas. Payoffs took many forms. Tex was informed that the oil lobby "sold" stock in businesses—some real, some not—to Congressmen for unsecured notes, then repurchased the stock at higher prices—and cancelled the notes. There were many other techniques, but Tex's particular favorite was the use of uniformed restaurant delivery boys who would leave large paper sacks on Congressmen's desks—the sacks filled with hundred dollar bills, with a ham sandwich on top—accompanied by a note saying that more orders of "sandwiches" would be ready for delivery after a key congressional vote.

Tex was committed to the Civil Rights movement, which was beginning to assert its influence. The stage had been set in May of 1954 by the Supreme Court's landmark desegregation decision, *Brown v. Board of Education*. After that, there was no way to turn back the clock. The growing influence of national network television was exposing to the whole nation the volatile racial issues which had previously been swept under the Congressional rug, as matters of only "local" concern.

In the 1954 election, the Democrats recaptured both Houses of Congress. Eisenhower went to Augusta for the holidays and Tex talked to Hagerty, whose role was steadily increasing, to get his reactions. Hagerty told him that Lucius Clay had come down right after the election for a heart-to-heart talk with Eisenhower, saying that the election had demonstrated that country needed a more progressive party to counter the backward-looking Republican "Old Guard," and only Eisenhower could bring that about, but that he must take a strong leadership role and immediately announce that he would run again in 1956 to preempt the ambitions of the right wing. Bill Knowland, who had lost his role as Majority Leader of the Senate with the 1954 Democratic sweep, had already passed the word that he intended to run for President in 1956, if Eisenhower did not make his intentions known soon. Hagerty said that Eisenhower had agreed with Clay, and said that if the Republican Party would not change, Eisenhower would enlist moderate Democrats to join Eisenhower Republicans in forming a new party. Tex began to think about the possibilities.

He put his thoughts in a piece of extraordinarily sharp and frank correspondence, including his personal plea for more attention to the young people of America.

JOHN REAGAN M⊆CRARY, JR.
THE DORSET
THIRTY WEST FIFTY-FOURTH STREET
NEW YORK 19, N. Y.

November 30, 1954

The President
The White House
Washington 25, D. C.

My dear Mr. President:

>   *As the smoke of one more campaign clears, and before the next one begins come January, I venture one comment and one suggestion.*

>   *Last night in Madison Square Garden, the best efforts of all the friends of Senator McCarthy could not gather much more than half the crowd that collected at midnight two years ago to ask you to come home and be President.*

>   *I have spent 20 years handling crowds in New York City, and two things I would judge by the crowd at the Garden last night:*

>   *Such a crowd can never make anybody President:*

>   *There has not been so much evil packed into the Garden since the pre-war Bundist meetings.   Tempers have never in my memory been uglier than they are now.*

>   *All of us yearn for firm leadership in the development of some counter-force to this welding of all the venomous groups in both Parties.*

>   *I know that the Gallup Poll shows that you have lost little if any of your own hold on the respect and affection of most American people.*

>   *But in my opinion, the Gallup Poll is once more missing the mark.*

Tex's letter to President Eisenhower (page 1)

- 2 -

I do not believe we could now assemble more than half of the people who turned out in your behalf two years ago.

The rest of America, I cannot judge; New York, I know as well as I know Jinx.   And in New York, among the young people and the independents who defied the elements and the politicians, there is a definite fall-away, from their one-time peak of faith in your leadership.

In the area we understand, we plan to go to work now for 1956.   Jinx worked inside the regular Republican organization in the last election -- as co-chairman to Jock for the Republican Fund, she met her quota of $200,000.

Whatever we do will be with the full knowledge of Jock, but probably outside the Republican Party.   We plan to work with women, with young people, and in Harlem through the churches as we did before.

It is my conviction that the roots of power of the Democratic Party can be found in the City Halls of New York, Chicago, Los Angeles, Philadelphia and other great cities.

The one man who understands this better than any other Republican is Jack Javits.

It is significant that Javits has emerged from this campaign as the nation's number one vote-getter, for any office, in either Party.

It is also significant that he comes from your District.

You may recall that I once came to Washington and urged you to help persuade Dewey to give him the nomination for Mayor last time.   Had Dewey been less blind, the Republicans would today control both City Hall and Albany. This is simple arithmetic.

I hope that you will find some way to draw Javits into your circle of valued friends.   I realize that Jack does not possess skill in any of the social graces that make him a quick friend -- he does not play golf or bridge nor does he enjoy fresh water fishing.   This is said not in sarcasm, but

Tex's letter to President Eisenhower (page 2)

- 3 -

only in realistic appraisal of the differences between Jack and all the other men who have earned your close friendship.

But there is one area in which you both can meet as instant friends -- *your concern for the young people of America.*

We believe that Jack can and will build soundly for the Republicans among first voters. We plan to help him. I hope you will find a way to extend your hand to him. It will be of great help inside the Republican Party organization here in New York State.

Neither Jinx nor I are very good at prayers, but whatever prayers we know and speak always include you and Mamie.

Very sincerely,

Tex McCrary

TM:sg

Tex's letter to President Eisenhower (page 3)

Jinx had cautioned Tex that his letter to Eisenhower was too personal and too strong, and he thought she was probably correct, when he was delighted to receive an answer from Eisenhower a few days later.

In 1955, the major item on the White House schedule was the upcoming Geneva Peace Conference with the Russians, and it brought Nelson Rockefeller and Tex together again. Rockefeller had started out in the Eisenhower Administration as Deputy to Oveta Culp Hobby at the Department of Health, Education and Welfare. He had then moved on as an Assistant to the Secretary of State, dealing with South American affairs, in which he had a long interest, including his ownership of a huge ranch in Venezuela, as well as in the development of Venezuelan oil production. Anyone with his own ideas, which Rockefeller certainly had, was not going anywhere in the State Department under the dictatorial Foster Dulles, particularly if his name was Rockefeller, so he arranged a slot for himself as a Presidential Assistant working on "Government Operations."

The 1955 Geneva Conference was planned to discuss European Security and the meeting had special significance in that, since the then still-unexplained death of Stalin in 1953, the question of the real source of power and direction in Russia remained a subject of world-wide concern. Rockefeller saw Geneva as an opportunity for a new Presidential initiative. In addition to his natural high energy, one of his great assets was his effective use of the Rockefeller family foundations as a kind of intellectual farm club—and one of his stars was Henry Kissinger. Tex knew that Eisenhower was deeply concerned over what he called a mistaken "Pearl Harbor complex," the fear of a sudden, unexpected attack that was driving a competitive, costly, and dangerous arms race, with both the United States and Russia possessing nuclear weapons. In this context, Rockefeller and Kissinger had come up with a plan for mutual deterrence of surprise attacks by a U.S. proposal for unrestricted aerial reconnaissance by both the United States and the Soviets over each other's territory, a plan which came to be called "Open Skies."

Tex thought that the idea was great. And it immediately appealed to Eisenhower, who planned it as the centerpiece of the U.S. position at the Geneva Conference in July of 1955. However, in Geneva, Khrushchev, who had emerged as the real source of Russian authority, adamantly and inexplicably, refused to consider the proposal. Tex could not find any explanation for Khrushchev's behavior, until he later learned the extent of his excessive drinking habits. Eisenhower was distressed at the failure of "Open Skies." Space reconnaissance satellites were under development, but they would not be available for several years, and to bridge the gap until the satellites were ready, Eisenhower approved the secret development of a remarkable high-altitude aerial reconnaissance aircraft, the U-2, ostensibly a weather research aircraft, but actually a "spy plane" for the Central Intelligence Agency—which was later to lead to a critical confrontation in U.S.—Soviet relations.

Squabbles with Congress continued into the summer when Eisenhower went on vacation to Colorado, where, on September 23, 1955, he was stricken with a heart attack. As time passed with no news, it became apparent that the heart attack was far more serious than had been initially acknowledged. Concern for the President's health also meant concern over Richard Nixon as his successor. In the absence of hard information

THE WHITE HOUSE
WASHINGTON

December 4, 1954.

<u>Personal and Confidential</u>

Dear Tex:

I am glad that you wrote me as frankly and fully as you
did in your letter of November thirtieth.

As for your comment about Jack Javits, I agree thoroughly. From my observations of him as a Congressman, I would say he is progressive, dynamic and able.
I have certainly been at some pains at various times to
let him know of my good opinion of his judgment and of
my approval of the general attitude that he seems to
display toward government and its relations to our
citizens. Moreover, at one time I urged him upon
the New York Republican leaders as their best candidate for Mayor. So I have some trouble in reducing
to concrete terms your suggestion that he and I should
meet as friends; I have never felt for him anything other
than friendship.

Next I refer to your statement that you could not now
assemble more than half the people who turned out for
your meeting almost three years ago. Accepting without question your statement that you are intimately acquainted with the pulse of New York and with your further
statement that there is a definite fall away from young
citizens' "faith in me," I still must remark that I am
not conscious of any serious contradiction, over the
years, in my public or private statements or any change
in the basic political and economic convictions to which
I fervently adhere.

So the reasons for the results you describe are not readily
apparent to me. I do refuse to be a demagogue -- but I
have always despised the breed. I have not, of course,
ever -- in my life -- indulged in personal, public vitupera-
tion. Incidentally, with respect to your comments on the

<u>Personal and Confidential</u>

Eisenhower's response to Tex's letter (page 1)

THE WHITE HOUSE
WASHINGTON

<u>Personal and Confidential</u>

Mr. McCrary - 2.

ugly tempers aroused by McCarthyism, I must tell you that
during the first five weeks I was in Denver this last summer,
his name was not once mentioned to me. The issues that boil
in New York are not always of primary concern to the rest of
the country, but even if they were, I would not, under any circumstances, glorify -- or at least publicize -- such an individual
by attempting a Presidential Philippic, with him as the target.
When any individual or any idea goes completely outside the
realm of logic and of reason, I doubt that elimination can be
achieved through argument! In fact, it is only the persistent
and senseless publicity he has achieved that has made the matter of any concern to our people.

My own reaction to this whole messy business has been to up-
hold Americanism and preach fairness, justice and decency.
Moreover, where I had any knowledge of facts in a case, I've
made a point of praising Marshall, Zwicker, etc. If young or
old want a President who will indulge in billingsgate -- and be-
mean the office as it has been bemeaned before -- they'll have
to find another.

Of course I am delighted that you and Jinx are going to devote
your great talents and energies to working with the groups you
mention. There is much groundwork to be done, and it cannot
be started too soon. As for myself, I would hope that you know
me well enough to believe that I have always done what I consider
in the best interests of America.   It is true that my convictions
of what is best for America may not always agree with the convictions of others, including yours. But I do have faith that we
are both working for the same great ends, which is the important
thing.

With warm regard,

Sincerely,

W. E.

Mr. John Reagan McCrary, Jr.,
30 West 54th Street,
New York, New York.

<u>Personal and Confidential</u>

Eisenhower's response to Tex's letter (page 2)

about Eisenhower's real physical condition, agitation inevitably spread. As Tex pieced the story together, Dulles exercised his authority as Secretary of State and senior Cabinet member to send the Chief of Staff, Sherman Adams to serve as liaison with Eisenhower in the Army Fitzsimons General Hospital in Denver. Nixon, recognizing the delicacy of his position, expressed his opposition and offered himself as the proper liaison figure. His offer was rejected by the other Cabinet members. Naturally, there was a "backroom" character to all of this. Senate Minority Leader Bill Knowland urged Nixon to exercise his role as Vice President, push his case, and "take over," the real goal being, of course, to have a right wing President in office, with the prospect of five, or perhaps nine, more years of right wing control.

Eventually, a schedule was established whereby each member of the Cabinet, by order of seniority, would make a brief hospital visit at appropriate intervals, including Richard Nixon. The right wing fumed in frustration, but their hands were tied. After six weeks, Eisenhower's doctors said he could leave the hospital, but would have to do so in a wheelchair, and could not return to work for an extended period. Recognizing that news photographers would be present, Eisenhower refused to leave the hospital, not wishing the public to see him so incapacitated, and he remained in the hospital until he could walk out on his own. He did not return to his farm at Gettysburg until mid-December of 1955, nearly three months after the heart attack, and he remained on the farm, without any date of return to the White House, or any indication of his intentions regarding the upcoming 1956 Presidential election.

Despite the uncertainty over Eisenhower's future, Tex had kept Eisenhower informed of plans for the 1956 campaign, including mention of a series of "Salute to Ike" dinners. While Eisenhower continued his public silence over his own willingness to seek a second term, Tex was surprised, and delighted, to receive another letter from him, dated January 23, 1956, which included, so far as Tex was then able to determine, Eisenhower's first disclosure of his intention to run for a second term, contained in a quotation from Stephen Vincent Benet's poem about Lincoln *"John Brown's Body,"* in a "Personal and Confidential" postscript.

Eisenhower's letter was a great relief to Tex, who considered a second Eisenhower term as crucial for the country, but naturally wondered what lay behind the elegiac tone of the Eisenhower letter. The later disclosure of Eisenhower's medical records revealed that his doctor, the renowned cardiac specialist, Paul Dudley White, had recommended to Eisenhower that, given the stress levels of the Presidency, he not run for a second term. Other doctors apparently concluded that a second term was feasible, under certain conditions. Recalling the relative passivity evident in some of Eisenhower's responses during his second term, Tex later came to suspect high levels of medications.

The first public announcement of Eisenhower's intention to run for a second term was made in late February 1956, and it was significant that it made no mention of Nixon or the Vice Presidency. When asked about his intentions regarding Nixon, Eisenhower answered that the decision for the Vice President was a matter for the Republican Convention to determine. Apparently Eisenhower then worked for several months to try to convince Nixon to resign as Vice President and accept a Cabinet position, on the grounds that Nixon needed more administrative experience. Indicative

THE WHITE HOUSE

WASHINGTON

January 23, 1956

Personal and Confidential

Dear Tex:

The optimistic predictions in your letter of the thirteenth
concerning the success of the Salute dinners were more
than borne out by the event.   I was tremendously
impressed that evening and though, of course, I was
deeply grateful for the many expressions of personal confidence, there was another implication that held my attention even more firmly.   It was the evidence that the
Republican Party had at last begun to develop rapidly in
convictions, in energy and in imagination!

The whole performance left Mamie and me with a warm
and friendly feeling.

To many of the people who were individually in charge of
the dinners I have sent notes of thanks, but I wanted to
write a special message to you and Jinx because of the
unfaltering enthusiasm with which you two have supported
everything this Administration has tried to do in order to
redeem the promises of the Crusade which began in 1952.

Needless to say, I was both intrigued by your use of the
Einstein formula to indicate your opinion of my importance
as a leader in the world (and, of course, flattered by the
result you arrived at).   I do want you to know that I am
not giving any concern as to what, under the changed conditions, this job might do to me.   The great and grave
question is, "Over a five year stretch what might I do to
the job?"

Personal and Confidential

Eisenhower's letter mentioning his intention to run for a second term (page 1)

THE WHITE HOUSE
WASHINGTON

<u>Personal and Confidential</u>

Tex McCrary -- 2

We like to deal in personalities; even when we discuss ideas, we frequently do so by referring to "Teddy's policies" or Wilson's plan."   But personalities are mortal and finite; a truly great idea can be eternal, or at least of centuries long importance.

It would be fatal if, through a combination of advancing years and gradual loss of energy on my part, the great foreign and domestic programs for which this Administration has stood should begin to suffer because of slackening energy and leadership.   I do not need here to outline all the considerations pro and con that have a bearing on the matter.

All this is, of course, confidential; but I would not want such faithful friends as you and Jinx to believe at this time of my life I would begin to give more attention to my own personal convenience and possibility of a long existence, than I do to the great issues that inspired the Crusade.

With warm personal regard,

Sincerely,

D.E.

Mr. Tex McCrary
30 West 54th Street
New York, New York

<u>Personal and Confidential</u>

Eisenhower's letter mentioning his intention to run for a second term (page 2)

THE WHITE HOUSE
WASHINGTON

Personal and Confidential

Tex McCrary -- 3

P.S.   Look in your copy of the newest edition of
"John Brown's Body," about the bottom of page 205 or
top of page 206.   You will find a part of Lincoln's
soliloquy where he speaks of his great desire to know
"God's will."

D.E.

John Brown's Body

What is God's will?

They come to me and talk about God's will
In righteous deputations and platoons,
Day after day, laymen and ministers.
They write me Prayers From Twenty Million Souls
Defining me God's will and Horace Greeley's.
God's will is General This and Senator That,
God's will is those poor colored fellows' will,
It is the will of the Chicago churches,
It is this man's and his worst enemy's.
But all of them are sure they know God's will.
I am the only man who does not know it.

And, yet, if it is probable that God
Should, and so very clearly, state His will
To others, on a point of my own duty,
It might be thought He would reveal it me
Directly, more especially as I
So earnestly desire to know His will.

The will of God prevails. No doubt, no doubt—
Yet, in great contests, each side claims to act
In strict accordance with the will of God.
Both may, one must be wrong.

Lord, I will keep my promise and go on,
Your will, in much, still being dark to me,
But, in this one thing, as I see it, plain.

I cannot read it but I will go on,
Old dog, old dog, but settled to the scent
And with fresh breath now from this breathing space.
Almighty God.
            At best we never seem
To know You wholly, but there's something left,
A strange, last courage.

"John Brown's Body"—A postscript to Eisenhower's letter to Tex

of Eisenhower's opinion of Nixon, neither State, Treasury, nor Defense was apparently included among the various positions offered. Naturally, Nixon declined. At the time, Tex wondered whether Eisenhower had not fully recovered sufficient emotional energy simply to drop Nixon and choose another Vice President for his second term. There would have been an inevitable outcry from the far right wing, but Eisenhower's national standing was so high that he could safely have ignored it. Through the years, Tex kept thinking of what a difference that change would have made for our country!

After returning to the White House, Eisenhower became increasingly concerned over conditions in the Middle East, particularly with respect to the oil situation. While the United States had historically been energy-independent from its own oil production, by 1956 U.S. oil imports were rising rapidly, and it was inevitable that the United States would eventually become dependent upon oil from the Middle East. (Tex recalled his uncle's predictions thirty years earlier) Nationalist ambitions were rising in the Middle East and in the Third World, however, in Congress the oil issue was regarded, not in relation to future U.S. oil requirements, but rather in the context of the Cold War, as a growing threat of Russia's potential to penetrate Middle Eastern politics and cut off the supply of oil to England and Europe. At that time, there seemed to be no thought of the prospect of a rise of a militant anti-western Islamic Middle East. No one then seemed to be thinking about the possibility of a threat to access to the world's largest oil reserves that would bring America into two wars in the Middle East, George H. W. Bush's Persian Gulf War in 1991 and George W. Bush's current "Holy War" on Iraq.

In 1956 England's economy depended upon Middle East oil, accessed through the Suez Canal in Egypt. As a schoolboy at Exeter, Tex had been fascinated by the romantic story of the Suez Canal; how the Frenchman, Ferdinand de Lessups, had engineered the digging of the Canal; then England's acquisition of control, artfully arranged by Prime Minister Disraeli as a present for Queen Victoria; the ceremonial opening in Cairo with the first performance of the spectacular opera, *Aida.* (to which Tex's aunt and uncle had taken him in New York). By treaty, England shared toll income from shipping with Egyptian King Farouk, notoriously corrupt, and corruptible, who was overthrown in 1952 by a revolt of Army officers led by an ambitious, charismatic colonel, Abdel Gamal Nasser, who soon became President of Egypt. Although Egypt itself was not a rich country, it was regarded by other Arab countries as the leading Arab state and Nasser was intent upon ending the British colonial position in Egypt and its control over the Suez Canal—all as part of his further intention of spreading active Egyptian leadership throughout the Arab world, already angered by Israel's territorial ambitions.

As Nasser's political power increased, he pursued rapid Egyptian development, both military and economic. At that time, the U.S.-Soviet standoff barred arm sales to the Third World by either party. However, a seeming opportunity to appease Nasser arose through the financing of a major dam on the Nile River at Aswan, which offered important agricultural and hydroelectric development for the Egyptian people. In "Cold War" terms, the cost was small, $70 million from the U.S. (Britain to contribute twenty percent), compared to the potential benefits.

However, Eisenhower's lengthy recovery from his heart attack had, unfortunately, left control of this project in the hands of Secretary of State Dulles. Dulles' handling of the matter reflected his autocratic character and narrow, legalistic approach. He seemed not fully to grasp the larger international issues, and instead treated the issue of Nasser's threat to violate the long-standing Suez treaty as simply a violation of a legal contract. Nasser immediately recognized the opportunity to lift the issue to the Cold War level. He arranged a major arms deal with Czechoslovakia—and paid for it with Egyptian cotton—which angered Southern Senators, always eager to protect their generous U.S. cotton subsidies to southern cotton growers. Dulles retaliated by canceling the U.S. loan commitment for improving the Suez Canal. The Soviets stepped in immediately and replaced the U.S. loan. Thus empowered, Nasser seized control of the Suez Canal from the British. The world situation spun out of control.

Anthony Eden, then Prime Minister in Great Britain, had never gotten along with Dulles (few did) and Eden concluded that England's economic future could not depend on Dulles' fits of pique. Control of the Suez Canal was vital to British access to Middle Eastern oil, as well as access to colonial interests in India and beyond to Malaya, Singapore, and Hong Kong. Accordingly, Eden secretly entered into discussions with France (which wanted to deflect attention from its problems of a rebellion against French colonial control in Algeria) and Israel (which wanted control of the Sinai) for a joint invasion of Egypt to deter Nasser's ambitions and establish control of the Suez Canal.

Anticipating American objection, the British, French and Israelis acted in secret to time their military action to coincide with the 1956 U.S. Presidential election, believing that fear of the loss of Jewish votes in key states would inhibit Eisenhower from opposition in the final days before the election on November 6th. Events became more complicated when, on October 23, in the final stages of the U. S. election campaign, Hungarians rebelled against their Soviet masters. The Russians immediately sent in troops. Allen Dulles and the CIA were caught unaware. With Eisenhower focused on "Freedom Fighters" in Hungary, the Israelis attacked across Egypt's Sinai Desert on October 28 and reached the banks of Suez in four days, a humiliating defeat for Egypt, and one felt throughout the Muslim world. On November 5, the day before the U.S. election, Britain and France dropped paratroops into Egypt. A potential world war seemed at hand. Again, the CIA was caught by surprise. Russia threatened immediate response, and the Brits, French and Israelis, although dependent upon U.S. military and financial aid, continued to assume that the U.S. would support their imperial ambitions, regardless of the inherent risk to world peace.

Facing this seemingly impossible situation, Eisenhower again "kept the peace." To the amazement of the world, he refused to support England, France and Israel. [Footnote: In his biography of Eisenhower, Steve Ambrose reports Eisenhower, thinking of the Presidential election a few days away, as saying "There goes New York, New Jersey, and Pennsylvania."] The countries of the Third World could hardly believe that the U.S. "colossus" would side with a Third World country against the colonial interests of America's traditional allies. Israel withdrew from the Sinai. England and France begged in vain for support for their position in Egypt. Then Russia jumped in to support Egypt, financing the Aswan Dam, and entering in a kind of alliance. With this support, Nasser then proceeded to establish the United Arab Republic, to absorb Syria, to kill King Faisal and his family in a coup in Iraq, and to move into Lebanon. Tex's Uncle Tom Taylor's warnings, that the wars of the future would be fought over oil, continued to echo in Tex's mind.

Disgusted by the CIA's repeated failures of intelligence, Eisenhower appointed Jimmy Doolittle to head a committee to investigate the CIA. Tex was told that Doolittle's subsequent report was critical of Allen Dulles' performance, particularly in clandestine operations, and he heard that Eisenhower had told Allen Dulles to hand over clandestine operations to General Lucian Truscott. Later, Tex learned that Allen Dulles had ignored Eisenhower's order, placed Truscott in charge of intelligence gathering, while he retained personal control of clandestine operations. For this to have occurred, and for the Dulles brothers to remain in office, Tex could only conclude that Eisenhower's energy level was not up to a fight that potentially destructive within his Administration

The 1956 election occurred in the shadow of the momentous events in the Middle East, in which the public had confirmed that they "liked Ike" even more, electing him to a second term by a vote of thirty-five million to twenty-five million for Adlai Stevenson, a lower total turnout for Eisenhower than his 1952 election, but an even greater percentage margin of victory. Once again, ticket-splitting between the votes for Eisenhower and the votes for members of Congress was further evidence that voters clearly distinguished between the role of the President, as the leader of the nation, and that of members of Congress, who, necessarily for their own re-election, represented the interests of their state or district.

Tex and Bill Safire had put a lot of work into the Eisenhower 1956 campaign, in all the major cities, ending up with another rally at Madison Square Garden. After Eisenhower's smashing 1956 victory, Tex recognized that his relationship with Eisenhower during the second term would inevitably be reduced. It was time to broaden his activities, while continuing to follow developments in the White House.

Between the television shows and politics, Tex and Jinx had been working eighteen-hour days, seven days a week. It was just too much, even for Jinx's enormous energy. They had good people taking care of their young sons, Paddy and Kevin, but that, too, was far from an ideal arrangement. Neither Tex nor Jinx wanted to go back to television full time. And, in any case, NBC had entered the morning television market, which Tex and Jinx had pioneered, with the "*Today*" show, which came to dominate the market. They kicked ideas around for a while, and eventually formed a company, Tex McCrary, Inc.—and waited for things to happen. One thing led to another, and suddenly a lot of things began to happen.

Tex had known Spyro Skouras for years. Spyro's father, Charlie Skouras, owned most of the movie houses in New York and was a good friend of Arthur Brisbane's, and they, together with Walter Annenberg, had engineered some real estate deals. During the War, Spyro was in the OSS, and he and Tex had crossed paths in London, Caserta and Cairo. After the war, Spyro went to Hollywood to build on his movie connections. When Bill Zeckendorf completed his plan with the Rockefellers to build the UN on the East River, he called Tex and said that he wanted to put a deal together in

Los Angeles. McCrary called Spyro, and Tex and Zeckendorf flew out to meet him. As Tex had anticipated, Skouras and Zeckendorf hit it off immediately. Tex was back and forth to Los Angeles regularly. The result of their efforts was Century City. The "Avenue of the Stars" runs through the center of the complex, paved with large stars, each bearing a famous Hollywood name. When the project was completed, Skouras and Zeckendorf took Tex to see it. Star Number One was engraved "Tex McCrary."

Tex's uncle, Tom Taylor, had been a director of Swift & Company, the giant meat packer in Chicago. Swift wanted to do more business in Argentina, and Tex was asked to arrange a visit and dinner for the President of Argentina, Arturo Frondizi. Argentina was the most advanced and richest country in South America. Tex had his Yale friend Ed McNally, of the map company Rand McNally, make a giant world globe the same size as the one he made for Eisenhower's office—except that Tex wanted this globe upside down, with Argentina on top. Frondizi was thrilled, and the globe made a powerful impression on the audience, which was made up of a good many of America's corporate leaders, including Henry Ford—who told Tex that he, too, wanted to expand in South America. Tex had carefully checked out Frondizi's personal history and he knew that he was crazy about cars; he suggested to Ford that Frondizi be invited to Detroit, shown the Ford factory, given a dinner—and a car, a pretty little Ford convertible—and President Frondizi rewarded Tex with the first television license for Buenos Aires. A hotel and several other projects were in various stages of preparation when a military dictatorship arrested Frondizi and took over the country. Tex was told that, despite the revolution, Frondizi's Ford convertible was still on display in a museum in Buenos Aires.

Tex knew Ted Morosco as a member of the Eisenhower Administration, a truly great man who deserves tremendous credit for his role as the Director of Development for Puerto Rico. Morosco told Tex that Puerto Rico needed a first-class hotel. A mutual friend, who was a pal of Conrad Hilton, called to say that he had recommended Tex to Hilton and set up an appointment—and he gave Tex some advice: "Don't get yourself hung up trying to learn 'hotel business' talk. Connie Hilton only builds hotels to have his name on them, hang a giant picture of himself in the lobby, and meet pretty girls." Hilton and Tex got along just fine. A Puerto Rico Hilton took shape quickly. The numbers looked good, and a Havana Hilton seemed a next step. Tex and Jinx went to Havana to get the project started—and fell in love with the place. Veradero Beach in those days was the most fabulous place that they had ever seen. "El Presidente" Batista controlled Cuba, and was, of course, rotten to the core—but eager for another grand hotel. They went ahead with the project and didn't pay too much attention to local politics, until one fateful night. Bill Safire and Tex had at the same time been developing a project with President Mendoza of Mexico, another old friend of Jinx's family, and Mendoza was staying with them at the *Hotel Nacionale* in downtown Havana. It was near midnight when Safire called to say that Castro was entering Havana to take control of the Cuban government. It was essential to get Mendoza to sanctuary in a foreign embassy. They got him into the Bolivian Embassy just ahead of Castro's troops—but that was the end of Cuba for Tex and Jinx.

In the course of all this, Tex put together what he thought was to be his most personally satisfying business achievement, the purchase of *The New York Herald Tribune* for Jock Whitney. The *Tribune* and the *New York Times* were the two leading national morning newspapers—the *Times*, leaning toward the Democratic side, and the *Trib* as a voice for moderate Republicans. The Reid family owned the *Herald Tribune*, and Tex's friend Brownie Reid was managing the paper. Tex had had a column in the *Trib* for several years (Bill Safire did most of the writing). Tex knew that, for family reasons, the Reid family wanted to sell. All of the pieces seemed to fit together perfectly.

Jock was then the U.S. Ambassador to the Court of St. James, and Tex flew to London to talk it over with him. Jock had been on the *Yale Record,* and had always been interested in publishing. After laying out the opportunity to Jock at the Embassy in London, Tex took him down to the lobby where a plaque listed the Ambassadors. The name of Jock's grandfather, John Hay, led the first column, with Whitelaw Reid's name at the top of the second. Tex pointed to the bottom of that column, at the name John Hay Whitney. Using the language of Tap Day at Yale, Tex said, "Jock, you've been tapped."

The events that followed were complex, and not always pleasant. Tex knew that owning the *Herald Tribune* would fulfill Jock's highest hopes for personal achievement. But, even though he had so clearly demonstrated his desire for a significant personal accomplishment and contribution, rather than just an inherited position, Tex also knew that Jock unaccountably held back when confronted with an individual public role. Part of the problem was his fear of conflict. After the war, Lawrence Rockefeller had started a venture capital operation as a good use of inherited wealth, and Rockefeller had encouraged Jock to do the same. Jock then set up an operation, J.H. Whitney & Co., initially run by his lawyer, Bill Jackson. While Jock wanted to buy the *Tribune*, he didn't want to have operational management responsibilities. Walter Thayer, a tough operator, was brought in. Trouble. Finally, when all other details had been settled, Thayer questioned Tex's finder's fee. Tex didn't want to have his fee be used as a deal-breaker, so he said that he would waive it. The deal closed. There were celebrations all around. A great New York newspaper was in good hands. Republicans rejoiced that Jock Whitney was in charge. Eisenhower called Jock with congratulations. Tex thought it was a happy ending.

Then Thayer cancelled Tex's long-standing column arrangement with *The Herald Tribune*. Tex lost his temper and told Jock that Thayer was a sharp dealer, unworthy of the Whitney organization, and if Thayer was going to cancel Tex's arrangement, Tex wanted to reinstate a finder's fee. That, of course, put Jock in a tough spot, as he was relying on Thayer to run all of his operating businesses in J.H. Whitney. After some thought, Jock, obviously troubled, sent Tex a letter offering to sell him the house that Tex and Jinx rented on his Long Island estate. The price was so low that it was really a most generous gift, evidencing Jock's friendship, but Tex was too angry to accept.

The truth was that Tex had far too many balls in the air. Running around was a lot of fun, and Tex made—and lost—a fair amount of money. But the personal cost was even higher. Strains on their marriage steadily increased. Jinx and Tex finally separated, but never divorced. Jock Whitney, saddened by the disagreement with Tex, but ever gracious, provided for Jinx to continue to live in the house at *Greentree* until Betsey Whitney's death. Jock died in 1982, Betsey lived until 1992. Whitney estate lawyers served an eviction notice on Jinx the day following Betsey's death.

[Footnote: Jinx attended a birthday party for Tex at the Racquet and Tennis Club and my wife, Maggie, and I spent a day with Jinx in her charming cottage in Locust Valley. Despite her long struggle with cancer, her natural beauty was apparent. She spoke of Tex with evident affection, he visited her on Sundays, his health permitting. She talked easily of their lives, the war, the adventures and excitements, especially the Eisenhower days, their friendship with Jock Whitney and the happy times living in the grand house on Jock's estate. She spoke openly and easily of the various stresses on the marriage and of her alcohol problems, which she was eventually able to master. She and Tex never divorced—but she said that their interests in life were incompatible. Despite the effects of her long illness, the qualities that had made "Tex and Jinx" the insider couple of their time, were still apparent.]

On October 4, 1957, the Soviets startled the world with the launch of the world's first space satellite, *Sputnik,* the beginning of the Space Age—another failure of intelligence by the CIA and a blow to U.S. prestige, along with a serious warning of technological advances by the Soviet military. If the Soviets had rockets which could launch a satellite into space orbit with such precision, it was inescapable that they had to have long-range missile capability for their Atom bombs. Now the heavy B-52 bombers of the Air Force and the big nuclear-powered Navy carriers were outmoded. A potential U.S. "missile gap" loomed.

Then, in December 1957, Eisenhower had a stroke. After some recuperation, he returned to his office, as international troubles continued to escalate. Nasser's aggressive expansion of his United Arab Republic, and, as Eisenhower had feared, generated an active arms race. The U.S. sent arms to Israel, Saudi Arabia, Iraq and Jordan, and sent U.S. Marines into Lebanon. The Russians sent arms to Egypt and Syria, while the French continued their arms sales to Israel.

In 1958 Chiang Kai-shek again cranked up his saber rattling from Formosa, again over the tiny islands of Quemoy and Matsu off the coast of China. And again, the "Old Guard" members of Congress—continuing to enjoy Chiang's financial support—jumped in on his behalf. The newly-appointed chairman of the Joint Chiefs of Staff, Air Force General Twining recommended the use of Atom bombs, a foolish temptation to a war of choice. Fortunately, Eisenhower put the matter in its place, saying, "Formosa, if lost, would constitute a serious military loss; but the loss of the Middle East would be a disaster for our nation."

Then the Russians announced the planning of a major International Exhibition in Moscow in 1960, and an American exhibit was planned. Tex was called and told that Eisenhower was not satisfied with the plans being developed by the State Department, and he wanted Tex's advice on the project. After he had looked at the plans, Tex agreed that something much better could be done. It seemed certain that the Soviets would play up *Sputnik* and their scientific and military advances—and America was not in a position to get into competition on those grounds at that time.

Instead, Tex recommended that, as a counter to the Russian militarism, American emphasis should be placed on the way that average Americans lived, in the form of a typical American house, such as the homes that Bill Levitt had built for GIs. The concept was received with enthusiasm, but it raised the question of whether such a house would be too small for the large crowds anticipated at the Moscow exhibition. He suggested that a standard house be built in two halves, with a wide pedestrian passageway between, so that large crowds could, in effect, walk through the interior. Eisenhower was delighted with the concept. Work went forward on that basis, and the house became known as "*Splitnik*."

Bill Safire was handling the "*Splitnik*" project, and "*Splitnik*" was very popular with the Russian people, the crowds far outnumbering those at the Russian military and space exhibits—which naturally angered Khruschev. Nixon came over for the opening ceremony, and Khruschev seized the opportunity to take on Nixon. In front of Russian crowds and on Russian television, Khruschev embarked on a bombastic and aggressive attack, totally dominating Nixon. Safire, seeing the problem, shouted, "This way to the American Exhibit,"—and pulled down the fences which had restricted the attendance. The Russian crowd surged forward, filling the "split" of the *Splitnik*." Safire got Nixon and Khruschev into the kitchen. It was so crowded that Safire had to kneel on top of the stove. U.S. photographers were kept out by Russian guards, but Safire helped Elliot Erwitt get the photograph of Nixon jabbing his finger in Khruschev's chest—a picture which Tex believed contributed more than any other single item to an impression of Nixon's "Presidential" qualifications.

Bill Hearst was among the U.S. correspondents standing outside. Tex grabbed him and said, "Bill, here's your headline: 'Nixon stands up to Khruschev;' Safire has the pictures." The Russians embargoed all film from being sent out of the country for several days, but Safire smuggled negatives out in his sock. The headline and the picture of Nixon jabbing his finger into Khruschev's chest went around the world, and would later be used by Nixon as perhaps his most effective political image.

Eisenhower's *Farewell Address* to the Nation in January 1961 was not the gentle remarks expected from the old soldier. Instead, Eisenhower delivered an entirely unexpected and powerful warning for the future. He noted that, as Tom Taylor had predicted years before, "change" was changing the world. Whereas once, "makers of plowshares could make swords as well . . . the Cold War has created a permanent armament industry of vast proportions . . . and this conjunction of an immense military establishment and a large arms industry is new to the American experience. The total influence—economic, political, even spiritual—is felt in every city, every statehouse, every office of the federal government. . . . In the councils of government, we must guard against the acquisition of unwarranted influence, whether sought or unsought, by the military-industrial complex . . . the potential for the disastrous rise of misplaced power exists, and will persist." He went on to say that "The solitary inventor, working on his own, has been replaced by task forces of scientists working in laboratories . . . but today, because of the huge costs involved, a government contract has become virtually a substitute for intellectual curiosity . . . the prospect of domination of the nations scholars by federal employment, project allocations, and the power of money is ever present."

At the time, few people understood how prescient Eisenhower's prediction, and warning, was to prove.

Chapter Fourteen

The Failure of an Eisenhower Succession: Rockefeller: What If?

Nelson Rockefeller had called Tex after the 1956 election and said he had an idea he wanted to talk over. They met for lunch in his private dining room in Rockefeller Center. Nelson, being Nelson, came right to the point. He said he had made a decision and he wanted Tex's advice. They had both supported Eisenhower because they believed in him, and in the importance of a positive Republican Party. Nixon was not a "Citizen For Eisenhower." Eisenhower didn't pick him for Vice President, didn't want him on the ticket, had not given him any real role or responsibilities. Nixon is essentially a creature of the Republican right wing. He is the wrong man for the country and for the future of the Republican Party. He is not what the country should have. For whatever reason, whether because of his heart attack, his stroke, or his energy level, Eisenhower didn't want to face the unpleasant task of getting rid of him, when he should have, before the 1956 election. Now Eisenhower is a "lame duck" politically and Nixon is in the driver's seat for 1960—even though he is unpopular all over the country.

Rockefeller pressed on. He said that when he was pushing the 'Open Skies' project for reconnaissance flights over the Soviet Union in 1955, he got involved with Charlie Wilson at the Defense Department. Wilson wanted to make Rockefeller Under Secretary of Defense. However, Nixon knew Wilson was going to resign and he didn't want to see Rockefeller in the position of Secretary of Defense—and as a challenger for the 1960 Presidential nomination. Nixon got his key right-wing, big business supporters to push Eisenhower to make the "safe" choice of Neil McElroy, the CEO of Proctor & Gamble who didn't know anything about defense or international affairs. It was now clear to Rockefeller that he had no future in the Eisenhower Administration. He believed that the only opportunity he had for higher office was to break through the wall that the right-wing had built around Eisenhower—and to run for Governor of New York in 1958. And then take on Nixon in 1960. What did Tex think? Tex thought it was a good idea. Averill Harriman, the sitting New York Governor, was resting on his oars, confident of the support of the New York City Democratic machine. Averill was a poor public speaker and had none of Nelson's enormous vitality. New Yorkers were ready, even eager, for a change.

Meanwhile, the mess in the Middle East—Nasser, Suez, Israel—was getting worse. The oil issue was becoming more important every day—and Rockefeller knew the oil situation far better than any other political figure. While the American public was not yet alert to the looming problem that oil would become, the country would inevitably have to come to face the oil issue—and America would need a President equipped to provide knowledgeable leadership on the subject.

Looking down the road to 1960, Tex thought that Rockefeller was the only person with the necessary knowledge, the national identity and name recognition, the personal energy and drive, and perhaps most important, with the Rockefeller fortune, which would free him from dependence on special interest money and the vested institutional power of the right-wing control of the Republican National Committee. They talked it over and Nelson asked Tex to become an advisor, and a lot of great young people from their old Eisenhower "Citizens" campaign joined up. The resources Rockefeller put into the race were a revelation, the best of everything, and in duplicate. Harriman was completely out-classed. Nelson Rockefeller became the Governor of the largest and most powerful state in the country, while elsewhere around the country the 1958 Congressional elections proved to be a disaster for the Republican Party. As the upset victor over Averill Harriman, the well-known entrenched Democratic governor, Rockefeller was suddenly everyone's first choice to carry forward the kind of progressive Republican Party that Eisenhower had consistently said was his ambition for the country. He threw himself into his job as governor with his usual enthusiasm—for about six months. Then, he began his run for the Presidency. He assembled a whole new staff, entirely separate from his governor's staff, all experienced, top-quality, highly paid people—at least fifty professionals—all on his personal payroll.

As news of Rockefeller's activities began to leak out, Nixon's ever-present anxieties increased, and Tex got a long, convoluted call from Jim Hagerty at the White House. He said that although George Humphrey had resigned as Secretary of the Treasury, he had maintained his close relationship with Eisenhower and, during a long visit at his quail-hunting plantation at Thomasville, Georgia, had persuaded Eisenhower that Rockefeller was a liberal, a "spender." and thus a threat to conservative government. The upshot of all this was that Eisenhower had told Hagerty to ask Tex to give up his role as an advisor to Rockefeller, and get behind Nixon.

Hagerty's call was troubling. Since Eisenhower's serious heart attack in September, 1956—and the disagreement between Eisenhower's doctors over his fitness for a second term—Tex thought he had noticed a visible slowing down, a lessening of vitality—and perhaps of awareness. And, of course, Humphrey's position was self-serving. He knew that if Rockefeller were President, he would pay no attention to him. Humphrey would hate that. Tex told Hagerty that, given time, he believed Eisenhower would come to see Rockefeller as he did, and as did most of the old Eisenhower "Citizens," as the best candidate. The Republican Party should have a candidate with national leadership qualities who had a positive connection with the public. No matter how one viewed it, Nixon did not meet that test. It seemed to Tex that by every reasonable standard Eisenhower should have seen that his long-held desire to repudiate the regressive right wing and establish a truly progressive Republican Party would have been best served by supporting Rockefeller. He was convinced that, had Eisenhower thrown his support to Rockefeller, he could have changed the future course of American politics.

But before hopes for a change in Eisenhower's attitude could play out, Rockefeller called Tex and in a subdued manner recited the conclusions of his presidential research team that the Republican National Committee people had locked up control of the 1960 Republican nomination for Nixon by rule changes, money and a network of ideologically dedicated right-wing worker bees in the state committees. Tex jumped in, said that all of Rockefeller's resources, his personal energy, enthusiasm, appeal, unlimited finances, media and public support would overcome the "death wish" of the Republican National Committee for a "safe" right wing nominee, particularly one so lacking in public appeal as Nixon. Rockefeller's researchers had simply taken at face value what they were told by state party people, the hangers-on who owed their jobs, or their positions in their communities, to party loyalty. His research team had not taken into account the dynamics of a political campaign or the impact of the Rockefeller personal dynamism. Rockefeller was free to be his own man, while Nixon was always locked to the dictates of his money sources. They both knew the power of a positive leader who was not seen as being "in the pocket" of the party bosses. Confronted by " We Want Rocky," a positive, upbeat "clean" candidate, the slippery, negative Nixon would be overshadowed, overwhelmed. Moreover, International issues were looming ever larger, and Rockefeller was far better informed, not only on the oil situation, but especially on the growing tensions in the Middle East, where Iran, Iraq, Saudi Arabia, Kuwait, together with Venezuela, were organizing what came to be OPEC, the Organization of Petroleum Exporting Countries. But, despite Tex's best efforts, Rockefeller remained essentially unresponsive. Tex had never seen him like that before. He left the meeting feeling glum himself. Rockefeller had nothing to lose. He couldn't imagine what was holding him back.

Looking back on those days, Tex always wished that he had taken an even stronger stand. He knew that Rockefeller was unhappy with his advisors' negative advice. The Presidency was what he really wanted, and he needed someone to urge him to do what he wanted to do. To the end of his life Tex believed that, if the Rockefeller of that time had taken on Nixon, he would have been elected President. Further, Rockefeller's international experience would have led him to avoid the Kennedy-Johnson mistakes, the disastrous decisions in Vietnam would not have occurred, and our nation could have escaped much of the turmoil that has so afflicted, and continues to afflict our national politics to this day.

However, it was not to be. Shortly after the meeting with Tex, Rockefeller issued a gracious public statement that he would not seek the Republican nomination, and he threw himself into his role as Governor with his usual enthusiasm. For a time he seemed content with his pursuit of his building plans for Albany and New York—until Jack Kennedy entered the Presidential race. Rockefeller called Tex, a long general chat in which it was clear that he missed not being part of the great game—and was searching for some way to get back in.

Later, Tex wondered how a Rockefeller versus Kennedy race would have played out and what difference it might have made for the country. Rockefeller and Kennedy were both very attractive men, both positive in their attitudes, sharply different from the artificial and negative Nixon. While Rockefeller had vastly more experience, Jack Kennedy would have had some advantage in his "star" quality, and Jackie would have been an asset compared to Rockefeller's wife, Todd, who would have found campaigning distasteful. Nevertheless, it seemed to Tex that the "Catholic" problem for Kennedy, along with some likely shadows from his father's past, would have made Rockefeller the clear winner (as the 1960 post-election data on the religious issue indicated). After his election Kennedy said that, even he, had thought Rockefeller would have beaten him, and he added that his father thought so, as well! Asked what his father would have said if he had lost, Jack, with his whimsy and insight into his father, replied, "He would have said, Joe (the older brother killed in the war) would have won."

As the Nixon–Kennedy campaign advanced, and tightened. Rockefeller could not keep out. He went public with a harsh criticism of Nixon, ending with, "We cannot march into the future under a banner whose only emblem is a question mark"—intended as a direct attack on Nixon, but which was also taken by Eisenhower as an implied criticism of him and his Administration. Nixon could not ignore Rockefeller's outright challenge, and he went to meet Rockefeller at the Rockefeller apartment, in effect hat-in-hand, a humiliating concession, and fully covered by the press. The result came to be called the "Compact of Fifth Avenue," in which Nixon agreed to include some of Rockefeller's proposals in the Republican Party platform, knowing that the platform was essentially a farce, and could safely be ignored at the convention. Despite the embarrassment of the process, Nixon was skilled at converting an apparent humiliation into an asset. Knowing that he had the "Old Guard" Republican National Committee nomination in his pocket, he could safely ignore them for the rest of the campaign, all the while seeming to appear publicly to have accommodated to a progressive position. Thus he could play it both ways.

For all of his concerns about Nixon, Tex's paramount concern ever since seeing Hiroshima, was the election of a candidate who could keep America out of war. Eisenhower had demonstrated his commitment to this principle. He had steadfastly maintained that there were wars of choice, and wars of necessity—and that American troops should only be used in wars of necessity. Tex took comfort from the fact that Ike was still alive, and even if Nixon were President, Tex did not believe that he could afford to break with Eisenhower on the issue of war.

In the 1960 election the general public seemed to be in a kind of passive drift. The economy was flat, the Cold War was continuing, and Soviet military advances in space were threatening. At the Republican Convention, Nixon named as his Vice Presidential candidate, Henry Cabot Lodge, the man who had originally rigged Nixon's appointment as Eisenhower's Vice President in 1952.

Tex thought that the energy level of the country had drained away during the last years of the Eisenhower Presidency—and that Kennedy's vitality and style might give the country a needed lift. Still, he had serious doubts about Kennedy's total lack of experience, especially international experience. While he understood the political motivations that had led Kennedy to choose Lyndon Johnson as his Vice President despite his ignorance of world affairs, Tex was uneasy about a sluggish U.S. economy; seriously concerned about what was going on in Europe, and deeply apprehensive about what was going on in Vietnam.

Chapter Fifteen

Jack Kennedy: The Dream of Camelot and the Nightmare of Vietnam

It all began with such promise on that crystal-clear January day, the strikingly handsome, vital young President, the quivering voice of the poet Robert Frost in the invocation, then Kennedy's inspiring words—"Let the word go forth, from this time and place, to friend and foe alike, that the torch has been passed to a new generation . . . and so, my fellow Americans, ask not what your country can do for you, ask what you can do for your country."

Kennedy spoke to a higher national purpose, a challenge to fulfill the American dream, an Inaugural masterpiece that forever established Kennedy's place in history. For Tex, the Kennedy Inaugural remained the single most impressive and inspiring of all the public ceremonies of his life. And the Kennedys brought a dazzling elevation of style to the White House with their intellectual and artistic associations and their glamorous parties. Tex was surprised and pleased to see Jackie, who had seemed so shy and insecure when she had tried out to work with him, emerge as a "First Lady" of such elegance and grace. And Jack Kennedy had all the qualities that Nixon lacked, personal charm, manner and style, a prestigious education, warm personal friendships, a glamorous wife, an elegant lifestyle and, perhaps most important, a sense of humor and a sense of irony. The Kennedys brought new possibilities to replace the stale corporate dullness that marked the end of the Eisenhower Administration.

The media was fascinated by the Kennedy aura. It seemed almost too perfect, too good to be true, the idealized image of what Americans wished for their nation. Then it was to end, so suddenly, shockingly, tragically, the rifle shots in Dallas, the unforgettable picture of the three-year old son saluting his father's funeral caisson. All to be transformed into myth. A reality lay behind that myth, the questions of war and peace, which lie in the hands of the President. Those questions had haunted Tex by what he had seen in his flight over Hiroshima, now made more terrible to contemplate by the development of the new H-bomb and the Intercontinental Ballistic Missile. While Jack Kennedy had all the appeal of a movie star, handsome, graceful, charming, witty, splendid company to his many friends, there was little, if any, qualifying international experience, or even of much real interest, by Kennedy or by his Vice-President, Lyndon Johnson, to equip them for the immense responsibility of leading America in the ever-shrinking, ever more dangerous world.

Baruch had visited Kennedy at the White House right after the Inauguration and he told Tex that, while he found Kennedy impressive as a person, he kept thinking of Oliver Wendell Holmes' comment after his first meeting with Franklin Roosevelt: "First-class temperament; second-class mind."

He and Tex became more disturbed as they watched the selection of the Kennedy Cabinet, people Kennedy did not know—and who did not know each other—the same kind of mistakes that Eisenhower had made, but at least Eisenhower had an unmatched personal depth of personal experience upon which to draw. The appointment of Dean Rusk, the obscure head of the Rockefeller Foundation, as Secretary of State, the senior Cabinet position, the chief advisor on foreign policy, the seat to which George Washington had appointed Thomas Jefferson, was appalling. And then Robert McNamara, the President of Ford Motor Company, was appointed Secretary of Defense. It reminded Tex of Eisenhower's disastrous appointment of Charlie Wilson, the ill-equipped head of General Motors. The foreign policy group was rounded out by Kennedy friend Mac Bundy, a young Harvard Dean, who was ambitious, intellectually pretentious and totally ill-equipped for the role of National Security Advisor. This group lacked the depth of experience and judgment to compensate for Kennedy's lack of international experience.

What followed was worse. Looking back with the perspective of many years, Tex saw in the foreign policy of Kennedy—and then of Johnson, although for different reasons—a more fateful national consequence, a linked series of decisions which were ultimately to cause the destruction of the Presidencies of Lyndon Johnson and Richard Nixon, to reverse the traditional character and role of the political parties, and lead to the failed Presidencies of Gerald Ford and Jimmy Carter—all beginning in Vietnam, and ultimately leading to the devastating economic impact of the Arab Oil Embargo and to America's escalating entanglement in the politics of oil and religion, Islam and Israel, in the Middle East.

Eisenhower had faced essentially the same set of problems, but he had been able to avoid the mistakes of the Presidents who followed him because he had the experience and judgment to resist the impetuous, reflexive military and Congressional recommendations to commit military forces, or to use the Atom bomb. At the end of Eisenhower Presidency, there were less than seven hundred CIA "advisers" in Vietnam—none in uniform. Prior to Kennedy's commitment of U.S. troops in uniform, the war in Vietnam was between North Vietnam communists and a dictatorial South Vietnam government—Asians fighting Asians. Then Kennedy began quietly to commit U. S. troops in uniform to Vietnam—the number steadily rising to over fifteen thousand. It seemed to Tex that it was almost inevitable that Kennedy's action would result in "Blood on the Uniform," that Kennedy's decision had made it a war of choice for America, and even worse, a colonial war—West against East—everything that Eisenhower had warned against.

The first real international exposure of the Kennedy Administration was the "Bay of Pigs" invasion of Cuba in April 1961, three months after the Inauguration. The Bay of Pigs was a CIA operation, the landing force consisted primarily of anti-Castro Cubans trained by the CIA, with air cover from U.S. Navy and Air Force planes with national markings removed. However, the scheduled air cover, essential to interdict movement of Castro's troops to counter the invasion, was inexplicably cancelled just before the landing. The invasion was a disaster. Castro troops captured or killed most of the landing force.

The White House made every effort possible to avoid responsibility resting on the Kennedy Administration, but the facts revealed a record of confused and conflicted decisions, even an alleged assassination attempt on Castro, known as *Operation Mongoose,* allegedly arranged through the CIA with Sam Giancana, the Chicago Mafia boss. This led to further questions of Mafia pressure to regain their old Cuban gambling casino operations, connected with Kennedy campaign cash contributions from Las Vegas Mafia casino connections, The White House "spin machine" tried to cover up by asserting that the Cuban invasion was an Eisenhower plan. But that excuse did not stand up. Even if the plan had been presented to Eisenhower in prospect, the ultimate responsibility for the final decision rested on Kennedy. Bobby Kennedy, as Attorney General, pulled all strings to direct responsibility away from the President, and great play was made of Cabinet involvement in the decision-making. Journalist friends who covered the White House told Tex that the part of the fault in the decision resulted from the way that Bobby ran the Cabinet. After the CIA presentation, Bobby had questioned the Cabinet members sequentially by order of rank, for a go or no-go decision. Given the constant emphasis by Bobby on Kennedy "toughness," it was inevitable that no member of the Cabinet would want to be seen as the first to reveal, by a "no go" vote, that he was, in the Kennedy phrase, "lacking in fiber." Only after each Cabinet member had said, "go," did Jack concur. The whole Cuban operation was a shady, disgraceful performance at every level, one which was seriously to impair U.S. international relationships thereafter, especially in Central and South America.

After the Cuban debacle, it was essential for Kennedy to change the subject as quickly as possible, and the White House laid on a European visit at the end of May 1961. Tex and Jinx watched with interest. Paris was easy. Jack took Jackie, whose combination of beauty, elegance and ability to speak French (a legacy of her *Prix de Paris* days with *Vogue* magazine) captivated French President de Gaulle. Her success was capped by Jack, typically graceful, introducing himself in his formal Paris address, "I am the man who accompanied Jacqueline Kennedy to Paris." The French were ecstatic.

Kennedy then went to a meeting with Khrushchev in Vienna in the first week of June. Khrushchev delivered a belligerent tirade, dressing down an embarrassingly unprepared and unresponsive Kennedy. Apparently sensing weakness, Khrushchev began to build the Berlin Wall to seal off East Germany from the West. There was no response from the U.S. Tex couldn't understand it. It seemed that the Kennedy Administration was unable to anticipate, or to respond effectively, in foreign policy matters.

Tex talked with Baruch, wondering what could have influenced Kennedy to such decisions? Baruch said that his father's influence loomed large. Tex knew something of Joe Kennedy going back to conversations with him during his visits to Brisbane's office at the *Mirror* nearly thirty years before. And, of course, Baruch had known him for many years before. From them, Tex had learned a good bit of fascinating information about Joe Kennedy, going back to the 1930's.

Following Joe Kennedy's well-regarded performance as the first head of the Securities and Exchange Committee, Roosevelt had then appointed him as Ambassador to the Court of St. James in 1937. Tex loved the story of the meeting when Roosevelt informed Kennedy of his appointment. Kennedy said that he hoped that he could be formally presented to the King of England wearing a formal day tailcoat, rather than the silk "knee britches" that were conventional in European diplomacy. Roosevelt asked why, and Kennedy said that he was embarrassed at the thought of exposing his "knock knees." Roosevelt said, "Really, Joe? Drop your pants and let me see." Confronted by the evidence, Roosevelt agreed that Kennedy would look better in a tailcoat and formal trousers.

As war clouds gathered during his time as Ambassador in London, Joe Kennedy became increasingly convinced that England was too weak to oppose Hitler, and in 1940 he made his views public in an interview with a Boston newspaper, saying, "Democracy is finished in England, and it may be here, too"—and unforgivable breach for an Ambassador. Roosevelt replaced him, and Kennedy, realizing that the door had closed on any political future for himself, turned his ambitions toward his sons, beginning with Joe, Jr.

Tex used to see Joe, Jr. in New York, always with a beautiful girl on his arm. When the U.S. entered the war, Joe, Jr. became a Naval Aviator and was sent to England, where they saw more of each other. He soon grew tired of flying boring Navy ocean patrols, and volunteered to fly a high-risk, one-way bombing mission against a Nazi rocket-launching platform on the French coast, so heavily protected that it had resisted all prior conventional bombing attacks. Joe piloted a Navy version of the B-24 packed with high explosives, and the plan was for him to parachute out near the target to be picked up by waiting patrol boats, while the pilotless plane would be directed by radio control from an accompanying RAF escort into the target. As Joe reached the designated point, his plane exploded. Despite extensive search, no trace of his body was ever found. Joe Kennedy was distraught at the loss of his eldest, seemingly most impressive son and, inevitably, the father's relentless ambition turned to the second son, Jack.

The father's preparation had begun early. During Jack's last year at Harvard in 1940, Joe Kennedy had enlisted the help of Arthur Krock, the *New York Times* Washington columnist, whose support Kennedy had obtained, as he had with many other journalists, by a variety of benefits—stock market tips, long visits to Palm Beach, use of his yacht, "loans," and other luxuries—to "assist" Jack with a thesis with a view toward its publication. Joe then took the final product to Henry Luce at *Time* and prevailed upon Luce to write a strong introduction, which contributed to the book, "*Why England Slept,*" being chosen by the prestigious Book-of-the-Month Club, an asset for Jack's political future, while simultaneously giving some credibility to his father's defeatist pre-war views.

Later, Tex heard that after Pearl Harbor, Joe had arranged a direct commission for Jack as an ensign in the Navy, with assignment to a Naval Intelligence slot in Washington, where Jack pursued his habit of lady-chasing to the extent of several embarrassing involvements, including an intense relationship with a Danish beauty whose prior associations and lifestyle had attracted the attention of J. Edgar Hoover, leading to a critical FBI report, a copy of which Hoover forwarded to Kennedy's father.

A longer stay in Washington did not seem to be appropriate, and Jack requested duty as PT-boat officer. He was sent to the Pacific, where his 60-knot, highly maneuverable PT-109 was rammed and sunk on night patrol by a 30-knot Japanese destroyer. Two crewmen were killed. Any other officer who had lost his boat, and two of his crew, under such circumstances would likely have faced severe disciplinary proceedings. However, Kennedy got the rest of his crew ashore, then swam to a neighboring island and arranged their rescue. Kennedy's father used all his connections to promote the event into heroic proportions. A laudatory article by the prestigious author John Hersey appeared in the *New Yorker,* in time to assist in Jack's election to Congress in 1946. This was followed by the development of a flattering movie, "PT 109," starring Cliff Robertson as Jack Kennedy, which was released to extensive national publicity in time to help Jack's capture of Henry Cabot Lodge's Senate seat in 1952.

In 1953, Jack married the beautiful Jacqueline Bouvier, who had tried out to become one of the "kids" with Tex and Jinx. They were impressed to see Jackie, while retaining her natural sense of dignified reserve, suddenly emerge as the very epitome of elegance and sophistication, a great compliment to Jack's dashing masculinity. Jinx saw more to the marriage than Tex did. She said, "That means Jack's going to run for President, and he knows he'll have to have a elegant, glamorous wife."

For all his manifest talent and charm, there was a reckless streak in Kennedy. Jinx raised the subject when she and Tex were in Los Angeles in the late 1950's while Tex was working with Bill Zeckendorf on the development of Century City. Jinx had been raised in Hollywood—Paulette Goddard was a kind of older sister to her—and Jinx said the "girl-talk" network was full of stories of Jack Kennedy's wild extramarital activities on his frequent visits. In 1956 Jack had made a run at the Vice President slot behind Adlai Stevenson, and it was clear that Jack was going for the Presidency in 1960. Under the circumstances, Jack's behavior seemed inexplicably impulsive and self-indulgent, especially as American politics at that time was still notably straight-laced (Stevenson was considered to have lost many votes in 1956 because he was a divorced man). Yet Jack, whose marriage to the elegant Jackie was a prominent part of his political image, bed-hopped constantly with a wide range of ladies, from established movie stars to mobsters' playgirls, in Washington, Palm Beach, New York and Los Angeles, where he openly engaged in wild parties with Frank Sinatra and known Mafia "bosses."

Tex couldn't understand it, but Jinx said he had been caught up in politics too long. Movies and television had changed the country. Now Americans are hooked on entertainment. Just think of all the Kennedy stuff simply as a movie script. There's this filthy rich, tyrannical father raised in the gutter politics of Boston, thwarted in his own Presidential ambitions, and dedicated to achieving the power of the Presidency through his son, a dashing, handsome war hero playboy. Then there's the tough, hero-worshipping, little brother always sent in to clean up the messes. And think of the scenes—from Palm Beach to Palm Springs—the "Mob's" casinos and the supporting cast, beautiful women everywhere, falling all over themselves. Frank Sinatra! It's irresistible! Life imitating art. And he might just get away with it—if all the details of the women and the Mafia don't come out. That seemed to Tex to be a big "if." But Jinx was right. The story didn't come out until much later.

In the run-up to the 1960 Presidential campaign, Joe Kennedy, realizing that the appearance of his control of the campaign would be undesirable, had kept himself secluded, out of public view, in Boston. He telephoned directions to Bobby, as the ostensible front man, while simultaneously spreading money around in key political spots where the source of the funds could not be disclosed, i.e., to the "bosses" of the Democratic machines in major cities, Mayor Daley in Chicago, the union bosses in Detroit, and a variety of other similar types around the country. Joe Kennedy used all his many connections. Articles appeared in *Life*, *Look*, and other national magazines, along with complimentary photographs in newspapers. Ted Sorenson, a man whose abilities Tex respected, was Jack's Senatorial chief of staff, ran the office, wrote Jack's speeches, and is generally credited with authorship of the book, *Profiles in Courage*, for which Jack Kennedy won a Pulitzer Prize (Sorenson was listed in the appendix as a research assistant).

The 1960 Kennedy Presidential campaign was enhanced by a variety of committees, including the much publicized "Academic Advisory Committee" recruited from Harvard, MIT and other prestigious institutions, including the ubiquitous John Kenneth Galbraith, and Walt Rostow.

Tex noted the artful hand of Joe Kennedy, guiding Jack in primaries where it was essential to demonstrate his capacity to defeat his principal competitor, Hubert Humphrey. Kennedy won the New Hampshire primary easily, and then was able to defeat Humphrey (from Minnesota) in his neighboring state of Wisconsin, where the Kennedy margin of victory came from high turnouts in the union labor wards in Madison and Milwaukee, where private cash distributions were though to have been helpful.

The most crucial Kennedy victory was the West Virginia primary, where the combination of poverty and fundamentalist Southern Baptist Protestantism seemed a barrier to a rich Catholic presidential candidate. The amount of cash distributed to the "usual suspects," the politicians, sheriffs and precinct captains and, interestingly, to Protestant clergymen, to tone down their usual anti-Catholic sermons, while considered to be "significant," has never been finally determined.

The Kennedy victory in West Virginia was then promoted as evidence that Kennedy's Presidential bid would not be precluded by the feared anti-Catholic prejudices elsewhere. However, enough money had been spread around to generate talk that Joe Kennedy had "bought" the West Virginia primary. Tex admired Jack's stylish, casual dismissal, "Well, naturally I asked him, and he said he might be willing to buy an election—but he'd be damned if he'd pay for a landslide."

With Jack's Presidential nomination assured by the sophisticated "lubrication" of critical Democratic delegates, the Democratic Convention proceeded to the choice of a Vice President. Kennedy's presumed favorite was Stuart Symington, Senator from Missouri, and Kennedy's announcement of Lyndon Johnson as Vice President came as a total surprise to Tex, given the sharp contrasts and apparent incompatibility between the two men. The origin of the decision remains obscure. The cover story at the time attributed the decision to the persuasive argument of Phil Graham, the charismatic publisher of the *Washington Post*. Bobby Kennedy, serving as the visible head of his brother's campaign, did not conceal his unhappiness. Speculation centered on Joe Kennedy as the decision-maker; however, rumors persist that some kind of threat from Lyndon Johnson or Sam Rayburn, Speaker of the House, lay behind the sudden decision.

[Author's Footnote: Tex was interested to learn that Charley Bartlett, a Pulitzer Prize-winning Washington reporter and close friend of Jack Kennedy's—the man who had introduced Kennedy to Jackie and was an usher in their wedding in Newport— was staying with Kennedy during the Democratic Convention in Los Angeles. Charley told me that, prior to the nomination, Jack and Bobby had decided on Symington. However, on the morning following Kennedy's nomination, Phil Graham, editor of the *Washington Post*, and the journalist, Joe Alsop, visited Kennedy and strongly recommended Lyndon Johnson, as the only man who could carry Texas and the South (heavily Baptist and anti-Catholic) for Kennedy. Kennedy questioned whether he could get along with Johnson and, more importantly, whether Johnson would accept. "Just ask him," Graham replied. "If he refuses, he will at least be flattered and be more inclined to help." Intrigued, Kennedy went to LBJ's office on the floor below him in the Biltmore hotel, intending to hold out the possibility, dangle the idea in front of him, just to get his reaction. Johnson cut him off, saying, "I accept." Shortly thereafter, Bobby Kennedy, who had not been privy to the Graham meeting and did not know of Kennedy's visit to Johnson, independently went to Johnson, and told him that Kennedy had decided on Symington. Johnson, naturally, was outraged, and he had Sam Rayburn, the Democratic Congressional leader, similarly angry, call Kennedy, furious at the insult. Recognizing the problem he could face in dealing with Congress, Kennedy said calmly, "Bobby was out of touch," and that the small embarrassment should be ignored. Joe Kennedy had rented Gloria Swanson's mansion on the ocean, and Bartlett and Kennedy went there to change for the evening. They were talking on the terrace when Bobby arrived, angry and dead-set against Johnson. Jack Kennedy tried to sooth him when Joe, in velvet dinner jacket and slippers, joined them, listened silently to Bobby rage on for a time, and then said, "Boys, in a couple of weeks you'll think it was the best thing you ever did."]

Kennedy was elected President by tiny margins in Texas and Illinois, the crucial states in the razor-edged victory. Kennedy ran well, while Nixon ran a poor race— poor planning, poor debates, poor execution. Voter turnout was a record sixty-four percent of the electorate (versus less than fifty percent in 2000). A few thousand votes in Texas and Chicago, neither known for clean elections, would have changed the result—which gave rise to Republican charges of Democratic mischief. However, the closeness of the vote masked the impact of religion. Data indicated that, whereas fifty percent of Catholics had voted Republican for Eisenhower, Catholics voted seventy-eight percent for Kennedy in 1960. However, in the Democratic supposedly "Solid South," the racist and Christian fundamentalist vote shifted to Nixon—an ominous implication of the future direction of Nixon's thinking.

Tex was also surprised that during the campaign there had been relatively little mention in the mainstream press of Jack Kennedy's extramarital adventures and associations with the Mafia in Hollywood and Los Vegas. His suspicions of Joe Kennedy's sense of need for protection on this front were supported by Kennedy's appointment of J. Edgar Hoover, to continue as head of the FBI. Hoover was well known to have kept his position by using the resources of the FBI to protect himself and to influence behavior of others. This assumption was similarly underscored by the next Kennedy appointment, Allen Dulles, to remain head of the CIA—all of this suggesting a concern over potential problems that might need discreet covering up. The appointment of Bobby Kennedy as Attorney General was widely criticized. Ever stylish, Jack commented that he wanted "to give Bobby some experience before he had to go out and practice law." However, Tex could see old Joe's hand, knowing that, as Attorney General, Bobby could be counted upon to maintain strict control over the Department of Justice, over J. Edgar Hoover and the FBI, and also to keep a heavy hand over Dulles at the CIA.

Then there was Vietnam, which was to loom as the lasting Kennedy legacy. Tex thought about what he had seen there in 1945, the vast corruption of the French rule. He knew what a mess it was then, and surely it had only gotten worse through the years The corruption of Diem and his French-related regime became ever more apparent, as the communist Vietcong forces steadily gained ground and power. Vietnam President Diem, with his wife, Madame Ngu—a real "Dragon Lady,"—and Diem's brother, all Catholics, began a persecution of Buddhists, the predominant religious affiliation in Vietnam. In protest, a Buddhist monk knelt in a Saigon square, poured gasoline over his body, and set himself on fire. Madame Ngu ridiculed the suicide as a "barbeque." Protests spread rapidly, more monks set themselves on fire, and the situation became uncontrollable. Henry Cabot Lodge was the Ambassador. And a cover story was released, asserting that the warfare was directed by "Communists."

Tex didn't believe it. He had seen the brutal abuse of the Vietnamese people by the degenerate French colonial administration when he was there in 1945. He believed that rebellion against the French-supported government of the Catholic President Diem, and his wife, Madame Nhu, was essentially a nationalist movement, doubtless Communist-supported, but not Communist-controlled. He later concluded that the "Communist" argument was intended to appeal for support from the simplistic, fear-peddling but powerful "anti-communist" majority in Congress.

As the situation in Vietnam continued to deteriorate, and pressure for more troops increased on the Kennedy Administration. On November 1, 1963, President Diem was overthrown by dissident generals, and assassinated. The real story remains murky, even after more than forty years. There were stories that Diem was preparing to negotiate with Ho Chi Minh to unite the two Vietnams and force U.S. withdrawal.

Some degree of U.S. involvement in Diem's assassination was widely suspected. And stories persist that both Lodge, and Kennedy, had involvement in, and/or authorized, the assassination. In any case, the future of the war depended upon a decision by the U. S. to take over the war. Kennedy ordered fifteen thousand uniformed troops to Vietnam.

[Author's Footnote: Charley Bartlett told me that, in the summer of 1963, Kennedy had said to him that he had come to the conclusion that the war could not be won, and that he intended to pull out. Delighted at the news, Bartlett asked, "When?" Kennedy replied the he would act after his reelection in 1964. Bartlett was shocked at the thought that his close friend Jack Kennedy would continue the war for purposes of his own reelection. Troubled by the thought that the temptation of reelection could work against the best interests of the country, Bartlett later became an advocate for a single six-year term for future Presidents, and he joined a group dedicated to promoting the idea—but the group later disbanded when somebody asked, "Do we really want the risk of six years of Jimmy Carter?"]

On November 22, 1963, Jack Kennedy was assassinated in Dallas. The entire nation was overcome with grief at the death of their idealized lost leader. The images remain etched in the nation's memories, of thee-year old "John-John," saluting his father's funeral caisson, of Jackie, black-veiled, distant, in shock, kneeling in mourning in front of the casket in the White House, other scenes almost too painful to recall, all the hoped-for anticipation of inspiring leadership, extinguished.

Despite the promising beginning, Baruch nevertheless thought that Kennedy's performance as President was shockingly inept. Now Lyndon Johnson was President. Baruch felt that Johnson was even less prepared than Kennedy to lead the nation. And he had no more idea than Kennedy of how to get the American troops out of Vietnam. Johnson was a master manipulator of Congress, but that was all he knew. And the Republican isolationists in Congress know nothing of the world. They have this crazy idea that Vietnam is somehow controlled by China, and that China is controlled by Russia, and therefore it's all a single, massive Communist conspiracy against America. Lyndon Johnson is profoundly ignorant of international affairs. The situation can spin out of control. Baruch feared the worst.

Baruch told Tex that it was wrong to think of Johnson only as a Texan, he was also a man of the South, and the South is different in many ways. The North won the Civil War, and winners don't think much about losers. But losers cling to their traditions and beliefs. The South respects the military virtues—authority, loyalty, personal honor. Remember how long dueling lasted in the South. And understanding the religious differences is crucial. In the North, religions are typically hierarchical, authoritarian, disciplined, and to some degree, remote and impersonal, whereas in the South, religious practice is local, personal and emotional—and plays a big part in Southern life. Johnson is a creature of politics, and Southern instincts and prejudices run deep.

Baruch pointed out that attention should be paid to the major changes that would inevitably affect the country. Air conditioning would open the South and West to new industry, immigration and, most important, to better education. Lyndon Johnson would take care of Texas. The West would benefit, with aviation and space industry in Los Angeles and strong science and electronics programs in major Western universities, Stanford, Berkeley, Cal Tech. All these changes would alter the national political balance.

Tex asked what did Baruch see as the most positive change? He said the best thing was that the country is finally free of Nixon. After losing the Presidency to Kennedy in 1960, he couldn't accept the public judgment. He ran for Governor of California in 1962—and lost again—ending with that whining, self-pitying, news conference, "You won't have Nixon to kick around anymore." He's thoroughly discredited now. The Nixon stain on American politics is behind us.

At that time, it never occurred to Tex that Baruch could be wrong.

Chapter Sixteen

"Hey, Hey, LBJ, How Many Boys Did You Kill Today?"

He couldn't stand to hear it, the cry endlessly chanted by crowds of college kids wherever Lyndon Johnson appeared. Nor could that supremely ambitious, vanity-obsessed man forget that he had been brought to the Presidency not by a national election, but by an assassin's bullet. And his legacy was Vietnam—which ultimately destroyed both him and his Presidency.

Afterwards, when no longer President, he said that he wished that he could have followed his "true love," his "Great Society," but instead he was caught up in what he called that "bitch" of a war. Why did Johnson continue to escalate what had been a losing French colonial war, Asians fighting Asians, into an American war of choice? A war which would ultimately escalate into a national disaster, the dark shadow of which continues to haunt America.

Did Johnson not know what Kennedy had confided in Charley Bartlett, and to others, that he had concluded that the Vietnam war could not be won—and that he intended to pull out after the 1964 election? It is certainly possible. The Kennedys, particularly Bobby, had isolated Johnson from nearly all discussions and decisions regarding foreign affairs. Of course, when Johnson became President, he could, and should, have made his own evaluation. At that time the total number of U. S. troops committed was still small, only fifteen thousand, and total U. S. deaths were less than one hundred. There was no legitimate government in place, no plan for a Vietnam "victory," no "exit" plan for America.

The Vietnam War was to drag on for ten years, finally ending with the humiliating picture of the last U.S. helicopter staggering off the roof of the U. S. Embassy in Saigon, overloaded with terrified people hanging on the landing skids. More than five hundred thousand U.S. soldiers had been committed, more than fifty-eight thousand had been killed, and more than three hundred thousand wounded.

Apart from the disaster of Vietnam, Tex believed that Johnson should also be viewed in the context of his domestic policies. At the time of his selection for the Vice Presidency, Johnson was Majority Leader of the Senate, unquestionably the most powerful figure in Congress. Although he had none of Jack Kennedy's extraordinary attractiveness and personal magnetism, Johnson's skill lay in knowing what was feasible within the political context of the Senate. He was the master of the sordid "inside game," the secret deals and the manipulation of personalities. He knew "where all the bodies were buried," what buttons to push, and his power rested in backroom, closed-door deals, greased by the liberal use of "pork."

However, for all his immense personal power in Congress, Johnson did not have a strong national following. Despite all the projects and "pork" that he lavished on Texas and the South, he was never quite trusted on the race issue by conservative southerners. Ironically, he was not trusted by liberal northerners for the same reason. To bridge this gap, he chose as his Vice President the premier Northern liberal, Hubert Humphrey.

Given Johnson's limited background, Tex was impressed by his adroit development of his "Great Society" concept, an integrated package of civil and voting rights, education reform, and other meaningful legislation, reaching well beyond Kennedy's public rhetoric—which Johnson brought to fruition in the Civil Rights Act of 1964. By this, Johnson advanced the Democratic Party, from the "State's Rights" Party of Harry Truman in 1948, into national "Civil Rights Party"—which confronted the Republicans with a direct challenge to their claim, as the Party of Lincoln, to be the standard-bearer for respect for human dignity.

It was ironical that Johnson, the consummate political dealmaker, should regard his civil rights legislation as his finest achievement (but also anticipating its likely exploitation by Republicans) as, "the right thing to do—but it will mean the end of the Democratic Party's base in the South." At the time, Tex didn't focus fully on the full implications of Johnson's statement—but it turned out that Dick Nixon was listening.

Despite Johnson's great Civil Rights achievement, Tex became, alternately, fascinated, appalled, disgusted, and ultimately horrified by Johnson's subsequent decisions and behavior. He thought that part of the answer lay in the fact that Lyndon Johnson and Texas had risen to national power together, and their rise revealed much of the underlying process of American politics. The McCrary family in Texas knew Lyndon Johnson well and Tex had learned much of the early background from them. The McCrary ranch was in the prosperous cotton country on the eastern side of the Tenth Congressional District, important because it included Austin, the capital of Texas. The district was divided into the eastern "cotton country" and the barren "hill country" to the west. When Tex went to Exeter in the mid-1920s, the "hill country" was destitute, without machinery or electricity, where farmers plowed behind mules. One of the McCrary neighbors in the "cotton country" was Richard Kleberg, owner of the biggest ranch in Texas. He was elected to Congress in 1932, and he took Lyndon Johnson, a young school teacher, to Washington as his secretary. Johnson made the most of his opportunities, and, after Kleberg retired in 1936, Johnson was elected to Kleberg's seat, at the age of twenty-eight.

Roosevelt's New Deal benefited Texas perhaps more than any other state, and in many ways Lyndon Johnson came to represent this change, not only in his district, but throughout the state. In Congress, Johnson ingratiated himself with the powerful leader of the House, fellow Texan, "Mister Speaker," Sam Rayburn, and was included in Rayburn's decision-making inner circle, known as "The Board of Education," where Johnson rapidly came to understand the mechanics of Congress, and the technique and benefits of directing government contracts to favored contractors. New Deal projects sprang up all over Texas—dams, electric power plants, highways, Army and Air bases, the giant Corpus Christi Naval Base—these were only the beginning. George Brown, with his engineering firm, Brown & Root—now a subsidiary of Halliburton—was an early sponsor of Johnson, (now a staunch supporter of George W. Bush) and Brown seemed to win most of the major government projects. The "competitive bidding" process was easily manipulated by an initial low bid, especially if the other bids were known, which could be obtained if one knew the "right" people. Once a government contract had been approved, profitability could be expanded dramatically by "change orders" and "adjustments," which were not subject to public review. Apart from the benefits to the contractors, such projects also generated substantial new employment and other economic benefits, all generating the economic transformation of Texas in a remarkably short period.

Lyndon Johnson encouraged the belief that he had brought it about—and in many ways he had. He relentlessly used this perception to take personal fundraising to a new level. The bankers on Tex's mother's side of the family were regularly exposed to this approach, which also lay heavily upon the beneficiaries of federal contracts, oil companies and businessmen, to whom Lyndon Johnson made it clear that they had a substantial return obligation to him as the person who had made it happen—and who would be in a position to continue to do so.

Apart from Johnson's own enormous energy and ambition, he also had an eye for talent, preferring to recruit student body presidents from the University of Texas, and Washington soon became full of very successful men whose careers began with Johnson. Lyndon assiduously worked both sides of the street, enriching both the state and himself. He used his Congressional influence to obtain for himself the license for the television station in Austin—and to maintain thereafter a television monopoly in the capitol city of Texas. He also arranged many highly lucrative real estate and investment deals, always careful to place legal title in his wife's name and thus become the richest President ever to hold office.

After the U.S. entered World War II, Johnson had obtained a direct commission in the Naval Reserve as a Lieutenant Commander, and he eventually concluded that his political future required some exposure to a war front. He arranged an inspection trip to the Pacific, flew as a passenger on an Air Force bombing raid where his plane encountered Japanese fighters. The politically ambitious General MacArthur awarded Johnson with the Silver Star, the third ranking U.S. combat decoration (regular crew members of the squadron did not receive similar decorations during their full combat tour) Johnson wore his ribbon proudly thereafter. Tex was told that at the decoration ceremony an assisting officer asked MacArthur what the wording should be for the decoration, to which MacArthur replied, "Think up something."

After the war Johnson ran for the Senate against a popular former governor, Coke Stevenson. By election day, Stevenson appeared well ahead, but the Johnson district chairmen were told to disclose low turnout figures during the day—and to keep tight control of ballot boxes in oil-rich counties controlled by Johnson friends. After the Stevenson final figures were recorded, the Johnson County's ballot boxes were opened. The last box revealed that Johnson had won by eighty-seven votes, out of nearly one million cast, earning the nickname "Landslide Lyndon." (Kennedy liked to refer to his Vice President as "Old Landslide.") Despite his idiosyncrasies, Johnson had accumulated unrivaled power in Congress.

It became more and more apparent that Kennedy, had kept Johnson out of the early military discussions on Vietnam, during which Kennedy ignored Eisenhower's requirement that the small number of American military "advisors" must wear civilian clothes, and committed American troops in uniform as a show of support for the Diem government. Up to that time, the American public had shown little, if any, appetite or interest in American involvement.

When Johnson became President following Kennedy's assassination, he certainly had an opportunity to reconsider and disengage. Given the Kennedys' tendencies to withhold information from the Cabinet (as in their subsequently revealed "back channel" dealings with Russia using respected reporter friends, Charley Bartlett and John Scali, as intermediaries during the Cuban missile crisis) it may be that the Cabinet truly had no knowledge of any intention to withdraw from Vietnam after the 1964 election. As further evidence of the dysfunctional atmosphere of the time, Tex heard that Johnson had told friends that the Kennedys had been trying to connect Johnson to a scandal around his former Senate aide, Bobby Baker, sufficient to force Johnson from the ticket in 1964 in favor of Bobby Kennedy.

Given this background, Tex was surprised that Johnson had kept the Kennedy Cabinet in place through the 1964 campaign, apparently believing it was important to maintain a sense of national continuity, and to demonstrate his respect for the fallen leader. It must have been difficult for a man as vain as Johnson, who had been forced to endure the indifference of the Kennedy's during his days as Vice President.

As President, Johnson showed evident discomfort and awkwardness in public appearances, suggesting a deep-seated sense of inadequacy—possibly a sense of illegitimacy at having taken the place of so popular a President under such tragic circumstances. Further, Johnson masked his insecurities with egregious acts of vanity, compounded by his bragging about them to others. He loved to show off the grandeur of his ranch, and he offended guests with a different sense of sportsmanship by shooting deer from the back seat of his open Lincoln convertible.

Johnson was justly proud of his passage of the Civil Rights Act, passed in the summer of 1964. However, within a week, to his consternation and distress, riots broke out in Harlem and the Bedford-Stuyvesant sections of New York. Looters overwhelmed police, and arson and acts of wanton destruction were carried into the nation's homes by television—a seemingly perverse response to Johnson's successful passage of legislation so obviously beneficial to blacks. Student riots followed elsewhere, most notably in September at the University of California in Berkeley, this time linking complaints of well-to-do students to their sense of lack of personal attention by the faculty with a generalized antagonism by blacks from poor neighborhoods in Oakland. Nevertheless, Johnson pressed ahead, converting his Civil Rights Act into a more expansive "Great Society Program," including "War on Poverty" and medical and educational benefits.

Johnson's whole career had been marked by his preference for secrecy. And, under the cover of his "Great Society Program," Johnson escalated military operations in Vietnam. Evidently fearing public disclosure of the magnitude of the military escalations before the 1964 election, Johnson went to Congress and declared that the situation in Vietnam was highly volatile and required the capacity for immediate response. To bypass the fact that the Constitution had established that the power to make war rested with the Congress, not with the President, Johnson asserted that conditions in Vietnam were so fluid that Congressional involvement would impede necessary military response. In August 1964, Johnson used that justification to extract from Congress the *Tonkin Gulf Resolution,* effectively a "blank check," giving Johnson personal control of the funding, operation and expansion of the Vietnam War without Congressional oversight or public disclosure. Thus Johnson was able to conceal from Congress, from budget officials, and from the American people, the ever-increasing troop deployments, costs and casualties of Vietnam before the 1964 election. Testimony in subsequent hearings revealed that the *Tonkin Gulf Resolution* was a sham, intended to provide "cover" for Johnson's secret escalation of the war.

As the 1964 Presidential election approached, Tex thought that the logical Republican candidate was Nelson Rockefeller. Nixon was discredited, living in seclusion in San Clemente, still licking his wounds from his loss of the California governor's race in 1962. Tex and Rockefeller had early planning conversations, but Rockefeller seriously handicapped his campaign by another of his self-indulgent distractions. He compounded the political problem of his recent divorce by insisting upon remarriage, shortly before the primaries, to an attractive woman, twenty years younger—who had left her four children and her husband, a doctor employed by the Rockefellers. The quick Rockefeller re-marriage was not well-received by the public. As a result, Arizona Senator Barry Goldwater—a personally attractive man whom Tex admired, but whose forthright disposition seemed ill-suited for high office—became the Republican nominee.

Tex was amazed that Johnson—while himself secretly escalating a major war concealed from Congress and the public—was able to overwhelm Goldwater by depicting him as an irresponsible warmonger. Johnson achieved this perverse result through a television spot which ran only once—but once was enough to assure its place in history. A sweet young girl was shown plucking a daisy, while a portentous voice in the background counted down from ten to one, and the scene dissolved into the mushroom cloud of an Atom bomb explosion. There was no sound track. Goldwater was not mentioned. But the television image of the mushroom cloud destroyed his candidacy.

Secure in his protection from public disclosure of his secret escalation of the Vietnam War, Johnson told Bobby Kennedy that he would not be considered for Vice President. Infuriated, Bobby resigned and announced that he was moving to New York to become a candidate for the Senate. The Kennedy magic prevailed, and the new New Yorker was elected to the Senate almost upon his arrival. A precedent to Hillary Clinton's similar success in 2000.

Confident of his reelection, Johnson continued to intensify the war. Tex later learned that National Security Advisor McGeorge Bundy had delivered a memo incorporating the views of McNamara, Rusk and the military leaders, laying out policy options for Vietnam in bureaucratic form, offering three choices: 1) withdraw; 2) continue at present levels, (i.e., keep losing); 3) go all-out to win. Given Johnson's personality, his sense of insecurity and his aggressive nature, the decision was obvious. Johnson took the third choice, indelicately declaring that he was going to "nail that coonskin to the wall."

However, Vietnam rapidly became a " quagmire" for Johnson, sucking in ever-more troops. Soon existing regular Army troop levels could no longer support the increasing Vietnam requirements and maintain preexisting commitments of U.S. troops to NATO, Japan, etc. The logical solution was to call up the Army Reserve and National Guard units—but that would require involving Congress. Instead, unwilling to accept exposure of the magnitude of the war he was secretly conducting, Johnson elected to rely on the military Draft, which up to that time had involved relatively small numbers, generally unemployed young men, as college students had been exempted.

Johnson continued to involve himself personally in the escalation of the war. He had his picture taken, pouring over maps with McNamara and Bundy, picking bombing targets, declaring his personal control, "They can't bomb an outhouse without my permission." Draft calls for college students steadily increased, and draft dodging became rampant. Public protests rose dramatically, escalating into destructive riots. Civil order came under siege. Within the black community, leadership passed from the early positive style of Martin Luther King, to others, many rabble rousers and criminals. Stokely Carmichael of *Black Power* and H. Rap Brown of *the Black Panthers* openly incited rioters, shouting, "Burn, baby, burn." Tex was disgusted to see high-visibility cultural, literary and social figures entertaining and supporting such grotesque persons in well-publicized Park Avenue parties.

Tex hated the cultural changes that he saw the Vietnam War bringing to America, particularly the alienation of the groups, youths and blacks, to which he had always tried to direct attention. Students at leading universities, whose fathers and grandfathers had volunteered willingly for duty in World War I, and World War II, were now abandoning their classes and trashing their campuses, shouting "Hell No, We Won't Go!" The flower of American youth was actively rejecting their parents' values, living apparently on their parents' incomes, without any sense of responsible motivation, wearing outlandish costumes, listening to protest music, living in groups with narcotics and free sex, courtesy of the "Pill."

At the end of January 1968, the North Vietnamese initiated a major military effort, the "Tet Offensive," a total surprise, another weekend attack, which caught U.S. troops off guard, and seemed to demonstrate the growing power of North Vietnam. Walter Cronkite, the most respected commentator on television, for the first time openly opposed the war. Johnson said later that when Cronkite turned against him, he knew his Presidency was over. General Westmoreland, U.S. Commander in Vietnam, asked for two hundred thousand more troops, which would have brought the total U.S. troops in Vietnam to over seven hundred thousand. A massive student rally surrounded the Pentagon, faced by a ring of soldiers with fixed bayonets Protesting young college girls stripped to the waist and chanted, "Make love, not war."

Would it never end? Secretary of Defense Robert McNamara broke down emotionally and was taken, sobbing, from the Cabinet room, to be replaced by Clark Clifford. The request for the additional two hundred thousand troops was dropped. The tide had begun to turn. But the damage to the American psyche, already wrought by the war, lingers to this day.

Tex had an awful sense of "déjà vu," of Korea and 1950, when Truman had backed MacArthur's escalation of that war, because he just didn't know what else to do. Tex had seen first hand on the battlefields, the mistakes and bloody costs of the decisions of Roosevelt in World War II and Truman in Korea. Then Kennedy had initiated, and Johnson had escalated, the pointless deaths and horrors of Vietnam. It appalled Tex to think of the hundreds of thousands of American lives lost as a result of the election of Presidents without sufficient international experience or knowledge of the world.

And, at that time, Tex could not foresee the same failings to come from a succession of men ill-equipped for the Presidency, Nixon, Ford and Carter. As the 1968 election approached, there was rampant dissatisfaction with Johnson's handling of the war. Tex didn't think Johnson could survive a challenge by a leading Democrat. But Who? All the potential candidates held back. At this point, an unusual political organizer, Allard Lowenstein, stepped into the picture and tried to persuade Bobby Kennedy to run against Lyndon Johnson. Polls at the time showed Bobby slightly ahead of Johnson, but Bobby hesitated, finally declaring that he had no intention of challenging Johnson. Lowenstein then turned to Eugene McCarthy, an admired and scholarly Senator from Minnesota—whom Tex regarded as one of the most interesting political figures of the time—who agreed to enter the race.

[Author's Footnote: Lowenstein was my co-counsel in the 1954 Yale Law School Moot Court competition and Tex was interested to learn more about him. After Yale, he had devoted his life to organizing young people to engage in reform politics, first in the United States, then later in Europe and Africa. Sadly, he was later murdered by one of his own political recruits.]

The first primary of 1968 was New Hampshire, on March 12th. It was the beginning of a cascade of startling political surprises, and tragic national events. Johnson was expected to win New Hampshire overwhelmingly. The election night result showed a dramatic victory for McCarthy. Although absentee ballots later gave Johnson a five-hundred-vote margin, the damage to Johnson's support was complete. On March 31st, Johnson announced that he would not accept renomination for the Presidency. Bobby Kennedy immediately entered the race. On April 2nd, McCarthy won the Wisconsin primary. On April 4th, Martin Luther King was shot to death in Memphis, Tennessee. A new wave of destructive riots broke out across America, one of the worst occurring in the nation's Capitol, with violent looting and arson.

On May 28th Bobby Kennedy faced McCarthy in Oregon, and McCarthy beat Kennedy badly. The crucial challenge then became California in early June. The Kennedy name still had magic in California, and Bobby Kennedy's poll numbers had started to rise—when he was shot and killed on June 5th in a hotel kitchen in Los Angeles.

Two Kennedy brothers assassinated! To Tex, it seemed the country had gone mad.

The Democratic National Convention convened soon after Bobby Kennedy's assassination. Despite McCarthy's demonstrated national appeal, the Democratic National Committee bosses could not stomach the risk of the maverick McCarthy, instead they duly nominated Hubert Humphrey, the incumbent Vice President, despite the shadow of Johnson's hated war hanging over him. Tex kept thinking of Truman and Korea, and now Johnson and Vietnam—two Democratic Presidents destroyed by a war of choice that they had pursued in Asia.

Tex thought that a Republican victory seemed assured in 1968, a kind of replay of 1952—of Eisenhower over Truman and his war in Korea—but this time the Republicans did not have an Eisenhower.

Chapter Seventeen

Nixon's "Secret" War, His
"Southern Strategy," and Disgrace

A previously obscure Canadian professor, Marshall McLuhan wrote a book on television, containing a phrase which has become part of our language, "The Medium is the Message." Tex was interviewed about the book and said, "McLuhan is not right. Television is the most powerful medium of communication, but it is not the message. The Messenger is the Message—and Nixon is the proof."

Nixon was elected president of the United States in 1968 to end Lyndon Johnson's hated war in Vietnam. In his acceptance speech at the Republican Convention Nixon said, "When the strongest nation in the world can be tied down for four years in a war in Vietnam with no end in sight . . . it's time for new leadership in America." Enough Americans believed him to elect him President. Four years later, the war was not over, and there were more than five hundred thousand American soldiers in Vietnam. Military casualties had more than doubled under Nixon's command, to a total of more than fifty-eight thousand.

America was in chaos, seemingly trapped in the deadly stalemate of Vietnam. Rioting, looting, destruction and death were rampant in the major cities all over America, while college students protesting the war (and the military draft) virtually shut down universities with violent "sit-ins," threats to faculty and administrators, with wanton destruction of faculty records, academic research files and damage to campus buildings.

Johnson's decision not to seek reelection in 1968 had left Vice President Hubert Humphrey in an impossible position, unable to extricate himself from Johnson's Vietnam war policies, and his domineering nature, so long as Johnson remained as President. New national leadership was required. And Humphrey had many good qualities—but the nature of their relationship was summarized in Johnson's caustic comment, "Hubert's popular because he says yes to everybody on everything; it's a good thing he's not a woman, he'd be pregnant all the time."

Johnson's withdrawal declaration had created a kind of leadership vacuum, and into the vacuum stepped the "New" Nixon. Tex thought that it had taken an extraordinary demonstration of single-minded perseverance for Nixon to have resurrected himself from a seemingly impossible situation. After his loss of the Presidency to Kennedy in 1960, Nixon had moved back to California to run for Governor in 1962. The result was his humiliating loss to Pat Brown, ending with Nixon's self-pitying, "Last Press Conference"—"You won't have Nixon to kick around any more," generating the lasting enmity of the press, embodied in Mary McGrory's memorable tag line, "Exit Nixon: Snarling."

Nixon then withdrew to a Southern California estate on the Pacific at San Clemente. Nixon's impressive personal residences, first in Key Biscayne and then in San Clemente—and how he had been able to finance them—were always a matter of some curiosity. Because it was Nixon, many assumed that something underhanded was involved—and that Bob Abplanalp was somehow connected. Tex knew and respected Abplanalp from his many charitable activities in New York, and he asked him about it. Abplanalp told Tex that people always thought there was something wrong with his relationship with Nixon. The fact was that Nixon was hanging around with a bad guy in Florida, and Abplanalp hated to see a man of Nixon's political prominence forced to accept hospitality from people like that.

Abplanalp's company, *Precision Valve*, manufactured high quality aerosol valves, protected by patents. He thus had no reason to try to make sales, buyers had to come to him. He invested in real estate and he told Nixon that if he wanted a home in Key Biscayne, he should pick a big house with a lot of adjoining waterfront land. Abplanalp would take his note and his mortgage for the whole cost. He didn't see any real long-term risk in oceanfront land in Key Biscayne, especially if it had been lived in by a President.

When Nixon was forced to resign from the Presidency, he wanted to disappear to seclusion in Southern California. He chose a property in San Clemente, part of a much larger parcel which adjoined the big Marine base, Camp Pendleton. He talked it over with Abplanalp who told Nixon to mark the land he wanted, Abplanalp would again take Nixon's mortgage, and then bought the whole remaining parcel for himself. Eventually reporters from the San Diego papers dug up the land transfers, and assumed there was something crooked. They came to see Abplanalp, very hostile, certain that he had an inside deal of some kind. No matter what he said, it didn't satisfy them. Finally he said, "All right, boys. You're convinced there's some kind of deal. Well, here's the real story. How many Marines are there in Camp Pendleton? At least twenty-five thousand, right? All young men, right? Well, I'm going to build the biggest whore house in California just outside the base."

Nixon's preference for isolation had always seemed strange to Tex. The press was informed that Nixon liked to walk on the beach at San Clemente, and he permitted himself to be photographed walking on the beach, alone—dressed in a dark business suit, white shirt, tie, and shoes. Hardly the image of a dynamic national leader. He remained in San Clemente, literally "on the beach" out of the public eye, until Elmer Bobst, head of a major drug company, later merged into Warner-Lambert, stepped into the picture. To Bobst and his New York big corporate CEO friends, neither Goldwater or Rockefeller, the likely candidates for 1968, were overwhelming favorites, thereby seeming to open an opportunity for a Presidential candidate who was nationally known, who needed big corporate money—and who would be dependent on their support. Nixon fit their needs.

Tex became interested when Nixon moved to New York, where Bobst and his group had arranged a partnership for him with a New York law firm. "Legal fees" presumably financed Nixon's little-noticed travels to meet privately with state and local Republican committees to line up conservative delegates to the 1968 Republican National Convention. Nixon paid particular attention to the hangers-on in the state party structures, those whose lived off their party jobs. Then he began quietly meeting leading figures around the country, and around the world. Tex could see what was coming, but the extent of Nixon's activities were little noticed publicly, while a steadily increasing flow of major corporate money was financing Nixon's return from political oblivion.

At the national level, Republicans were sharply divided between Western ideological conservatives behind Barry Goldwater and moderate Eastern Republicans behind Nelson Rockefeller, whom Tex supported. So bitter was the antagonism between the supporters of Rockefeller and Goldwater that, while neither side wanted Nixon, he seemed preferable to the detested alternative. And so it came to pass that Nixon, effectively by default, became once again the choice of the Republican Party.

After all of Eisenhower's long hesitancy over Nixon's suitability for the presidency—Tex had frequent visits to the White House during Eisenhower's first term and there was no indication of any positive personal relationship between them; no personal visits in the White House or at the Gettysburg farm; no morning coffee, no drink at the end of the day. But that was before Eisenhower's serious heart attack in September 1955. He was not the same man afterward. Tex was surprised that in 1964 and again in 1968, although he was by then seriously ill, Eisenhower endorsed Nixon for President. Later, after his fifth heart attack, and just before his death, Eisenhower named Nixon to give the eulogy at his funeral. Jinx thought that the marriage of Ike's grandson, David, to Nixon's daughter had come to influence Eisenhower's thinking.

During the campaign, Nixon's communication approach was based on static background pieces, spliced to appear to show him answering questions from voters. However well done, the public saw the artifice for what it was. No matter the quality of Nixon's speeches or ads, the old antagonism between Nixon and the press continued—and the lines were fiercely drawn. The atmosphere was nothing like that of the Eisenhower days. Eisenhower liked people, so people liked Ike. Not so with Nixon. Where Ike was open, positive, upbeat, Nixon seemed closed and negative. He was not a man who seemed to have any interest in making friends. His public record and his speaking style continued to feature attacks and exaggerations—and the press would not let Nixon escape his record. He had attacked Truman, and Democrats, for "twenty years of treason." He played both sides of the issues, attacking Kennedy in 1960 for allowing Russian atom-armed missiles in Cuba—at the same time always denying he would invade. In the 1968 presidential campaign, he linked Johnson's Civil Rights Bill to race riots and student lawlessness.

Nixon's selection of Agnew for the Vice Presidency was, like Nixon himself, a kind of "accidental" choice. Agnew was an unknown figure, a self-made man who had risen through the tainted politics of Maryland to become Governor. The day after rioting by blacks in Baltimore in early 1968, Agnew ordered a meeting of all black leaders in the city, and delivered a speech bitterly denouncing them for not having stopped the rioting. The racist overtones of Agnew's speech had caught Nixon's attention, an early foreshadowing of Nixon's forthcoming 1972 "Southern Strategy."

The 1968 election posed a problem for Tex. In 1960, he had voted, reluctantly, for Nixon—Jinx had held her nose—because he thought that international issues were the biggest national problem, and Nixon had had eight years as Vice President under Eisenhower, while Kennedy had no qualifying background or experience, and had shown little real interest. So, in 1968, Tex found himself, again reluctantly, voting for Nixon—because Nixon had said that he would end the Vietnam War. Not that by then

Tex would have believed anything Nixon said, just because he said it, but because it seemed to Tex that Nixon had every reason to do so.

Nixon's early selection of Bill Safire as advisor and speechwriter was certainly important, and he was also pleased by the appointments of Pat Moynihan as advisor for social policy, and Henry Kissinger for international affairs. Tex knew, and liked, some of Nixon's money men, Peter Flanigan and Jerry Milbank, from his working relationship with them in the Eisenhower days. He did not know Maury Stans, and he knew John Mitchell only through Nelson Rockefeller. But then there seemed to be no cause for concern. Once again, Tex would be wrong about Nixon.

Vietnam, and attendant riots and civic disorders, overwhelmed all other factors in the 1968 election—and provided Nixon with a substantial early lead over Hubert Humphrey, who could not separate himself from the discredited, but still President, Lyndon Johnson, looming behind him. A major complicating factor was the third-party campaign of George Wallace, former governor of Alabama, a known racist, serving as a southern protest against the civil rights commitments of Kennedy, Johnson and Humphrey. As the election neared, Humphrey finally shook off the Johnson restraints, began to campaign strongly, and rapidly narrowed Nixon's lead—but not quite enough. Nixon was elected with 43.4% of the popular vote; Humphrey received 42.7%; and Wallace, 13.5%—winning five southern states, and almost winning three others. The combined Humphrey and Wallace vote represented an anti-Nixon vote total of 56.2%—and Tex feared that the racist Wallace vote might become crucial in the future. But he never imagined it would become the cornerstone of Nixon's forthcoming "Southern Strategy," and later support for George W. Bush's 2004 Presidential campaign, decisions that would reverse the fundamental principles of the Republican Party, the Party of Lincoln, the party that freed the slaves of the South. Tex thought of the end of the American Revolution at Yorktown when where the British surrendered and their band played a tune of the times, "The World Turned Upside Down."

Because of Tex's work for Eisenhower, and doubtless because of Bill Safire's role as his speechwriter, Nixon sent word that he would like to meet with Tex, apparently to contribute ideas. Tex jumped at the chance to get to know the key members of the White House staff and to get a feel for Nixon's White House. Nixon's welcome was brief, but professionally courteous. J. R. Haldeman, tightly wound and tight-lipped, ran the White House staff. It was masculine, youngish, very serious, affecting a hard-edged, strictly business manner. Tex was immediately struck by Nixon's isolation from his senior staff, and by the strict hierarchical structure. He made a special effort over Pat Nixon, whom he had met at parties in New York, and Rose Woods, Nixon's faithful secretary.

As he came to know the situation better, the more *Alice in Wonderland*-like it seemed, "curiouser and curiouser." Access to Nixon was extremely limited—and strictly enforced. Presidential Orders to the top staff in the West Wing came in the form of an early morning memo from Haldeman, one page, single-spaced, no paragraphs. Nixon began to refer to himself, in the third person, affecting an almost regal style, "RN wishes . . ." It was almost as if he looked at the Richard Nixon who was President as a separate personality. Gradually Tex came to understand that, not only had Nixon created a compartmentalized, hierarchical structure, he had deliberately set up competitive conditions between key people: National Security Advisor Henry Kissinger versus Secretary of State Bill Rogers in international affairs; Mitchell versus Haldeman for Nixon's ear; Haldeman versus Rose Woods for control of the inner office. Nixon isolated himself, using the Oval Office for formal meetings and other similar occasions, but preferring to spend part of his days, and many of his evenings, in his suite of offices in the Old Executive Office Building.

More important, there was something seriously lacking in Nixon's connection with the public. Real leaders always have some extra quality about themselves that is essential to their relationship with people. This had been evident in the polling data in the first 1960 debate between Nixon and Jack Kennedy, which was broadcast both on radio and on television. Polls showed that those who heard the speech on radio concluded that Nixon came out ahead; whereas those who saw the debate on television thought Kennedy the clear winner. It was evident that people responded negatively to pictures of Nixon, particularly to pictures of Nixon talking, perhaps because it reminded them of the "Old Nixon." In thinking it over, it seemed to Tex that this might be helped by images where the focus was on Nixon doing things—Presidential actions and events—rather than the carefully staged White House photo "ops" of Nixon answering prepared questions. He recalled a similar situation in the early days of the Eighth Air Force in England, when there were so few B-17s and the British press constantly compared America's efforts unfavorably to the much larger RAF bombing raids—comments which were passed rapidly to America and negatively affected morale at home. Then, Tex had been able to convince General Eaker that, if people at home could see what our airmen were actually doing, the visual reality would help overcome the impersonal printed numbers. Tex thought perhaps something like that could work to help Nixon. That approach was, of course, picking up on Walter Lippmann's concept—that public opinion was formed from "pictures in people's heads," a subconscious association of impressions. The challenge was to get that closed and suspicious Nixon White House to open up to new approaches and/or activities.

When Tex learned that Nixon was returning from a *SALT* disarmament talk in Moscow and planned a speech to Congress thereafter, he called Dwight Chapin, Nixon's personal assistant in the White House and suggested that he not do the usual, dull coverage when Air Force One lands at Andrews, then the helicopter to the White House, and then later a limo to the Hill. Instead, integrate the action, have the helicopter land on the Capitol steps so the President is seen going immediately and visibly to Congress. Chapin worked fast. The visual impact of the President's helicopter approaching the dome of the Capitol was dramatic. The scene came off, to a good public response.

Nixon seemed to wish that the public would regard him as a person who outthought others, who could startle the world with surprise moves. Somehow, he apparently thought that his perverse sense of "Leadership by Secrecy" would make people more confident about him. Thus, his isolation, his secret meetings with Mitchell, or with Kissinger, behind the back of his Secretary of State, Bill Rogers, as about his trip to China—"only Nixon could go to China!" In anticipation of that trip, Tex was asked for an idea. He remembered from his wartime visit that women in China do not typically appear in public or political situations—and, as an indication of the freedom of our society, Tex urged that Pat Nixon go on the trip. Further, red is a symbolic color in China; therefore, Pat should wear an elegant red coat and be visible whenever possible. It worked well—and Pat said she was pleased.

Tex later received a memo from Haldeman, forwarded by Chapin.

Xerox for
Tex
Moore

THE WHITE HOUSE

WASHINGTON

April 5, 1972

MEMORANDUM FOR: DWIGHT CHAPIN

FROM: H. R. HALDEMAN

The President informs me that Mrs. Nixon has a very high
regard for Tex McCrary, based on a long time association.

He suggests that McCrary can be used effectively to sell
Mrs. Nixon on various projects we might want her to do and
that we have difficulty presenting to her.

Keep this in mind.

*Tex — personal & Confidential —
The next time were together —
which — I'll call & set soon —
we should discuss this —
                    Regards*

Memo from Haldeman to Tex

In memos, phone calls and visits to the White House, Tex kept pushing the themes which he had tried with Eisenhower; the education of American youth; outreach on the problems of the inner cities, the blacks, drugs, violence; positive steps in the national interest, instead of politically-targeted special interests. But none of this seemed to have any effect. He felt that he was just wasting his time. The Nixon White House had become a giant hole into which all ideas seemed to disappear.

In the 1972 campaign, Nixon's "Southern Strategy" was openly revealed—a blatant appeal to the white racist voters of the "Old Confederacy" who had voted for Wallace in 1968. It was hard to believe that Nixon could so blithely abandon the hundred-year-old history of the Republican Party by reaching out to these voters The only explanation that Tex could imagine was that, in some way, Nixon's isolation of himself, and perhaps his impersonal sense of himself, had led him to envision a "new" Nixon, a leader of a new Party, or of a new kind of Party.

Tex talked with Bill Safire about Nixon's 1972 "Southern Strategy"—and pointed out that the South had lost the Civil War. But Bill, because of his position in the Nixon Administration, could only say that he understood Tex's position. However, Tex thought that, by then, Bill felt much the same way. In fact, Bill had made up his mind to leave the White House in 1972 to become the distinguished columnist for *The New York Times*.

Safire later wrote a remarkable book, *Before the Fall*, of his time in the first term of the Nixon Administration, in which he begins his description of what evolved into Nixon's "Southern Strategy" with a delightful quote, suggesting Nixon's approach in terms of the "Schorenstein Rationale." "Hymie Schorenstein was a Brooklyn district leader in the 1920s who refused to spend a nickel on the local campaigns, instead sending his donations to the campaign of Franklin Roosevelt for Governor. To his pleading candidates he said, "You ever watch the ferries come in from Staten Island?' When that big ferry sails into the ferry slip, it never comes in strictly alone. It drags in all the crap from the harbor behind it." Then, after a dramatic pause, Schorenstein would conclude, "Roosevelt is our Staten Island ferry."

Safire suggested that Nixon supposed himself to be a new kind of "Staten Island Ferry," which would establish a new, broader Party, one which would "drag in" disaffected, alienated potential voters. However, the practical result was to replace the two-party system with a "two-ideology" system, backed up in this case with cultural and psychological divisions, and adding to the us-against-them separation, fomenting distrust, fear, and occasionally hatred on both sides. Safire's insight is apparent today, "a nation frozen in a two-ideology system, rather than a two-party system" The Republican Party has changed its character from "a political party which offers a home," and is instead now locked into "an ideology, which offers cold comfort."

Just before the 1972 convention, Dwight Chapin told Tex that Haldeman had asked for his comments on the draft of the 1972 Nixon Republican Convention Program. This was his last memo of the Nixon Administration, a powerful indictment.

PERSONAL & CONFIDENTIAL   *7/19/72*

To: Dwight Chapin, Dick Moore for B. Haldeman

From: Tex McCrary

Subject: CONVENTION IMPACT

*1. After discussion of the Convention program with both of you during
which I voiced vehement objections to an opening impression from which
the President will have to struggle to escape, I have since quietly reviewed
every aspect and accent and focal point, every headline, picture and caption
that will come out of it, and this is my summary judgment:*

*2. This is not Nixon's Convention, it is Goldwater's. This is not the
Spirit of '76 or even '72 -- it is '48 and '64. It is the Convention that produced
the LBJ Landslide, and Truman's upset of Tom Dewey.*

*3. It makes the McGovern Convention by comparison look like "Oklahoma"
and "South Pacific" and "My Fair Lady" and "Funny Girl" and "Fiddler on the
Roof".*

*5. You boast that you open with a woman -- Anne Armstrong is not a Woman,
she is fat cat Texas King Ranch.*

*6. The dominant name that hits the eye first is Ronald Reagan, who could
not carry his own State even against Pat Brown this year. In a year when
George Wallace made Tax Reform an issue with as much appeal as busing,
Ronald Reagan is the millionaire Governor who paid no State taxes.*

*7. Reagan will overshadow the only black face in the opening lineup,
Ed Brooke -- who is scarcely a hero to Blacks and has been often as maverick as
Javits.*

*8. In a year where there is a chance to crack the critical Jewish vote in
the key cities, the only Jew prominent in the lineup is Sammy Davis Junior --
who will be remembered throughout the South as a Black who married a white
girl and then discarded her. And you have him singing the National Anthem!
Why not Sinatra, whom somebody wanted to take to Moscow.*

*9. In a year when, with the help of the Jewish Vote and a split in Labor, you
might crack Chicago and Los Angeles and Miami and New York City, the only
voice of the Cities is lost behind Reagan and Brooke in the keynote quartet --
Mayor Lugar of Indianapolis. And Labor is as speechless here as in McGovern's
show.*

Letter from Tex to Dwight Chapin (page 1)

Page 2

10. *When Dwight said that "we have to work Goldwater in somewhere", he needn't worry -- barry is already everywhere, the Spirit of '64.*

11. *It is true that you have a touch of class in Jimmy Stewart and even Clint Eastwood and Johnny Cash; and nostalgia in John Wayne and even Pat Boone; and both class and nostalgia in Mamie Eisenhower -- but from the opening shot of this monumental bore, I keep expecting to see Bob Dole or Reagan introduce Jimmy Hoffa and Harold Geneen and Carswell and Haynsworth and Martha Mitchell and Hedda Hopper and all the other grinning ghosts working to help McGovern win in the closing week, as Humphrey was winning at the finish in '68.*

12. *The feel and smell of this Nixon Convention of '72 is frighteningly reminiscent of the euphoria that beat Tom Dewey -- I staged his closing Madison Square Garden Rally in '48 and watched an audience walk out on his speech, and next day on NBC I said, "last night, Tom Dewey lost the election...."*

13. *The insensitivity of this spectacle is frighteningly reminiscent of the insulated arrogance of the Taft Gang, which we attacked in the Madison Square Garden Rally for Eisenhower in '52. And in Chicago, starting with the young Texans, we brought to that Rally, Taft was routed the way the McGovern Gang took Humphrey and Wallace and Muskie and Jackson and Meany and...and Daley.*

14. *Now I know where that battlecry for the '72 campaign came from -- "Nixon Now More Than Ever" is "In Your Heart You Know He's Right", plus 8, and spelled backward.*

15. *Johnny Unitas in this lineup has only three pass receivers -- Mamie and Pat and the President....and nothing but holes in his pocket to give him protection until he can get rid of the ball.*

16. *The President's acceptance speech better be better than Lincoln's Gettysburg Address -- and it better be full of quotes that will get him finally into Bartlett's, and give him a campaign headline equal to "I never shoot blanks".*

17. *You better figure out a way fast to get Kissinger and Connally into the Convention lineup; and get Agnew into blackface to play Jimmy Brown.*

18. *Alsop wrote that "the only man who can beat Nixon is Nixon" -- he can add the architects of this Convention to that list of one.*

19. *After the Peking trip, I wrote across the bundle of headlines: "Look out for loose boards...."*

Letter from Tex to Dwight Chapin (page 2)

Page 3

20. In this Convention structure, it's hard to find anything but loose boards.

*21. In introducing Agnew at the Heritage Dinner, I tried to make two points:
"Not since Disraeli has any immigrant Jew been brought to such pivotal power
as Richard Nixon has given to Dr. Henry Kissinger....
In America, no political party can become, or deserves to become a majority
party, until minorities feel at home within it...."*

*This Nixon Convention, as outlined, even to Archie Bunker, is pure early
California WASP, ripe for Raid.*

*22. In terms of Showbiz, there isn't a belly laugh or a roar, not even a
chuckle or a knuckle in the whole lineup -- no sex, only ex.*

*In terms of drama, no suspense, no guteemotion except Mamie, no encore!
In terms of news, no headline. In terms of history, as sharply focussed and
significant and electric as Dave Mahoney's plans for the Bicentennial.*

*New subject: Had a good meeting with three key guys on Agnew staff --
Sommers, Damgart, and Goodearle. Based on working with them by phone
on Zionist and Heritage dinners, they seemed genuinely hospitable, not at
all resentful or suspicious at my offer to sit with them from time to time for
suggestions, review and preview. They accept that even though Connally is
my friend, I am not "his man".*

*As I suggested to Dick, perhaps the best way I can be helpful to all of you
from now on is to be as helpful as possible to Agnew -- I think your Boss is
going to need a good fullback to score on the ground, until his instincts and
scars tell him it is safe to put the ball in the air.*

*New subject: Around John Price in Queens, which is Archie Bunker Country
and the key to New York State, we will work to set up a perfect prototype
campaign for a strategic urban area; in that territory, Agnew will have more
candlepower than any movie star, second only to the President, if he comes
in for the climax.*

*My guts and scars tell me that this weird campaign will be won in Hanoi,
Wall Street, and places like Queens -- not on Pennyslvania Avenue.*

Letter from Tex to Dwight Chapin (page 3)

Chapter Eighteen

The Arab Oil Embargo: "That Damn Fool Nixon Turned His Back on the World's Largest Oil Reserve to Fight a Losing War in a Small Asian Country that Grows Rice!"

By 1970 public support was slipping away from Nixon. Apparently Nixon didn't, or couldn't, realize this. Instead, he told his staff that his administration lacked "vitality"— and asked for ideas. Of course, the underlying problem was that the public did not see the secretive Nixon as a "leader." Naturally, Haldeman and the senior staff knew better than to point that out, and instead wrote memos that the problem was that the Cabinet was "dull and boring" It needed somebody who could give it a lift, somebody "Big."

In Texas, "Bigness" is a word used to convey a larger-than-life quality. John Connally personified "Bigness." Tex had had his eye on Connally for a long time, as a man who had evidenced real national leadership qualities. Tex's family had begun to talk about Connally after Lyndon Johnson had picked him out of the University of Texas in 1939 to join Johnson's staff. Connally impressed everyone, tall, handsome, highly intelligent, charming, easy and graceful in manner, married to an equally attractive wife, Nellie. While Johnson was forceful in person-to-person situations, he was weak in front of an audience, perhaps revealing an innate insecurity; whereas Connally was a master of any situation. He became Johnson's legislative assistant in Congress in 1939, ran Johnson's Senate campaign in 1941, learning an important lesson in Texas politics. Inexperienced and overconfident, they let their district chairman report final voting figures on time. His opponent, more sophisticated in Texas ways, reported after Johnson's votes were final, and, knowing the votes he needed—in the time-honored Texas tradition—was able to find an extra thousand for himself. After Pearl Harbor, Connally joined the Navy and had a distinguished record as an intelligence officer on a Navy carrier in the Pacific. He rejoined Johnson after the war, impressed everyone, and as Johnson rose in power in the Senate, Sid Richardson, the richest oil man in Texas, recruited Connally as his principal associate.

Tex first got to know Connally when he flew down in 1952 with Jackie Cochran to raise money for Citizen's for Eisenhower, and they stayed in touch. In 1956, a Senate seat opened, one which Connally could have won easily. However, Connally said that he believed one would have to be a Senator for two terms, twelve years, before acquiring enough seniority to make the job really meaningful. It was clear that Connally had his eye on a higher position.

In 1960, he worked for Jack Kennedy, and was rewarded with the position of Secretary of the Navy. His selection was criticized on the grounds that one of the biggest oil men in Texas should not be the Secretary of the Navy, the nation's biggest purchaser of oil. Nevertheless, Connally performed well as Navy Secretary, and with Connally regularly in Washington and New York, Tex began to see him more often. Connally felt that the Navy job was a bureaucratic dead-end, so, he ran for, and won, the Governorship of Texas in 1962. When Jack Kennedy came to Texas in November of 1963, Connally escorted him around Dallas. He was in the car, seated next to Kennedy, when Kennedy was assassinated. Another bullet, perhaps two, hit Connally, serious, nearly fatal wounds. He recovered, and was reelected Governor in an authentic landslide. But he became bored. And his association with the Kennedy assassination had heightened Connally's visibility as a national figure.

By this time, Texas had evolved from its self-conscious localisms and had moved away from its one-party Democrat status into two distinct wings, both calling themselves "Democrat." Connally was the head of the "moderate conservative" wing, essentially indistinguishable from the moderate Republican wing nationally, and Nixon asked him to head up "Democrats for Nixon" in the 1968 campaign. John Connally had the "star" quality that Nixon was looking for. Connally had many friends, and the word was passed around. Nixon was captivated, and offered Connally a Cabinet position. Tex later learned that Nixon was taken aback when Connally blithely said he would only accept either Secretary of State or Secretary of the Treasury. In as much as Henry Kissinger at the State Department was already deeply involved in Nixon's Vietnam machinations, Nixon fired the sitting Secretary of the Treasury, David Kennedy, and appointed Connally Secretary of the Treasury in 1971, although he had no visible qualifications for the position,

However, the hallmark of Connally's career was his extraordinary capacity as a "quick study." He took as his tutor William McChesney Martin, former Chairman of the Federal Reserve, and had so mastered his subject that he sailed through his Senate confirmation, and was able to win approval and enthusiasm from both U.S. business leaders and European statesmen for his understanding of "political economics." Nixon became so fascinated by Connally that he closeted himself for long talks with Connally at all hours. Nixon said openly that, "every Cabinet should have a future President in it." The word went around that, if one wanted to get approval on a project, it was necessary "to get Connally's approval first, or Nixon won't sign it."

Tex's sources in the White House said that it was understood that Nixon would drop Vice President Agnew and name Connally to the Vice Presidency before the 1972 election. However, in the early summer of 1972, John Mitchell resigned as Attorney General to take over the 1972 campaign as head of the Committee to Re-Elect the President. Polling had indicated that "The Committee to Re-elect the President" drew a much stronger response than "Re-elect Nixon" but Tex was amazed that no one seemed to notice that the public usage of "CREEP" might also send an inappropriate message.

Connally told Tex that Mitchell had talked Nixon into deferring the dropping of Agnew and the appointment of Connally as Vice President until after the election, on the grounds that Agnew, however incompetent (and soon to be demonstrated to be a criminal) had support among right-wing racists and religious fundamentalists, and that it was "counterproductive" to alienate them on any kind of issue before the election.

Connally resigned as Treasury Secretary to lead *Democrats for Nixon* in the 1972 campaign. However, in June of 1972, during the week that Mitchell was advocating keeping Agnew, CREEP burglars, operating under Mitchell, were breaking into the Democratic National Committee headquarters at the Watergate Office Building. There was an initial brief flurry of press attention, but it soon quieted down. However, Tex sensed a ticking bomb, and wondered how long it would take for the obvious questions about the burglary—"Who?" and "Why?"—to reach the public. Nixon's Watergate "cover-up" held through the 1972 election and, after Nixon's reelection, Connally registered as a Republican. Shortly thereafter, another crisis "cover-up" surfaced. Vice President Agnew was discovered to have taken bribes throughout his political career, continuing to accept cash from Baltimore businessmen, in effect, on the steps of the White House. Agnew resigned, and was later able to escape jail through a plea bargain.

By then, Nixon's troubles had mounted to the point where his first priority had to be getting as much defensive protection as possible in Congress. He couldn't risk another fight with Congress over naming Connally Vice President, and his safest bet seemed to be to buy support in Congress by appointing the amiable and well-liked Congressman from Michigan, Gerald Ford. However, the newly passed Twenty-Fifth Amendment to the Constitution required Congressional approval for a Presidential appointment of a Vice President, and, by then, "Watergate," and his other sins and omissions, had begun to catch up with a increasingly beleaguered Nixon. Connally told Tex that, as the possibility of Nixon's impeachment increased, Nixon had made it clear, both to Ford, and to him, that Ford was an interim appointment only, and that Nixon was going to support Connally for President in 1976.

Meanwhile, questions about the Watergate break-in had intensified. In May 1973, Attorney General Eliot Richardson appointed Archibald Cox as a special prosecutor to investigate the Watergate break-in. From what he had seen in Nixon's need for all the secrecy with which he had surrounded himself, Tex sensed that this was the beginning of the end of Nixon.

With Nixon increasingly absorbed in defending himself in the Watergate affair, events continued to unfold in the Middle East that were to change, and profoundly threaten, the existing economic and international relationships of the United States. While Tex and Connally were deep in discussions about plans for Connally's run for President in 1976, they were both acutely sensitive to increasing Arab aggressiveness toward Israel, which held ominous consequences, not only for Israel, but also for all the Western powers dependent upon oil from the Arab Middle East. From the time of the British Mandate in the Middle East after World War I, England had maintained stability in the area; however, the balance of power began to change after the Egyptian-Israeli War in 1967. By 1972 British finances had become so depleted that they could no longer maintain their last military base, at Aden on the Persian Gulf, and Britain quietly asked the U.S. to take over their role.

By 1972, America was importing more than a third of its oil requirements. Oil prices had been steadily rising across the country and inflation was becoming a major national problem. But Nixon remained obsessed by Vietnam. Press criticism of his failure to fulfill his 1968 election promise to end the Vietnam war had been steadily escalating and a resolution of the war seemed essential for his reelection in 1972. For Nixon, his re-election came first. Decisions regarding America's energy and economic

future would have to wait until after the election. Connally told Tex he couldn't believe it, "That damn fool, Nixon, has turned his back on control of the world's largest
reservoir of oil to fight a losing war in a small Asian country that grows rice."

Turmoil in the Middle East continued to escalate. After the death of Nasser, a Muslim Pan-Arab zealot, in 1970, Anwar Sadat, an Egyptian nationalist, a realist, had
taken over in Egypt. To restore Egypt's leadership role in the Arab world, Sadat
wanted to recover the Sinai Desert, which had been lost to the Israelis. He asked both
Britain and the U.S. to prevail upon Israel to withdraw—but he got nowhere. He prepared carefully. The Russians promised military equipment. The Saudis backed him
up, and the Egyptians struck at dawn on October 6, 1973, *Yom Kippur,* the Jewish Day
of Atonement. Israeli military defenses were lightly patrolled, all government and
business offices closed, families gathered at homes, the whole country effectively
closed down. Egyptian pilots in Russian MIG-16s nearly destroyed the Israeli Air
Force on the ground. The Egyptian army, in Russian tanks, broke through thinly defended Israeli lines, and raced across the Sinai Desert. Syrian tanks attacked from the
north. Israel Prime Minister Begin begged for U.S. help.

Nixon, by then ever more deeply absorbed in his Watergate defense, left Kissinger
effectively in charge. A U.S. Air Force supply chain of military equipment and aircraft
was set up. To cover up the extent of American involvement, big Air Force transports
were scheduled to land in Israel under cover of darkness, after a refueling stop in the
Azores. But there was only one runway in the Azores long enough to handle the big
transports. Strong crosswinds delayed landings, so that deliveries in Israel were made
in daylight. The U.S. cover story was broken, and U.S. involvement was out in the
open as an active military partner of the Israelis.

Arab anger was further inflamed, and the Russians pushed the story around the
world. By October 16, 1973, the Israelis, resupplied with new U.S. military arms, aircraft and equipment, had turned back the Egyptians—another humiliating Arab defeat—attributed throughout the Arab world to American support of Israel. The next
day, October 17, the Organization of Oil Exporting Countries, OPEC, imposed what
came to be known as the *Arab Oil Embargo* on the U.S. Connally told Tex that the
Saudis had tried to stay out of it but pressure from other Arabs was too much. The
Saudis agreed to enter the war—with the oil weapon. They embargoed oil shipments
to the United States, reduced production—and gas prices in the U.S. tripled.

Connally was angry. He said, "Goddamn it, Tex, the American public just doesn't
seem to know or care anything about what's going on in the world. Americans don't
know history, and don't know international economics. They know they want industrial
growth and increased personal income here at home—but they don't understand that
America—and the developed world—runs on oil." He went on to say that more than
half of the oil reserves in the world are under the desert in the Middle East. All the
Americans hear is about the Arab-Israeli problem—but that's a big over-simplification,
dictated by domestic politics and public perception. The reality is much more complex.
What's really at stake is the economy of our country, and the oil supply of the free
world. (Tex thought he was hearing his uncle Tom Taylor's warnings years before). The
international oil companies—the "Seven Sisters"—had worked together and dealt with
the oil-producing countries individually. But then things got out of hand. It started in
Egypt. Ironically, Egypt had no oil itself, but Egypt had been the historic leader of the

Arab world. Through the 1950s England had kept things under control—until Nasser took the Suez Canal and kicked the Brits out. It was all downhill afterwards. Throw Israel into the mix—originally with narrowly defined borders—but openly declaring its intention to expand over all of the "Holy Land." Just think how the Arabs liked that. They finally got themselves together. So now it's not only an oil issue, not only just a war, it's a religious war, Muslims versus Jews. In 1956, when John Foster Dulles cancelled the U.S. loan on the Aswan Dam commitment to Nasser, Russia jumped into the picture—and started to provide arms to Nasser. So, now, it's Jews, Muslims and Christians—and the Arabs say it's the Crusades all over again! Now oil prices are skyrocketing, and our economy is going to hell."

In the White House, events were spinning out of control. On October 20, 1973, only three days after the start of the *Arab Oil Embargo*, the Watergate scandal broke open with what came to be known as "The Saturday Night Massacre." Nixon demanded that Attorney General Eliot Richardson fire the Watergate Special Prosecutor, Archibald Cox. Richardson and his deputy both refused, and then both resigned. It was the beginning of the end for Nixon.

The United States government seemed to be coming apart. Nixon became even more isolated in his "secret" office in the Executive Office Building. The White House staff saw him even less. Behind-the-scene intrigues eroded the integrity of the White House. Now that the White House tapes of his meetings are available, Nixon's language seems almost unimaginable in its anger and vindictiveness. Tex watched it all, as the national agony dragged on into summer of 1974. Finally, facing inevitable impeachment and criminal prosecution, Nixon resigned his Presidency on August 8, 1974.

In the chaos left by Nixon, it was obvious that Gerald Ford was ill-suited and ill-prepared for the task he faced as President. During the Congressional hearing on his appointment as Vice President, Ford had denied that he would pardon Nixon, were Nixon to be impeached. Five weeks after Ford became President, he gave Nixon a "full and complete pardon for any and all crimes." For all his amiable nature, Ford's Presidency was doomed from that moment. Was there some kind of a deal? What was Ford thinking?

Upon taking office as President, Ford faced the necessity of naming his Vice President. Ford knew that he needed an experienced and nationally respected figure. He also needed support among progressive eastern Republicans, and, above all, it was essential to have someone who knew the oil business, and was equipped to address the Arab Oil Embargo. Ford picked Nelson Rockefeller, clearly the best choice for Vice President. Had Ford subsequently listened to and worked with Rockefeller—who knew more about oil than anyone in Washington—Ford could have been helped. Rockefeller recommended a $100 billion program for the development of synthetic fuels. Naturally, the powerful oil lobby immediately mounted strong opposition in Congress. Unprepared and uncertain, Ford hesitated. Was it ignorance, or was it lobbyists? In any case, the Rockefeller recommendation got nowhere. America was effectively without Presidential leadership.

The Arab Oil Embargo steadily forced oil prices higher. The historic attitude of the oil companies to mask their operations in secrecy now worked against them. Urged on by the oil lobbyists, the Congressional Democrats seized the opportunity to blame the oil price increases on the Ford Administration, virtually ignoring the Arab-Israeli factor. Disregarding the escalating reality of the crisis in the Middle East—and always eager to attack big corporations—the Democrats began an investigation, charging the oil companies with "obscene profits." Tex couldn't believe the breakdown of national leadership—in both parties.

Although Vice President Rockefeller was, by far, the most knowledgeable man in America to bring leadership to the oil crisis, President Ford, focused on domestic politics and his prospects in the upcoming 1976 election, began to see Connally as the Vice President who could give him the best chance to retain the Presidency. Ford consulted party leaders, including Barry Goldwater, who agreed that Connally was the best choice. Ronald Reagan had his hat in the ring for President in 1976 and, hoping to head him off, Ford offered him the V-P slot, knowing that, as an already declared candidate, Reagan would refuse. However, Reagan recommended Kansas Senator Bob Dole. Because of his "insider" contacts, Tex heard about these backdoor conversations, and he couldn't understand any part of it. In a national Presidential election, what could Ford, a former Congressman from Michigan, gain by teaming up with a Senator from Kansas? For all their good nature, two inward-focused, isolated men. It was crazy!

Tex was troubled by Rockefeller's resignation. He was at that time unquestionably the most qualified person for the Presidency in America. Tex couldn't understand why Rockefeller didn't put up a fight to keep his position as Vice President, but once again Rockefeller's strange reluctance to assert himself at crucial moments overcame him, and he backed away, resigning as Vice President in November, 1975. Ford immediately named Bob Dole as Vice President.

Tex thought that Ted Kennedy, now a Senator bearing the magic family name, had a lock on the Democratic nomination and would inevitably beat the dull Republican Ford-Dole ticket. Then Kennedy went on national television in an interview with Roger Mudd. After some introductory chatter, Mudd asked Kennedy the obvious question—why did he want to he President? Kennedy must have known it was coming. But he stammered and stumbled around, and simply could not get out a clear answer. After that interview, there was no way Kennedy could continue with an effective campaign, even against such a nationally lackluster pairing as Ford-Dole.

Meanwhile, in Atlanta, some aggressive Democratic thinkers, recognizing a sudden vacuum in the Presidential roster, had set out to prepare a candidate from the "New South," which was rapidly growing in population and industry. They picked Jimmy Carter, an Annapolis graduate who, after surviving a tour of duty under the nuclear expert, Admiral Rickover, had resigned from the Navy to run a family peanut farm in rural Georgia. Seeing talent in Carter which had previously eluded others, they promoted him into the governorship of Georgia, with an eye on a Presidential opportunity. Carter had no national or international experience. Even Carter, with innate modesty, questioned his own qualifications for the Presidency—until he went to his first Governors' Conference, always a bubbling cauldron of Presidential ambitions. Seeing the other aspirants "up close and personal" dispelled Carter's fears over his own lack of national or international background. However, he recognized the gaps in his experience and knowledge, and he asked his advisors for books that could fill the gaps. His advisors, more sophisticated, told him not to worry; none of the other Presidential competition knew much either. Campaign advertising and the media's own self-interest would develop "issues," and the press—and the public—never seemed to look much deeper. Apparently the important thing about Carter was that he was a devout church-goer, therefore, presumably, an inherently good man. That would come across to a disillusioned public. The only essential was to appear "current," aware, on top of things—and the way to get "current" was to read newspapers and watch television. They gave him a reading list and he followed it closely.

In the face of the obvious need for American leadership in an ever-increasingly internationally-connected world, Tex was disgusted at the idiocy of local party politics in Presidential elections, a process inevitably focusing attention on local and state interests, rather than on national and international issues. Excepting Eisenhower, since the first Roosevelt both party's had offered Americans Presidential candidates primarily domestically oriented, and with limited, if any, real international experience.

The 1976 Presidential election took place in a period of national despondency. The Arab Oil Embargo, with its attendant sharp increase in the price of gasoline and all energy costs, had brought on a severe recession, compounded by drastic inflation. The press began to track a "Misery Index," a combination of the price of oil and the inflation rate. A grim prospect for Ford and Dole. Tex believed that if Rockefeller had resisted Ford's effort to push him out, Rockefeller as Vice President—a man widely respected, internationally knowledgeable, especially on oil issues, and free of any Nixon taint—Ford would likely have won. And he felt confident Ford would have won with Connally. But the voting public was not in a mood to accept a ticket of Ford-Dole, and the Republicans lost to the unknown, and seemingly inexperienced, unelectable, Jimmy Carter of Georgia.

To teach the nation humility, Carter followed his Inauguration ceremony at the Capitol by walking to the White House, holding hands with his wife. He wore a sweater around the Oval Office, and told the nation to turn down their thermostats at home. He didn't say "repent"—but you knew what he meant. About this time a book appeared, *Small Is Beautiful*, by E. F. Schumacher, with the phrase, *Less Is More*, which seemed to sum up Carter's message. Growth was unbecoming—and America should restrain itself in foreign affairs.

But by then, the Arab Oil Embargo had America—and the world—by the throat. The price of Middle-Eastern oil had risen steadily from $3 per barrel toward $40 per barrel, forcing prices up throughout the world. Oil price escalation clauses were written into business agreements and serious financial figures estimated that oil prices would rise to $90 per barrel, and there was even speculative talk of $100. [Author's Footnote: As this book is being written in, oil is over $70 a barrel, the equivalent of more than $90, in 1974 dollars, and there is still no national energy policy.]

Americans were accustomed to the "Cold War," where Russia was the obvious enemy and, however threatening, there were ways to deal with Russia. But the oil crisis was the beginning of the awareness in America that the economy of the nation had become dependant on the power of others, to which there seemed to be no effective response. As energy is essential to all industrialized countries, increases in the price of oil drive up all other prices, rapidly causing both economic recession and inflation at the same time. Interest rates rose toward twenty percent. Businesses could not long survive at that level. And there were more problems to come.

Jimmy Carter had become President in a world economic crisis over oil, further compounded by that most dangerous of conflicts, a religious war, originating in the Arab anger at the Christian "West" for supporting the establishment of the Jewish State of Israel in Arab Palestine. Carter piously responded with preachments. Iranian mullahs, taking him at his word, seized the American Embassy in Tehran in November 1979 and held the staff as hostages. For six months Carter's responses were ineffectual. Then Carter attempted a pitifully small rescue attempt in April 1980. The result was smoking wrecks of U.S. helicopters in the desert, eight American soldiers dead, and a humiliating retreat. The image of America as a "Paper Tiger" spread through Arab lands, and elsewhere around the world. There was no way the Presidency of Jimmy Carter could survive.

Tex and Connally continued to talk regularly. Connally said that the economic-political dynamics were changing dangerously, and nobody seemed to understand what was really going on. The rate of industrial expansion was obvious to everyone, but only a few people were aware of the essential interrelationship of industry and oil—and only a very few people understood what was really going on in the Middle East. America's future depended upon reliable access to oil from the Persian Gulf—and that access was in real danger. The *Yom Kippur War* in 1971 was the triggering event, and it had changed all the dynamics of the region. Nobody seemed to remember that the Arabs nearly won. But for the last-minute rescue by American aerial support and equipment, Israel was finished. It was more a matter of minutes than of hours. Nobody in America seemed to realize how close it was. Now there was an economic crisis, but all tied up with religious conflicts. The Arabs see Israel as the point of an American spear aimed at the heart of Islam—a Jewish-Christian attack. Connally believed that history demonstrates that religious wars are the source of the greatest crimes against humanity; "Murder in the name of God!" And the Saudis believed that their God has given them the power of control of oil lying under "The Holy Places." The Arab military was not too impressive—but human sacrifice is a big deal in the Islamic world.

Connally declared that the United States, as the most industrialized, and industrial-dependent country, simply had no choice but to recognize, and deal with, the inescapable fact that America's oil requirements necessitates dealing with the Islam-Jew-Christian issue in the Middle East. Rockefeller had understood the problem, but Ford would not listen to him.

Connally said he was planning to run for President in 1980—and he wanted Tex's help. He declared that Carter was a dead duck—really a national disgrace—and there was no other national figure out there. Ronald Reagan had Ford on the ropes in the 1976 Republican convention, but Ford's Republican National Committee friends pulled their old vote-rigging tricks and knocked him out by a few votes. Reagan has a lot of charm, but there's a big difference between California sunshine and the real world outside. By then, Connally was really wound up. He said that at the national level, the Republican Party didn't have a heavyweight in the ring, somebody who's been around the world and knows a few things. America's got plenty of problems facing it, big problems. Oil was the top of the list. And he knew oil.

Tex asked Connally if he saw anybody else around, other than the tired old political names? Connally surprised Tex, saying said that there were those who believed that the biggest problem was understanding how the U.S. Government works, so therefore the next President should be an "insider," somebody who is experienced in government at the top level, and there's a guy Connally had watched setting himself up to make that play—Don Rumsfeld. He came from Chicago, went to Princeton, was a Navy pilot, ran for Congress, served three terms, and moved into Nixon's White House. As he saw the shadows gather around Nixon, he got Nixon to make him Ambassador to NATO, so he was out of the line of fire before the end came for Nixon. Then, when Ford moved up to President, he was desperate for knowledgeable people in the White House, and Ford made Rumsfeld his Chief of Staff. Then Rumsfeld pulled a "sleeper" out of the White House woodwork to be his deputy, a guy from Wyoming named Dick Cheney. Rumsfeld got the idea that he had a shot at Vice President in 1976. A major power play ensued—and a number of potentially competitive players were effectively moved out of the way. Rockefeller was pushed out as Vice President. George H. W. Bush, considered as a prime Presidential opponent for Ford in 1976, then representing the U. S. in China, in effect as Ambassador, was made Director of the CIA, from which he could not move to the Presidency. Kissinger's wings were clipped, he lost his key position as National Security Adviser, while remaining Secretary of State—and Rumsfeld became Secretary of Defense at the age of thirty-four, with Cheney moving up to Chief of Staff.

When Carter was elected, Rumsfeld had returned to Chicago to head Searle, the big drug company, and Cheney had moved to Wyoming where he was elected as the single Congressman from that state. Connally said they were the only people in Washington who seem to know where they wanted to go. They were worth watching. Just look at all the dead bodies they left behind!

Meanwhile, Connally went on planning his own campaign for 1980, and Tex was looking forward to working with him, when Connally suddenly faced a new challenge. Connally had made a number of enemies along the way, and they cooked up a phony lawsuit. A local Texas political operator, Jake Jacobsen, claimed that Connally had kept $10,000 in cash which had been raised in connection with the activities of the milk lobby. Connally said dismissively, "In Texas, ten thousand dollars won't get you into a cheap poker hand"—but with unerring judgment, Connally picked Edward Bennett Williams as his defense counsel. Williams demolished Jacobsen. But the notoriety of the trial drew unwanted attention to Connally as a Texas "wheeler-dealer." Then he made a crucial mistake. He thought he could resolve the Middle East problem. In a speech at the National Press Club, he outlined his plan for a trade-off: Israel to withdraw from the West Bank in exchange for a binding agreement on world oil prices from the Arabs. To Connally, and to many others, there was a certain logic to the concept—but Connally, now deeply engaged in the thoughts of a world statesman, was blind to the support for Israel in Congress. He was excoriated from all directions. Overnight Connally's star had set. His political career was over. He pulled out of the race.

Disappointed at Connally's fate, Tex took a time-out from national political leadership issues, and concentrated on other projects. He was troubled by the rising, hostile culture of the Vietnam generation, hippies and draft dodgers, sex and drugs—while the men and women who had fought our country's wars were being ignored, denied their due respect, even ridiculed. He had continued to serve as the master of ceremonies for the Navy League dinners in New York, and one night someone mentioned that so many of the men who had won the nation's highest award for heroism, the Medal of Honor, were dying, and soon there would only be a few left. He went to work to establish a Medal of Honor Society, not only to honor and remember our nation's heroes, but also to serve as an example and inspiration. A few years ago the Society honored Tex with the creation of an annual Tex McCrary Award for Journalism.

As the military began to close down facilities in New York, and around the country, Tex began to wonder how to keep some physical evidence of military history and national service in New York City. Tex's brother had been a Navy carrier pilot during the war, and he had been instrumental in preserving an aircraft carrier scheduled for scrap as a memorial in Charleston harbor When Tex learned that the aircraft carrier *Intrepid*, with a distinguished war-time history was also to be cut up for scrap, Tex told the story of the *Intrepid* at a Navy League dinner, and asked whether anyone present knew any way to preserve it as a museum in New York City. After dinner, Jack Fisher, a member of the prominent real estate family, told Tex that he and his wife would like to do it. Tex put it together, and it now plays an important symbolic role in New York as a major attraction for tourists and other visitors, as well as a site for ceremonial occasions. Tex served as arranger and master of ceremonies for many banquets, including political introductions for, among others, George H.W. Bush and Colin Powell.

Tex liked to visit Hong Kong, where his son, Michael, was publisher of the *Hong Kong American* newspaper there. The change in Hong Kong since Tex had first seen it during World War II was incredible—and it gave him an idea. When he was first there at the end of World War II, the old *Peninsula Hotel* faced directly onto the water. Now it was several blocks back from the water. Hong Kong had faced the limitation of space for expansion—and solved it by expanding into the harbor with major landfill. Tex began to wonder, could this be done in the Battery, in lower Manhattan, where the Hudson River side had become a dangerous area of abandoned warehouses and rotting docks. Tex was disturbed to see the beginnings of the move of financial power uptown, led by City Bank, and he talked it over with Nelson Rockefeller. Many people today are unaware of the importance of the Rockefeller family's contributions to the development of New York City, apart from the architectural monument of Rockefeller Center. Nelson, as Governor, was always looking for large-scale projects of lasting value, not only for financial reasons, but also for civic contribution. The Rockefellers also had large land holdings in the Battery area in addition to their control of the Chase Bank, where Nelson's brother David was chairman.

The whole Wall Street-Battery area was then almost solely limited to business, and there was no suitable living community, despite the potential benefit of direct access to the waterfront, otherwise largely unavailable in New York City. Tex began to talk about developments, including upscale housing, apartments and restaurants, which could establish a living community. He talked with major apartment developers, and finally got Sam Lefrak to come to Hong Kong to see for himself what had been done there—and could be done in New York. Out of all of this came major redevelopment, the World Trade Center (started while Rockefeller was Governor) and Battery Park City. Tex moved into one of the first Battery Park City apartments, and lived there—until the events of 9/11.

A phone call drew him back into the national scene.

Chapter Nineteen

Ronald Reagan: "Morning in America" . . .
"Mr. Gorbachev: Tear Down That Wall"

"Hi, Tex, it's Nancy Reagan."

The call came out of the blue. Nancy and Ron were old friends—but they hadn't talked for a while. After friendly greetings, Nancy said, "Ronnie would like to talk with you." He came on the phone, "Tex, I hope I'm not out of line in asking, but I want to do a little proselytizing. I know you have been talking with "Big John" (Connally) but I'm going to announce for the President in a few months—and I'd like to have you in my corner." They talked on, and Tex said that he needed a little time to think it over, as he had been close to Connally for a long time, and felt an obligation. Reagan said he understood completely, and hoped that Tex could work things out.

Natural leaders have a special relationship with the public. Not talent, not special qualities of speech or technical skills, but something else, an emotional connection at another level. Tex thought the only way to describe it is a kind of trust—trust, in the sense that people feel they "know" them, have confidence in their judgment, and believe that they will do what is they think is right for the country. Also, Tex believed that natural leaders seemed to convey a higher vision for the country rather than just the narrow interests of the "Party." Franklin Roosevelt had this kind of trust; Eisenhower had it; Jack Kennedy had it; John Connally had it—until the end. And Ronald Reagan had it—but it had taken Tex longer to recognize it.

As the 1980 Presidential election approached, Tex thought America was in a mess. The economy was in serious trouble and President Carter seemed unable to address the Arab Oil Embargo, the severe recession and the rampant inflation. The evening news shows began with Walter Cronkite, America's most respected television voice, who ended his nightly news program with "America Held Hostage," citing the cumulative number of days since the Iranian mullahs had seized the American Embassy in Tehran and held the staff as hostages—a continuing humiliation for the country, still working through the long, painful, drawn-out aftermath of Vietnam.

America was desperate for new, inspiring leadership. But who? The Democrats were stuck with Carter. They doubtless wanted to get rid of him but they couldn't dump a sitting President, no matter how he got there, and especially with no replacement at hand. The leading early Republican entries were Ford and Dole, both certain losers, humiliated by their loss to Jimmy Carter in 1976; Senator Howard Baker, amiable, but hardly a national leader; George H. W. Bush, who had held top positions at the UN, in China and in the CIA—but had not left a strong mark; and Ronald Reagan, the popular governor of California, whom Ford had barely nosed out at the 1976 Republican convention by Ford's use of his powers, as the incumbent President, to manipulate delegates. So, what about Reagan?

Tex and Jinx had known the Reagans in California over the years, but Tex hadn't paid sufficient attention to Reagan's political career as Governor of the state. A nice guy, but Tex had tended to think of him as a western conservative, sort of a further manifestation of the Goldwater phenomenon. But then Tex simply had not paid attention to what Reagan was saying. And as Tex had originally looked over the national field for 1980, John Connally had seemed the best choice.

But then he got that call from Nancy Reagan. He had known her as Nancy Davis, before she married Ronald Reagan. She was a graduate of Smith College, and they had many Eastern friends in common. After her marriage to Reagan, Tex and Jinx had continued to see them through the years whenever they were in Los Angeles. Early in his career, Reagan had been a Hollywood Democrat, but later had converted his political registration to Republican, and Tex had asked him about it. Reagan told him that his political conversion arose when, as President of the Screen Actors Guild, he faced agitators (later identified as Communists) who whipped a conventional union meeting into a mob scene, ready to burn down the studio. Reagan came away convinced that Democrats were gullible, far too willing to accept direction from outside ideological agitators. His suspicions were confirmed when, as Governor of California, he was the speaker at the University of California when an organized mob threatened to shut down a convocation. As Reagan confronted them, he recognized many of the agitators as the same Communists who had stirred up the mob scenes in Hollywood years before. This convinced Reagan that there was something more sinister lying behind the destructive "student " movement, as well as in the Black Power and murderous Black Panther "protest" groups, then being entertained by rich, gullible social types in Park Avenue apartments.

Reagan obviously had all the personal appeal that Nixon and Carter had so visibly lacked—but when he had first surfaced as a potential Presidential candidate, Tex had been troubled by Reagan's conservative Southern California fund raisers—limited men, rich car dealers and real estate developers—not the ideal kind of backing for the leadership of the nation. Following their call, Reagan sent Tex tapes of some of his speeches. What Tex heard on the tapes was different from what he had expected. This was not simply another right-wing voice from Southern California; instead, Reagan spoke to the whole of America—not in terms of "Party" positions, but in a larger, conceptual sense. There was none of the conventional political, "us" versus "them," nor of right or wrong—simply a voice of America, as most Americans thought of it, the way Americans wanted America to be, as Reagan phrased it, "A shining city on a hill."

Now Tex understood. Against the prevailing despondency in the country, Reagan had that "something special,"—hard to describe, but "you knew it when you saw it." In the theater world it's called "star quality"—that certain something that makes a person seem to "fill up the room." He brought with him the image of his movies, the strong man, best friend, good guy. Reagan knew that successful movies depended on a positive story line, with a few key scenes—and Reagan knew how to play them. Above all, he could handle the unexpected, step out beyond the script. This was a voice that America needed to hear, a positive voice speaking the common values of a fractured society, an appealing figure who could inspire trust.

Years before, Baruch had predicted that the availability of air conditioning would lead to a massive shift in the population base and political composition of the South and the West, and would ultimately alter the political dynamics of the country. California was fast overtaking New York as the most populous state in the nation. While the financial base of the Republican Party had previously rested in the East, in the headquarters of the major industrial corporations, now there was big, new political money, and fast-growing technology-based companies in California, and in Arizona and Texas. This represented a new political force, and Reagan was representative of that change. Reagan, twice elected governor of California, now had the political win campaign managers, John Sears, a young, pushy, Wall Street lawyer who had managed—badly, in Tex's opinion—Reagan's 1976 campaign. Sears was a control freak, listened to no one, trusted no one. All the experienced men whom Tex knew felt the same way. They told Reagan their concerns, but he appeared to let it slide. However, Reagan was not a known political figure in New York, or in the East, and Tex knew he could help him there. He called Reagan and said he would come on board.

His first step was to get Reagan better exposed to the top New York columnists and media people. He called around to develop interest, arrange meetings and interviews. Bill Safire was particularly helpful. Interest in Reagan shot up. Tex urged Reagan to open his campaign in New York. He did so—and he came across very well.

Tex wrote Reagan a long letter (by this time they were addressing each other as "Cousin" because of the shared Reagan name). Reagan's gracious reply is typical of the man.

Recognizing that Ronald Reagan's "movie star" aura would attract audiences where there was no possibility for verbal communication, Tex recommended that, rather than the traditional, passive, wave, he should also adopt a hand-sign which conveyed positive emotion and energy—his famous "thumbs up"—and Tex further recommended that whenever possible he should use both hands, which would require a wider photograph, and thus force newspapers to give his story a three-column coverage. Reagan was pleased, and sent Tex a picture of himself, with two thumbs up. The picture had a big red lipstick kiss on it from Nancy, and Reagan added that "people were catching on and, best of all, signaling back."

Tex was concerned about Reagan's age being used against him, and what he perceived as an approaching hearing problem. Reagan rejected his concerns, so Tex recorded a phone call in which he asked Reagan a series of questions at different volume levels. Reagan's responses were off-point and occasionally not responsive at all. When Tex played the recording back to him, Reagan was distressed—and he got a hearing aid.

JOHN REAGAN McCRARY

1/22/80

Dear "Cousin" Ron:

Attached you will find pictures I shot of your snow-
bound headquarters in Alaska, in moonlight. In my
"Annual Report" Christmas letter, started in Alaska
and finished here, I touched on some of the points
of my increasing uneasiness about Sear's conduct of
your campaign. You think very sharp up there on
"America's Soviet Frontier", where Russian planes
are blips on the DEW-Line radar screens on Saturday
nights...

In writing you in the wake of Iowa, I want to set the
sequence of my feelings quite clearly, because I
continue to have both respect and affection for my
"Protestant 'cousin", as you described yourself in your
letter last August, when you wrote,"Again Tex, my
heartfelt thanks and great relief that John Reagan
McCrary has not declared war on this Protestant cousin".

You and Bill Casey and Bill Simon and Charlie Wick
and Max Rabb all know that I tried to be helpful when
you wisely chose to "launch" in my town,Manhattan.
But very shortly after that, after two talks with
Sears, the uneasiness began.

I heard you flounder, unprepared, in the press con-
ference about New York City. And on the "Today Show",
I was struck once more by what you called " a slip of
the tongue" when you failed to recognize the name of
Tom Watson in Greenbrier--you answered, "who?" when
Tom Brokaw asked you about the age of Giscard D'Estaing.
That was another blip on your radar screen, or should
have been.

At lunch in New York on the Sunday before your Launch,
I heard you answering questions I had not asked, and
only Charlie was sitting between us. And Ray Donovan
reported the same problem. I wondered then:

When is Ron going to have to decide whether he comes
over deaf, or dumb?

I wrote you about that problem of booby-trap questions
and answers in press conferences after the "Watson-
Watkins" goof in Greenbrier; that was really when my
worries began.

Letter from Tex to Reagan (page 1)

Page 2

But the bottom line and the headline and the by-line
on all my worries then and now is John Sears: Bluntly,
I don't want to see another Haldeman building a wall
around another President.

And this is not hindsight, Ron; I put it straight in
a 30 page memo to Bill Casey on November 16, copy
delivered also to Bill Simon. Key bits of it:

"Dear Bill: Attached, xeroxes of relevant material
about the role of Sears as puppeteer for a synthetic
Reagan..."

"Quite frankly, Bill, I am more than disenchanted. I
believe that Sears will turn Reagan into 'Ronald Re-
run', terminal.

"I wish you would send all this to Bill Simon; if
you don't, I will. Reagan doesn't have the Nomination
any more locked than Taft did at this time in 1952;
I think you know that I knew how to beat Taft; I
also know how to beat Reagan -- even without an Ike:

"Just leave him in the hands of Sears. Over, but not
out...not quite yet."

I am sure you remember, Ron, that I did not call you
to get into your campaign; you called me, Nancy first,
then you:

"I hope you don't think I'm out of line, Tex, but I
know you have moved away from Big John...and frankly,
I want to do a little proselytizing...You know I'm
going to announce...not right away...but when I do,
I want you in my corner..."

I told you then and I repeat: When you deal directly
with people, Ron, you are very persuasive. I spent a
week thinking, as I told you I would, and then I
pitched in to help -- first with Charlie and Bill
on your launch.

But very quickly, as others had, I discovered that
there was no way I could get past John Sears and "in
your corner". You graciously thanked me for my
suggestions, my "Texas-size memos" as you described
them, but then you added, "You make some excellent
points, and I will go over them with John".

By the time I sat with Sears and Charlie, it was
loud and clear that I was "the enemy" to Sears.

Letter from Tex to Reagan (page 2)

Page 3

In New Hampshire, you are on turf I know like the
back of my knuckles. With the help of the Media,
and a corn-roots organization, Bush sacked you in
Iowa. By the time New Hampshire celebrates your
birthday in February, and Republicans put a number
on the age factor, you are going to have to scramble
to do what I urged you to do in those first memos:

Equate Age with Wisdom -- get a Karsh campaign photo--
relate to Churchill, not Maggie Thatcher -- and
read up on "the other Teddy, the forgotten Roosevelt",
read especially his, "In the Arena" --Debate!

When I broke with John Connally, I sent him a copy
of Ike's D-Day communique, in which the last line
locked onto Connally, and to you:

"The fault...is mine alone"...for failure.

I have been rough on Sears, but the truth is Truman's
desk top sign -- "The Buck Stops Here"--in your
saddle.

Very soon, you will have to face a tough question
that I put to you in Greenbrier, when I asked, and
taped your answer:

"If Connally or Baker or Bush win the nomination in
Detroit, would you repeat the offer you made in 1976..
for the good of the Party, for the good of the country,
...would you again offer to run as Vice President?"

You dismissed the possibility that you might be asked
to run as Veep, with the joke about "only the lead
dog gets a change of scenery", but you did make clear
that you would support the ticket so that the fumble
of '76 would not be repeated, by you, or anybody. And
that was the substance of the resolution that Bernie
Kilbourn introduced the following Saturday in Minneapolis at the national convention of State Chairmen --
unanimously passed.

Now that it is clearly a two-man race for the Republican nomination, don't you think you, personally,
should talk to Bush -- not through Sears this time,
and seal in blood an agreement each to support the
other after Detroit?

Incidentally, I am leasing a parking lot right across
the street from Madison Square Garden, where the Republican Ticket, winners and losers, can field a Truth
Squad under an Army tent, to set the record straight
for the Media, three times a day, during the Donny-

Letter from Tex to Reagan (page 3)

Page 4

brook of the Democratic Convention in the Garden.

The pair of you, Reagan and Bush and the Republican Veep, could score headlines three times a day, while the Democrats are still picking their first team.

After you launched in New York, Bob Grey said to me, "you and I have spent a lifetime trying to help Republican candidates...and fighting staff in order to be helpful..."

I got to 69 four months ahead of you, Cousin, and I'm too damn old and weary to play that game any longer.

Good luck to you and your First Lady, abrazo to you!

Very sincerely,

Tex

Letter from Tex to Reagan (page 4)

RONALD REAGAN

February 13, 1980

Mr. John Reagan McCrary
TEXCOMM, Inc.
10 West 66th Street
New York, N.Y. 10023

Dear Cousin Tex:

Your letter of January 22nd is not easy to answer, but I
appreciate your writing and the pictures of my iceberg
headquarters.

I've read all the Eastern press about my new image,
that Sears is pulling the strings and I'm the puppet.
On top of this, I read about how I'm coasting, riding
above the fray. If seven states in four days is coasting,
then I guess I am. The truth is that press treatment is
phoney and made out of whole cloth.

I made the decision not to debate in Iowa because I
honestly thought it would be divisive. I was wrong -
maybe all the years of preaching have paid off and the
party is together (except I suspect there is an Eastern
Establishment determined to stop Reagan - this Reagan).

Anyway, having realized my mistake, I am going to debate
in New Hampshire and wherever else they go for that foolish-
ness.

Tex, no one has been trying to moderate me. I'm saying the
things and preaching the policies I've always believed in
and I'm campaigning the way I choose to do it. I'm in
charge.

Yes, Tex, it's possible I didn't hear the question at
Greenbrier or the one at lunch with you and Charlie. I've
had one bad ear since the late 30's when an actor shot a
'38 off right beside my right ear. I imagine that would
be seen now as a result of age by the same people who are
putting out the garbage about puppets, etc.

I never thought the nomination was a sure thing and I don't
think so now, but I'm going to fight like h--l.

                              All the best,

                              Ron
                              RONALD REAGAN

9841 AIRPORT BOULEVARD. SUITE 1430. LOS ANGELES. CALIFORNIA 90045
Reagan's reply to Tex

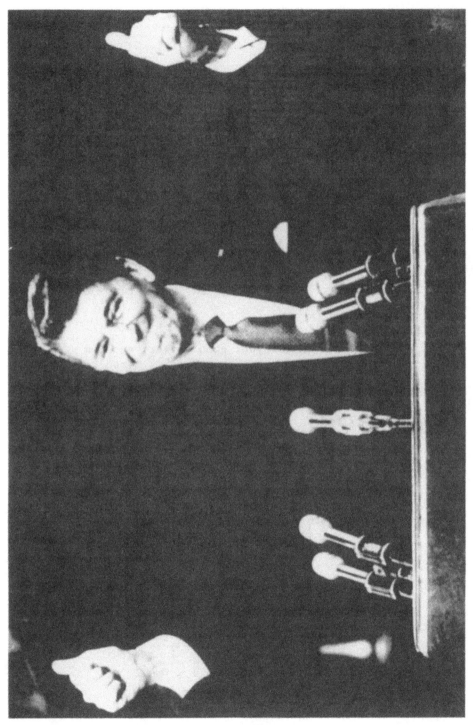

Photo that Reagan sent to Tex, showing "two thumbs up"

RONALD REAGAN

習 頂 危
根 好 机

July 3, 1980

Mr. John Reagan McCrary
The Greenbrier
White Sulphur Springs
West Virginia 24986

Dear Tex:

Thanks very much for your good letter, and I'm
glad you approve of the "thumbs up". I don't
know where or how I started using it, but I
have found I get far more of a response from
people along the street or in a crowd than with
the old V for Victory sign so I'm glad you
approve, and I'll continue using it.

This won't be much of a reply because Nancy and
I are rushing to get off for a few days at a
ranch across the border where there is no telephone, TV, or even a morning paper. I appreciate very much all the sound suggestions you
had in your letter, and I'm passing them on to
Bill Casey. I'll catch up with him when I get
back.

Again, thanks and I hope we see you soon. Nancy
sends her best as do I.

                          Sincerely,

                          Ron

                          RONALD REAGAN

9841 AIRPORT BOULEVARD, SUITE 1140, LOS ANGELES, CALIFORNIA 90045

Reagan's note to Tex, thanking him for recommending the "thumbs up"

Reagan did not enter the Iowa caucus—a bad recommendation by John Sears—which George Bush "won," a non-binding event but inevitably given attention by the press as the first step in a campaign. This time Reagan reacted. He fired Sears, and asked Bill Casey to manage the campaign. Tex knew Casey from New York state politics and he ran into him occasionally in Caminari's, a Locust Valley restaurant, favored by some of the polo crowd. He had an interesting background. During World War II, General Donovan, head of the OSS, had promoted Casey over the heads of many older, better-known men, to head the spy side of the OSS. Casey did a good job running the Reagan campaign and later, after the election, Reagan appointed Casey to head the Central Intelligence Agency. At the time, Tex wondered if Casey's secretive nature, combined with strongly-held opinions, were well-suited to that position.

New Hampshire by tradition holds the first national primary, an important confrontation between Reagan and Bush. A television station offered a debate between them, if the two candidates would pay for it. Bush refused, so Reagan picked up the whole ticket. This put Bush on the spot, he could hardly refuse to appear—but he wanted it confined just to the two of them, excluding the other candidates, Howard Baker, Bob Dole, John Connally, and John Anderson. Reagan invited them all. When they all duly appeared in the studio, Bush was angered and, with the cameras running, sat silent while his campaign manager, Jim Baker, argued against including the others, and threatened to have Bush pull out. In the confusion, Reagan, alert to the television opportunity, rose from his seat, grabbed the mike, and said, "I paid for this microphone." The audience burst into applause. After that, Jim Baker couldn't let Bush pull out in front of national television. The program went on, but Reagan had stolen the scene. Bush never seriously challenged Reagan thereafter.

At the Republican Convention, although Reagan seemed well ahead, the Republican National Committee did not want Reagan. He was not "their man." The National Committee bosses began to push a proposal for a "Co-Presidency" of Ford and Reagan. A crazy idea! Typical of the "bosses" at the National Committee! They thought Ford was their creation—and they knew that Reagan owed them nothing. Tex wondered how long Americans would put up with the local, state-focused, self-serving "National" Committees.

Tex wrote a strong memo to Reagan.

In all of his prior political involvements, Tex had paid attention primarily to the character and policies of the people he supported—and he had always been opposed by what he called the right wing troglodytes and schemers of the Republican National Committee, who only seemed to care about their control over the candidates. Now it was apparent that the selection process for the President involved a kind of mutual reciprocity between the state party bosses and the Republican National Committee people, each with the primary objective of keeping their respective powers and positions. Winning the Presidency would be nice, but it was not essential for their careers. Thus they naturally favored a dependable "Party" man, rather than a person with true national leadership qualities who might be less responsive to their local interests. And it

JOHN REAGAN McCRARY   August 5, 1980

MEMORANDUM

To: THE REPUBLICAN TICKET, 1980
     Governor Reagan and Ambassador Bush

Subject: "Thinking the un-thinkable".

From:· Tex McCrary

No copies of this one to Paul, or anybody else.

Note: Ron, you have been responsive to every memo,
letter, note and needle -- especially the needles --
from your "Protestant cousin". Only one to you, George.
Via Dick Moore. No response.

As both of you know, I carefully "shopped" the Candidate's
circuit, testing my suggestions with each of you, before
I wound up trying to help the one who took the trouble
to phone and invite me into his "corner". I split over
Sears, came back when Bill Casey filled that slot.

I will continue, Ron, to send directly to you suggestions
out of my own many fumbles, and those I have shared with
the predecessors of both of you in the White House. As
Ike said so often, as General and President, "Damnit,
when do I have time to think?!?!" I have that luxury over
both of you from now on.

I will watch the Democratic Convention as I watched the
Republicans, from a distance, with carefully selected
"Juries" of voters and observers, in London, Paris, and
Zurich next week. Sorry nobody picked up my parking lot
"Truth Squad". As promised, Ron, you will get my photo-
clipping-cartoon analysis of your scorecard so far:

"How did you get to where you are from where you were....?"

So far, the "score" on my own suggestions is pretty
skimpy -- the "thumbs up -- can do -- ding how!" salute
does seem to have captured your spirit, Ron. And even
though the crowds don't yet play it back as they did the
"V" to Churchill, they will. It is contagious -- George
and Maureen use it eloquently. See attached. But what
follows in this "Texas-size bundle" is far more serious
than a symbolic salute:

Strong memo from Tex to Reagan (page 1)

Page 2

Attached you will each find carefully marked copies of
a book you have certainly both read, probably hurriedly,
pertinent now: "Six Crises", Nixon's. The marked crises
deals with Ike's triple illness, and the inexorably
sensitive relations between President and Vice President
for the last 50 years.

I would hesitate to send this to you, Ron, if you had not
so candidly dealt with the age factor in your soul-
searching interview with THE TIMES, in which you triggered
the flinch-word, "senility".

President Eisenhower dealt with equal candor with that
factor in his "Personal and Confidential" letter to me on
January 23, 1956, in which he told me clearly before even
Mamie knew, that he would run again; I sent you a copy of
that letter. The key paragraphs:

".I do want you to know that I am not giving any concern
as to what under the changed circumstances, this job might
do to me. The great and grave concern is, 'Over a five
year stretch, what might I do to the job?'

"It would be fatal if, through a combination of advancing
years and gradual loss of energy on my part, the great
foreign and domestic programs for which this Administration
has stood, should begin to suffer because of slackening
energy and leadership. I do not need here to outline all
the considerations pro and con that have a bearing on the
matter.

"This is, of course, confidential; but I would not want
such faithful friends as you and Jinx to believe at this
time of my life, I would begin to give more attention to
my own personal convenience and possibility of a long
existence, than I do to the great issues that inspired
our Crusade...."

And then he quoted the whole of Lincoln's solioquy from
"John Brown's Body", winding up:

"Lord, I will keep my promise, and go on.
Your will, in much, still being dark to me,
But, in this one thing, I see it plain:

"I cannot read it, but I will go on,
Old dog, old dog, but settled to the scent
And with fresh breath from this breathing space,
Almighty God, we never seem
To know You wholly, but there's something left,
A strange last courage...."

....cont'd

Strong memo from Tex to Reagan (page 2)

Page 3

Inserted in each copy of Nixon's "Six Crises" is a
reproduction of a relevant Chinese character, which my
son taught me -- it was the preface of the original
edition, the Chinese character for "Crisis".   It should
have a special meaning for you, George, on your present
mission to Mainland China:

> One character means, "Danger".
> The other means, "Opportunity".
> Together, they mean "Crisis".

Only finally did President Eisenhower and Vice President
Nixon take wise steps, together, to avoid the ultimate
crisis of command;   Kennedy and Johnson and Ford and
perhaps Carter learned from their belated precaution.

But short of total crisis -- and these times are far more
critical than the eight Eisenhower years -- the snipers
from ambush will do their utmost, as you already know, to
create friction between you.   As forewarning, attached also
is a copy of the first shot by a cartoonist. There will be
more, many more, and far more savage.   Remember the cartoon
of Nixon and Ike at the foot of the Capital steps after
his heart attack?

Caption, Nixon: "Race you to the top of the steps, Mr.
President!"

And remember the flap when Ike was defending his decision
to keep Nixon on the ticket, saying: "He's had great
training to be President someday...why, he has participated
in every major decision of my Administration...."

A reporter, digging in: "Really, Mr. President...for
instance...which ones...?"

Ike: "Well....well...let me see now...give me a week and
I'll think of one...."

Not said meanly, but honestly; and all hell broke loose,
and Nixon bled internally for months.   A carnivorous Press
will sniff and snarl and snap at every opportunity to
draw blood from both of you.

(You dealt early with your hearing problem, explained it
to me, and Lou Cannon printed it, and sympathy replaced
suspicion.)

By way of conditioning for the carnivores, I urge you
both to read the marked passages of Nixon's anguish, and
then discuss the whole problem in the spirit of the first
one-word quote you scored in a TIMES front-page headline,
George: "Candor".

....cont'd

Strong memo from Tex to Reagan (page 3)

Page 4

(Nixon never scored a headline quote on THE TIMES front page until "I am not a crook".)

I was involved in the bush-whacking of Nixon by Eisenhower's staff, especially Adams; I talked to Sherm about clarifying and expanding the Vice President's role, used the phrase "Executive Vice President" -- but Ike only understood "brigadier" and "Chief of Staff".

"Executive Vice President" is a phrase and rank and role that everybody would understand today; it says everything, and means whatever you both want it to mean. There was a mad scramble in Detroit to define the "role and mission" of a Veep. You both won the strongest ticket for governing -- you never needed Ford for the Election.

But out of that scramble, there certainly must have emerged some new and specific sectors of responsibility for an "Executive Vice President". The mission to Mainland China is clear evidence of clear command thinking. Especially if you think Executive Vice President.

You have already scored a perfect "Executive Vice President" assignment in George's Mission to Peking -- far more delicate and important strategically than Nixon's trip to South America, or the "kitchen debate" in the "typical American home" I built in Moscow when he was Veep. Peking is your Middle East problem -- the capital city of China, Peking vs. Taipei, is like Jerusalem. But there is another point about Peking:

I urged you from Tokyo and Manila and Taipei as you may remember, Ron, to go first to the Far East, between Detroit and New York -- the European trip you had planned would, as you realized, raise more questions than "Le Cowboy" or anybody could now answer.

George's China and CIA experience makes it a natural to go to Peking. And now instead of ridicule, the Europeans must respect the signals you called. And the teamwork -- almost West Point's "Mr Inside and Mr. Outside" -- must be applauded. And you did it with no help from Kissinger. Bravo!

That was always one trouble with Jerry Ford: His problem was not what LBJ said -- "too much football without a helmet", because we wore helmets in those days. Jerry's trouble was that he always played Center, spent four years looking at the world upside down between his own legs, only moved the ball backwards, and then only a couple of feet, and on signal -- and too often the signals came from Kissinger. You have called your own, together.

...cont'd

Strong memo from Tex to Reagan (page 4)

Page 5

There is obviously much work both of you need to do offshore: in Europe of course, but also in the two countries
that you, Ron, first linked in a new North American
"Alliance", Mexico and Canada.

Portillo in Havana cozied up to Castro, and in Montreal
last week, I found an amazing lot of sympathy for Carter,
even before his "Checkers defense" for Brother Billy. See
the attached Gallup Poll in Canada:

53% of Canadians would rather see Carter win on Election
Day, on 12% Reagan.

Only the North and South Poles are frozen, but this poll
needs a lot of heat.

On the homefront, here in New York where you launched,
before the Urban League, you recovered the ball that staff
dropped with the NAACP; you were as bold and as effective
as Catholic Kennedy was before my fellow Texan Baptists,
who beat Al Smith.

And your quote from Chappy James was as moving as your
moment of silent prayer in Detroit. Incidentally, there
is another living ally in Mayor Tom Bradley, host to the
1984 Olympics -- he was born and raised in my hometown of
Calvert, Texas.

Postscript suggestion: You know that words are both
weapons and boobytraps; words that spell out the difference
between NAACP and the Urban League, and speak your own
shared objectives might be: "You have won the right to
one-man-one vote; now together, let's win your right to
one-man, one-job -- a real job."

Suggestion: To lift the process of "casting" a Cabinet,
first and second teams, up above the snakepit of politics,
why not retain the best headhunter in America to flush
out all the Veeps from corporations and universities and
hospitals and R&D outfits, to brand your Administration
early with a bunch of young tigers, take-charge men and
women, strength in depth, offense and defense, on the
field, on the bench, and even down in the farm clubs.
Sound out the editors of FORBES and FORTUNE and INC. for
up-and-coming Veeps.

George, why don't you get the YPO to start a "Veep"
organization, nationally?

(Aside: George, why don't you start using more baseball
lingo -- and you, too, "Dutch" Reagan!)

                                        ....cont'd

Strong memo from Tex to Reagan (page 5)

Page 6

Back to a more serious note: Right after Stevenson conceded, I stood in a room in the Commodore while Baughman briefed President Eisenhower, lifelong soldier, on how different life would be from now on under the watchful eye of the Secret Service -- even on the golf course at Burning Tree and Augusta.

My first TV program from Washington, after the Inauguration, "The President's Week" on NBC Sundays, dealt bluntly with that peril.

I urged Eisenhower and Kennedy and Johnson and Ford to consolidate the Secret Service -- take it out of Treasury -- team it with the FBI and the CIA, to create a single special force to guard the life of the President and the Vice President. Such a synchronized force could have saved Kennedy.

We live in an age of terrorism unprecedented since Nobel's dynamite launched the Nihilists; and TV has created a whole crop of crazies -- Jerry was a man without enemies, but two women tried to kill him.

It is reckless not to think of this unthinkable.

I'll close this bundle on lighter notes for both of you:

1. Get Karsh to make a portrait of both of you, paired, teamed, to capture the can-do, ding-how, thumbs up spirit. Karsh made a portrait of you as Governor, Ron -- he still knows best how to capture a portrait of leadership, as he proved first with his classic shot of Churchill.

2. Both of you, especially you, George, should consider at least a drop-in at the Navy League Dinner, November 6, hard in the wake of Election Day. Al Haig is the speaker. I preside. Perfect place for a first appearance, together, as President and Vice President-Elect.

3. See attached clipping on Grace Tully, FDR's secretary for 17 years. She typed that "rendezvous with destiny" phrase, and all the rest down to his speech to the joint session of Congress after Yalta, and for the first time spoke of "the weight and pain of the steel upon my limbs". Grace used to sit beneath an air vent in the basement of the White House, under the Oval Office, and take short- hand notes on FDR's "private" meetings, long before the Watergate Tapes.

....cont'd

Strong memo from Tex to Reagan (page 6)

Page 7 .

Suggest: Nancy and Bar should invite every living
former President's <u>secretary</u> to lunch, the last week
in January, 1981, in the White House -- and don't forget
<u>Nell Yates</u>, secretary to Dwight Chapin, now Number Two
to Jimmy Carter.

Over to you all,

Strong memo from Tex to Reagan (page 7)

had always been this way. Going back in history, the Republican "Party People" had fought against Teddy Roosevelt; similarly, the Democrat "Party People" opposed Franklin Roosevelt; the Republicans didn't want Eisenhower; had backed Nixon, as "dependable," as they had Ford—and now they feared the independence of Ronald Reagan. As Reagan's support steadily increased, the obviously impractical "Co-Presidency" idea faded away.

The national election was a fore-gone conclusion. Reagan overwhelmed the hapless Jimmy Carter. Reagan was a natural leader, secure in himself, at ease with his own ego. The public could sense, perhaps intuitively, his own confidence. He understood that the great majority of American people had underlying instincts which transcended the contrived structures and labels of contemporary political inter-party debate. He avoided the trap into which nearly all politicians fall, trying to play every issue, no matter how fleeting, for temporary advantage. Reagan kept his eye on the crucial issue, the chief concern of the country—the "Cold War" and the threat of Soviet power—which had dominated American thinking since the 1960s.

For Reagan, winning the Presidency was only the first step. Governing came next; and governing required a plan; the people to execute the plan; and how well those key people could work together. Tex was pleased to see Reagan offer the Vice-Presidency to George Bush, the man whom he had beaten for the nomination, a gracious conciliatory move. He was further impressed when Reagan named Jim Baker, Bush's campaign manager, as Reagan's Chief of Staff. Tex had heard about Baker—all of it good—from mutual friends in Texas. Having seen the problems of internal conflicts in the Eisenhower, Kennedy and Nixon Cabinets, he knew that Reagan would need a talented man in that crucial spot. Further, Tex knew that Reagan would need a "Working Cabinet" to resolve the deep conflicts between his early backers, the "California Conservatives," and the moderate "Eisenhower" Republicans.

However, Tex saw trouble coming with the first Cabinet appointment, Al Haig, as Secretary of State. Haig had been Nixon's Chief of Staff, a former four-star Army General, NATO commander, a known right-wing autocrat, a terrible choice for a position requiring sensitivity and tact. Tex couldn't understand it. The last thing Reagan needed was anyone connected to Nixon, especially in such an important position. Where had the idea come from? Tex asked around, and he discovered that Nixon had been sending lengthy secret policy memos to Reagan, and the appointment of Haig was Nixon's number one recommendation. Tex was appalled at the nationally discredited Nixon having such "backdoor" influence in the Reagan White House. Then the Secretary of Defense slot went to Caspar Weinberger, a California conservative, former Chairman of the California Republican Party, Nixon's director of the Office of Management and Budget, and Secretary of Health, Education and Welfare. Don Regan, formerly the aggressive head of the Merrill Lynch investment firm was appointed Secretary of the Treasury. Tex was particularly disturbed at the appointment of Bill Clark, a major California supporter, as National Security Advisor, seemingly without any qualifying experience for such a sensitive position. Then Reagan appointed his campaign manager, Bill Casey, to be Director of the Central Intelligence

Agency because of his distinguished record as head of the spy side of the OSS in World War II. And Casey immediately went "undercover" himself, ultimately to disastrous results.

It was apparent to Tex that all these ambitious men, who had risen to high positions by fierce competitive drives, would not serve as a "Working Cabinet"—a situation which placed immense pressure on Jim Baker, as Chief of Staff, to try to keep the Cabinet functioning. Tex was impressed with Baker's calm, sure-footed manner during the campaign and they had friends in common in Texas. Baker was the grandson of the founder of Baker and Botts, then the leading law firm in Texas, a Princeton graduate, a Marine officer, a graduate of the University of Texas Law School. He was a close friend of George Bush and had managed Bush's unsuccessful campaign for the U.S. Senate in 1970. Baker served as Under Secretary of Commerce for President Ford, then ran Ford's Presidential campaign in 1976 and ran himself, unsuccessfully, for Governor of Texas in 1978. Tex thought that Baker evidenced a unusual combination of intelligence, energy, experience and ambition, balanced with composure and courtesy—personal characteristics which, Tex hoped, would enable him to deal with the competing prima donnas of the Cabinet.

On March 31,1981, three months after taking office, President, Reagan was shot by a crazed college kid who wanted to impress a movie actress. Reagan was taken to the hospital, coughing blood from his lungs. To avoid having the public upset by the sight of a seriously wounded President being carried into a hospital, Reagan gallantly pulled himself out of the car, stood erect, buttoned his jacket, and walked in—where he collapsed with a bullet pressing on his heart. The country was in a state of shock. Given the magnitude of his wound, Reagan's recovery was slow; but the sense that "he had taken a bullet for his country" deepened the public attachment to him.

In July 1981, Reagan startled the country by appointing Sandra Day O'Conner as the first woman to the Supreme Court of the United States. Like most Americans, Tex and Jinx were delighted at this long overdue recognition of women in American life.

Fortunately, national affairs remained fairly quiet through Reagan's recuperation during the second half of 1981. Naturally, there was considerable concern over what course the Reagan Presidency would take. Tex remembered that, for Reagan, the issue of good guys versus bad, had been a constant theme throughout his movie career. He had defined his films in terms of an over-riding moral issue to be resolved in a positive way and, as time passed, Tex began to see that, in a larger sense, Reagan had conceived of his Presidency in a similar fashion, as a commitment to personal freedom, both economic and political.

Tex believed that his fundamental conviction was that democracy was superior to dictatorships or authoritarian governments. America had destroyed the authoritarian dictatorships of Hitler, Hirohito and Mussolini, and now, Reagan, as President, was determined to remove the power of the Russian Communist dictatorship. To that end, Reagan had conceived of a kind of script for his Presidency: First, to restore overwhelming U.S. economic and military strength; and then, to use that power to break the threat of what he called the dictator-driven "Evil Empire" of the Soviet Union. The power of the "Evil Empire" lay in the strength of its military, which in turn depended on the underlying industrial capacity. Reagan was convinced that the United States, with its free market efficiency, could so outperform the slave-labor base of the Soviet economy, that Russia would ultimately fall behind in the industrial support of their military. Without the threat of their Army, the Kremlin would be forced to recognize that the Soviet Union could not hold together. The "Evil Empire" would then break up, and eventually disintegrate.

Reagan committed his Presidency to that end. He devoted his first term to the revitalization of the sluggish U. S. economy and to rebuilding powerful military strength. During his second term, he planned to break the "Cold War" mind-set between Russia and the West. He introduced an economic/industrial program based on what came to be known as "Supply-Side Economics," an incentive for capital investment by reducing the top personal income tax rate from seventy percent to below fifty percent. Tex thought that such a cut also reflected a psychological dimension of economics, that a positive outlook and new investment were inherently interrelated. The second element of Reagan's strategic plan was to strengthen, and then to display, America's increasing military strength. That took longer, and some mistakes were made along the way.

In September 1983, National Security Advisor Bill Clark asked to be moved to Secretary of Labor. Chief of Staff Jim Baker was tired of having to deal with the personal bickerings in the Cabinet and indicated he would like to move to the National Security Advisor slot. However, the bellicose California conservatives, eager to assert their aggressive foreign policies, opposed the Baker appointment. Reagan disliked disputes and, to avoid controversy, he simply let Bud McFarlane, then the deputy National Security Advisor—although significantly limited by lack of top executive and policy experience—move up to fill that crucial position. Apparently the President thought so as well. Later, Tex was fascinated to read in Reagan's autobiography, *An American Life*, a rather melancholy recognition, "My decision not to appoint Jim Baker as National Security Advisor, I suppose, was a turning point for my administration, although I had no idea at the time how significant it would prove to be."

McFarlane, as National Security Advisor, soon became a kind of captive agent of the wily and forceful CIA Director, Bill Casey. On the third weekend of October 1983, a cascade of events shocked the country. Late Saturday night a truck carrying 12,000 pounds of TNT drove into the garage of the Beirut hotel where U.S. Marines were quartered, and exploded. Two hundred forty-one Marines were killed, and more than three hundred Marines were wounded. A tragic loss.

The Reagans were visiting in the Eisenhower cottage at the Augusta National Golf Club as the guests of Secretary of State George Shultz and New Jersey Senator Nick Brady and the President and his group were informed of the Beirut bombing at 2:30 A.M. Sunday morning. They assembled in the dining room and decided to remain in direct and secure contact with the White House, rather than try to travel back immediately.

Later that Sunday morning, Reagan learned of danger to six hundred American students enrolled in Grenada at the St. George Medical School. The Organization of Eastern Caribbean States asked for U.S. intervention to prevent an attempted takeover of Grenada by Communist sympathizers. A U.S. military rescue mission was ordered to Grenada. Extensive television coverage of the mission to rescue U.S. students preempted much of the coverage of the disaster in Beirut, and obscured the far more important events taking place in the Middle East. Tex believed that, had Jim Baker had been National Security Advisor, the situation would have been handled very differently—and America's subsequent difficulties in the Middle East would likely not have risen to the dangerous levels that followed.

Late in 1983, Reagan began a series of international travels which were to last into the early summer of 1984. Tex was pleased to see it happen. Reagan needed to get around, see and be seen. The visits included Europe, then Japan and Korea, followed by Ireland, England and France. On June 6, 1984—forty years after the American Forces landed in Normandy in D-Day 1944—Reagan spoke at *Pointe du Hoc*, where U.S. Rangers had climbed the cliffs in the face of withering German fire. Facing a large audience, including a group of aging Rangers, Reagan said: "These are the boys of *Pointe du Hoc*. These are the men who took the cliffs. These are the champions who helped free a continent. These are the heroes who helped end a war." Spirits soared across the country.

Reagan's election to a second term in 1984 was virtually assured. He was opposed by Walter Mondale, another of those decent public servants from Minnesota; but for all practical purposes it was no contest. In a debate with Mondale, reporter Henry Trewhitt raised the "age issue," asking whether Reagan felt that he would have difficulty functioning in a crisis (Reagan was approaching his seventy-fifth year). Reagan replied with his classic line, "Not at all, Mr. Trewhitt. And I want you to know that I will not exploit, for political purposes, my opponent's youth and inexperience." It was "no contest" from then on, as Mondale knew and, greatly to his credit, acknowledged with a wry chuckle. Reagan won his second term as President with 525 Electoral College votes, an all-time record, with his opponent, Mondale, winning only his native state, Minnesota, by a tiny margin.

In his second term, Reagan doubtless relied more on his staff, and he agreed to what seemed to Tex to be a fatefully unfortunate key personnel switch. Don Regan, an arrogant and demanding Secretary of the Treasury, was a man whose drive for personal power had led him to conclude that Jim Baker, as Chief of Staff, was the real controller of events, especially with an aging President whose energy levels seemed to be declining. As Tex understood what followed, Don Regan proposed that he shift positions with Baker, with Baker to become Secretary of the Treasury. By then, Baker, more frustrated than ever by the continued Cabinet in-fighting which Reagan would not take steps to control, wanted a job with direct responsibilities. He presented his case to the President, who passively agreed, with the transfer to take place at the start of the second term.

Tex was troubled when he learned of the job switch. He didn't like and didn't trust the dour Don Regan in any position, let alone in the crucially sensitive position of Chief of Staff to the President. And, as he had feared, the job rapidly became too much for Regan. One of the consequences was a major embarrassment, now known as "Iran-Contra." It appeared that CIA Director Bill Casey, working through National Security Advisor McFarlane, had convinced President Reagan to help "Freedom Fighters" from El Salvador destabilize the Communist government in Nicaragua. A Marine Lieutenant Colonel, Oliver North, a National Security Council staffer, another protégé of Bill Casey, became project coordinator. Eventually, a complicated story leaked out, in bits and pieces. As Tex understood it, Defense Department weapons were transferred to *Mossad*, the Israeli intelligence unit. Then very shady Middle Eastern types got into the picture. The weapons went to Iranians. Money and other arms went to the "Freedom Fighters" in Nicaragua. Another Congressional "Circus Act" of investigations began. All the usual Senatorial huffing and puffing. What did the President know? And when did he know it?

A huge embarrassment for everyone. Tex believed that there was more to the story than what has been disclosed. And he was convinced that this sorry business would not have occurred on Jim Baker's watch. However, for all the difficulties and missteps along the way, Reagan achieved the objective to which he had devoted his Presidency. He had overcome the obsessive fear of Russian Communism that had paralyzed so much of prior U.S. policy.

Then Reagan set out to break the power of the "Evil Empire" of the Soviet Union. As an actor, Reagan knew the necessity of building to a climatic scene. He had perceived the weaknesses in the internal Soviet power structure—and he played his card. Reagan visited Berlin in June 1987 and met with Gorbachev. Then he spoke to the German people at the infamous Berlin Wall, separating free West Germany from Soviet-dominated East Germany. Up until that time, the Berlin Wall had been a symbol of mutual belligerency between the East and the West. Reagan was greeted with enthusiasm. The speech began quietly, and then Reagan—in what Tex believed Reagan had intended as the high moment of his Presidency—built to his final climax: "Mr. Gorbachev, Tear Down That Wall!"

Suddenly, Reagan's simple four-word challenge had exposed "The Wall,"—not as a sign of Communist military strength and power—but as a symbol of weakness, repression and fear of freedom. Reagan had understood how to accomplish what American Presidents since Eisenhower had lacked the capacity to imagine. He had shifted the burden of the argument, from confrontation to contempt.

The "Wall" came down—and, with it, the end of the Cold War and, ultimately, the end of the "Evil Empire" of the Communist Soviet Union. An historic success for Reagan, the culmination of his plan for his Administration. He had finished his Presidency with dignity and honor. Tex was pleased to have played a part.

After leaving office, Ronald Reagan retired to California, where he was later diagnosed to be suffering from Alzheimer's disease. It was sad to watch the slow decline of a President who had restored America's belief in itself. He thought of Reagan often, wondering how to describe his effect on the American people. Then, in Lou Cannon's biography of Reagan, *The Role Of A Lifetime,* Tex read what he thought was an ideal summation: "Walter Lippmann once said of Charles De Gaulle that his greatness was not because De Gaulle was in France, but because France was in De Gaulle." Tex thought that statement equally applied to Reagan: America was in Reagan.

Chapter Twenty

Bush "41": The Aborted Ending of the Gulf War

Tex could never understand the puzzling Presidency of George Herbert Walker Bush. He was one of the most attractive, personally gracious men Tex had known. His experience seemed to have provided every qualification. His Presidency seemed so promising—and yet it ended so listlessly.

Tex had met him at Yale, at a Skull & Bones event. Bush had been captain of the baseball team, was generally considered the top man in his class—and he had come to Yale with an already impressive record. He had volunteered for Naval Aviation directly out of Andover in the spring of 1942. He was the youngest pilot in the Navy when he won his wings. He was sent to the Pacific, flying torpedo bombers off aircraft carriers, earning the Distinguished Flying Cross and three Air Medals in more than fifty missions. Toward the end of his tour, his plane was hit by anti-aircraft fire. After ordering his crew to bail out—and receiving no answer—he bailed out himself, landed in the ocean, where he floated for hours before being rescued by a U.S. submarine. Despite anguished search, no trace of his crew was discovered. Bush was offered the opportunity to return to the U.S, but he chose to finish his combat tour.

At the end of the war, he entered Yale, where the name George Herbert Walker Bush carried impressive family connections. His grandfather was George Herbert Walker, the leading investment banker in St. Louis, and founder of the Walker Cup prize in golf. In 1919 Walker was recruited by E. H. Harriman to move to New York as head of the Harriman firm. George Bush's father, Prescott Bush, tall, distinguished, a member of Skull & Bones and the famous Yale singing group, the "Whiffenpoofs," married Walker's daughter, Dorothy, joined the Harriman firm, and after a distinguished investment career, was elected a U.S. Senator from Connecticut. Their union produced George Herbert Walker Bush.

After graduating from Yale, George Bush had turned down a promising career on Wall Street—and had gone to Texas. Tex asked around, and was told that Bush's father had recommended the plan, that while he would have a good career on Wall Street, the real growth opportunity at that time was in the oil business in Texas. Tex assumed that presumably this plan recognized that on Wall Street George Bush might not stand out quite so dramatically among many other similarly educated men of suitable background, whereas in Texas his Wall Street and family connections would give him substantial advantages.

At that time, the underlying motivation for investment in the oil business was confiscatory federal income tax rates, over ninety percent. Most high-income people would rather give their money to almost anything, rather than pay taxes to the Federal government—and Lyndon Johnson, Robert Kerr and other "Big Oil" Senators had carved out generous capital gains tax benefits for oil exploration and development. As a result, the big oil companies had easy access to capital in New York. George's father, Prescott Bush, had many such clients at Brown Brothers Harriman, prominent among them, Dresser Industries, a Texas oil services company, where Prescott Bush was a director, and where George Bush went to work. [Footnote: Dresser Industries later merged with Brown and Root, which had risen to power in a long series of deals with Lyndon Johnson, and was subsequently merged into Halliburton—the giant oil company which Dick Cheney headed before becoming Vice-President.]

Apart from the major oil companies, there were lots of "wildcatters," experienced Texans who knew the land—but had little capital, and no exposure in New York. What was needed was a trustworthy scout in Texas. George Bush fit the bill—and Prescott Bush and his Wall Street friends would do the rest. Tex followed George's career: first as an oil field supply agent for Dresser Industries, then on to Zapata Petroleum, then to Zapata Offshore, a drilling company, where he subsequently became president. He entered politics, ran unsuccessfully for the U.S. Senate in 1964, and then his political career took off. He was elected to Congress in 1966, served two terms and ran, again unsuccessfully, for the Senate in 1970. Nixon then appointed him Ambassador to the United Nations, then head of the Republican National Committee. President Ford appointed him U.S. Representative to China (effectively the Ambassador) then head of the Republican National Committee, and finally head of the Central Intelligence Agency. In 1980 Bush ran for President, lost to Ronald Reagan, who then offered him the Vice Presidency, as the man who had finished in second place. Bush served dutifully as Vice President through Reagan's two terms—and it was assumed that that he would be the automatic choice for a continuity of the Reagan Presidency.

However, as the 1988 Presidential election approached, a large field, perhaps sensing opportunity, entered the Republican race against Bush. Senator Bob Dole of Kansas was the most experienced, but primarily in domestic issues, and with no significant international exposure (other than military service in Italy, where he was seriously wounded). Jack Kemp, pro football quarterback, former Congressman, former Secretary of Housing and Urban Development, (and later to become Bob Dole's Vice Presidential choice in the Dole's 1996 campaign) known for his doctrinaire "supply side" fiscal policy, in effect, a one-issue guy, but a strong personal campaigner. Al Haig was foreign policy—with a harsh edge, people remembered his bravado statement from the White House, "I'm in charge here" on the day that Reagan was shot. Pete DuPont, Governor of Delaware, was attractive personally, and the respected Senator Howard Baker was lurking in the wings.

It was hardest to figure out was a newcomer, Pat Robertson, the son of a Senator from Virginia, a television evangelist, a most aggressive self-marketer, with a powerful TV personality. Tex hated the mixing of religion with politics—wars tended to be the result. Robertson was a Yale Law School graduate and a skillful executive, who had built a major national religious organization, the Christian Coalition, and had attracted a large television audience of religious fundamentalists seemingly mindlessly committed to him—while Robertson was accumulating control of a substantial personal fortune.

As the incumbent Vice-President, Bush was the favorite. Most informed people around him, believed that Bush would make the obvious choice for Vice-President, the highly experienced and respected Jim Baker, Bush's friend of long standing, then serving as Reagan's Secretary of the Treasury. Instead, Bush, inexplicably, chose Dan Quayle, an obscure Senator from Indiana. An incredible decision. There was nothing distinguished about Quayle, no reputation outside Indiana, no marginal state to be picked up, as Indiana was a dependable Republican state. A completely wasted opportunity! Bush then compounded this bizarre Vice Presidential selection by picking as his campaign manager, a young right-wing firebrand from South Carolina, Lee Atwater, one of the new breed of ideological "win at any cost" campaign managers, with close alliances with southern religious fundamentalists. This was not the Bush Tex thought he knew.

The 1988 Presidential campaign began, as usual, in Iowa—and, as expected, Bob Dole, from the neighboring state of Kansas, "won" the Iowa caucus. Robertson came in a strong second, dropping Bush to third, a serious blow. Bush managed to pull out a win in New Hampshire, but Robertson surprised again by winning a major state, Michigan, with a previously unnoticed, but intensively organized, campaign among "true believers" of the fundamentalist religious right. It was particularly surprising— and represented an ominous forewarning of a new kind of politics from the far right, a sudden and dramatic shift from a former hard-core anti-tax economic base, to an intense, rapidly-growing, and single-minded emotional commitment to a politics of Calvinistic religious absolutism.

Despite his early victories, Robertson's campaign then developed a serious problem. His political literature described him as having been a "combat" Marine in Korea. This usage struck the wrong note among Marines—who regard all Marines as combat-ready—hence any reference to oneself as a "combat" Marine was a serious violation of the code. Moreover, Marine officers who were with Robertson in Korea noted that Robertson had not served in a combat role—presumably through his father's Senatorial influence—but had, in fact, served in rear areas as the regimental "liquor supply" officer. Congressman Pete McCloskey, himself a Marine officer decorated for leadership under fire in Korea, repeated the story—and Robertson sued McCloskey for libel. The trial drew national attention. After devastating testimony from other Marine officers regarding Robertson's conduct in Korea, his suit was dismissed with prejudice, effectively an acknowledgement of McCloskey's criticism.

With Robertson discredited, Bush won the South Carolina primary, which carried him on to the Republican nomination. However, there were far-reaching negative implications arising out of the South Carolina campaign. Lee Atwater had established alliances with far-right religious fundamentalist and racist groups—particularly virulent in South Carolina, but also influential in other southern states—the taint of which were to cling to Bush—and, later, to his son. Bush continued to make favorable appearances, but his speeches tended to a certain awkwardness. He later spoke of his lack of interest in what he called "the vision thing"—but vision is an essential quality of leadership. He was gifted with an intense personal competitive drive, perhaps reflecting the Walker side of his family.

Although not directly involved in the Bush campaign, Tex followed events closely. The Reagan "continuity" factor had given Bush an enormous head-start in the Presidential campaign in 1988, and "first string" Democrats—recognizing the amount of lead-time and money-raising now required—decided not to risk a loss on their record, and to wait for 1992. As a result the Democratic Party nominated Michael Dukakis, Governor of Massachusetts. From the beginning, there was little chance for Dukakis. He was not well known nationally; he was identified by Republicans as a "Massachusetts liberal," and his campaign was marked by mistakes. Moreover, Dukakis was not impressive personally. He was small in stature, and was poorly advised to put on a military helmet and be photographed, peering "mouse-like" out of an Army tank. Unkind press stories made comparisons to "Snoopy," the cartoon dog on the popular "Peanuts" comic strip. The 1988 Presidential campaign was virtually no contest. Bush was elected President with fifty-four percent of the vote, to Dukakis' forty-six percent.

The high point of the campaign occurred in the Vice Presidential debate between Dan Quayle and Lloyd Bentsen, a decorated B-24 pilot in World War II, who had defeated George Bush for the U.S. Senate from Texas in 1970, was reelected three times, before being picked as the Democrat Vice Presidential candidate in 1988. Clearly outmatched, Quayle compared his experience to that of Jack Kennedy. Bentsen replied, "I knew Jack Kennedy. Jack Kennedy was a friend of mine—and you're no Jack Kennedy." Tex believed that—despite the support of Ronald Reagan and his own two terms as Vice President—Bush would have lost to Bentsen, had the Democrats nominated Bentsen instead of Dukakis. The 1988 Presidential election was really no contest. Bush easily defeated Dukakis, although Bush made unnecessary future trouble for himself by declaring, "Read My Lips; No New Taxes."

Then in 1990 trouble erupted in the Middle East: a dispute over oil between Iraq and Kuwait. It seemed apparent that any such issue between two of the major players in the world oil market was, on its face, a matter of serious concern for the United States. The dispute escalated, and in late July 1990, the U.S. Ambassadress, April Glaspie, advised Saddam Hussein, the dictator of Iraq, that the U.S. had "no position" with respect to oil and border disputes between the two countries. It seemed inconceivable that the U.S. should appear not to be concerned about a dispute, potentially affecting world oil supplies, and especially recognizing the major disparity in military power between the large and modern Iraq military and that of Kuwait. Apparently acting on his perception of the Glaspie position, Saddam Hussein invaded Kuwait in August of 1990. Saddam's army, equipped with Russian tanks and other sophisticated weapons, swept through Kuwait, and massed on the border of Saudi Arabia, the world's largest reservoir of oil.

Suddenly faced with an immediate threat to so much of the world's oil supply, Bush's initial response seemed strangely passive. The British Prime Minister, Maggie Thatcher, instantly alarmed, came to the U.S. and met with Bush, where she was quoted as saying, "Don't go all wobbly on us, George." He emerged from that meeting and declared, rather awkwardly, "This will not stand."

A major military build-up ensued. The Saudi royal family, thoroughly frightened, welcomed U.S. troops and aircraft. With U.N. cooperation, thirty nations joined the U.S. coalition, contributing about two hundred fifty thousand troops to a U.S. force of four hundred twenty-five thousand U.S. troops in Saudi Arabia by early January 1991. The Chairman of the Joint Chiefs was General Colin Powell, a black man, an ROTC graduate from CCNY, a decorated veteran of two combat tours in Vietnam, and a man of great personal dignity and force of character. As the U.S. forces faced the Iraqi Army at the Kuwait border, General Powell famously spoke to the nation, "When we meet the Iraqi army, first we are going to cut it off, then we are going to kill it." American aerial bombing attacks began on January 17, 1991, continuing until the ground attack began on February 24th. Powell's words were accurate; the Iraqi army was "cut off and killed" in Kuwait in four days. Then came a puzzling event. At a small meeting, Bush and his political advisers decided to declare the Gulf War ended, after "ninety-nine hours." It seemed inexplicable that Bush decided to leave Saddam in power in Iraq, armed with four armored divisions, the elite core of his army—and the basis of his power.

The American public was elated at the apparent victory. The troops returned and General Norman Schwarzkopf led an impressive "Victory" parade down Pennsylvania Avenue in Washington in May 1991. Bush's popularity reached the ninety percent level in national polls, and he seemed unbeatable for reelection to a second term in 1992. Apparently the "A" players in the Democratic Party thought so as well, as they elected to pass the 1992 race, assuming that the result of the Gulf War had rendered Bush invulnerable.

Nevertheless, as the election approached, the inevitable Congressional recriminations began. Democrats—who had initially opposed entry to the war, and voted against the commitment of troops or the use of military force—began to complain that Bush had not gone far enough in the war. And then the carping Democrats were joined by the right wing of the Republican Party, and the domestic economy began to slide. Through it all, Bush's passivity continued. He seemed disinterested in campaigning for a second term. The country, already in a slow-down, began to slip into recession.

With the more visible Democrats on the sidelines, a new, unfamiliar figure, Bill Clinton, the young governor of Arkansas, appeared as a Democratic candidate for President. And then Ross Perot burst on the scene—a phenomenon of modern media, of national television and especially the cable and radio talk shows, where Perot became an instant celebrity. Perot was a small compact, fast-talking dynamo, a Naval Academy graduate who resigned his commission to become a top salesman at IBM. Then he started his own company, *Electronic Data Systems*, which he ran autocratically—and built into a great success, as well as a major fortune for himself. At the beginning of the 1992 election year, with the country facing uninspiring offerings from both national parties, Perot's blunt, provocative comments, coupled with his seemingly limitless wealth, began to attract notice.

In the spring of 1992, Larry King, leader of the cable talk market, asked Perot to come on his program. The result was grand theater. Perot totally ignored King's questions, talked through him, and across him, and generally took command of the show. He spoke dismissively of both parties—and all candidates—with pointed "one-liners." As to his own plans, he asserted that (1) he was not a candidate;(2) the "people" were the "owners" of the country—and should take their country back; (3) he was the "servant" of the people—and, if they wanted him, he could "get under the hood" and "fix things"; but first (4) "he would have to see some sweat"—specifically, they (the public "owners") would have demonstrate their commitment by getting him registered as a candidate for President in all fifty states. Within a couple of months, the national polls showed Perot at 33%, several points higher than Bush, who led Clinton, in third place. Apparently public disillusionment with the choices offered them by the Republican and Democratic parties had reached the stage where they were so disgusted that they would prefer anything but what the parties throw up. Then, Perot, after having steadily increased the public interest and energy, suddenly—and without any explanation—withdrew from the race.

The two major parties went on to nominate George Bush and Bill Clinton at their respective Conventions. Then, in early October of 1992 Perot suddenly re-entered the race, claiming that he had withdrawn in the summer because he feared that "Bush people" might "interfere" (how, was never explained) with his daughter's wedding in late August. Although Perot's poll numbers had fallen sharply after his withdrawal, his numbers immediately began to rise again. Perot was an obvious "flake," a man who had suddenly, and without any explanation, withdrawn three months before—and who had now, equally suddenly, reentered with a crazed story. Again, he offered nothing but "one-liners," no discussions of the future, of economic policies, or of foreign affairs. Yet the public continued to respond in increasing numbers—apparently eager for any change.

In the 1992 election, Clinton received 43.3% of the votes cast; George Bush 37.7%; with Perot drawing 19.9% The combined total for Clinton, young and unknown, and Perot, was 63.2%, with Bush, the incumbent President who had just won an important war, receiving only 37.7% of the vote. What was happening in America? What was it about this man, George H. W. Bush, otherwise so personally attractive, that he should leave such a discordant public image? Tex thought perhaps it was because his whole career, prior to the Presidency, was one of discharging defined roles, always performing either the prescribed procedures or following the specific instructions (or perceived requirements) of his position. And there were inconsistent aspects to his life, beginning with his move to Texas, a life-style so out of character with his aristocratic New England background and manner. He persisted in wearing Texas boots—which may have fit his feet—but did not seem to fit the man. And then there was the fact of his unexplained illness, and the decision to treat it chemically, requiring a delicate daily balance of drugs. His energy and vitality were clearly affected, as became evident through his losing campaign.

What did all this mean? Clearly it was a rejection of George Bush and of the Republican Party. It was hard to fault Bush's background, credentials or personal qualifications. There was nothing overtly negative about him—as there clearly was with Johnson and Nixon. However, it was also clear that, despite Bush's record of high office, people just didn't feel they "knew" him. He lacked the personal "authenticity" of an Eisenhower, Kennedy or Reagan, that powerful, but elusive, "Trust," so essential for real leadership. Bush seemed to lack force in his public speeches. In contemporary language, "he just didn't seem to get it."

On a personal level, Tex was saddened to see George Bush, a man whom he had known and respected, permit himself to be recast by the new breed of political advisors into something so unlike himself that neither Tex, nor others who knew him, could recognize the public Bush as the same person they had known. Was our political system so bereft of people with real leadership qualities that an unknown, unproven figure like Bill Clinton could come from the governorship of Arkansas and be elected over a man with Bush's extensive experience? What were Americans looking for in a President? Were they so captured by television that choosing a President for the Superpower of the World was simply another aspect of entertainment? As the distasteful trends in Bush's race against Clinton continued, public respect declined for both political parties. Congress polarized into hostile far-right/far-left intransigence. There were gross abuses of campaign finances, together with rapid growth of "special interest" power groups. The result was a general decline of public respect for the self-serving autocracy in both Democratic and Republican Party leadership.

After Bush's loss to Clinton, Tex used to see him from time to time at Skull & Bones events. Then an old family friend asked Bush to give a talk at Texas A&M. At dinner, the Chairman of the event told Bush that he wanted the Bush Presidential Library at Texas A&M—and that he would guarantee all financing. Bush replied gracefully—but both Tex, and Bush, firmly believed that Bush's library would be at Yale. However, the sad fact was that Bush had by then so antagonized sufficient members of the Yale "Vietnam generation" faculty and alumni that a library for Bush at Yale had become a "bridge too far." For all of the Bush family connections to Yale—the Bush Presidential Library resides today at Texas A&M.

While the hopes envisioned for President George Herbert Walker Bush ended in disappointment in 1992, who could have imagined that his son, George Walker Bush, would be elected President eight years later, in 2000—and would be quoted in a column in *The New York Times* as having said, "I saw what happened to my Dad, who got elected, and said, "what do we do?"

Chapter Twenty-One

Bill Clinton: "All Sail; No Keel"

Standing alone, Bill Clinton as President seemed a kind of character from a morality play—a man gifted with great talents which lifted him to high station, but who was unable to discipline himself—and ended in disgrace. However, the Clinton Presidency had a larger context, in its political origin, in its structure, and in its implications for the future. Clinton was not a typical Party Democrat. He called himself a *New Democrat*, supported by a new group called the *Democratic Leadership Council*. The DLC had been formed as a progressive spin-off from the Democratic National Committee, organized by Senator Sam Nunn, whom Tex greatly admired, and other Southern senators and governors, including Bill Clinton of Arkansas. Clinton also served as a bridge to *The Renaissance Group,* a kind of think tank and policy discussion forum founded at Hilton Head Island by Phil and Linda Lader, with annual meetings over the New Years weekend. It was soon apparent that Clinton planned to run for President. Tex was very interested in the "centrist" approach, and the possible future development in American politics.

[Author's Footnote: Tex and I had long discussions about the possible future of a "centrist" role, as I had been involved with *The Renaissance Group* through Charles Fraser—a friend from Yale Law School—the gifted developer of Sea Pines Plantation which transformed Hilton Head Island and the first to introduce intelligent and eco-friendly large scale recreational land planning—his multiple talents sadly lost in a boating accident. Fraser introduced my wife Maggie and me to the Laders, which led to our first-hand exposure to the extraordinary personal charm of Bill Clinton.]

Everything that Tex had learned in his long life had reinforced his conviction that high-level experience and judgment were the essential elements for a person's qualification for positions of great authority. So his first thought was that Clinton's leap—in a single bound—from Governor of Arkansas to the Presidency of the United States seemed a bit much, especially for one about whose character, background and judgment so little was known nationally. He watched with interest, as Clinton became the first example of the "Vietnam Generation"—in all its manifestations—to seek the highest office in the land. He came from distinguished universities: Georgetown, Oxford, where he was a Rhodes scholar; and the Yale Law School. Recognizing his limited public recognition, Clinton arranged to give three lectures at Georgetown, excellent policy pieces, clearly demonstrating a powerful intellect. As he had intended, the speeches were picked up by the national media, giving beneficial visibility to his campaign, and serving as a lead-in to the New Hampshire primary.

The Clinton campaign image was aided by his choice of a fast-beat, positive, forward-looking campaign theme song, "Don't Stop Thinking About Tomorrow," which he played on his saxophone to audiences, and on television, a "first" for a Presidential candidate in a national campaign. His campaign director, James Carville, brash, fast-talking and clever, drove home the campaign theme "It's the economy, stupid!" The fact that Clinton's campaign staff hardly conveyed a "Presidential" style in their manner, speech, style and dress seemed to be ignored by the press and the public.

Troubles began to appear in New Hampshire, "women" problems, then a record of apparent draft dodging, then drug use. Clinton ducked and weaved adroitly—"I didn't inhale"—the media seemed to let each subject drop. Was it an accident? Was it his manifest charm? Or was it some latent sense of complicity among the "new" media, themselves members of the Vietnam Generation? It certainly wasn't from lack of coverage—there was plenty of ink—but not nearly enough thoughtful examination of the implications of the accumulating negative information about Clinton's personal behavior. Clinton's election was not the result of a powerful campaign; instead it seemed to be a virtual default by Bush. Following his election, Clinton seemed to squander the time before the Inauguration, and was embarrassed by a series of missteps in Cabinet appointments and general disarray in his White House staff—essentially the same group that he had had with him throughout the campaign. Clinton's first Presidential initiative reflected that fact—an effort to integrate "gays" into the Armed Forces—especially awkward, coming from a successful draft-dodger.

The centerpiece of the Clinton agenda, a plan to reorganize the national health system, was headed by his wife, Hillary. And political battle lines were drawn. The calculus of both parties rests on the assumption that Americans vote their economic interests. The presumed Democratic inducement rested on the offer of more new benefits from the government—to be paid for by taxes, implicitly on the rich—with the strategic objective to jump, from the numerical advantage already held by the Democrats among low-income voters—to provide government benefits more extensively to the middle class.

Meanwhile, Congressional behavior, long marked by southern courtesy of manner and speech, was undergoing change. The slide to record low levels began with the arrival of young, aggressive, conservative Southerners who—believing that their ambitions would be frustrated by the entrenched seniority of old, racist Democrats in Congress—chose to run as Republicans, and were elected—signaling the end of the Democratic "Solid South" which had existed since the Civil War.

Foremost among the new Southern Republicans in Congress was Newt Gingrich, a former history professor from a small college in Georgia. He was disgusted that senior Republicans had put up with Democratic Congressional dominance for so long—effectively since Roosevelt—and he began to agitate against the long-standing Democratic "closed shop" control of Congressional committees.

Congressmen always seek easy ways to look good to the voters, and Tip O'Neill, the powerful Democratic Majority Leader, had permitted C-Span to televise Congressmen delivering speeches to what appeared to be a full and attentive Congress. In fact, the speech was delivered to a blank backdrop, and then was superimposed on an image of a full House. However phony, it was a great prestige-builder and campaign tool. Gingrich's public demonstration of the sham production technique was a stinging and effective attack on Democratic Congressional integrity and leadership.

Gingrich then set out to "nationalize" the focus of the Republican members of Congress with a "Contract with America." Tex was fascinated. Gingrich had recognized that, while most Americans liked their own Congressman enough to keep him in office, they regarded the Congress, as a whole, as a collection of self-serving people, interested in their own advancement, rather than in the good of the country. Working with Frank Luntz, a perceptive political advisor, Gingrich conducted extensive polling and focus group analyses to identify the top ten "issues" most important to Americans. These "issues" were then incorporated into a formal document, the "Contract with America," which obligated the signers to bring each "issue" in the Contract to a vote within a hundred days. It was a brilliant move, a striking success—the Congress was finally doing something positive—resulting in a the Republicans winning a majority in the 1994 Congressional election, and the loss of Democratic control of both Houses of Congress for the first time in forty years.

The 1994 Congressional elections were a disaster for Clinton and, even worse, he had to face Gingrich as Speaker of the House, with a united Republican majority behind him. However, Gingrich, flushed with success, was unable to control his vanity and badly overplayed his hand, twice forcing shutdowns of the national government over intransigent disputes with Clinton. The negative public reaction was compounded by Gingrich's childish petulance over which door he could use to exit Air Force One. The *New York Daily News* ran a front-page picture of Gingrich with the headline, " Cry Baby." The press picked up the theme which began to shift attention to Gingrich's personal behavior and away from public disgust at the conduct of our national government.

Gingrich's "Contract with America"—and Democratic past abuses of power—had provided Republicans with a great opportunity in the approaching 1996 Presidential election, especially with Clinton beginning to face more "women" problems. However, leading Republicans in Congress, apparently jealous of Gingrich's sudden capture of national attention, did not come to his support, effectively ending Gingrich's power. Not having to face Gingrich was a relief to Clinton. And again, the Republican Party leaders gave Clinton a pass by nominating a moribund Bob Dole as the Republican candidate. The dismal aspect of the election was underscored by the fact that Clinton, while beating Dole, nevertheless lost Democratic seats in Congress—hardly an indication of broad national respect or support for the leadership of either party.

Despite his reelection, Clinton was unhappy about his Presidency. He felt he couldn't even trust his White House staff because of their ties to what he regarded as a too-liberal Democratic Congressional leadership. He retained, in secret, Dick Morris, a subtle advisor, who wrote speeches on the basis of a concept of "Triangulation," which took Clinton back to a more centrist position, generally reflecting the *Democratic Leadership Council* perspective. However, Clinton's second term was overtaken by disgrace. Scandalous behavior—intimate relationships with a young intern in the Oval Office, as well as other "women," all very messy—and all leading to a Republican spasm of righteousness—and a Motion of Impeachment in Congress; an event which riled emotions to a fever pitch.

In the end, all sides were embarrassed, particularly the Republicans, who really lost control, pursued a sordid Impeachment process—but did not receive sufficient votes to remove Clinton from office. It was a bad performance, negative and vindictive, really a shameful reflection of the degeneration of Congress into petty personalities and partisanship.

The grotesque burlesque of the Impeachment proceedings damaged Clinton, and he did not recover through the remainder of his term, when he made a final error of judgment. On the last night of his Presidency he issued one hundred seventy-seven pardons to a variety of mostly undeserving types, among them campaign donors, fugitives from the law, etc., etc. It was a sad ending indeed, especially for a person with Clinton's great natural talents, intelligence and empathetic sensitivity.

Hillary moved to New York, and was promptly elected to the U.S. Senate.

Chapter Twenty-Two

Citizens for Colin Powell:
The Appeal of "The Sensible Center"

The distasteful aspects of the Clinton Administration were partially compensated for Tex by his role in a gallant effort to elect Colin Powell President of the United States in 1996.

Powell was the most respected person in America. He embodied the essential core elements of leadership—authenticity and, above all, trust—both so lacking in most contemporary political figures. And he had gained that respect the old-fashioned way—he had earned it. Powell exemplified all the qualities Americans admire and respect—and, as President, he could reestablish a positive, unifying sense of national purpose and direction, so woefully lacking in the apathy and divisiveness in the country.

Tex had admired Colin Powell for years, and he had seen, first-hand, Powell's effect on people when he had come to speak at a dinner Tex had put together on the aircraft carrier *U.S.S. Intrepid*. Powell gave an inspiring address. After the applause died down, Tex, as master of ceremonies, said, "General Powell has spoken of great American leaders. Tonight I think we have found another." That was when Tex first began to think of what a Powell presidency might do for the country.

By the fall of 1994, the country was uncertain, and disgusted. The Clinton White House was disorganized and ineffectual, and Congress was petty, vituperative, and destructive—the worst in memory. In short, the country was without leadership—and without the prospect of a national leader emerging from either party.

When The Citizens for Colin Powell Presidential Draft was introduced publicly, Tex signed up immediately, and began to make calls to his many friends around the country. The calls produced the same response: "Absolutely, Colin Powell is what the country needs, but he can't be elected. It's not only because he is black, it's also the Party system, the money sources that control the selection process. Neither Party will support Powell; he would not be "their man;" only a billionaire with a hankering for celebrity could afford the cost of a campaign, etc. . ."

Politics was all about money now—and the money sources want special deals. And where do those deals come from? Congress. From the "Party" point of view, winning the Presidency is nice, but playing the Congressional money game is what it is all about—a locked circle. Who can deliver the big bucks needed for the big blocks of TV, which in turn bring in the blocks of controlled votes. And the game gets bigger every election cycle, exponential growth. That's it. Big money, very big money, very big television time—and the Parties have control of it.

The important Presidents, those who had made a difference—all of them had come from outside of the Party. Going back to his boyhood, Tex recalled that the Republican Party had wanted William Howard Taft over Teddy Roosevelt. Later, the Democratic Party wanted Al Smith instead of Franklin Roosevelt. The Republican Party wanted Bob Taft over Eisenhower, and when they lost to Eisenhower, Henry Cabot Lodge maneuvered Nixon on the Eisenhower ticket as Vice-President in the name of "Party solidarity," when nobody, except the far right-wing Southern Californians wanted Nixon. Tex liked to speculate on the possibilities of that decision. Nixon, alone, had no real leadership qualifications. He was simply a front for others. Without the prestige of his Vice Presidency under Eisenhower, Nixon could not have risen to the Presidency on his own, and the consequences of Nixon as the Party choice would not have contaminated our country in so many ways for so many years. Later, the Republican Party similarly favored Gerry Ford (with Dole as Vice-President, instead of Rockefeller) over Ronald Reagan in 1976, which resulted in the election of Jimmy Carter. Then the Republican Party bosses wanted Dole as the Presidential candidate in 1996. Dole was a decent man—but he had been a loser on the Presidential ticket before.

Tex pointed to the success of the Eisenhower effort in 1952 as a favorable comparison for Citizens for Colin Powell. Both were natural, proven leaders. But there were major differences. Eisenhower had already agreed to be a candidate, if nominated. Moreover, the CEO community was solidly behind him with the powerful leadership of Cliff Roberts (with his control of the membership at Augusta) together with a more cohesive collection of national wealth and corporate power than exists today. An old friend, a CEO of a major corporation, refused to take a leadership role, saying that he could not take the risk for his company because "the change of a couple of commas and semi-colons in one of those late-night Congressional 'reconciliation meetings' could put his company out of business."

Republican governors and state party chairmen of the early primary states were canvassed. There was consensus that Dole would lose, but there was a general reluctance on their part to come out openly against Dole, as presumably the choice of the Party's bosses. But recognizing Dole's weaknesses as a candidate, they were reluctant to endorse Dole "until they had to." Many governors held back endorsements, and the governor of New Hampshire waited until the very last weekend, before the important "first in the nation" New Hampshire primary.

State Party chairmen fall into two categories: paid professionals, typically from large states; and "volunteers" generally from the small states, often with businesses dependent on state contracts, highway contractors, real estate developers. They, too, felt that they could not afford to go against the "Party" dictates. Further, there was a general sense that a Dole loss was less important than retaining control of Congress, because control of Congress represents a principal source of projects and money in most states.

Americans condemn the role and power of lobbyists, but there is a reason for their existence, the log-rolling, "pork"-trading, game that goes on in Congress, a self-serving, irresponsible breach of fiduciary responsibility, and a principal cause of the ballooning national debt, a burden on the future, one which had grown exponentially for more than seventy years.

The Citizens for Colin Powell campaign plan focused on Powell's long-time chief interest — the young people of America, as the future of our country. The plan was for Powell to make one visit in each primary state, speak in the largest auditorium in the city with the largest university. A substantial portion of the seats would be provided to students, with the remainder allocated to campaign contributors. Given the prospect of high public and media attention, helped by the recent publication of Powell's autobiography, *My American Journey*, substantial national coverage could be expected.

Visits by Citizens' leaders at civic lunch clubs or similar events around the country had provided an interesting response. In essence, an echo of Eisenhower's repeated admonition to "lead from the center." Voters said they were sick of politics, sick of both Parties, sick of all the bickering, pettiness and pork. They wanted a President that they felt they could trust, not just another political hack always mouthing the latest poll or Party formula. They wanted a national leader, person of "authenticity," one whose life experiences validated his character and judgment. Powell met their test.

However, the media and polling people keep devising lists of "issues" and grading candidates on that basis. But voters know that those issues are complex, not matters of a simple yes/no response. They want a President whose life experiences indicate that he, or she, will think the problems through, obtain the best advice available — and decide what's best for the country as a whole. Of course no one can be right all the time. They accept that. They see the Parties as simply political calculating machines, always looking for the money or groups that can deliver blocks of votes, however unappealing the candidates. On top of that, the Republican Party is so insecure that they are willing to adopt the "pro-life" dogma of the religious right.

From the beginning of the Citizens For Colin Powell effort, it had been apparent that Powell's wife, Alma, had sacrificed a lot in support of his military career and, understandably. she was less than comfortable with the Citizens For Colin Powell campaign effort. She had to move her home and family so many times during his military career that she wanted to have a home and a family life of her own. Who could blame her?

Ultimately, Powell held a press conference to declare that he would not be a candidate. Had Prime Minister Rabin of Israel, a close friend of the Powells, not been assassinated during that period, Tex believed that there was reason to hope that, in an open election, a black man could have been elected President of the United States.

Chapter Twenty-Three

The Evil of Two Lessers: Bush "43" and Cheney and the Loss of the Popular Vote

John McCain was a naval aviator who had been shot down over Hanoi, badly wounded, early in the Vietnam War. He was the son, and grandson, of Navy admirals, and the Vietnamese offered to release him, in exchange for his denunciation of U.S. policy in Vietnam. His steadfast refusal resulted in five and a half years of torture and suffering—a remarkable act of heroism, and an inspiration to America. After his return from years of torture in a Vietnam prison and had recovered his health, McCain was elected to Congress from Arizona, and in 2000 announced his candidacy for President of the United States.

Tex had found his next candidate. McCain represented just what our country needed, especially after the sordid ending of the Clinton Administration. Tex was then in his ninety-first year. He had seen a lot through those years, and he was disgusted by the conduct of recent national leadership, both by Republicans in Congress and Clinton in the White House. He believed the country needed a President who was his own man, a demonstrated leader, not a captive of some pressure group or a manipulated puppet of money interests.

America's greatness was that, in times of internal conflict, a leader would emerge with a message of inspiration, thereby returning the country to the values that transcend personal or political advantage, that put the national interests ahead of private interests. He thought back over the Presidents he had seen, and only four seemed worthy of that high office, and the trust of the American people. Franklin Roosevelt's "New Deal" was first in mind, then Dwight Eisenhower, whose confidence had maintained American stability through the rise of Russian atom threats; then John Kennedy, and his unforgettable, "Ask not what your country can do for you, ask what you can do for your country." Then Ronald Reagan, who inspired the country to remember the idealized vision of America as "a shining city on a hill." Tex believed that McCain's example reached the same potential level of national confidence and inspiration. And he was convinced that McCain would win over Al Gore, Bill Clinton's Vice-President. Gore was the son of a former Senator from Tennessee, but he had been overshadowed through his Vice—Presidency by the pyrotechnics and embarrassments of Clinton himself.

Tex thought the significant Republican challenge seemed be the Texas Governor, George W. Bush, the son of George H.W. Bush, the former President. On the face of it, George W. Bush had none of the experience of his father. In fact, Bush had, to use the most favorable word, an undistinguished record, rescued by friends from repeated business failures and bouts with alcohol, until finally some friends arranged a role as "front man" for the Texas Rangers baseball team, where his natural enthusiasm and team spirit seemed well suited. He sat in the president's box behind the player dugout, where television cameras broadcast his enthusiastic responses to every play. That exposure naturally aided his election to Governor. In Texas, appearance counts for a lot.

Although he was affable and high-spirited, there was nothing in Bush's career, other than his name and the support of his father's friends in the oil business, to recommend him for President. He had been a "cheerleader" at Andover, followed by a companionable career at Yale ("Bones" like his father), then a questionable direct commission in the Texas Air National Guard, just a few days before a draft call for Vietnam. At that time the National Guard had a particular attraction in that most Guard units were not sent overseas. Following completion of initial pilot training, Bush apparently did not report for active duty for nearly a year, military records seemed to have been lost, and he received an honorable discharge before the end of his prescribed enlistment period. However, Tex knew something about Texas politics, and the influence of the oil business. And he knew that in Texas, where the legislature held the power, and with the oil lobbyists standing behind them, all such little details didn't really seem to matter.

McCain won the first primary, in New Hampshire, and then went on to win in other states across the country from Connecticut to Arizona, including Vermont, Rhode Island, and, most importantly, Michigan. But then the primaries turned south, to South Carolina, long a cesspool of political racism and backwoods religious fundamentalism. Bush's chief political advisor was Karl Rove, a disciple of the deceased Lee Atwater who had directed Bush's father's campaign—an adroit practitioner of the "Big Lie" and the "Smear." And so it happened in South Carolina. McCain was doing well, when just before the primary, television stations covered the state with a charge that McCain had fathered a "colored" child. A despicable "Big Lie." In reality, McCain and his wife had adopted an Asian refugee child, an act of compassion and charity in the best sense—as Karl Rove, Bush's campaign manager, and Bush well knew. But they also knew that in South Carolina the word "colored" mean "black." Thus, the "Smear." Rove and Bush knew how prejudiced Southern voters would react.

Another sinister aspect was the ready availability of instant money, in multi-million dollar amounts, to finance such reprehensible tactics, and all without any apparently traceable source. The South Carolina "colored child" sabotage was spread through other Southern states—and the Southern vote carried Bush to the nomination of the Republican Party. But for the reprehensible Bush-Rove tactics, Tex was convinced that McCain would have been elected President—and McCain's experience, judgment and leadership abilities would not have led our country into George Bush's war of choice in Iraq, based on a series of lies.

Tex believed that Al Gore would be so handicapped by the lingering taint of the Clinton behavior that he would not present a meaningful challenge to Bush. But when the votes were counted on Election Day, Gore had won the national popular vote over Bush by more than half a million votes. However, the Presidential election is not won by popular votes, but by states, through the archaic metaphysics of the Electoral College—which provides a major disproportionate advantage to states with smaller populations, in the South, the Mid-West and the mountain states, now known as the "Red States"—and all infected by Karl Rove's "colored child" "Big Lie" and racial "Smear."

Despite the Gore's five hundred forty-four thousand vote victory on a national popular vote count basis, the final Electoral College decision turned on one state, which faced election count difficulties, Florida, with its twenty-seven Electoral College votes—and where Bush's brother, Jeb, was Governor. After the close of the Election, the initial closing count showed Bush the winner by a small margin; however, there were many thousands of uncounted and/or disputed votes in Palm Beach County—and a recount began. Recounts and attendant litigation proceeded for more than a month, until the U. S. Supreme Court, in a five-to-four decision, declared recounts ended, effectively awarding George W. Bush the Presidency of the United States by a margin of 537 disputed votes in Florida.

Bush asked Dick Cheney, then head of the giant oil company, Halliburton, to head a search committee to select the Vice Presidential candidate. Cheney, a long-time resident of Texas, promptly moved back to his prior home state of Wyoming and declared that he was the choice for the job.

Tex was appalled at what he saw happening in our country!

Bush's first Cabinet appointment was Colin Powell as Secretary of State. This gave Tex some comfort, knowing that Powell's experience and worldwide respect would lend much-needed stature to the new Administration. The appointment of Don Rumsfeld as Secretary of Defense followed. Tex remembered him from when Gerry Ford—then newly President after Nixon's resignation and desperate for help in a White House suddenly empty of staff—had picked Rumsfeld to be his top aide—with Rumsfeld reaching down in the White House woodwork to bring Cheney along as his deputy. Rumsfeld subsequently ended up as Ford's Secretary of Defense, while Cheney went to the White House as Chief of Staff. After Ford lost the Presidency effectively by default to Jimmy Carter, Rumsfeld cleverly distanced himself from government and went on to a successful corporate CEO career, while Cheney elected to be the sole Congressman from Wyoming, a state with some oil production. Later, George H. W. Bush appointed Cheney as his Secretary of Defense, who had served as a liaison to the Middle Eastern oil sheiks during the Gulf War.

As the George W. Bush Presidency began in 2001, Rumsfeld, as the new Secretary of Defense, asserted himself immediately on military and international matters, while Vice President Cheney virtually disappeared, to pursue his interests in secret. He briefly emerged as head of an Energy Task Force, ostensibly to develop a national Energy Plan. Everything about the Energy Task Force was secret, the names of members, subjects of discussion, meeting dates and locations, even the names of the Task Force staff. Inquiries from Congress and the Government Accounting Office were ignored.

Another "Secret Presidency." Memories of the Nixon days resurfaced. Tex hated what he saw happening in the new Bush Administration.

Chapter Twenty-Four

The 9/11 Attack on America and War in Iraq

On September 11, 2001, the sirens of emergency vehicles awakened Tex in his apartment in Battery Park City, a few short blocks south of the Twin Towers, the tallest buildings in New York. He turned on his television which showed that a hijacked jet had crashed into the Twin Towers. He pulled on some clothes, grabbed his ever-present camera, and ran toward the incredible sight. His first thought as he looked up at the burning Tower was that Pearl Harbor must have been like this. He had been through bombing attacks before—but this was New York, his city, the greatest city in the world. How could this be happening? Who could have attacked us like this? Who was behind it?

He was photographing the raging fires when the first Tower collapsed. He could remember being struck by the shock wave, and being lifted off his feet. Later, he could recall regaining consciousness in what seemed total darkness, deafened by roaring sounds, and almost suffocated by the dense, swirling ashes. He sensed the direction of the Hudson River, and tried to grope his way. He recalled falling again. His next memory was of being carried on a stretcher off a boat on the Jersey shore.

He had been found unconscious, and was put on one of the many boats carrying the injured from Manhattan to New Jersey. He must have given his name—it was on a paper pinned to his chest—but he had no recollection of it. A doctor, the president of a hospital, was screening patients, and he recognized Tex's name. The hospital was filled with the most seriously injured, and the doctor took Tex to his home. For several days, his friends assumed he was dead, until they heard his voice on a telephone. As soon as he was able, Tex returned to New York. His apartment was in shambles and friends had located a small apartment for him in mid-town. Although seriously weakened, his spirits slowly recovered, and he began to see friends—and to contemplate the meaning of 9/11. As the story emerged, it appeared that nineteen Arabs, fifteen of them Saudis, had hijacked four large commercial jet airliners as part of a carefully planned attack. The first two planes had destroyed the Twin Towers, the third struck the Pentagon, and the fourth, presumably intended to hit the Capitol, crashed in Pennsylvania, as gallant passengers rushed the cockpit.

A Saudi prince, Osama bin Laden, part of the Saudi royal family claimed credit for the attack and bin Laden began to have video tapes delivered to Arab television stations, asserting, among other things, that his attack on the U.S. was in retaliation for U.S. support of Israel and the U.S. military presence in Saudi Arabia on land considered "holy" to Muslims. Tex recalled John Connally telling him years before, that Arabs regarded the establishment of Israel on Arab land as "a Second Coming" of the Christian Crusades of the Eleventh Century.

Osama bin Laden was then living in Afghanistan with Al Qaeda terrorists harbored by the Taliban party. Bush sent troops to Afghanistan to capture bin Laden—and to crush the Taliban, but, despite every effort, bin Laden has remained at large.

Following the 9/11 attack on America, President Bush had used the event to justify his going to war to destroy Saddam's dictatorship in Iraq—although the Bush Administration did not produce any evidence of bin Laden's involvement in the attack. Tex was increasingly concerned over Bush's flaunting a kind of "cowboy, go it alone" attitude. Despite the obvious fact that fifteen of the nineteen 9/11 attackers were Saudis, Vice-President Cheney continued to assert that Iraq was behind the 9/11 attack—and that therefore a war with Iraq was necessary to destroy Saddam's "weapons of mass destruction." Tex was puzzled by Cheney's argument. What was going on? Was it possible that Bush and Cheney were using the 9/11 attack as an excuse for a pre-planned war on Iraq?

Was this some kind of replay of the Gulf War in 1991, where Bush's father ("41") had assembled more than thirty countries to drive Saddam's Iraqi invasion army out of Kuwait. At the time, Tex could not understand why Bush ("41"had then stopped short of destroying Saddam's elite Republican Guard armored divisions—the basis for maintaining Saddam's power in Iraq—when Saddam's Guards divisions were virtually at Bush's mercy. Was it possible that the son didn't talk with the father, that Bush "41" didn't talk with Bush "43?" Or was it vice versa?

During 2002, reports of U.S. air strikes on key elements of Iraqi defenses steadily increased, an obvious preparation for yet another U.S. involvement in war in the Middle East. Why? To what purpose? Then, as Tex had feared, the Iraq war began on March 20, 2003, with a massive U.S. aerial attack on Baghdad. The magnitude of the attack was clearly intended to intimidate. Precision bombs struck Saddam's palaces. Secretary of Defense Rumsfeld spoke of the "Shock and Awe" of overwhelming U.S. power. The Iraqi army seemed to melt away, and Baghdad fell with only limited military resistance. The war seemed to be over in short order.

To celebrate the quick, and then apparently decisive, conclusion of the Iraq war—and to divert public attention from the alleged "weapons of mass destruction" justification for the war—an impressive ceremony was prepared for May 1, 2003. A Navy aircraft carrier, the USS Abraham Lincoln, returning from the war in Iraq, was kept at sea off San Diego so that President Bush could land on the carrier in a Navy plane and step out in a full military flight suit, under a massive banner, reading, "Mission Accomplished." Tex was repelled by the pretension and phoniness, of the whole process, really evidence of Bush's contempt for the intelligence of the American people.

Then, Halliburton—where Dick Cheney had been chairman before becoming Bush's Vice-President—was selected, sole source and without competitive bidding, to rebuild Iraq's infrastructure. Was it possible that there was some connection to Cheney's secret Energy Task Force? The whole situation reminded Tex of the famous scene in the movie, "The Wizard Of Oz," where the great character actor Frank Morgan, pretending to be the "Wizard," directed the action hiding behind a curtain, while repeating, "Pay no attention to that little man behind the curtain."

Meanwhile in Iraq, a guerilla war broke out, in the form of suicide bombers, fed by a steadily increasing influx of volunteers from Saudi Arabia. U.S. casualties began to mount. Tex had seen, first-hand, the bloody cost of Japanese "kamikaze" suicide attacks in the Pacific. He kept thinking of his uncle's prediction that the wars of the future would be fought over oil. Now, a war over access to oil required by a rapidly industrializing world had become overlaid by a religious war, spreading across the Muslim Middle East.

Everything that Tex had learned—from Exeter and Yale, from his mentors, his uncle Tom Taylor, Brisbane and Baruch, from what he had seen and learned from the wars—World War II, Korea, Vietnam and Iraq, together with the attendant political campaigns—all had convinced him that America's role in the world was to lead by example, not by force. But what were we doing now? He hated the thought of Bush's pandering to the religious bigotry of the far right wing—the so-called "Redneck" vote of the "Red" states—seemingly isolated from the realities of the world, and obsessed by the religious fervor of their opposition to abortion, while remaining indifferent to Bush's pursuit of his imperious commitment to an open-ended war in Iraq.

Tex was then in the ninety-third year of his remarkable life, a life which had ranged across the century of America's entry onto the world stage, emerging from isolationism to become the reluctant superpower, and culminating in a kind of "Manifest Destiny" attitude of what Tex had come to call the "Imperial Presidency" of George W. Bush. The leadership of our country had been the consuming interest of his Tex's life, and he had been privileged to be an "insider" for so much of it. He said he didn't want to focus on the past but, nevertheless, he was frightened by what he foresaw in the future.

The American Century had begun so positively with the vision and leadership of Teddy Roosevelt. Then Wilson took the nation into World War I. The country had then endured three weak Republican Presidents and the Depression before it rose again with FDR. After Roosevelt's death early in his fourth term, his Vice President, Harry Truman, took office and began what came to be called "The Marshall Plan" to rebuild war-torn Europe. American power peaked with the Eisenhower Presidency, then began a slow erosion—excepting a positive period under Reagan—to the year 2000, when a divided Supreme Court had to intervene, in a five-to-four decision, to "elect" George W. Bush—who had not won the popular vote—as President of the United States.

Tex was angry at the process and disgusted at the result. He said that since 1945, when he made his first low-level reconnaissance flight over Hiroshima to examine the site of the first use military use of the Atom bomb, the question of how Presidential decisions were made had become all the more crucial. Now, other than the U.S., at least five nations have atom weapons, four near the Middle East—Iran, Russia and Pakistan—(Israel, although undeclared, is also presumed to be included), along with

North Korea. Against this looming threat, Tex was deeply troubled by the character and leadership of George W. Bush. His war in Iraq reminded him of Korea and Vietnam, other bloody "wars of choice" engaged in by Presidents Truman and Johnson, who had risen to the highest office by the death in office of Roosevelt and Kennedy, without apparent qualifications for the responsibilities of the office, and who didn't know how to get out of losing wars.

The reality is that the President of the United States is not a truly nationally elected leader. Tex shuddered at the thought that, while Americans live in a world economy with internet communications and manned space ships, they must vote for the President in a state by state process of inward isolationism, a product of the Electoral College system established in 1787 and not materially changed since—despite the fact that Jefferson himself had suggested a Constitutional Convention every twenty years just to keep up with the obviously accelerating rate of change in the country.

How we choose our President defines who we are as a people. Tex believed that the choice of the leader of our nation should not be dependent upon political pandering to the worst prejudices of the voters in the most backward states, where the arcane dictates of the Electoral College effect on Presidential elections is so disproportionate to the voting population that the twenty-six states with the smallest populations—representing in total only eighteen percent of the population of the country—have the voting potential to elect fifty-two senators—and effectively control the country.

He thought this process was a political perversion in America in the 21st century. Always looking to the future, he said that, given what he had seen through his long life, if he had the strength he'd devote whatever energy he could muster to organize a national campaign to adopt a national Direct Election of the President.

Epilogue

Tex McCrary's long life ended on July 29, 2003. Jinx died a month later.

A memorial service was held in New York on the morning of September 15, 2003. Many friends gathered, with many commemorative comments, and many tears.

Bill Safire devoted his *New York Times* column that day to a touching reminiscence of their long friendship, titled "Of Tex and Jinx," ending with the final lines of a poem by Walter Benton,

> "The last we saw of them was when they kissed,
> Then beautifully naked walked as if into a sea of bright blue water
> leaving their bodies like old clothes upon the shore."

Tex didn't believe in endings, he believed that ideas live on, so this book closes with the words he always used to close conversations or writings that he cared about,
"To be continued . . ."

John Reagan McCrary

CPSIA information can be obtained
at www.ICGtesting.com
Printed in the USA
LVHW102354070221
678678LV00007B/67